EWING GALLOWAY

*Like most of the **beautiful** government buildings in Washington, the Supreme Court of the United States is based on a Roman model. "Equal justice under law" is a Roman **idea**, one of Rome's greatest gifts to our country.*

# LATIN *for Americans*

*First Book*

*I must admit that as I have grown older, I have changed m[y]
mind about the study of the classics. I never liked them when [at]
school. I did not yield responsively at all to the many urgent an[d]
sometimes painful appeals which were made to me to grasp th[e]
full charms and precision of the classical languages. But it seem[s]
to me that, if the teaching of the classics dies out in Europe an[d]
the modern world, and with it the knowledge of Greek an[d]
Roman literature and the vast picture presented by that lo[ng]
epoch of time, then a great unifying force in Europe might easi[ly]
become extinct.*

Winston S. Churchill

Oslo, 1948

# LATIN *for Americans*

## *First Book*

B. L. ULLMAN KENAN PROFESSOR OF CLASSICS AND CHAIRMAN OF
THE DEPARTMENT, UNIVERSITY OF NORTH CAROLINA

NORMAN E. HENRY LATE TEACHER OF LATIN, PEABODY HIGH
SCHOOL, PITTSBURGH, PENNSYLVANIA

*THE MACMILLAN COMPANY* • New York

# Contents

*From Roma to Astoria—1800 years*

*The Emperor Trajan (98–117 A.D.) built a column about 125 feet high in Rome, on which is carved in a spiral band the story of his military campaigns. The effect is that of a motion picture—if you do the moving. The column is now surrounded by churches and other modern buildings. See also p. 424.*

*In 1811 an expedition sent out by John Jacob Astor founded Astoria, Oregon. Its name is a Latinized form of Astor. In 1926 this column, in imitation of Trajan's Roman column and of the same height, was erected to honor the founder of the city. Its spiral band tells the history of the region.*

*From Astoria to Roma—7000 miles*

# Introduction

The first question that most Latin teachers, long familiar with earlier editions of this book, are likely to ask is "Just what changes have been made in this revision?" The changes in format and size are obvious. As to content, the changes are numerous and sometimes extensive. The following are the most important:

1. The number of lessons has been reduced from 78 to 77.

2. A few basic words have been eliminated, a few others have been added, and the order of occurrence has frequently been changed.

3. Some reading selections are entirely new (e.g., Lessons V, XIII); others are entirely rewritten (e.g., Lessons III, IV, VII, XIV).

4. The major changes in grammar presentation have been three: a. the first and second declensions are taught together, beginning with Lesson IV; b. the perfect tense has been moved forward from Lesson XXXI to Lesson XIII—and the imperfect has been postponed from Lesson V to Lesson XXVIII; c. the third declension has been moved forward from Lesson XLVIII to Lesson XLIII.

5. The grammatical changes indicated in the preceding paragraph caused extensive changes in reading selections, exercises, etc.

6. Some of the grammatical matter has been played down and simplified. A number of technical grammatical terms have been eliminated. The English explanations of grammar have been simplified where possible.

7. The sentences in the Latin-English and English-Latin exercises have frequently been shortened. The number has been reduced somewhat. Many entirely new sentences have been substituted for the old.

8. Brief tabular summaries comparing and contrasting English and Latin grammatical usages have been added to most of the Unit Reviews.

9. The "Hints for Reading Latin" in Lesson XXVIII have been expanded.

10. Even greater emphasis than before has been given to clarifying the difference between Latin and English word order (see especially Lessons V and XXIII).

11. Some important matters have been put earlier, e.g., the discussion of "word sense," formerly in Lesson XXVIII, is now in Lesson XXI.

12. A new feature, "Lazy Latin," has been added in Lessons XXXVII and LXXV.

13. Another new feature is the discussion in the "Word Studies" of towns in the United States with ancient names.

14. The "Glimpses of Roman Life" (revised) now regularly precede each Unit Review.

15. Two new plays have been written for the present edition by Dr. Lillian B. Lawler of Hunter College.

As in the two preceding editions of this book, the title *Latin for Americans* is based on some of the leading features of the book. Among these are the comparisons between ancient and modern life in the "Glimpses of Roman Life" and in the reading selections; the emphasis on the American way of life, good citizenship, and democracy throughout the book; the prominence of the English word studies, which occur in every lesson; the emphasis on correct grammatical usage in English; the many illustrations of American buildings that imitate the ancient models and of other American material; the quotation of Latin phrases used on American buildings and as American mottoes; and the listing of American towns, firms, and organizations having ancient names. It is firmly believed that this book, by making young Americans more deeply aware of their cultural heritage, will help make better Americans.

The reading selections, which come first in every lesson, furnish the material for the study of forms, syntax, vocabulary, and word study. The exercises and practice drills may be expanded or reduced by teachers to meet the needs of individual classes. This is especially true of the exercises calling for translation from English into Latin, which some teachers may wish to minimize or omit.

Some grammatical material, shown by investigation to be of little importance, has been eliminated. When a Latin construction is like English and is intelligible without explicit teaching, no attempt is made to add unnecessary explanations. As in earlier editions, no knowledge of English grammar is assumed, and basic English grammar in simple form is presented as needed.

It should be remembered that this book gives special attention to the verb; its importance for both Latin reading and English derivation is recognized by the introduction of many verbs in reading selections and vocabularies and by rapid development of verb forms. In this way reading power is attained more quickly.

The thirteen "Glimpses of Roman Life," together with the illustrations and the reading selections, furnish a basis for study of Roman civilization. In addition, references are given for further study. The questions for discussion suggest comparisons between ancient and modern life.

The Latin and English Word Studies, covering such matters as prefixes, suffixes, loan words, phonetic changes, interesting derivations, Latin phrases, abbreviations, and quotations, have always been a particular feature of this series. They are closely integrated with the reading selections and are not disjointed presentations of material which has little or no organic connection with the rest of the book. They are the more valuable because the vocabulary of the reading selections consists in large part of the words which are most important for English derivation. At the same time the words are those most common in Latin authors.

The illustrations are an essential part of the instructional material. Much time, effort, and thought have been devoted to the selection of a useful and attractive group of pictures. Among them will be found pictures of classical buildings in the Americas and elsewhere, Latin inscriptions on American buildings, and other material which shows the continuing influence of Roman civilization. The illustrations of postage stamps with classical motifs should interest pupils who are stamp collectors.

Teachers are urged to secure copies of the Manual which accompanies this book. The many useful teaching suggestions and the supplementary information it contains will make any Latin teacher's job easier and his classes more interesting. The *Progress Tests*, by B. L. Ullman, Edith Kovach, and A. W. Smalley, are extremely helpful to teachers and pupils.

B. L. Ullman

Chapel Hill, N. C.

*The Emperor Justinian (sixth century) appointed a commission to collect and select from the great body of Roman laws, edicts, and decisions of the preceding one thousand years. Here he is shown with his committee examining the results. Being in codex form (like our modern books), it is called Justinian's Code, still the basic law code of many nations. At left and right are shown the earlier law books, in papyrus rolls.*

# ⚘ Our Roman Heritage

Twenty-five hundred years ago Rome was one of many small towns in Italy. Its language, Latin, got its name from the district of Latium in which the town was situated. As the power of Rome spread, first over Italy and then over most of the civilized world of that day, its language came to be used everywhere. On the map on page 104 you can trace the growth of the great Roman Empire. You can see how it became a sort of United States of the Mediterranean World. Rome was at the same time **urbs et orbis,** *city and world.*

Not only did Roman culture spread to all the people living in the Roman Empire, but as centuries passed it became the foundation of European civilization. This European civilization was carried to all parts of the world by the English, French, Spanish, Portuguese, and others. So all the world owes a debt to ancient Rome. One reason for studying Latin is to learn something about the Roman civilization in order to understand our own better. How did an ancient Roman live? What did he think? How did he solve the problems that we too must face? How did he govern his vast empire? How did he find happiness? You will discover the answers to these and many other questions in your study of Latin, and you will find those answers very interesting. For the Romans were human beings like ourselves. You will like to read the stories of their lives. They were not perfect; you will learn that they had their faults and that there were bad Romans as well as good ones.

The Romans have handed down not only their ideas but also their language. The Romance languages are the various forms which the Roman (Latin) language has taken in the course of centuries in various parts of the Roman Empire. They are Italian, French, Spanish, Portuguese, Rumanian, and even, to a large extent, English, since about sixty per cent of our English words are taken from Latin. Such words are called derivatives. French, Spanish, and Italian become very easy after a study of Latin. Latin America (meaning Mexico, Central America, and South America) is so called because

*The newly decorated chamber of the House of Representatives in Washington contains marble plaques of men who made important contributions to American law. Among the Romans are (left) Papinian (third century, A.D.) and the Emperor Justinian (see p. x).*

the people speak Spanish or Portuguese—modern forms of Latin. The people themselves are sometimes called Latins.

One of the chief reasons for studying Latin is to get a better knowledge of English. Most of the more difficult words in English are from Latin or Greek. In a few weeks you will learn or know better the meaning of *impecunious, emigrate, mandate, predatory,* and many others. Soon you will know why a *submarine* is so called, what a *Pyrrhic* victory is, and the meaning of such words as *neutrality* and *repatriate*—all words found in the daily newspapers. Your English spelling will improve.

The study of Latin will make it much easier for you to understand English grammar. Then, again, there are Latin words, phrases, and mottoes used in English, such as *radius, per annum,* and *e pluribus unum.* Many abbreviations used in English are Latin, such as i.e. for *id est,* "that is"; cf. for *confer,* "compare."

The very fact that for some fifteen centuries Latin was the international language of educated people in Europe makes it important today. Up to a few centuries ago thousands of books were written in Latin about almost everything, from astrology to zoölogy. It was an international language of conversation as well. To some extent it is still written and spoken.

No matter what line of work you will enter, you will find Latin useful. If you plan to be a doctor, you will learn that nearly all

Class A medical schools require or recommend Latin—most of them four years of it. If you intend to be a lawyer, Latin will prove useful and necessary in many ways—as, for example, in understanding the many Latin phrases used in law, such as *habeas corpus*. Teachers of many subjects, such as English and history, should or must know Latin. The technical terms in science and other subjects, the terms that make those subjects difficult, are chiefly from Latin or Greek. They become easier when the root words out of which they grew are studied.

When we consider the influence of Rome, we do not wonder that Latin is an important subject of study in England, France, Germany, Italy, and all over Europe, as well as in North and South America and other parts of the world. In the United States more pupils are studying Latin than ever before. Latin is truly international and is a bond between many nations.

**DISCUSSION**    1. How many events of Roman history can you think of?
**QUESTIONS**     2. What famous Romans do you remember?
                3. What Roman gods can you recall?
                4. What do you know about the city of Rome as it is today?
                5. Make a list of the Latin words, phrases, legal terms, scientific terms, mottoes, proverbs, and abbreviations that you know.

*The Roman Forum as it was. Here "justice under law" ( see p. ii) was born.*

JAMES SAWDERS

*Wax-covered writing tablet from Etruria, in Italy, over 2600 years old. The ABC's are scratched on the wooden rim as a model to imitate. The letters run from right to left, as in the Semitic alphabet.*

## The Alphabet

Civilization owes more to the invention of writing than to anything else. It has truly been said that the pen is mightier than the sword—or, in more modern language, than guns and bombs. The earliest forms of writing, invented before history began, told their stories by means of pictures. Such methods have lasted into modern times; the writing of the American Indians is an example. No less important than the invention of writing was that of the alphabet, which made it much easier to learn to read and write. The alphabet was invented by Semites in western Asia, but in its earliest form was handicapped by its lack of vowels (*a, e, i, o, u*). These were added by the Greeks when they got the alphabet from the Semitic Phoenicians, a people related to the Jews and Arabs. The Etruscans, northern neighbors of the Romans in Italy, learned it from the Greeks and taught it to the Romans. The Romans made some changes in the values and forms of the letters and passed them on to the modern world along with the rest of their culture. Their alphabet is one of the great contributions of the Romans to our civilization. It is impossible to measure its influence. It is by far the best of existing alphabets and is one of the great international forces of our day. A few years ago Turkey abandoned the Arabic alphabet, a descendant of the early Semitic, in favor of the simpler and more widely used Latin alphabet. European nations do not understand one another's languages and have many a quarrel, but nearly all except Greece and Russia (which uses a modified form of the Greek alphabet) write out their thoughts in Latin letters. The Latin alphabet is a symbol of a common culture.

Since Roman days the alphabet has changed little. The Romans used *i* for *i* and *j*. Three centuries ago it became the custom in

4

English to use a long form of *i* for *j*, and thus our *j* was formed. Similarly the Romans used only one character for *u* and *v*, but we have introduced the useful distinction between them, even in Latin. The original identity of the two is shown by another modern letter, *w*, which is a double *u* in name and a double *v* in form. The letters *j* and *w* are not found in Latin words in this book.

The Romans made no distinction between capitals and small letters. Our small letters gradually developed out of capitals in late antiquity.

### Pronunciation

The pronunciation of Latin is quite different from that of English, especially in the vowels ( *a, e, i, o, u* ), and is more like that of Spanish, Italian, French, German, and other foreign languages. It is not difficult, because it follows a few simple rules. Latin has no silent letters. For tables of sounds see pages 383–384.

### Pronunciation Exercises

1. Pronounce: ā, Mārs, pār, ab, iam, dat, nār′rat, ma′lā, ē, mē, pēs, ex, sed, per, cer′tē, lē′ge, quī, hīc, vīs, in, quid, fit, di′gitī, mī′litis, nōn, prō, mōns, nox, post, mors, cō′gor, ro′gō, iūs, cūr, lūx, nunc, cum, dux, iūs′tus, cur′rū, aes, quae, Aet′nae, aut, clau′sae, poe′nae.

2. Read the following verse. Can you tell from the rhythm and arrangement of words what it is?

> Mī′cā, mi′cā, par′va stēl′la!
> Mī′ror quae′nam sīs, tam bel′la,
> Splen′dēns ē′minus in il′lō,
> Al′ba ve′lut gem′ma, cae′lō.

*An inscription of the third century* A.D. *on the base of a statue of a chief Vestal Virgin, Terentia Flavola. This still stands in the Roman Forum. See* *p. 315.*

3. Read the following ·translation by George D. Kellogg of the first two stanzas of "America":

Tē ca′nō, Pa′tria,          Tē ca′nō, Pa′tria,
Can′dida, lī′bera;          Sem′per et ā′tria
    Tē re′feret                 Inge′nuum;
Por′tus et ex′ulum          Lau′dō viren′tia
Et tu′mulus se′num;         Cul′mina, flū′mina;
Lī′bera mon′tium            Sen′tiō gau′dia
    Vōx re′sonet.              Caeli′colum.

4. The following are ancient Latin quotations, some of which you probably have seen:

*a.* **Vē′nī, vī′dī, vī′cī,** *I came, I saw, I conquered* (Caesar's famous dispatch to the senate after a victory).

*b.* **In hōc sig′nō vin′cēs,** *In this sign* (referring to the cross) *you will conquer* (motto of Constantine, the first Christian emperor).

*c.* **Nōn nō′vit vir′tūs calamitā′tī cē′dere,** *Courage knows not how to yield to disaster.*

*d.* **Iniūriā′rum reme′dium est oblī′viō,** *Forgetfulness is the cure for injuries.*

*e.* **Pos′sunt qui′a pos′se viden′tur,** *They can because they think they can.*

*f.* **Aman′tium ī′rae amō′ris integrā′tiō est,** *The quarrels of lovers are the renewal of love* (Terence; quoted by Winston Churchill in a message to Franklin D. Roosevelt).

5. The two verses that follow were used by Roman children in some of their games:

*a.* **Ha′beat sca′biem quis′quis ad mē vē′nerit novis′simus,** *May he have the itch who comes to me last.*

*b.* **Rēx e′rit quī rēc′tē fa′ciet; quī nōn fa′ciet nōn e′rit,** *He will be king who does right; he who does not will not be king.*

 UNIT I

# Easy Reading

The Plymouth Rock Monument, commemorating the three-hundredth anniversary of the landing of the Pilgrims at Plymouth, Mass., in 1620, is in a classical style.

PHILIP GENDREAU

*Via. A street in ancient Pompeii as it was 1900 years ago. The boys had to fetch the water even in those days.*

*Britannia. London as it was under Roman rule. The Romans ruled England from the first to the fifth century A.D. Many ruins of Roman London have been uncovered, especially in the holes made by bombs in World War II.*

# *Lesson i*

## ĪNSULAE

Britannia [1] est īnsula. Eurōpa nōn est īnsula. Italia paene [2] est īnsula; Italia paenīnsula [3] est. Sicilia et [4] Corsica īnsulae sunt. Viae et silvae et īnsulae et paenīnsulae in Eurōpā sunt. Silvae et viae in īnsulā Britanniā sunt. Cuba est īnsula. Est America īnsula? Āfrica et Asia nōn īnsulae sunt.                                                            5

QUESTIONS    1. How many islands are mentioned?
             2. How many peninsulas?

## Reading Latin

As you read through a Latin sentence, try to get the meaning of each word as you come to it. Sometimes you will find a clue in an English word derived, or formed, from the Latin word, as *insular* from **īnsula;** sometimes you will have to guess from the rest of the sentence. Some words not explained in the lesson vocabularies are purposely used in the Latin passages. If you cannot guess their meaning, look them up in the Latin-English Vocabulary at the end of the book. Pay close attention to the endings; they will cause you all sorts of trouble if you don't. When you understand the passage, answer the questions; then translate, that is, express it in good English. Do not always use the English meanings of the Latin words as given in the vocabulary, but find English words of like meaning which exactly fit the sentence. Remember that Latin has no words for *a, an,* and *the*.

## Sentences

The Latin and English passages above are made up of *sentences* —that is, words grouped together to express thoughts.

---

[1] *Britain.* The meaning of names such as this is usually so clear that they are not listed in the lesson vocabularies; if necessary, they may be looked up in the Latin-English Vocabulary at the end of the book.

[2] *almost.*

[3] Try to find the meaning of this word from its English derivative and from the meaning of **paene** and **īnsula.**

[4] *and.*

Coin of Queen Elizabeth of England issued in 1953. The Latin inscription reads: "Elizabeth II Dei gra(tia) Britt(anniarum) omn(ium) regina f(idei) d(efensor)," "Elizabeth II by the grace of God queen of all the Britains, defender of the faith." The spelling with two tt's is a sign of the plural, as we abbreviate pages by pp.
WIDE WORLD

Each sentence has two parts: the *subject*, about which something is said, and the *predicate*, which says something about the subject:

*The road* (subject) *is long* (predicate), **Via longa est.**

### Nouns

1. When a word is used to name a person, place, or thing, we call it a *noun*. It happens that the subject of each sentence in the Latin passage just studied is a noun.

2. We say a noun is *singular* in number when it names one person, place, or thing: *island,* īnsula. We say it is *plural* in number when it names more than one person, place, or thing: *islands,* īnsulae. Note that in Latin, as in English, the endings of nouns are changed to show plural number. Pick out the singular and the plural nouns in the second paragraph on page 1.

3. The *case* of a noun is determined by its use in a sentence. In English we sometimes change the ending to show the case: *the boy's hat.* In Latin this is almost always done.

### The Nominative Case

1. In Latin, as in English, the subject of a sentence is in the *nominative* case.

2. A noun used in the predicate after a linking verb (*is, are, seem,* etc.) to complete its meaning is in the nominative. This is called the *predicate nominative.* Such verbs really stand for the sign of equality (=).

1        2     1        2<br>
Britannia est īnsula, Britain is an island; Britain = an island

The case endings for the nominative, singular and plural, of nouns of the *first declension,* as it is called, are:

|  | SINGULAR | PLURAL |
|---|---|---|
|  | –a | –ae |
| as in the Latin word | via | viae |

## English Word Studies

Many English words have been borrowed from Latin without change. Some first declension nouns of this sort have kept the Latin nominative plural as well as the singular:

*alumna, alumnae; antenna, antennae* (or *antennas,* when used in radio); *larva, larvae; minutiae* (singular rare)

Others usually have the English plural in *–s:*

*area, arena, camera, cicada, copula, corona, formula*

Remember that the English pronunciation is used for all of them; therefore *–ae* is pronounced like *e* in *me.* See the English dictionary for the pronunciation and meaning of these *loan words,* as they are called.

*Isolation = Insulation.*

**Vocabulary**
est, *is*
īn′sula, *island* (insulate)
nōn, not
sil′va, *forest, woods* (Pennsylvania)
sunt, *are*
vi′a, *way, road, street* (viaduct)

*Note.* The words in parentheses are English derivatives of the Latin words. Be sure that you understand these derivatives and can use them in English sentences. Write the Latin words of each lesson vocabulary in a notebook together with additional derivatives. Your teacher will give you directions about the notebook.

*Mons Aetna. The volcano as seen from Taormina.*

# *Lesson ii*

### SICILIA

Sicilia est īnsula magna in Eurōpā. Magna est fāma Siciliae.[1] Fortūna Siciliae nōn magna est. Familiae[2] magnae sunt et vīta[3] dūra[4] est. In Siciliā est Mōns[5] Aetna. Aetna est magna. Fāma Aetnae[6] magna est.

5    Viae in Siciliā nōn bonae sunt. Viae novae nōn longae sunt. Silvae magnae in Siciliā nōn sunt.

QUESTIONS   1. Where is Mt. Etna?
               2. Are there good roads in Sicily?

### Adjectives

An *adjective* is a word used to describe a noun or to limit its meaning. We say that an adjective *modifies* its noun. Pick out the adjectives in the second paragraph of page 1.

In English, an adjective is not changed to show number and case. *This* and *that*, however, change in the plural to *these* and *those*.

---

[1] *of Sicily.*    [2] *families.*    [3] *life.*    [4] *hard.*    [5] *Mt.*    [6] *of Etna.*

In Latin, an adjective shows by its ending both the number and the case of the noun which it modifies.

1. **Silva magna,** *a large forest.*
2. **Silvae magnae,** *large forests.*

An adjective may be used directly with a noun, as in the above examples, or in the predicate, as follows:

1. **Via longa est bona,** *A long street is good.*
2. **Viae longae sunt bonae,** *The long streets are good.*

## Position of Adjectives

In English the adjective almost always precedes the noun it modifies; we rarely use such expressions as *the house beautiful, Captains Courageous.*

In Latin the adjective precedes only in sentences in which it is more important or emphatic than the noun.

**Exercises   A.** Read in Latin and get the meaning; then translate.

1. Īnsula est magna.
2. Via est nova.
3. Viae sunt longae.
4. Viae longae sunt bonae.

5. Fortūna est bona.
6. Via bona est longa.
7. Fāma est bona.
8. Crēta est īnsula.

*Sicilia. Ruins of a Greek temple at Agrigento. Sicily was colonized by Greeks.*

PAUL PASCAL

**B.** For the English words supply Latin words with the correct endings.

1. Longa Īnsula est (*large*).
2. Īnsulae sunt (*long*).
3. Fortūna magna est (*good*).
4. Īnsula nova est (*long*).
5. Eurōpa nōn est (*island*).

**C.** Copy these sentences and add the correct endings.

1. Īnsula nov___ est magn___.
2. Viae bon___ sunt nov___.
3. Magn___ est fām___.
4. Viae nov___ sunt bon___.
5. Fortūn___ est nov___.

*Law and Medicine. Vatican City issued the stamp at the left, with a Latin inscription, for the International Juridical Congress in 1934, just 1400 years after the acceptance of the Code by Justinian. At the right is an Italian stamp for an international health congress. Shown are the snake and rod of Aesculapius, the Roman god of healing. Physicians today use a modified form of this. At the bottom, St. Peter's and the Colosseum.*

**Vocabulary**

| | | |
|---|---|---|
| bo′na, *good* | | (bonus) |
| fā′ma, *report, fame* | | (famous) |
| fortū′na, *fortune* | | (fortunate) |
| lon′ga, *long* | | (longitude) |
| mag′na, *large, great* | | (magnify) |
| no′va, *new, strange* | | (novice) |

**Roman Numerals in English**

Roman numerals are also used in English, as in dates, etc. (see the lesson headings of this book): I = 1; V = 5; X = 10; L = 50; C = 100; D = 500; M = 1000. The other numerals are formed: (*a*) by *adding* to a numeral one or more numerals of equal or smaller value after it: II = 2; VII = 7; CCLVIII = 258; (*b*) by *subtracting* from a numeral by placing a smaller numeral before it: IV = 4; IX = 9; XCV = 95. A smaller numeral placed between two larger numerals subtracts from the following numeral: CCCXLV = 345.

*Puella. She is playing jacks with knucklebones, either real ones from sheep's knuckles or imitations made of silver, clay, or other substances. She is evidently just back from the beauty shop. From a statue about 1800 years old.*

# Lesson iii

## ROSAE

Quid[1] puella parva portat? Rosās[2] portat. Ubi rosās parat? In silvā multās rosās parat et in magnā corbulā[3] portat. Ubi silva est? In īnsulā longā silva est. Cūr[4] puella parva rosās portat? Rosās amat. Rosās amātis, puellae? Rosās amāmus. Multae puellae, magnae et parvae, rosās amant. Rogā[5] puerōs![6]    5

**QUESTIONS**
1. Where does the girl go?
2. What does she do there?
3. Who loves roses?

## Verbs

1. A *verb* is a word that tells what a subject does or is. It is either the whole predicate or part of it:

He *carries*, **Portat;** The girl *is* small, **Puella parva *est.***

Pick out the verbs in the third paragraph of page 1.

2. Verbs also "tell time," that is, they tell us whether something happened in the past or is happening now, etc. We call the time of a verb *tense*. In Latin verbs, as in most English verbs, the form of the verb indicates the tense of the verb. For example, *see* is in the present tense, *saw* is in the past tense.

---

[1] *what.*    [2] *roses.*    [3] *basket.*    [4] *why.*    [5] *ask.*    [6] *boys.*

*Rosae. In this wall painting from Pompeii winged Cupids are busy selling flowers.
At the right, two are bringing in the flowers on a goat; in the center, flowers are being
unloaded; at the left, they are being arranged for display, and a customer (a wingèd
Psyche) is looking over the stock. This is one of a set of charming paintings showing
Cupids in various occupations, found in the House of the Vettii at Pompeii, a town
near Naples which was buried by an eruption of Mt. Vesuvius in 79 A.D. See p. 201.*

3. The *first person* represents the person speaking (*I, we*), the
*second person* the one spoken to (*you*), the *third person* the person
or thing spoken about (*he, she, it, they*). Verbs are sometimes
changed to show the person intended: *I have, he has.* Sometimes
they are changed to show *singular* or *plural number: I am, we are.*
But the distinction of person and number is usually made in English
only by use of the personal pronouns (*I, you,* etc.): *I have, they
have.*

4. In Latin, however, the personal pronoun subjects are usually
omitted, and *personal endings* show person and number. As a result,
a verb may be a whole sentence by itself: **Portāmus,** *We carry.* The
verb *agrees* with the subject in person and number, for the subject is
the boss of the sentence. The commonest endings are:

| | | |
|---|---|---|
| *1st person* | **–ō** (or **–m**) = *I* | **–mus** = *we* |
| *2d person* | **–s** = *you* | **–tis** = *you* |
| *3d person* | **–t** = *he, she, it* | **–nt** = *they* |

**Infinitive**

In English, the *infinitive* is the verb form that is introduced by
*to: to be, to go, to prepare.* But sometimes we use the infinitive without *to: I dare not leave, Hear him talk, Let me go, Make him come.*

In Latin, the present infinitive of all regular verbs ends in **–re:**
par**ā***re.*

## Present Stem and Present Tense

Drop the infinitive ending –re of a verb and you have the *present stem:* **portā(re)**. The present tense is formed by adding the personal endings to this stem. The hundreds of verbs in Latin are divided, according to the present stem, into four classes called *conjugations*. The present stem of the first conjugation ends in –ā. The present tense of **portō** (stem **portā–**) is *conjugated* by putting together its various forms as follows:

| SINGULAR | PLURAL |
|---|---|
| portō, *I carry, am carrying, do carry* | portāmus, *we carry, are carrying, do carry* |
| portās, *you carry, are carrying, do carry* | portātis, *you carry, are carrying, do carry* |
| portat, *he, she, it carries, is carrying, does carry* | portant, *they carry, are carrying, do carry* |

1. *Remember* that all vowels are shortened before –nt and final –m or –t and that –ā– disappears entirely before final ō in the first singular.

2. *Observe* the three ways to translate each Latin verb form— *common, progressive,* and *emphatic.* In English, when *am* and *do* are used as auxiliary verbs, that is, verbs used in the conjugation of other verbs, they have no Latin equivalent. Note the difference between **Portat,** *He is carrying,* and **Nauta est,** *He is a sailor.* One cannot say **Est portat.** Latin has no auxiliary verbs.

3. *Remember* that when a noun is used as subject the pronoun (*he,* etc.) is omitted: **Portat,** *He carries;* **Puella portat,** *The girl carries,* not *The girl she carries.*

**Practice**    Give the present of the verbs **parō** and **amō**, translating each form in three ways.

**Exercises**    **A.** 1. Amō; parās; portat.
2. Portāmus; parātis; amant.
3. Īnsula nova est parva.
4. Ubi est silva magna?
5. Ubi est Longa Īnsula?
6. Multae puellae sunt parvae et bonae.

**B.** 1. Puella (*is preparing*).
2. Puellae (*are carrying*).

3. Ubi sunt (*large forests*)?
4. Ubi est (*the little girl*)?

**C.** 1. Via bon__ est nov__.
2. Vi__ sunt bon__.
3. Ubi sunt puell__ parv__?
4. Portā__ (*we*); para__ (*they*); amā__ (*you, plur.*).

**Vocabulary**    a'mō,[7] amā're, *love, like*          (amiable)
et, conjunction,[8] *and*
mul'ta, *much*; plur., *many*          (multitude)
pa'rō, parā're, *get, get ready, prepare*     (preparation)
par'va, *small*
por'tō, portā're, *carry*                  (porter)
puel'la, *girl*
u'bi,[8] adverb, *where*

## English Word Studies

1. The following are additional loan words, borrowed from the Latin first declension, often found in high-school textbooks of science (remember that the letters are pronounced as in other English words and not as in Latin):

*amoeba, amoebae* (or *amoebas*); *nebula, nebulae* (or *nebulas*); *papilla, papillae; vertebra, vertebrae* (or *vertebras*)

Use the above in English sentences after looking up their meanings.

2. A "porter" is one who *carries* things. What is a *portable* radio? What does it mean to *import* things? What is an *amateur*? What is meant by *amity* among nations? From what Latin word is *insular* derived? Explain this sentence: "Puerto Rico is an *insular* possession of the United States." Another derivative of the same Latin word is *isolation*; what is meant by a policy of *isolation* for the United States?

---

[7] In Latin, the first person singular of the verb is put first, that is, it is the form you will find in a Latin dictionary; but in English, the "dictionary" form is the infinitive without *to*.
[8] For definitions of conjunction and adverb see p. 388.

*Viae in Italia. Two ancient roads in Italy; at the left, a street in Ostia, the seaport of ancient Rome; at the right, the Via Tusculana, at modern Frascati, southeast of Rome.*

# *Lesson iv*

## VIAE BONAE

Via Appia in Italiā est. Nōn nova est sed fāma eius[1] est magna, quod[2] longa et bona via est. Multae viae Rōmānae erant[3] bonae. Ubi sunt malae viae? Multae viae Americānae sunt malae, sed multae bonae sunt. In Italiā et in Americā bonae et malae viae sunt et erant.

Multī carrī et equī in viīs[4] Rōmānīs erant. Ubi nunc equī sunt? 5 Ubi sunt carrī? Servī magnī et parvī in viīs Rōmānīs erant. Nunc in Americā servī nōn sunt.

QUESTIONS  1. Why is the Appian Way famous?
2. Answer in English or Latin the questions asked in the Latin above.

---

[1] *of it.*  [2] *because.*  [3] *were.*  [4] *on the roads.*

*The Temples of Vesta and Castor in the Forum as they are today. These ruins enable an artist to make a picture like that on p. 3, where these two temples are at the extreme left.*

### Gender

In English, and sometimes in Latin, *gender* is a distinction in the form of words corresponding to a distinction of sex. It is shown by change of word (*father*, **pater**; *mother*, **māter**), by change of endings (*master*, **dominus**; *mistress*, **domina**), or by use of a prefix (*he-goat*, *she-goat*). *Father*, *master*, *he-goat* are *masculine* or "he" words; *mother*, *mistress*, *she-goat* are *feminine* or "she" words.

In English, nouns that are the names of sexless things are *neuter*.

In Latin, however, many such nouns are masculine or feminine: **via** (f.), *way*; **carrus** (m.), *cart*. The gender is indicated, not by the meaning of the word, but usually by its ending.

Nouns of the *first declension* are feminine (except a few that name males); those of the *second declension* ending in –**us** are masculine; the plural ends in –**ī**; **equus**, *horse*; **equī**, *horses*.

Adjectives are in the same gender as the nouns to which they belong: **puella parva, equus parvus, servī bonī.** They therefore *agree* with their nouns in number, case, and gender. We say they *modify* the nouns.

**Practice**
1. Give the nominative plural of **īnsula, equus, fortūna, carrus, servus, fāma.**
2. Give the Latin for *you* (sing.) *get, they are carrying, we do love.*

**Exercises A.** 1. Viae malae sunt.
2. Servus est parvus.
3. Ubi sunt equī et carrus?
4. Carrī magnī sunt sed equī sunt parvī.

**20**

**B.** 1. (*Wagons*) nunc nōn sunt.
2. Nunc (*the girls*) parant.
3. Ubi est (*the large island*)?
4. (*The large slaves*) portant.

**C.** 1. Bon___ est equus.
2. Carrī long___ sunt.
3. Serv___ magn___ portant.
4. Ubi sunt vi___ long___?
5. Puella est parv___ et bon___.

**Vocabulary**
car′rus, *cart, wagon* (car)
e′quus, *horse* (equestrian)
ma′lus, ma′la,[5] *bad* (malice)
nunc, adverb, *now*
sed, conjunction, *but*
ser′vus, *slave* (servile)

## English Word Studies

The following are some nouns of the –**us** type preserved in English in their original form. Note that in English the Latin ending –ī is pronounced like –*i* in *mile:*

GIMBELS COIN DEPARTMENT
*This commemorative coin was issued in 1952 in honor of President Eisenhower when he was chief of NATO. His portrait is on the other side. The Latin inscription reads "Federated Europe. Liberty. 2½ Europinos; value in silver, ½ dollar."*

| SINGULAR | PLURAL |
|---|---|
| alumnus | alumni |
| bacillus | bacilli |
| genius | genii (or geniuses, with different meaning) |
| gladiolus | gladioli (or gladioluses) |
| radius | radii (or radiuses) |

Adjectives include *bonus* and *quietus* (both nouns in English). What is a Christmas *bonus*?

Look up the plurals of *campus, circus, discus, focus, fungus, stimulus* in the English dictionary.

---

[5] The nominative singular masculine and feminine are given from now on.

*Pueri ludunt. At left and right, two marble games; in the middle, a hitting game.*

## *Lesson v*

### "PICUS-NICUS" [1]

Puellae et puerī [2] picum-nicum amant. Aquam et "cocam-colam" et multum cibum parant et in [3] silvam portant. Mārcus dīcit: [4] "Quid [5] portātis, Clāra et Anna?" "Cibum bonum portāmus." Puerī et puellae lūdunt [6] et cantant. [7] Sed nunc cibum puellae petunt. [8] "Ubi
5 est cibus?" Anna dīcit. "Hīc [9] erat cibus sed nōn est," dīcit Clāra; "ubi est Mārcus?" "Mārcus hīc erat sed nōn est. Mārcus et cibus hīc erant sed nōn sunt." Puerī et puellae dīcunt: [10] "Mārcus malus est; Mārcum accūsāmus. Fortūna mala est. Sed Mārcum inveniēmus! [11] Poena magna erit. [12] Ubi est Mārcus, ubi est Mārcus?"

**QUESTIONS**  1. What did the boys and girls take to the woods?
2. What happened to the food?

### Accusative Case: Direct Object

The *direct object* is the word which is directly acted upon by the verb. It is put in the *accusative* case. In spite of its name it has nothing to do with accusing. In English we call it the objective case.

In Latin, and sometimes in English, the accusative singular ends in **–m,** the plural usually in **–s:**

---

[1] A word made up just for you: *picnic.*
[2] *boys.*
[3] *into.*
[4] *says.*
[5] *what.*
[6] *play.*
[7] *sing.*
[8] *look for.*
[9] *here.*
[10] *say.*
[11] *we will find.*
[12] *will be.*

| Declension: | SINGULAR | | PLURAL | |
|---|---|---|---|---|
| | FIRST | SECOND | FIRST | SECOND |
| | –am | –um | –ās | –ōs |
| as in: | viam | servum | viās | servōs |
| Compare English: | him | | roads | |

1. **Anna Clāram amat,** *Anna loves Clara.*
2. **Clāra Annam amat,** *Clara loves Anna.*
3. (a) *I saw him.* (b) *He saw me.*

*Observe* in the above sentences:

1. In Latin, the accusative of a noun is usually distinguished from the nominative by its ending.

2. In English, as seen in 1 and 2, a noun does not show by its ending whether it is used as subject or as object. Its case depends upon the word order and sense. But personal pronouns (*I, you, he,* etc.) have separate forms for the accusative, as seen in 3 (a) and (b).

3. To put it another way, the greatest difference between English and Latin is this: in English, word order shows the connection between words and therefore determines the meaning; in Latin, the connection and meaning are shown by the endings. It does not make much difference whether you say **Anna occīdit** (*killed*) **Clāram** or **Clāram occīdit Anna,** but it makes a great deal of difference (at least to Anna and Clara!) whether one says *Anna killed Clara* or *Clara killed Anna.*

*Caution.* Do not confuse direct object and predicate nominative (p. 10). **Est** and **sunt** are forms of the linking verb *be.* Any noun they link to the subject must be in the same case as the subject.

**Practice**   **A.** Pick out any direct objects in the following sentences:

1. John's father is a rich man.
2. This boy found a dollar last week.
3. The butcher sold me two pounds of pork.
4. My brother saw many clowns in the circus.

**B.** Translate the words in italics:

1. I saw several *horses.*
2. Do you like the *woods*?
3. She is a very nice *girl.*
4. I see a beautiful *island.*
5. They are going to pave this *street.*

*The Forum as it once was, showing the Temples of Julius Caesar and Castor; at the right, part of the Basilica Julia, a courthouse.*

### Verb and Subject

1. **Servus fortūnam accūsat,** *The slave blames fortune.*
2. **Viam parāmus,** *We are preparing a road.*
3. **Puella et servus aquam portant,** *The girl and the slave are carrying water.*

*Observe* that:

1. The verb in each of the above sentences shows the person and number of its subject by its personal ending.

2. Two singular subjects connected by **et** require a plural verb (see sentence 3).

3. The verb stands last. But this is not always true, as we shall see later.

**Exercises  A.** 1. Equus parvus est.
2. Fortūnam accūsās.
3. Viam bonam nunc parātis.
4. Servum bonum nōn accūsāmus.
5. Carrī parvī equōs nōn portant.
6. Servus et puella multam aquam portant.

**B.** 1. (*Water*) portāmus.
   2. Servus (*the wagon*) parat.
   3. Puellae (*Anna*) accūsant.
   4. Anna (*the girls*) accūsat.

**C.** 1. Ubi sunt silv__?
   2. Aqu__ port__ (*he*).
   3. Viās bon__ parā__ (*we*).
   4. Serv__ (*plur.*) accūsāmus.
   5. Equ__ (*sing.*) accūsā__ (*you, plur.*).

**Vocabulary**
accū′sō, accūsā′re, *blame, accuse* (accusation)
a′qua, *water* (aquarium)
ci′bus, *food*
e′rat, *he, she, it was;* e′rant, *they were*
poe′na, *penalty, punishment* (penal)

*This ancient Roman ship is shown on a stamp of Tunisia, in northern Africa, once a Roman colony, now under French protection.*

**English Word Studies**

1. What is an *aquarium*? Do you know what a *ciborium* is? What is a *penal* institution?

2. The influence of Greece and Rome was strong in the building of our country. One indication of this is to be seen in the classical names of many towns. For example, there is an *Aetna* in Tennessee, and, in the English spelling *Etna*, the name is found in nine other states from Maine to California. The same influence is shown in names of business houses, factories, etc. Do you know of any named *Etna* in your community or elsewhere? The Chicago telephone directory lists *Aetna* (*Etna*) fifty-one times; Detroit's, thirty-two times; Cleveland's, twenty-eight times. There is a street called *Appian Way* in Cambridge, Mass.

# ~~~ Glimpses of Roman Life

### ROMAN ROADS AND TRAVEL

Though the Romans had no railroads, automobiles, steamships, or airplanes, they had better facilities for getting about than the modern world had until the introduction of steamships and steam railroads a hundred years ago. This was due to their wonderful system of roads. Only in the last few years, as a result of automobile travel, have our roads begun to compare with the Roman roads. Road engineers still admire the ancient Roman highways. The secret of these roads was that they were built like walls, sometimes over three feet thick.

The Romans became excellent road builders because they needed good highways to maintain communication between the various parts of their extensive empire. Even in the early days when Rome was conquering Italy, it started its policy of road construction. The most important road in Italy, the Appian Way (see p. 36), was built by Appius Claudius in 312 B.C. It led to Capua, about 130 miles from Rome and the most important city in southern Italy. Later it was extended across Italy to Brundisium, the seaport from which travelers sailed to Greece and the Orient. It was over 400 miles long. Parts of this and other Roman roads are in use today. In World War II our soldiers discovered and used a Roman road in Sicily. It is estimated that the Romans built about 50,000 miles of hard roads—enough to circle the globe twice.

Horses, mules, carriages or omnibuses, and litters were used by travelers who did not wish to go on foot. Along all the roads there were milestones to indicate distances. Often there were benches on which the weary traveler might rest. Watering troughs for animals and fountains for men were provided. Travel was slow, of course. Fifty to sixty miles a day was fast time for people in a great hurry. Ordinarily, twenty-five to thirty-five miles was a fair daily average. A trip that we now make comfortably in a night while asleep in a Pullman car took ten or twelve days.

*Lunch counter, or bar, in an inn at ancient Herculaneum, near Naples. Travelers could buy here wine, bread, cheese, fruit, and other simple foods.*

If the roads were better than ours, the hotel accommodations were much worse. In fact, there were only small inns, which were usually dirty and uncomfortable. The wealthier classes stayed overnight at country villas belonging to themselves or their friends, or in the town houses of people they knew. It was not uncommon for rich Romans to have half a dozen or more villas scattered throughout Italy.

Travel by water was avoided as much as possible. Roman ships were small sailing vessels which were also equipped with oars (pp. 25, 231). Sailing was dangerous, and the boats stayed near the shore as much as possible.

**DISCUSSION** 1. The Romans were great road builders—why?

**QUESTIONS** 2. Can you judge a people or a community by its roads?

3. What effect has rapid transportation had on the development of the United States?

**READING** Showerman, pp. 485–502; Davis, pp. 454–456; Johnston, pp. 309–315; Mills, pp. 424–429.[1]

---

[1] For full titles of these books see p. 405.

*The Forum at Rome, with the Temple of Saturn at the left, the open Forum behind it, the Colosseum in the rear; in the center background, the Arch of Titus and the Temple of Castor; at the right, the Palatine Hill.*

# Unit I Review

## LESSONS I–V

### ENGLISH WORD STUDIES

1. What is a loan word? How should *–ae* be pronounced in the English words *alumnae, larvae,* and *vertebrae?*

2. What do you think the following italicized words mean, judging from the Latin words from which they come?

an *accuser, amateur* sport, a *novel* idea, a *portable* typewriter, to live in *amity,* a *subservient* manner, a *bonbon, magnitude.*

## VOCABULARY

The English meanings of these Latin words will be found with corresponding numbers on the following page. Study both pages and then ask someone to test you by reading the words in the Latin list. As each word is read, give the English meaning.

| NOUNS | | | |
|---|---|---|---|
| 1. aqua | 4. equus | 8. poena | 12. via |
| 2. carrus | 5. fāma | 9. puella | |
| 3. cibus | 6. fortūna | 10. servus | |
| | 7. īnsula | 11. silva | |

| ADJECTIVES | | | |
|---|---|---|---|
| 13. bonus | 14. longus | 16. malus | 18. novus |
| | 15. magnus | 17. multus | 19. parvus |

| VERBS | | | |
|---|---|---|---|
| 20. accūsō | 21. amō | 23. est | 25. portō |
| | 22. erat, erant | 24. parō | 26. sunt |

| ADVERBS | | | |
|---|---|---|---|
| | 27. nōn | 28. nunc | 29. ubi |

| CONJUNCTIONS | | |
|---|---|---|
| | 30. et | 31. sed |

## GRAMMAR SUMMARIES

### Nouns

| *In Latin* | *In English* |
|---|---|
| 1. *Number* is shown by ending. | 1. *Number* is shown by ending. |
| 2. *Gender* usually depends on ending. | 2. *Gender* usually depends on sex. |
| 3. *Case* is determined by ending; word order is free, i.e., it can be changed without changing meaning. | 3. *Case* is determined by word order, which is therefore not free. |

### Adjectives

| *In Latin* | *In English* |
|---|---|
| 1. Change form to show number, gender, and case of noun. | 1. Do not change form to show number, gender, and case of noun. |
| 2. Generally follow the noun. | 2. Regularly precede the noun. |

**Verbs**

|  *In Latin* | *In English* |
|---|---|
| 1. Endings to show person and number. | 1. Few endings to show person and number. |
| 2. Pronoun subjects usually omitted. | 2. Pronoun subjects regularly used. |

## VOCABULARY (English Meanings)

NOUNS
1. water
2. cart, wagon
3. food
4. horse
5. report
6. fortune
7. island
8. punishment
9. girl
10. slave
11. forest
12. way

ADJECTIVES
13. good
14. long
15. large
16. bad
17. much
18. new
19. little

VERBS
20. accuse
21. love
22. was, were
23. is
24. get
25. carry
26. are

ADVERBS
27. not
28. now
29. where

CONJUNCTIONS
30. and
31. but

## UNIT PRACTICE AND EXERCISES

**Exercises** **A.** Give the Latin for the words in italic type:

1. I saw *large wagons.*
2. He owned *a small island.*
3. My sons are *small.*
4. These horses are *small.*
5. We must have *good water.*
6. Anna is *a good girl.*
7. It was *a long road.*
8. Anna loved *horses.*

**B.** In what number and case are each of the following: **fortūna, īnsulam, equī, servōs, via**? Give the correct form of **magnus** with each of the above words.

**C.** 1. Give the present tense of **amō** and translate each form.
   2. Translate: **sunt, parant, accūsāmus, est, portātis.**

 UNIT II

# Rome and America

*Denver's Civic Center is in classical style.*

*The Lee Mansion in Arlington, Va., has Doric columns.*

*The Forum of Julius Caesar as restored by an artist on the basis of the ruins below. At the right, the Temple of Venus.*

*The three standing columns of the Temple of Venus in the Forum of Caesar are in the foreground; in the background, the Colosseum; at right center, the original Roman Forum.*

# *Lesson vi*

## RŌMA

Rōma prīmō[1] parva erat. Fōrma Rōmae erat quadrāta;[2] plāna nōn erat. Posteā[3] magna et clāra rēgīna[4] terrārum erat. Rōmānī[5] Rōmam amāvērunt.[6] Viae Rōmae longae erant. Magnus numerus carrōrum et equōrum in viīs[7] erat; nunc paucōs[8] carrōs et equōs in viīs vidēmus.[9] In viīs servī cibum et aquam portābant;[10] nunc servī cibum et aquam nōn portant. Cōpia aquae bonae magna cūra erat Rōmānīs.[11] Est cōpia aquae clārae Americānīs[12] cūra? America prīmō parva erat; nunc magna et clāra est.

Nunc fāma Rōmae magna est. Fāma Americae magna est. Multī Americānī Rōmam amant et ruīnās Rōmae saepe[13] spectant. Pictūrās Rōmae in hōc librō[14] spectātis?

QUESTIONS    1. What was Rome called?
              2. Do Americans ever see Rome?
              3. Why is a good water supply important?

## Genitive Case

In English, possession is shown by (1) the possessive case or by (2) the objective with *of*:

| | SINGULAR | PLURAL |
|---|---|---|
| 1. | *the boy's father* | *the boys' father* |
| 2. | *the father of the boy* | *the father of the boys* |

In Latin, the possessive case is called the *genitive*. Its endings in the first and second declensions are:

| *Declension:* | SINGULAR | | PLURAL | |
|---|---|---|---|---|
| | FIRST | SECOND | FIRST | SECOND |
| | –ae | –ī | –ārum | –ōrum |
| *as in:* | viae | servī | viārum | servōrum |

---

[1] *at first.*
[2] *square.*
[3] *afterwards.*
[4] *queen.*
[5] *the Romans.*
[6] *loved.*
[7] *on the roads.*
[8] *few.*
[9] *we see.*
[10] *carried.*
[11] *to the Romans.*
[12] *to Americans.*
[13] *often.*
[14] *in this book.*

**33**

1. **viae īnsulae,** *the roads of the island.*
2. **numerus equōrum,** *the number of horses.*

*Translation Hint.* In English, when the subject follows the verb, the sentence (unless it is a question) begins with *there.* In Latin, no such word is used:

**Sunt multae viae,** *There are many roads.*

**Practice**      Give the Latin nominative, genitive, and accusative, singular and plural, of *water, supply, wagon, land, number.*

**Exercises**   **A.** 1. Equōs amāmus.
2. Cōpia est aquae bonae.
3. Fōrma terrae plāna nōn est.
4. Cūrae puellārum parvae sunt.
5. Numerus servōrum magnus erat.
6. Silvās clārās īnsulae magnae spectātis.

     **B.** 1. Parvus est numerus (*of the girls*).
2. Poena (*of the slaves*) magna erat.
3. Cōpiam (*of good water*) portāmus.
4. Terram novam (*we are looking at*).

     **C.** 1. Numerus equ___ (*of the horses*) erat magn___.
2. Ann___ (*Anna's*) cūrae erant mult___.
3. Cōpiam cib___ bon___ par___ (*they are preparing*).
4. Fāma īnsul___ parv___ (*of the small islands*) magna erat.

**Vocabulary**

clā′rus, clā′ra, *clear, famous*            (clarity)
cō′pia, cō′piae, f.,[15] *supply, abundance*    (copious)
cū′ra, cū′rae, f., *care, concern*          (curator)
fōr′ma, fōr′mae, f., *shape*               (form)
nu′merus, nu′merī, m., *number*      (numerical)
plā′nus, plā′na, *level*                  (plane)
spec′tō, spectā′re, *look at*         (spectacle)
ter′ra, ter′rae, f., *land, earth*       (territory)

### Latin Phrases and Abbreviations in English

**i.e.** (**id est**), *that is.*
**cf.** (**confer**), *compare.*
**Fortuna caeca est,** *Fortune is blind.*
**etc.** (**et cetera**), *and the rest, and so forth.*
**Magna Charta,** *the Great Paper,* or document, which is the corner-stone of English liberty.

---

[15] Memorize the nominative, genitive, and gender, in addition to the meaning, of each noun in the lesson vocabularies.

*Magna pecunia. The early Romans had no coined money and used sheep and oxen (pecus) instead. Later they used bronze bars like this, with the figure of an ox. As each bar weighed five pounds it was really "big money."*

# Lesson vii

## EURŌPA

Ad Eurōpam nāvigābō; tōta [1] familia nāvigābit. Magnam pecūniam ad Eurōpam portābimus et multās pictūrās ad Americam portābimus. Magnās undās spectābimus. Sed aquam plānam, nōn magnās undās, amāmus. Ad īnsulās clārās, Britanniam et Siciliam, nāvigābimus. Familia Galliam,[2] Italiam, Germāniam spectābit. 5 Nautae nāvem[3] novam parābunt. Cibum nōn parābimus, nam[4] in nāvī[5] magna cōpia cibī bonī est. Nāvigābitis ad Eurōpam et magnum numerum pictūrārum ad Americam portābitis?

**QUESTIONS**
1. Who is going to Europe?
2. Who will see Italy?

---

[1] *whole.*
[2] *Gaul (France).*
[3] Accusative singular of **nāvis** (*ship*).
[4] *for.*
[5] *on the ship.*

**35**

### Future Tense

The *future* tense refers to something that *will* happen at some *future* time.

In Latin, the future of the first conjugation is formed by adding the tense sign –**bi**– (corresponding to *shall* and *will* in English) to the present stem and then attaching the same personal endings as in the present:

| SINGULAR | PLURAL |
|---|---|
| portā**bō**, *I shall carry* | portā**bimus**, *we shall carry* |
| portā**bis**, *you will carry* | portā**bitis**, *you will carry* |
| portā**bit**, *he, she, it will carry* | portā**bunt**, *they will carry* |

*Observe* that the future sign –**bi**– loses **i** before –**ō** in the first person singular and changes to –**bu**– before –**nt** in the third person plural.

**Practice**
1. Give the future indicative of **spectō**, **nāvigō**, and translate.
2. Tell the form of **amātis**, **accūsābit**, **nāvigāmus**, **parant**.

*The Appian Way (see p. 26), as it looks a few miles from Rome.*

**Exercises** **A.** 1. Ad silvam cibum portābunt.
2. Servōs bonōs nōn accūsāmus.
3. Ad terram novam nāvigābimus.
4. Magnae undae ad īnsulam sunt.
5. Ubi magnam cōpiam cibī parābis?
6. Nautae ad īnsulam plānam nāvigābunt.
7. Anna ad familiam cōpiam aquae portābit.

**B.** 1. Multōs carrōs (*he will prepare*).
2. Ad terrās novās (*we shall sail*).
3. Undās magnās (*they will look at*).
4. Ad familiam nautae pecūniam (*I shall carry*).

**C.** 1. Est cōpia cib___ bon___.
2. Cōpiam pecūni___ parā___ (*we shall get*).
3. Ubi sunt silv___ īnsul___ (*of the island*)?
4. Familia nautae (*sailor's*) ad īnsulam nāvigābit (*will sail*).

**Vocabulary** ad, preposition [6] with acc., *to, toward* (with verbs of "coming" and "going"); *near* (with verbs of rest)

| | | |
|---|---|---|
| fami′lia, fami′liae, f., *family* | | (familiar) |
| nau′ta, nau′tae, m., *sailor* | | (nautical) |
| nā′vigō, nāvigā′re, *sail* | | (navigation) |
| pecū′nia, pecū′niae, f., *sum of money, money* | | (pecuniary) |
| un′da, un′dae, f., *wave* | | (undulate) |

*Impecunious.*

### English Word Studies

From what Latin word does *impecunious* come? Explain it in the sentence: *I never saw a more impecunious person.* From what Latin words are *unfamiliar* and *navigable* derived? An "abundant" harvest is one that overflows in big *waves.* Use *inundate* in a sentence.

---

[6] For definition of preposition see p. 388.

# *Lesson viii*

## COLUMBUS

Columbus ad Hispāniam [1] nāvigat. Isabellae, rēgīnae [2] Hispāniae, nūntiat: "Terra nōn plāna est; probābō et terrās novās mōnstrābō." Sed Isabella pecūniam nōn dōnat. Tum [3] amīcus Columbī litterās ad Isabellam portat, et Isabella Columbō pecūniam mandat. Columbus
5 grātus amīcō victōriam nūntiat.

Columbus nāvigat, sed via longa est et cūrae multae sunt. Magnus numerus nautārum malōrum Columbum accūsat. "Ad terrās novās nāvigābimus," Columbus nautīs malīs nūntiat; "Vōbīs [4] nōn poenam sed praedam dōnābō."

10 Sed subitō [5] nauta clāmat [6] "Victōria!" et terram grātam Columbō mōnstrat. Columbus cūram nāvis [7] nautīs mandat et terram novam spectat. Litterās ad Isabellam portat et Isabellae praedam dōnat.

Nunc Columbī fāma magna est. Americānī grātī Columbum laudant.[8]

QUESTIONS   1. What does Columbus say to Isabella?
2. What does Columbus do when land is sighted?
3. Find in an encyclopedia where Columbus got the idea that the earth is round.

## Dative Case: Indirect Object

The noun that indicates to or for whom the direct object is given, shown, or told, etc., is called the *indirect object* and is put in the *dative* case.

In Latin, the endings of the dative in the first and second declensions are:

|  | SINGULAR | | PLURAL | |
|---|---|---|---|---|
| *Declension:* | FIRST | SECOND | FIRST | SECOND |
|  | –ae | –ō | –īs | –īs |
| *as in:* | viae | servō | viīs | servīs |

[1] *Spain.*  [3] *then.*  [5] *suddenly.*  [7] *of the ship.*
[2] *queen.*  [4] *to you.*  [6] *shouts.*  [8] *praise.*

**Nautae pecūniam dōnō,** *I give money to the sailor,* or *I give the sailor money.*

*Observe* the following points:

1. In addition to the direct object (**pecūniam,** *money*) in the accusative, an indirect object (**nautae,** *sailor*) to show the receiver may be used.

2. In Latin the indirect object is expressed by the dative, but in English it may be expressed either by the dative, as in the second translation, or by the objective with *to* (or *for*).

3. In English there is no separate form for the dative.

4. In Latin and English the dative is placed before the accusative. This, however, is not always its position in Latin.

5. In Latin the genitive and dative singular of the first declension have the same ending. In both declensions the dative plural has the same ending.

*Caution.* After verbs of motion like "come" and "go," *to* is expressed in Latin by a preposition (**ad** with the acc.):

1. He went *to the city* as fast as he could (accusative with **ad**).

**Ubi ignis est?**

2. He told his story *to the officer* and showed *him* his driver's license (datives of indirect object).

**Practice**   **A.** Give the Latin nominative, genitive, dative, and accusative, singular and plural, of *family, money, horse, care, number.*

   **B.** Tell the case to be used in Latin in translating the words in italics:
   1. I showed *Anna* the book.
   2. I told my *friend* the whole story.
   3. We carried our bags to the *station*.
   4. The whole family moved to *California*.
   5. He presented his library to the *city*.

This is the kind of map of the world that was used by all the early explorers, probably including Columbus. It is taken from a Latin translation, made in the fifteenth century, of the book on geography written by the ancient Greek scholar Ptolemy. Remember that Columbus was trying to reach India, which he thought he reached, and that is why the natives he found in America were and still are called Indians. Note how prominent India and the Indian Ocean are in this map.

**Exercises**  **A.** 1. Servō poenam nūntiābimus.
2. Familiae pecūniam dōnābit.
3. Puellae litterās mandāmus.
4. Annae viās silvae mōnstrābō.
5. Nautīs victōriam grātam nūntiābō.
6. Anna Clārae magnam pecūniam dōnābit.
7. Carrī ad īnsulam parvam aquam clāram portant.

**B.** 1. (*To many families*) pecūniam dōnat.
2. (*To Anna*) poenam nūntiābit.
3. (*To the sailor*) litterās mandābō.
4. (*To the sailors*) viam mōnstrant.
5. (*To many lands*) nāvigābimus.

**C.** 1. Naut___ (*plur.*) pecūniam dōnābimus.
2. Nautae _____ (*to the islands*) nāvigābunt.
3. Naut___ (*sing.*) litterās mandābō.
4. _____ (*to Anna*) litterās portā___ (*she will carry*).
5. _____ (*to Clara*) cibum dōna___ (*she gives*).

*This model of a Roman freighter, propelled by sails and oars, is based on pictures in mosaic floors in Ostia. They were made by using colored stones (cf. p. 61). Compare it with a picture of one of Columbus' ships.*

**Vocabulary**

| | |
|---|---|
| amī′cus, amī′cī, m., *friend* | [amō] [9] |
| dō′nō, dōnā′re, *give, present* | (donation) |
| grā′tus, grā′ta, *pleasing, grateful* | (gratify) |
| lit′tera, lit′terae, f., *letter* (of the alphabet); plur., *a letter* (epistle), *letters* (if modified by an adjective such as **multae**) | (literary) [10] |
| man′dō, mandā′re, *entrust* | (mandate) |
| mōns′trō, mōnstrā′re, *point out, show* | (demonstration) |
| nūn′tiō, nūntiā′re, *report, announce* | (pronunciation) |
| prae′da, prae′dae, f., *loot* | (predatory) |
| pro′bō probā′re, *test, prove, approve* | (probation) |
| victō′ria, victō′riae, f., *victory* | (victorious) |

### English Word Studies

Try to see the relation between the meaning of the English derivative and the Latin word from which it comes, and then use the derivative in a sentence:

1. A "literary" man is a man of *letters;* a "literal" translation is one that is almost *letter for letter.*

2. A "mandate" is something *entrusted* to a person or a group, as the government of a weak nation.

3. A "novelty" is something *new.*

4. A person who is on "probation" is being *tested.*

In the same way explain *familiar, undulating, navigable.*

---

[9] When a new word in the vocabulary is related to a word previously studied, the latter instead of an English derivative is given in brackets.

[10] Except for *letter,* all the English derivatives have one *t,* based on an older spelling **litera.**

**41**

*Gallia. This model of the Roman aqueduct near Nîmes, France, was made by pupils of Mrs. P. Emerson Burton of the Edward D. Libbey High School, Toledo, Ohio.*

# Lesson ix

### GALLIA

Rōmānī Galliam occupant et Gallī[1] fortūnās et familiās silvīs mandant. Sed memoria iniūriārum Gallōs ad pugnam incitat. Gallī Rōmānīs nūntiant:

"Terram nostram[2] occupātis et pugnīs vāstātis. Praedam magnam
5 ad Italiam multīs carrīs portātis. Sed pugnābimus et victōriīs vītam[3] et pecūniam nostram servābimus. Iniūriīs et poenīs nōs[4] ad pugnam incitātis. Victōriās grātās Rōmae nōn nūntiābitis."

Gallī pugnant, sed multae et clārae sunt victōriae Rōmānōrum. Pugnīs Gallī vītam et terram nōn servant.

10 Ubi est Gallia? Gallōs accūsātis quod pugnāvērunt?[5] Pugnās Gallōrum memoriae mandābitis? Americānī quoque[6] pugnant et vītam et terram servant.

QUESTIONS   1. What did the Gauls do with their families?
2. What did the Romans do to Gaul?
3. Why is France today called a Latin country?

---

[1] *the Gauls,* i.e., the people of Gaul (**Gallia**).
[2] *our.*
[3] In English we use the plural.
[4] *us.*
[5] *fought.*
[6] *too.*

42

## Ablative Case

In English, the object of any preposition is in the objective (accusative) case.

In Latin, the object of some prepositions is in the accusative case; of others, in a case called the *ablative*, the endings of which are:

|  | SINGULAR | | PLURAL | |
| --- | --- | --- | --- | --- |
| *Declension:* | FIRST | SECOND | FIRST | SECOND |
|  | –ā | –ō | –īs | –īs |
| *as in:* | viā | servō | viīs | servīs |

## Ablative of Means

Many ideas expressed in English by a noun preceded by a preposition are expressed in Latin by a noun in the ablative case without a preposition, as the following common type:

**Litterīs victōriam nūntiant,** *They report the victory by (means of) a letter.*

*Observe* that **litterīs** (abl.) shows *by what means* they report, and that no preposition is used.

**Practice**  Tell the form of **memoriam, vītā, amīcōrum, iniūriā, fōrmae, servīs; occupābis, servātis, incitāmus, mōnstrābō, dōnās.**

**Exercises  A.** 1. Pugnīs īnsulam vāstātis.
2. Memoriā iniūriae nautās incitās.
3. Cibō multās familiās servābitis.
4. Aquā vītam equōrum servābimus.
5. Victōriīs vītam et terram servant.
6. Puella memoriae litterās mandābit.
7. Litterīs magnam victōriam nūntiābit.

**B.** 1. (*With money*) nautās incitāmus.
2. (*With care*) vītam amīcī servābō.
3. (*To friends*) victōriam nūntiābō.
4. Memoriā iniūriārum nautās (*arouses*).
5. (*By the victory*) īnsulam servābimus.

**C.** 1. Victōri___ (*by victory*) terram servā___ (*they will save*).
2. Aqu___ (*with water*) silvam serva___ (*they save*).
3. Pecūni___ nautās incitā___ (*I shall urge on*).
4. Serv___ (*of the slaves*) poenam nōn probāmus.
5. Amīc___ (*to friends*) pecūniam dōnā___ (*I shall give*).

**43**

**Vocabulary**

| | |
|---|---|
| in'citō, incitā're, *urge on, arouse* | (incitement) |
| iniū'ria, iniū'riae, f., *wrong, injustice* | (injurious) |
| memo'ria, memo'riae, f., *memory* | (memorial) |
| oc'cupō, occupā're, *seize* | (occupation) |
| pug'na, pug'nae, f., *battle* | (pugnacious) |
| pug'nō, pugnā're, *fight* | (pugnacity) |
| ser'vō, servā're, *save, guard* | (conservation) |
| vās'tō, vāstā're, *destroy* | (devastate) |
| vī'ta, vī'tae, f., *life* | (vital) |

## English Word Studies

1. Explain *curator, spectator, pugnacious, reservoir, incite.* From what Latin words are *vitamin, preserve, vitality, injury, devastation* derived? Give an example of a *conservation* policy in your state.

2. Latin phrases in English:

**persona non grata,** *an unacceptable person.*
**Nova Scotia,** *New Scotland,* a province in Canada.
**ad nauseam,** *to* (the point of) *seasickness* or *disgust.*
**aqua vitae,** *water of life,* formerly applied to alcohol.

*In the land of Gaul: the Roman amphitheater at Nîmes, France, now sometimes used for bullfights, which are not unlike the shows held there in ancient days.*

*Puellae undas spectant.*

# Lesson x

## PUELLAE

Anna: Ubi est Cornēlia?

Clāra: Ad prōvinciam novam nunc nāvigat.

Anna: Cūr[1] ad prōvinciam nāvigat?

Claudia: Prōvinciam amat et semper[2] laudat.

Anna: Puellae, spectāte undās magnās. Fortūna Cornēliae nōn 5
bona est. Cūra mea magna est.

Claudia: Deus[3] vītam Cornēliae servābit.

Clāra: Cornēlia servō litterās mandābit, et servus eās[4] ad
familiam portābit.

Claudia: Clāra, mōnstrā Annae gemmās[5] tuās novās.        10

Clāra: Spectā, Anna. Gemmās meās amō.

Anna: Gemmās tuās laudō; magnae et bonae sunt. Meae gemmae
parvae sunt.

Māter:[6] Fīliae, portāte aquam ad casam[7] et cibum parāte.
Servōs nōn habēmus.[8] Quīnta hōra nunc est.        15

Clāra: Magnam cōpiam aquae portābimus, māter. Quīnta hōra
est, Anna. Cibum parābimus. Valē.[9]

---

| | | | | |
|---|---|---|---|---|
| [1] *why.* | [3] *God.* | [5] *jewels.* | [7] *house.* | [9] Imperative: |
| [2] *always.* | [4] *it.* | [6] *mother.* | [8] *have.* | *good-by.* |

**45**

JAMES SAWDERS

*The famous church of the Madeleine in Paris is built like a Roman temple, with its Corinthian columns and a Latin inscription.*

**QUESTIONS**
1. Why is Cornelia unlucky?
2. Which girl has the jewels?
3. Which girls are sisters?

## Summary of First and Second Declensions

| | ENDINGS | | | | nauta bonus, *the good sailor* | | USE |
|---|---|---|---|---|---|---|---|
| | SINGULAR | | PLURAL | | SINGULAR | PLURAL | |
| DECL.: | FIRST | SECOND | FIRST | SECOND | | | |
| *Nom.* | –a | –us | –ae | –ī | nauta bonus | nautae bonī | Subj.; Pred. Nom. |
| *Gen.* | –ae | –ī | –ārum | –ōrum | nautae bonī | nautārum bonōrum | Possessive |
| *Dat.* | –ae | –ō | –īs | –īs | nautae bonō | nautīs bonīs | Indirect obj. |
| *Acc.* | –am | –um | –ās | –ōs | nautam bonum | nautās bonōs | Direct obj. |
| *Abl.* | –ā | –ō | –īs | –īs | nautā bonō | nautīs bonīs | Means, etc. |

*Observe* that:

1. In the first declension the genitive and dative singular and the nominative plural have the same ending (–ae).

2. In the second declension the genitive singular and the nominative plural have the same ending (–ī), and so do the dative and ablative singular (–ō).

3. The dative plural and the ablative plural of both declensions have the same ending (–īs).

4. In the first declension most of the endings contain –a, for this is the *A-Declension*. In the second declension several of the endings contain an –o, for this is the *O-Declension*. In the nominative and accusative singular the –o changed to –u.

### Base

That part of a word to which endings are attached is called the *base*. Drop the genitive singular ending and you have the base: **viae,** base **vi–; servī,** base **serv–.** You cannot get to first base in learning your Latin without knowing the base of a word.

*Mexico City's Memorial to Benito Juárez, the Abraham Lincoln of Mexico. The columns are in the Doric style. The chief difference between Doric, Ionic, and Corinthian is in the capitals, or tops, of the columns. Doric is the simplest. The Romans preferred Corinthian.*

JAMES SAWDERS

*The Colosseum at Rome, which once looked like this, was an amphitheater (cf. p. 44). It got its name from the colossal statue at the left—like the tail wagging the dog.*

### Declension

To *decline* a noun or adjective is to give all its case forms, singular and plural. That is quite different from declining a second helping of cake.

**Practice**     Decline together in all cases, singular and plural, **amīcus meus, numerus magnus, victōria parva, nauta malus;** *coca-cola.*

### Present Imperative

The verbs you have studied so far have been either in the *infinitive* form or in the *indicative mood.* The latter is used to make statements or ask questions.

Commands are expressed in both Latin and English by the *imperative mood.*

In Latin, the present imperative singular is the present stem of the verb (p. 17), as in **portā,** *carry.* In all conjugations except the third, the plural is formed by adding –te to the singular: **portāte,** *carry.* It usually stands at or near the beginning of the sentence.

**Practice**     Form the singular imperative of *fight, praise, sail, report;* the plural imperative of *give, accuse, save.*

**Exercises**  **A.** 1. Servā pecūniam tuam et pecūnia tua tē (*you*) servābit.
2. Amā fīliam tuam et fīlia tua tē amābit.
3. Nunc quīnta hōra est; nāvigābimus.
4. Mōnstrāte viam amīcīs.
5. Nautae vītam servōrum laudant et servī vītam nautārum laudant.

**B.** 1. (*Arouse*) servum et pugnābit.
2. (*Show*) puellīs litterās meās.
3. (*Entrust*) fāmam tuam fortūnae.
4. Puellae, (*look at*) equōs magnōs.
5. Nautae, nunc ad prōvinciam (*sail*).

**C.** 1. Laudā— (*imper. plur.*) fīliās.
2. Amīcī, laudā— fīliās bon—.
3. Dōnā pecūniam tuam amīc— (*sing.*).
4. Vāstā— (*imper. plur.*) prōvinci— (*sing.*).
5. Servā— (*imper. plur.*) vītam puellae cib—.

*The Temple of Mars (at the left) and the Forum of Augustus once looked something like this. What remains of them is near the original Forum.*

**Vocabulary**   fī′lia, fī′liae, f., *daughter*          (filial)

                 hō′ra, hō′rae, f., *hour*          (hour)

                 lau′dō, laudā′re, *praise*      (laudable)

                 me′us, me′a, *my, mine*

                 prōvin′cia, prōvin′ciae, f., *province*   (provincial)

                 quīn′tus, quīn′ta, *fifth*      (quintet)

                 tu′us, tu′a, *your* (referring to one person)

### Latin Words in the Romance Languages

The Romance languages, which are derived from Latin, have received many words from it with little or no change. This may be seen at a glance from the following list of words selected from the vocabularies of previous lessons.

*Something "good" to know.*

| FRENCH | SPANISH | PORTUGUESE | ITALIAN |
|---|---|---|---|
| accuser | acusar | acusar | accusare |
| aimer | amar | amar | amare |
| ami | amigo | amigo | amico |
| bon | bueno | bom | buono |
| char | carro | carro | carro |
| famille | familia | familia | famiglia |
| forme | forma | forma | forma |
| lettre | letra | letra | lettera |
| province | provincia | provincia | provincia |
| terre | tierra | terra | terra |

Judging from the Latin, what does each of these French, Spanish, Portuguese, and Italian words mean? Make a similar column of English words, so far as possible.

# Glimpses of Roman Life

## DRESS

The most obvious difference between ancient and modern clothing was that civilized men did not in the old days wear trousers. These garments were worn only by barbarians. After the barbarians destroyed the Roman Empire, their dress became the fashion for all Europe. The same is true of the mustache (without beard). No Roman ever wore one, and it was just as much the mark of the barbarian as trousers were. Down to the second century A.D.[1] most Romans were smooth shaven.

All Roman men wore as an outer garment a long shirt called a tunic, made of white wool. Senators and knights had crimson stripes down the front and back, the senators' stripes being broader than those of the knights. A belt was worn over this, and the upper part was bloused out over the belt. When a Roman was engaged in some active occupation, he pulled his tunic up to his knees. Such a garment alone was worn in the house.

Over the tunic the Roman citizen might wear the toga. This garment was the official dress of Roman citizens, and only citizens were allowed to wear it. It was made of white wool. The toga worn by boys and government officials had a crimson border. When boys grew up, they changed to the plain white toga. Important citizens always wore this garment when appearing in public, but the ordinary Roman wore it much less frequently.

The toga was really a sort of blanket which was thrown over the left shoulder, pulled across the back and under the right arm, and again thrown over the left shoulder. It was not fastened in any way, and it must have been quite a trick to learn to wear it.

Roman women also wore a tunic. Over this the married women wore a **stola,** a long dress with a flounce at the bottom. For street wear a shawl, called a **palla,** was added.

Wool was the chief material for clothing; next came linen. Silk was rare and expensive, while cotton was almost unknown.

---

[1] The first century A.D. covers 1–100 A.D.; the second, 101–200, etc.

MUSEUM THOUGHTS
Portrait of a Lady (c. 75 A.D.)

Julia to the barber went
And got herself a permanent.
Since the perm was unsurpassed,
"Fine!" she said. "But will it *last*?"

(I approximate the sense
Of *"Estne vere permanens?"*)
Then the vehement coiffeur,
Warmly reassuring her,
Guaranteed with confidence
The permanence of permanents.

Rome is gone and all her pride,
Still the dainty curls abide;
Venus, Mars, and Jove are dead,
Still remains the lovely head.

Let a thousand years go by,
Let our gods and empires die,
Time will never set a term
To the life of Julia's perm.
*Mundo semper erit gratus*
*Iste capitis ornatus.*
                                    —Morris Bishop [2]

In the house men and women wore sandals or slippers; outdoors they wore shoes. Those of officials were red. No stockings were worn, though in cold weather old and sickly people sometimes wound cloth around their legs.

Hats were rarely worn, except on journeys. Such as there were had broad brims and were flat. Women often wore ribbons and elaborate pins in their hair. Styles in hairdressing changed constantly as with us, but bobbed hair was unknown among adult women.

QUESTIONS
1. What was the distinctive garment of Roman men? Of women?
2. When did the Romans begin to wear mustaches and trousers?

READING
Showerman, pp. 56–64; Johnston, chap. VII; Mills, pp. 309–312.[3]

---

[3] For full titles of these books see p. 405.

# Unit II Review

## ENGLISH WORD STUDIES

Give the nominative, genitive, gender, and meaning of the Latin noun suggested by each of the following derivatives:

*copious, curate, informal, injure, literature, memorable, pecuniary, penalize, predatory, undulating, pugnacity, vitamin.*

### "To" Expressions

Tell whether the dative case or **ad** with the accusative will be needed to express the *to* idea in the following:

I hurried *to school.* The teacher explained the problem *to me.* When I went *to class,* the teacher sent me *to the board* and I showed *the class* how to do it.

## VOCABULARY

### NOUNS

| | | | |
|---|---|---|---|
| 1. amīcus | 6. fōrma | 12. numerus | 18. unda |
| 2. cōpia | 7. hōra | 13. pecūnia | 19. victōria |
| 3. cūra | 8. iniūria | 14. praeda | 20. vīta |
| 4. familia | 9. littera | 15. prōvincia | |
| 5. fīlia | 10. memoria | 16. pugna | |
| | 11. nauta | 17. terra | |

### ADJECTIVES

| | | | |
|---|---|---|---|
| 21. clārus | 22. grātus | 24. plānus | 26. tuus |
| | 23. meus | 25. quīntus | |

### VERBS

| | | | |
|---|---|---|---|
| 27. dōnō | 30. mandō | 34. occupō | 38. spectō |
| 28. incitō | 31. mōnstrō | 35. probō | 39. vāstō |
| 29. laudō | 32. nāvigō | 36. pugnō | |
| | 33. nūntiō | 37. servō | |

### PREPOSITION

40. ad

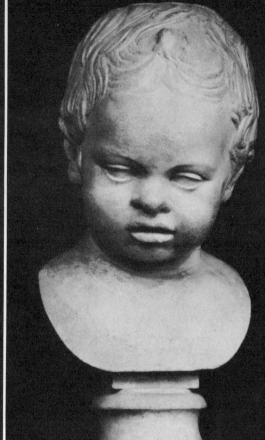

*Pueri parvi Romani. Two statues in a Roman museum.*

## VOCABULARY (English Meanings)

| NOUNS | | | |
|---|---|---|---|
| 1. *friend* | 6. *shape* | 12. *number* | 18. *wave* |
| 2. *supply* | 7. *hour* | 13. *money* | 19. *victory* |
| 3. *care* | 8. *wrong* | 14. *loot* | 20. *life* |
| 4. *family* | 9. *letter* | 15. *province* | |
| 5. *daughter* | 10. *memory* | 16. *battle* | |
| | 11. *sailor* | 17. *land* | |

| ADJECTIVES | | | |
|---|---|---|---|
| 21. *clear* | 22. *pleasing* | 24. *level* | 26. *your* |
| | 23. *my, mine* | 25. *fifth* | |

| VERBS | | | |
|---|---|---|---|
| 27. *give* | 30. *entrust* | 34. *seize* | 38. *look at* |
| 28. *urge on* | 31. *point out* | 35. *test* | 39. *destroy* |
| 29. *praise* | 32. *sail* | 36. *fight* | |
| | 33. *report* | 37. *save* | |

PREPOSITION
40. *to*

## GRAMMAR SUMMARIES
### Case Names

| In Latin | In English |
|---|---|
| 1. Nominative | 1. Nominative |
| 2. Genitive | 2. Possessive |
| 3. Accusative | 3. Objective |

### Case Uses

| | In Latin | In English |
|---|---|---|
| SUBJECT | 1. Nominative | 1. Nominative |
| DIRECT OBJECT | 2. Accusative | 2. Objective |
| INDIRECT OBJECT | 3. Dative | 3. Objective with *to* |
| POSSESSION | 4. Genitive | 4. Possessive |
| VARIOUS USES | 5. Ablative with or without preposition | 5. Objective with various prepositions. |

*Modern Rome is in and all around ancient Rome. The slanting street, which is new, runs east through the imperial fora to the Colosseum; the original Roman Forum is at the extreme right. In the foreground, a modern monument.*

UNITED PRESS

**Tense**

<table>
<tr><td>In Latin</td><td>In English</td></tr>
<tr><td>Tense is usually indicated by endings (Portābit).</td><td>Tense is often indicated by an additional verb (He will carry; He has carried).</td></tr>
</table>

## UNIT PRACTICE AND EXERCISES

**Exercises**  **A.** Decline **vīta mea, nauta malus.**

**B.** State the case required and then give in Latin:
1. *level land* (direct object)
2. *your daughter* (possessive)
3. *little girls* (indirect object)
4. *my wagons* (means)
5. *large horses* (direct object)

**C.** This is a rapid-fire drill. Give the form required as quickly as you can.
1. Translate: **occupābō, mōnstrās, dōnā, amīcōrum, pecūniā; laudābunt, servāre, nāvigātis, incitant.**
2. Translate: *of the victory, with money, we report, he will entrust, you* (sing.) *will be showing, they give, he fights.*
3. What forms are: **iniūriīs, numerō, undās, pugnābunt, grātam, spectātis, bonō, tua, mandās?**

 UNIT III

# Latin and the Romans

*Dice players quarreling in an inn; one says "get out," the other (in bad Latin), "it's two, not three." Just like a comic strip.*

*Pygmies walking on stilts and picking grapes. Can you do it? These two pictures are from wall paintings found in Pompeii.*

*An inscription in Latin to the palm goddess in Rio de Janeiro, Brazil. The date below (1906) is in Roman numerals and the building is classical in design.*

*The cathedral in Buenos Aires, Argentina, looks like an ancient Roman temple, with its Corinthian columns and its sculptured triangular pediment. Our Latin American neighbors have the same Roman cultural heritage that we have.*

# Lesson xi

Patriam nostram[1] amāmus et semper amābimus. Disciplīnā fāmam patriae augēbimus. Disciplīna nōs[2] nōn terret. Lingua patriae nostrae nōn Latīna est. Sed linguā Latīnā scientiam[3] nostrae linguae augēmus. Lingua Latīna prīmō[4] nōbīs[5] nova erat sed nunc nōn terret. Linguam Latīnam laudāmus et semper in memoriā habēbimus. 5 In Britanniā, in Italiā, in Galliā, in Americīs, in multīs terrīs et prōvinciīs multī magistrī[6] linguam Latīnam nunc docent et semper docēbunt. Magistrī magnum numerum discipulōrum[7] docent. Lingua Latīna magnam fāmam habet.

QUESTIONS    1. When did Latin scare us?    2. Why study Latin?

## Second Conjugation: Present and Future Tenses

The verbs that have occurred in previous lessons contain the stem vowel –ā– and belong to the first conjugation. All verbs which show the stem vowel –ē– in the present and future tenses belong to the *second conjugation*. The only difference from the first conjugation is in the stem vowel and in the present first singular, which keeps the stem vowel, though shortened: **doceō.**

---

PRESENT

| SINGULAR | PLURAL |
|---|---|
| doceō, *I teach, am teaching, do teach* | docēmus, *we teach, are teaching, do teach* |
| docēs, *you teach,* etc. | docētis, *you teach,* etc. |
| docet, *he, she, it teaches,* etc. | docent, *they teach,* etc. |

FUTURE

docēbō, etc., *I shall teach,* etc.

Give in full after reviewing **portābō** (p. 36). For help, see p. 397.

---

**Practice**    1. Conjugate **habeō** in the present tense and **augeō** in the future; then translate.

---

[1] *our.*    [2] *us.*    [3] *knowledge.*    [4] *at first.*    [5] *to us.*    [6] *teachers.*    [7] *pupils.*

*The Colosseum as seen from the Temple of Venus and Rome. From the moving picture "Three Coins in the Fountain."*

2. Give the singular imperative of *fight, teach*; give the plural imperative of *have, scare.*

3. Translate: *they will have, he increases, we show, he will teach, you (plur.) scare.*

**Exercises  A.** 1. Anna, docē linguās.
2. Multās linguās nōn docēbō.
3. Magnae undae servōs terrēbunt.
4. Magnae undae cūrās nautārum augent.
5. Victōria numerum servōrum non augēbit.
6. Prōvinciīs magnam victōriam patriae nūntiābimus.
7. Amīcus meus magnam pecūniam et parvam disciplīnam habet.

**B.** 1. Nautae Annam (*are scaring*).
2. Fīlia linguās (*will teach*).
3. (*Love*) linguam patriae tuae.
4. Cibum multum nōn (*we do have*).
5. (*Increase*) fortūnam tuam disciplīnā.

**Vocabulary**  au'geō, augē're, *increase*                    (augment)
disciplī'na, –ae,[8] f., *training, instruction*    (disciplinary)
do'ceō, docē're, *teach*                      (docile)
ha'beō, habē're, *have, hold*                (habit)
lin'gua, –ae, f., *tongue, language*          (linguistic)
pa'tria, –ae, f., *fatherland, country*        (expatriate)
sem'per, adv., *always*                    (sempiternal)
ter'reō, terrē're, *scare*                    (terrific)

---

[8] From now on only the genitive ending will be given instead of the full form.

## English Word Studies

1. From what Latin words are *terrible, subterranean, territory, accurate, doctrine, document* derived? When is the word *doctor* used to mean one who teaches? What is a *linguist*? What does our word *discipline* usually mean? What was its original meaning?

2. A number of Latin verb forms are preserved as English words. First conjugation: *veto, habitat, ignoramus, mandamus.* Second conjugation: *tenet.* For their meaning, see the dictionary.

The Latin ablative of the first declension is preserved in English in the word *via*: "I am going to New York *via* (by way of) Pittsburgh." The ablative plural is found in *gratis*, a shortened form of **grātiīs**: "He is giving this *gratis*" (for thanks, i.e., for nothing).

*Hunting big game in Africa. From a magnificent mosaic floor found a few years ago in a Roman villa in central Sicily, dating from about 400 A.D. This is only a small part of the floor in the main hall. And other rooms had mosaics too (cf. p. 125).*

TIME

*London, ancient and modern. Bombing in World War II brought to light portions of Roman London. Here in Billiter Square the lowest depth reveals the Roman period, the next level shows bombed-out ruins of the recent past, in the background modern buildings loom up.*

# Lesson xii

## BRITANNIA

Magna īnsula Britannia in amīcitiā Galliae manet. Caesar in Galliā pugnat et amīcitiam Britanniae et Galliae videt. In Galliā māteriam et cibum parat et ad Britanniam nāvigat. Ibi amīcōs Gallōrum pugnīs terret sed in Britanniā nōn manet. Īnsulam videt,
5 nōn occupat, sed glōriam suam [1] auget. Caesar grātiam et amīcitiam Rōmānōrum meret,[2] quod [3] magnae sunt victōriae Caesaris.[4] Multīs litterīs Rōmae victōriās nūntiat. Magna est grātia patriae quod Caesar patriam servat. Multam praedam carrīs et equīs ad patriam portat. Nunc Caesar magnam glōriam habet.

QUESTIONS
1. What did Caesar do in Britain?
2. Why did Caesar win the gratitude of his soldiers?

---

[1] *his.*  [2] *wins.*  [3] *because.*  [4] *of Caesar.*

**Prepositions of Place: In**

In the preceding lessons the various uses of the prepositions *with, of, to, for, by* with nouns have been expressed in Latin by means of case endings without prepositions. But some English expressions require the use of corresponding prepositions in Latin.

**In** with the ablative = *in* or *on:*

**in silvā,** *in a forest.*
**in viīs,** *on the streets.*

**Sentence Analysis**

Before writing the translation of an English sentence into Latin, you may find it helpful to place above every noun the case and number required in the Latin sentence, as follows:

     Nom. S.     Acc. S.     Dat. S.
1. The *man* gave a *book* to the *boy*.

     Gen. S.  Nom. S.     Acc. S.  Abl. S.
2. My *friend's son* saved his *life* by *flight*.

**Practice**
1. Decline **equus tuus** and **vīta longa.**
2. Give in Latin: *good friendship* in the acc., sing. and plur.; *good food* in the gen., sing. and plur.; *a small number* in the abl., sing. and plur.; *a famous language* in the dat., sing. and plur.

**Exercises** **A.**1. Laudāte amīcitiam.
2. Magna erat grātia puellārum.
3. Nautae in terrā nōn manēbunt.
4. In viīs multōs servōs nōn videō.
5. Disciplīnā glōriam patriae augēbimus.
6. In silvīs multōs equōs nōn vidēbitis.
7. In patriā magnam pecūniam nunc habēmus.

**B.**1. (*On the streets*) carrōs vidēmus.
2. Multa māteria (*in the forest*) est.
3. Equī (*on the island*) nōn manēbunt.
4. (*In the provinces*) multōs servōs vidēbimus.

**C.** Translate into Latin.

1. Remain and see my friends.
2. They will remain on the island.
3. I shall see your daughter on the street.
4. By friendship you will increase your influence.

*Roman shops as shown in a model. The vegetable stall in the center is deserted while the lady at the left looks at jewelry and the men at the right patronize the bar.*

**Vocabulary**  amīci'tia, –ae, f., *friendship*          [*amō*]
glō'ria, –ae, f., *glory*                    ( glorious )
grā'tia, –ae, f., *gratitude, influence*     [*grātus*]
i'bi, adv., *there*
in, prep. with abl., *in, on*
ma'neō, manē're, *remain*                    ( mansion )
māte'ria, –ae, f., *matter, timber*          ( material )
vi'deō, vidē're, *see*                       ( provide )

### Latin Forms of English Names

1. Many English names of boys and girls are derived from Latin words: *a.* unchanged, or *b.* changed:

*a.* Alma, *kindly*; Clara, *clear, bright*; Leo, *lion*; Stella, *star*; Sylvester, *belonging to the woods.*

*b.* Mabel, from **amābilis**, *lovable*; Belle, from **bella**, *beautiful*; Florence, from **flōrentia**, *flourishing*; Grace from **grātia**, *grace*; Margaret, from **margarīta**, *pearl.*

2. The following names were in common use among the Romans:
August, Augustus, *venerable*; Rufus, *red-haired*; Victor, *conqueror*; Vincent (**vincēns**), *conquering.*

3. Other Roman names still used in English are:
Emil and Emily (**Aemilius, Aemilia**); Cecilia (**Caecilia**); Claudia; Cornelius, Cornelia; Horace (**Horātius**); Julius, Julia; Lavinia; Mark (**Mārcus**); Paul (**Paulus**).

Find out whether any members of your class have names derived from Latin which are not included here.

*Servus laborat. A Roman wine shop. The slave carrying in the wine jars has bloused out his tunic (see p. 51); the merchant who is bossing the job has not. As glass was expensive, clay jars of various sizes were used for liquids. From a relief sculpture in marble.*

# Lesson xiii

## PUERĪ RŌMĀNĪ

Lūcius, puer [1] Rōmānus, in Viā Altā amīcum Mārcum videt.

Lūcius: Ubi est socius tuus Quīntus?

Mārcus: Ad īnsulam nāvigāvit.

Lūcius: Cūr [2] ad īnsulam nāvigāvit?

Mārcus: Īnsulam amat. In aquā diū [3] manet; in silvā ambulat.[4]  5
In īnsulā multōs amīcōs habet.

Lūcius: Cūr nōn cum [5] sociō tuō ad īnsulam nāvigāvistī? Cūr hīc [6]
mānsistī?

Mārcus: Servōs līberāvimus et labōrāre dēbeō.[7]

Lūcius: Magnum numerum servōrum habēmus et semper habui- 10
mus. In casā, in viā, in silvā labōrant, māteriam portant, agricolae
sunt. Servī grātiam nostram meruērunt, sed eōs [8] tenēbimus.

Mārcus: Quod [9] servī nostrī agricolae bonī erant et semper
labōrāvērunt eōs nōn tenuimus sed līberāvimus. Nunc amīcī sunt
et amīcitiam eōrum [10] semper memoriā tenēbō.  15

**QUESTIONS**  1. Where is Quintus?

2. Why isn't Marcus there?

3. Whose slaves have been freed?

---

| | | | |
|---|---|---|---|
| [1] *boy.* | [3] *a long time.* | [5] *with.* | [7] *I have to.* | [9] *because.* |
| [2] *why.* | [4] *walks.* | [6] *here.* | [8] *them.* | [10] *their.* |

**65**

## Perfect Tense

In English, the *past* tense refers to an action that is completed: *He **went** yesterday.*

The *present perfect* refers to an action that is completed, but from the point of view of the present: *He **has** just **gone.*** One does not say *He has gone yesterday.*

In Latin, the *perfect* tense is used like both the past and the present perfect of English, though it more often corresponds to the past.

## Perfect Stem and Perfect Tense

Verbs of the first conjugation studied so far form the perfect stem by adding –v to the present stem: **līb-erā–, līberāv–.** Many verbs of the second conjugation form the perfect stem like **doceō** below, but no rules can be given for the others. From now on the first person singular of the perfect will be given in the vocabularies as the third form. This should be memorized. Drop the –ī and you have the perfect stem.

The endings of the perfect tense, added to the perfect stem, are used in no other tenses:

| ENDINGS | FIRST CONJUGATION | SECOND CONJUGATION |
|---|---|---|
| –ī | portāvī, *I carried, I have carried, I did carry* | docuī, *I taught, I have taught, I did teach* |
| –istī | portāvistī, *you carried, etc.* | docuistī, *you taught, etc.* |
| –it | portāvit, *he carried, etc.* | docuit, *he taught, etc.* |
| –imus | portāvimus, *we carried, etc.* | docuimus, *we taught, etc.* |
| –istis | portāvistis, *you carried, etc.* | docuistis, *you taught, etc.* |
| –ērunt | portāvērunt, *they carried, etc.* | docuērunt, *they taught, etc.* |

**Practice**
1. Conjugate the following in the perfect tense: **labōrō (labōrāv–), teneō (tenu–), mereō (meru–), maneō (māns–), mōnstrō (mōnstrāv–), augeō (aux–), habeō (habu–), terreō (terru–), videō (vīd–).**
2. Translate: *he has praised, we entrusted, they scared, we shall destroy, I saw.*

**Exercises**  **A.** 1. Servō litterās mandāvī.
2. Multōs sociōs habuistis.
3. Agricola in terrā labōrābit.
4. Magnī equī puellās terruērunt.
5. Cōpiam aquae clārae parāvistī.
6. Multōs servōs in casā vīdimus.
7. Amīcus meus in prōvinciā nōn mānsit.
8. Agricolae grātiam patriae meruērunt.

**B.** 1. The slave held the horses.
2. We saw a large number of horses.
3. The farmers have got the food ready.
4. The girls will carry the food to the house.

*A Roman theater at Leptis Magna in Libya, North Africa, shown on an Italian postage stamp; Italy once ruled that region. Why don't you make a collection of stamps with ancient buildings and figures and those with Latin inscriptions?*

**Vocabulary**  
agri'cola, –ae, m., *farmer*
al'tus, al'ta, *high* (altitude)
ca'sa, –ae, f., *house*
labō'rō, labōrā're, labōrā'vī, *work* (laborious)
lī'berō, līberā're, līberā'vī, *free* (liberator)
me'reō, merē're, me'ruī, *deserve, earn* (merit)
so'cius, so'cī,[11] m., *comrade, ally* (associate)
te'neō, tenē're, te'nuī, *hold, keep* (retention)

### English Word Studies

From their meanings tell which of the following words come from **servāre** and which from **servus**: *serf, conserve, serve, servant, reserve*. What is an *equestrian*? A *copious* portion? A *nautical* mile? What does the derivation tell us about the meaning of *social, social service, social security, socialism*?

The Latin perfect tense of the first conjugation is preserved in English *affidavit*.

---

[11] Nouns (not adjectives) ending in –ius usually shorten –ii to –i in the genitive singular: **sociī** becomes **socī**.

The accent is not changed. The nominative plural always ends in –ii: **sociī**.

*Servi. Slaves and prisoners practicing for the fights in the amphitheater. From "Demetrius and the Gladiators."*

# Lesson xiv

### SERVĪ

Servī Rōmānī erant captīvī. Rōmānī multīs pugnīs singulās terrās vāstāvērunt, et magnus erat numerus captīvōrum. Captīvōs ē Graeciā, ē Galliā, ex Asiā, ex Āfricā in Italiam mōvērunt. In familiā Rōmānā erant multī servī, bonī et malī.

5  Servī aquam in casās portāvērunt; medicī [1] et agricolae erant; dē vītā, dē glōriā, dē amīcitiā docuērunt. Multī clārī Graecī erant servī et amīcī Rōmānōrum. Litterae [2] Rōmānōrum memoriam servōrum servāvērunt. Poena servī malī magna erat. Servōs bonōs multī Rōmānī līberāvērunt.

10  In quādam [3] casā Rōmānā Maximus servōs vocāvit: "Mārce et Stātī, [4] hōra quīnta est; portāte singulī māteriam dē silvā; Cornēlī, vocā socium tuum et movēte carrum ā viā et equōs ab aquā. Tum [5] parāte cēnam; amīcōs meōs in Altā Viā vīdī et ad cēnam vocāvī." Servī māteriam portāvērunt, carrum et equōs mōvērunt. Tum cibum
15 parāvērunt et ad mēnsam [6] portāvērunt. Post [7] cēnam amīcī mānsē-

---

[1] *doctors.*     [3] *a certain.*     [5] *then.*     [7] *after.*
[2] *literature.*   [4] *Statius (Stā'shius).*   [6] *table.*

runt, et Maximus amīcīs pictūrās mōnstrāvit. Interim [8] servī in culīnā [9] labōrāvērunt. Tum amīcī Maximī servōs laudāvērunt et eīs [10] pecūniam dōnāvērunt. Maximō singulī "valē" [11] dīxērunt.[12]

**QUESTIONS**  1. How and where did the Romans get their slaves?
2. Name four things that the slaves did.
3. To how many slaves does Maximus refer?

## Vocative Case

In Latin, as in English, the case (*vocative*) used in addressing a person has the same form as the nominative, except that the vocative singular of –us nouns and adjectives of the second declension ends in –e. But in –ius nouns –ie becomes –ī:

**Spectāte undās, parve Lūcī et parva Claudia.** *Look at the waves, little Lucius and little Claudia.*
**Līberā captīvōs, amīce Mārce,** *Free the captives, friend Marcus.*

Unless emphatic, the vocative does not stand first in the sentence.

**Exercises**  **A.** 1. Mārce, vocā servōs ē casā.
2. Sociī equōs ē Viā Quīntā movēbunt.
3. In malā fortūnā bonōs amīcōs habuimus.
4. Cornēlī, movē carrōs singulōs dē silvā altā.
5. Captīvī, portāte māteriam dē silvīs ad aquam.
6. Servī malī multam praedam ab īnsulīs portāvērunt.

**B.** 1. We have called the girls to dinner.
2. My daughter had a large number of friends.
3. Brutus, move the prisoners from the island.
4. One-at-a-time [13] they sailed from the island to the new land.

**Vocabulary**
ā, ab,[14] prep. with abl., *from*
captī′vus, –ī, m., *prisoner*  (captivate)
cē′na, –ae, f., *dinner*
dē, prep. with abl., *down from, from, about*
ē, ex,[14] prep. with abl., *out of, from*
mo′veō, movē′re, mō′vī, *move*  (movement)
sin′gulī, –ae, plur., *one at a time*  (singular)
vo′cō, vocā′re, vocā′vī, *call*  (vocation)

---

[8] *in the meantime.*   [9] *kitchen.*   [10] *to them.*   [11] *good-by.*   [12] *said.*
[13] Words connected by hyphens are to be expressed by one word in Latin.
[14] The shorter forms ā and ē are used only before words beginning with a consonant (except *h*), ab and ex before vowels and sometimes before consonants.

**69**

### Prepositions of Place: *Ab, Dē, Ex*

$$\left.\begin{array}{l} \text{ā, ab} \\ \text{dē} \\ \text{ē, ex} \end{array}\right\} \text{used with the ablative} = from$$

Examples: ā viā, (*away*) *from the road.*
dē silvā, (*down*) *from the forest.*
ex aquā, (*out*) *from the water.*

*Ā viā.*          *Dē silvā.*          *Ex aquā.*

Though all three prepositions mean *from,* **ab** means *away from the outside*; **ex,** *out from the inside*; **dē,** merely *from* when it is not important to distinguish. Sometimes **dē** means *down from.*

### Latin and English Word Formation

A great many Latin words are formed by joining prefixes (**prae** = *in front;* **fixus** = *attached*) to root words. These same prefixes, most of which are prepositions, are those chiefly used in English. With these prefixes we are continually forming new words. Through them English *lives* and grows.

Examples of the prefixes **ab–, dē–** and **ex–** are:

**ab–** (**abs–, ā–**): *a-vocation, ab-undance, abs-tain.*
**dē–**: *de-fame, de-form, de-ter, de-viate, de-portation.*
**ex–** (**ē–, ef–**): *ex-alt, ex-patriation, ex-pect* (from **spectō**), *e-voke, ex-president.*

Define the above words according to prefix and root. For root words, see previous vocabularies. Distinguish the meanings of *vocation* and *avocation.*

The following are other examples of the prefix **ex–** in English: *ex-cuse, e-dict, ex-empt, ef-fect, e-gress, ex-it.*

You will find it helpful to keep a list of prefixes in your notebook and to add examples of their use in English words.

*Magister pueros docet. The boys, sitting in comfortable chairs, are reading from papyrus rolls in this sculptured relief in Treves, Germany.*

# Lesson XV

## MAGISTER

Magister noster Americānus vir bonus est. Puerī bonī magistrum laudant; puerī malī magistrum nōn laudant. Magister puellās et puerōs dē agrīs et silvīs, dē virīs clārīs, dē glōriā et fāmā patriae nostrae, līberae et sacrae, docet. Disciplīnam magistrī amīcī probō.

Carrum parvum, sed nōn equum magister habet. In carrō ad 5 lūdum¹ venit.² Sine³ equō? Sine equō, nam⁴ equus in agrīs manet. Sed magister carrum nōn movet; carrus sē⁵ movet.

Amīcus meus Paulus magistrum nōn amat; magister Paulō praemium⁶ nōn dōnāvit. Sed Paulus praemium nōn meruit. Malus erat in lūdō; puellās terruit.          10

Lūdus noster pūblicus est. Amīcus meus Cornēlius in lūdō pūblicō nōn est. Amīcī semper erimus,⁷ nam amīcitia sacra est.

Lūdī Rōmānī nōn pūblicī erant. Multī magistrī Rōmānī quī⁸ in lūdīs docuērunt nōn līberī sed servī erant.

**QUESTIONS**   1. How does the teacher get to school?
2. Why doesn't Paul like the teacher?

---

| ¹ *school.* | ³ *without.* | ⁵ *itself.* | ⁷ *we shall be.* |
| ² *he comes.* | ⁴ *for.* | ⁶ *reward.* | ⁸ *who.* |

**71**

*Archives Building, Washington, D.C., another public building that looks like a Roman temple, as do so many in Washington and all over the United States.*

### Second Declension: Nouns and Adjectives in –r

Nouns and adjectives of the second declension whose base ends in –r omit the ending –us in the nominative singular. Such words therefore end in –er or –r in the nominative. The genitive singular shows whether –e– is retained before –r in the other forms. Examples are:

| Nom. | ager | noster | | puer | liber |
|------|------|--------|--|------|-------|
| Gen. | agrī | nostrī | | puerī | līberī |
| Base | agr– | nostr– | | puer– | līber– |

(The other forms are regular; if you need help, see pp. 392, 393.)

In memorizing vocabularies, always note carefully: 1. the *nominative*, 2. the *genitive*, 3. the *gender* of every noun.

*Note.* 1. Nouns and adjectives like **puer** and **līber** have the –e– throughout; those like **ager** and **noster** have it only in the nominative singular, while **vir** has no –e– at all. Most –er words are like **ager**; no others are like **vir.**

2. The English derivative will usually show whether –e– is retained or not; for example, *pu·e·rile, lib·e·ral, mis·e·rable*; but *agriculture, sacred, magistrate.*

3. Adjectives agree with their nouns in gender, number, and case but not always in endings: *puer bonus.*

1. Decline **magister novus, vir līber.**
2. Tell the form of **equīs, pūblicī, agrum, cōpiārum, virō, nostrī, līberōs, sacrā, plānārum.**

**Exercises A.** 1. Incitā, Mārce, equum ad agrum.
2. Magister noster linguam clāram docet.
3. Magister tuus puerō malō pecūniam nōn dōnāvit.
4. In Americā magnōs agrōs et virōs līberōs vidēbitis.
5. Memoria clārōrum nostrōrum virōrum sacra est.
6. Virī nostrī agrōs sociōrum amīcōrum nōn vāstāvērunt.

**B.** 1. Give Anna the boy's money.
2. Our country is free and sacred.
3. The men moved the timber out of the forest with horses.
4. I saw many horses in the fields of our friends.

**Vocabulary**

amī′cus, –a, *friendly*        [*amō*]
a′ger, a′grī, m., *field*        [*agricola*]
lī′ber, lī′bera, *free*        [*līberō*]
magis′ter, magis′trī, m., *teacher*        (Mr.)
nos′ter, nos′tra, *our*        (nostrum)
pū′blicus, pū′blica, *public*        (publish)
pu′er, pu′erī, m., *boy*        (puerile)
sa′cer, sa′cra, *sacred*        (consecrate)
vir, vi′rī, m., *man*        (virile)

### English Word Studies

1. Several Latin words of the –er type are in common use in English.

Nouns: *arbiter, cancer, minister, vesper.*
Adjectives: *integer, miser, neuter, sinister* (the first two are used as nouns in English).

2. **Assimilation.** Some prefixes change their final consonants to make them like the initial consonants of the words to which they are attached. This is called *assimilation* (**ad** = *to*; **similis** = *like*).

The prefix **ad–** is generally assimilated. Define the following words—all of them formed from Latin words in the previous vocabularies: *ac-curate, af-filiate, al-literation, an-nounce, ap-paratus, a-spect, as-sociate, ad-vocate.*

Additional examples of assimilation of **ad–** are: *ab-breviate, af-fect, ag-gressive, ac-quire, ar-rogant, at-tend.*

*Roma. The Palatine Hill, where Rome was born. In the foreground, the Basilica Julia in the Forum.*

# Lesson xvi

## COLŌNĪ RŌMĀNĪ

Puer Rōmānus sum. Es puer? Colōnī sumus et in agrīs multās hōrās labōrāmus. Estis colōnī? Ubi habitātis? Multī agricolae ad urbem [1] Rōmam migrāvērunt. In urbem equō et carrō frūmentum [2] portāmus sed ibi nōn manēmus. In urbe multī virī habitant sed nōn 5 in agrōs migrant. Agrī nostrī magnī sunt, sed casa nostra parva est. Līberī sumus, sed labōrāmus; multōs servōs nōn tenēmus. Pecūniam nōn habēmus.

Nūntius pūblicus ad agrōs venit [3] et victōriās virōrum nostrō-rum nūntiat. Nūntiī disciplīnam et animum habent.

QUESTIONS  1. For what purpose do these farmers go to Rome?
          2. Why do these farmers have few slaves?
          3. In what ways are people in cities today dependent on the farmers?

---

[1] *city* (accusative).   [2] *grain.*   [3] *comes.*

## Present of *Sum*

The verb *to be* is irregularly formed in English and Latin, as well as in other languages, and so does not belong to one of the "regular" conjugations. The present infinitive of **sum** is **esse**. The present indicative is conjugated as follows:

| | | | |
|---|---|---|---|
| sum, | *I am* | sumus, | *we are* |
| es, | *you are* | estis, | *you are* |
| est, | *he, she, it is* | sunt, | *they are* |

Remember that **sum** is a linking verb and does not have a direct object. Give the Latin in the proper case for the underlined words:

1. They are sailors.
2. We are settlers.
3. They move the prisoners.
4. He is a slave.
5. I teach my friend.
6. You are boys.

**Exercises A.** 1. Animus virōrum est magnus.
2. Colōnī ex Eurōpā migrāvērunt.
3. Ad līberam Americam nāvigāvērunt.
4. Servī estis et in agrīs labōrātis.
5. Multī līberī virī in īnsulā magnā habitant.
6. Sociī nostrī in īnsulam captīvōs mōvērunt.
7. Carrīs dē silvīs ad aquam māteriam portābitis.

**B.** 1. Give the loot to the settlers.
2. We are messengers of a great victory.
3. The messenger's horse is in our field.
4. The prisoners will carry the timber into the fields.

*A postage stamp of the Republic of Lebanon, on the shores of the eastern Mediterranean, showing an ancient Roman temple at Baalbek (see p. 191).*

**Vocabulary**

| | | |
|---|---|---|
| a'nimus, –ī, m., *mind, courage* | (unanimous) |
| colō'nus, –ī, m., *settler* | (colonize) |
| ha'bitō, habitā're, habitā'vī, *live* | (habitation) |
| in, prep. with acc., *into*; with abl., *in, on* | |
| mi'grō, migrā're, migrā'vī, *depart* | (migration) |
| nūn'tius, nūn'tī, m., *messenger* | [nūntiō] |
| sum, es'se, *be* | (essence) |

**75**

### Prepositions of Place: *Ad, In*

1. **ad** with acc. = *(up) to*

2. **in** with acc. = *into*

**ad aquam**                    **in aquam**

**Carrōs** $\left\{ \begin{array}{c} \textbf{ad} \\ \textbf{in} \end{array} \right\}$ **aquam movent,** *They move the carts* $\left\{ \begin{array}{c} to \\ into \end{array} \right\}$ *the water.*

Compare a like difference between **ab** and **ex** (p. 70).

1. **in** with acc. = *into*

2. **in** with abl. = *in* or *on*

**in aquam**                    **in aquā**

### English Word Studies

The prefix **in–** is often assimilated (p. 73). Define the following, formed from words found in recent vocabularies: *in-gratiate, in-habitant, im-migrant, im-port, in-spect, in-undate.* What is the difference between *emigration* and *immigration*? Additional examples of assimilation of **in–** are: *im-bibe, il-lusion.* Words that have come in through the French often have **en–** or **em–** for **in–** or **im–**: *enchant, inquire* or *enquire.*

What is meant by the *colonial* period of our history? What is a *laboratory*?

A wall painting at Pompeii shows a tiny wooden horse being brought into Troy.

# Lesson xvii

**TROIA**

Graecī et Troiānī[1] ad Troiam[2] pugnāvērunt. Troiānī barbarī
erant, quī[3] in Asiā habitāvērunt. Annōs x pugnāvērunt. Tum Ulixēs,[4]
clārus Graecus, cōnsilium novum in animō habuit. Graecōs signō
ēvocāvit et eīs[5] cōnsilium mandāvit: "Multam māteriam ex silvā ad
castra portāte. Ex māteriā equum altum parāte. Barbarīs praemium  5
novum dōnābimus." Equum parāvērunt et in equum virī singulī
ascendērunt.[6] In equō scrīpsērunt:[7] "Graecī Minervae praemium
dōnant." Tum ad Troiānōs equum mōvērunt. Ad īnsulam parvam
nāvigāvērunt et frūmentum parāvērunt. Barbarī equum et castra
dēserta[8] Graecōrum vīdērunt. Equum vocāvērunt signum sacrum et 10
in oppidum[9] mōvērunt. Nocte[10] Graecī ab īnsulā revertērunt[11] et
ūnus ex Graecīs[12] signō ex equō virōs ēvocāvit. In oppidum sociōs
vocāvērunt. Troiam occupāvērunt et vāstāvērunt. Fortūna Troiānōrum mala erat.

---

[1] the Trojans.    [4] Ulys'sēs.    [7] wrote.    [10] at night.
[2] Troy.    [5] to them.    [8] deserted.    [11] returned.
[3] who.    [6] climbed.    [9] town.    [12] one of the Greeks.

**77**

*The state capitol of Arkansas, at Little Rock, a good example of Roman influence on our public buildings. What other buildings look like this?*

QUESTIONS
1. Where did the Greeks go from Troy?
2. When did they return?
3. How did the Greeks in the horse know when to come out?
4. In April, 1940, German soldiers, disguised as crews of merchant ships, seized Norwegian ports. Why did the newspapers call this a "Trojan horse" trick?

READING Hamilton, pp. 259–290 (Mentor ed., pp. 179–201); Sabin, pp. 277–292; Colum, pp. 118–121; Norton and Rushton, pp. 378–405 (397–398).

## Neuters of the Second Declension

The second declension contains, in addition to the masculine nouns ending in –us, –er, and –r, neuter nouns ending in –um. The only difference between them and the –us nouns is in the singular nominative and the plural nominative and accusative. Adjectives too have neuter forms.

|  | SINGULAR | PLURAL |
|------|----------------|--------------|
| *Nom.* | signum parvum | signa parva |
| *Acc.* | signum parvum | signa parva |

(The other forms are regular; if you need help, see pp. 392, 393.)

**Practice**

1. Decline **frūmentum bonum** and **praemium grātum.**
2. Give in Latin: *a new standard* in the acc., sing. and plur.; *a famous reward* in the abl., sing. and plur.; *a great plan* in the gen., sing. and plur.; *a small camp* in the dat.

**Exercises  A.** 1. Amīcus meus multa praemia merēbit.
2. Cōnsiliō bonō vītam amīcī nostrī servābimus.
3. Litterīs ad castra virōs barbarōs ēvocāvit.
4. Agricolae ex agrīs in castra frūmentum portāvērunt.
5. Captīvī singulī virīs nostrīs cōnsilium nūntiāvērunt.
6. Castra sociōrum nostrōrum in magnā īnsulā sunt.
7. Fabī, nūntiā signō victōriam amīcīs tuīs.

**B.** 1. We shall give our friends great rewards.
2. The settlers then moved the grain with horse and wagon.
3. The strange shape of the horse did not scare the prisoners.
4. The colonists will sail from Europe to America.

**Vocabulary**  bar′barus (m.), –a (f.), –um (n.), *foreign*; as noun,
    *foreigner, barbarian*        (barbarous)
cas′tra, –ō′rum, n. (plur. in form; sing. in meaning),
    *camp*        (Lancaster)
cōnsi′lium, cōnsi′lī,[13] n., *plan, advice*    (counsel)
ē′vocō, ēvocā′re, ēvocā′vī, *call out, summon*    [*vocō*]
frūmen′tum, –ī, n., *grain*    (fruit)
prae′mium, prae′mī, n., *reward*    (premium)
sig′num, –ī, n., *sign, standard, signal*    (sign)
tum, adv., *then*

### English Word Studies

1. The following are Latin words of the –um and –ium type preserved in their original form in English:

---

[13] Nouns (not adjectives) ending in –ium usually shorten ii to ī in the genitive singular: cōnsilii becomes cōnsilī. The accent is not changed.

| SINGULAR | PLURAL | SINGULAR | PLURAL |
|---|---|---|---|
| addendum | addenda | dictum | dicta (or –ums) |
|  | agenda | maximum | maxima (or –ums) |
| bacterium | bacteria |  |  |
| candelabrum | candelabra (or –ums) | memorandum | memoranda (or –ums) |
| curriculum | curricula (or –ums) | minimum | minima (or –ums) |
| datum | data (remember to say "these data") | spectrum | spectra (or –ums) |
|  |  | stratum | strata (or –ums) |

2. What is a *signatory* to a treaty? How did **barbarus,** meaning *foreigner,* come to mean *barbarian?* Are all foreigners barbarians? Are we considered barbarians by other nations? Can you give other examples of national prejudice?

3. Over twenty-five states have towns named *Troy*; South Dakota has both a *Troy* and a *Trojan*. The Los Angeles, Rochester, and St. Louis telephone directories have thirteen listings of Troy, and in Los Angeles there are thirty-eight listings of *Trojan*. There is a town called *Roma* in Texas and ten towns named *Rome* in other states. *Gallia* is in Ohio.

WARNER BROS.

*The wooden horse as it appears in the motion picture "Helen of Troy."*

*Actors in a Roman comedy. They wore masks indicating the type of part being played.*

# ~~~ Glimpses of Roman Life

### SLAVES

In the earliest days the Romans had few slaves but as prosperity increased they came to depend on them more and more. Slaves did much of the work on the farms and in the industries; but of course the industries were not nearly as highly developed as today. Many slaves were prisoners of war, obtained by the conquest of foreign nations. A large number of those who came from the Near East and spoke Greek became teachers, doctors, musicians, actors, book-keepers, etc. The slave was often superior to the master as a result of background and early education. He was generally of the same race as his master.

*Silver for the slaves to polish. Many dishes of silver, gold, and bronze kept the slaves busy. Here are some of the thirty-four Roman silver spoons, bowls, trays, etc., of the fourth century A.D., found near Mildenhall, England, in 1942 in ploughing a field. As this was during the War, the Mildenhall Treasure did not become known until 1946. The collection is valued at $200,000, and each of the two finders received $4,000.*

The lot of the slave was not as hard as we might imagine, though he was often enough mistreated by a cruel master. Slaves were given an allowance, and the thrifty slave could hope to save enough in the course of years to buy his freedom. Masters often granted freedom out of gratitude for services rendered. Many of these freedmen became very rich and influential. A fine example of the intimate relation of master and slave is that of Cicero and his secretary Tiro, a brilliant man who invented a system of shorthand. Some of Cicero's letters show the greatest affection for Tiro.

The wealthy people kept large numbers of slaves, all of whom had their special tasks. One might be in charge of polishing the silver, another of writing letters, another of announcing the guests or the hour of the day, etc.

Disobedient slaves were punished in various ways. The master had the right to kill a slave, but naturally he was not often inclined to do so, as he would be destroying his own property. Flogging was a common punishment. Another was to send a city slave to the farm, where the work was harder. Runaway slaves when caught were branded on the forehead with the letter **F**, which stands for **fugitĭvus.** You can guess the meaning of the word from its English derivative.

**QUESTION**  What differences are there between Roman slavery and that which once existed in our country?

**READING**  Showerman, pp. 71–73; Davis, pp. 124–138; Grose-Hodge, pp. 160–165; Johnston, pp. 98–124; Mills, pp. 346 ff.

# Unit III Review

## LESSONS XI–XVII

## VOCABULARY

NOUNS
1. ager
2. agricola
3. amīcitia
4. animus
5. captīvus
6. casa
7. castra
8. cēna
9. colōnus
10. cōnsilium
11. disciplīna
12. frūmentum
13. glōria
14. grātia
15. lingua
16. magister
17. māteria
18. nūntius
19. patria
20. praemium
21. puer
22. signum
23. socius
24. vir

ADJECTIVES
25. altus
26. barbarus
27. līber
28. noster
29. pūblicus
30. sacer
31. singulī

VERBS
32. augeō
33. doceō
34. ēvocō
35. habeō
36. habitō
37. labōrō
38. līberō
39. maneō
40. mereō
41. migrō
42. moveō
43. sum
44. teneō
45. terreō
46. videō
47. vocō

ADVERBS
48. ibi
49. semper
50. tum

PREPOSITIONS
51. ā, ab
52. dē
53. ē, ex
54. in

## ENGLISH WORD STUDIES

1. Give and define three English nouns that retain Latin nominative forms, singular and plural, of the first declension; three nouns of the second declension, masculine; and three nouns of the second declension, neuter.

2. Give prefix and Latin root word from which the following words are derived, and define:

*defame, approve, advocate, invocation, immigrant, emigrant, avocation, vocation, deter*

A *duck* in a Roman mosaic floor. The Romans were fond of representing birds, animals, and fish on their floors.

3. Choose the word in parentheses which in your opinion most nearly gives the meaning of the italicized word. Tell why you select it.

  *a.* *amicable* relations (friendly, social, free, hostile)
  *b.* a *puerile* act (poor, childish, manly, effeminate)
  *c.* a *docile* creature (wild, untamed, stubborn, easily taught)
  *d.* an animal's *habitat* (habit, appearance, living place, color)
  *e.* a *migratory* bird (singing, wandering, tame, nocturnal)

## VOCABULARY (English Meanings)

NOUNS
1. *field*
2. *farmer*
3. *friendship*
4. *mind*
5. *prisoner*
6. *house*
7. *camp*
8. *dinner*
9. *settler*
10. *plan*
11. *training*
12. *grain*
13. *glory*
14. *gratitude*
15. *tongue*
16. *teacher*
17. *matter, timber*
18. *messenger*
19. *fatherland*
20. *reward*
21. *boy*
22. *sign*
23. *comrade*
24. *man*

ADJECTIVES
25. *high, deep*
26. *foreign*
27. *free*
28. *our*
29. *public*
30. *sacred*
31. *one at a time*

VERBS
32. *increase*
33. *teach*
34. *call out*
35. *have*
36. *live*
37. *work*
38. *free*
39. *remain*
40. *deserve*
41. *depart*
42. *move*
43. *be*
44. *hold*
45. *scare*
46. *see*
47. *call*

ADVERBS
48. *there*
49. *always*
50. *then*

PREPOSITIONS
51. *from*
52. *from, about*
53. *out of, from*
54. *in, on; into*

## GRAMMAR SUMMARIES

### Case Uses

|  | In Latin | In English |
|---|---|---|
| PLACE | 1. **In** with ablative | 1. *In* with objective |
| ADDRESS | 2. Nominative or vocative (**–us** nouns only) | 2. Nominative |

### Tenses

| In Latin | In English |
|---|---|
| Perfect | Past<br>Present Perfect |

### Agreement of Adjectives and Nouns

An adjective in Latin must agree with its noun in gender, number, and case. This agreement is shown by endings. In order, therefore, to modify nouns of different genders, every adjective thus far studied has a threefold declension; for example:

*The Virginia state capitol at Richmond, built in 1785–92, was modeled after a Roman temple in Nimes, France; Thomas Jefferson furnished the plans.*

**magnus, magna, magnum,** etc. (For full declension see p. 393.)

*Caution.* Since **nauta** and **agricola** are masculine though belonging to the first declension, an adjective to agree with either must have the second declension forms, as **nauta bonus, nautae bonī,** etc.

## UNIT PRACTICE AND EXERCISES

**Practice**
1. Decline **līber, barbarus.**
2. Decline **nūntius sacer, agricola novus, signum nostrum.**
3. Conjugate in full and translate: **migrō** in the present, **maneō** in the perfect, **doceō** in the future.
4. What forms are: **tenent, socī, tenuistis, nūntiī, docēbitis, linguīs, nūntī, habēbis, habitāre, amīce?**
5. Translate: *he increases, they have, we have lived, he taught, I shall remain, they are calling, you* (sing.) *deserve, we blame, you* (plur.) *will see, call out* (sing.), *remain* (plur.).

**Exercises** **A.** Choose the right words in the parentheses to complete the sentences correctly. Give your reason for each choice and translate.
1. Agricola (agrōs, agrī) habet.
2. Agrī sunt (magnī, magnōs).
3. Agricolae (in agrōs, in agrīs) labōrant.
4. In īnsulā (multī colōnī, multōs colōnōs) vidēbō.
5. In patriā nostrā (multās, multōs) agricolās habēmus.

**B.** Fill in the blanks and then translate the sentences.
1. Serv__, portā aquam.
2. Amīcī meī sunt mult__ et bon__.
3. Agricola est bon__.
4. Colōnī multōs servōs habu__.

 UNIT IV

# Romans and Americans

*The Forum at Pompeii; Mt. Vesuvius in the background.*  AMERICAN EXPORT LINE

The Pantheon, a Roman temple famous for its dome. From an eighteenth century painting by Pannini in the National Gallery of Art, Washington, D.C. (see p. 189).

# *Lesson xviii*

## BELLUM ET VICTŌRIA

Colōnī equīs et carrīs frūmentum ad castra portāvērunt. Sociīs amīcīs arma et frūmentum dōnāre parāvērunt. Virī pugnāre et augēre numerum captīvōrum barbarōrum mātūrāvērunt. Sociī multōs agrōs vāstāvērunt et colōnīs praedam multam dōnāvērunt. Sociōs ob [1] auxilium et cōnsilium laudāre mātūrāvērunt: "Sociī bonī, semper 5 amīcī erimus. Multa signa amīcitiae vestrae [2] grāta sunt. Magna est concordia nostra in bellō. Concordia nostra barbarōs terrēbit. Patriam nostram līberāre dēbēmus."

Novum fuit multōs nūntiōs, equōs, carrōs in viīs vidēre. Longum fuit bellum, sed magnae fuērunt victōriae. Patria victōriās memoriā 10 tenēre dēbet.

QUESTIONS   1. How did the allies aid the colonists?
2. Where were messengers seen?
3. What made up for the length of the war?

### Future and Perfect of *Sum*

Review the present tense of the verb **sum** (p. 75). The future tense of **sum** also is slightly irregular in its habits:

---

| | |
|---|---|
| erō, *I shall be* | erimus, *we shall be* |
| eris, *you will be* | eritis, *you will be* |
| erit, *he, she, it will be* | erunt, *they will be* |

---

*Note.* The perfect is regular, though based on a different stem: **fuī, fuistī**, etc. (see p. 401).

### Infinitive Used as Subject

1. Since the infinitive is a form of the verb used as a noun, it may be used as the subject of a verb; as

**Amīcōs habēre grātum est,** *To have friends is pleasing.*
**Errāre hūmānum est,** *To err is human.*

---

[1] *on account of.*        [2] *your.*

The City Hall in New Orleans is in classic style, with Ionic columns. Many public buildings everywhere are classical in design.

EWING GALLOWAY

*Note.* Though the infinitive is used as a noun, it is not declined. It is in the neuter gender. Therefore the predicate adjective must also be neuter, as **grātum** in the example above.

2. The infinitive may be used as a predicate nominative; as

**Vidēre est crēdere,** *To see is to believe.*

### Infinitive Used as Object

With many verbs the infinitive may be used as direct object, like other nouns; as

**Servōs līberāre parat,** *He prepares to free the slaves.*

**Exercises A.** 1. Puellae cēnam bonam parāre dēbent.
2. Pecūniam habēre est multās cūrās habēre.
3. Multōs equōs in agrīs vidēre grātum fuit.
4. Puerō praemium nostrum mōnstrāre mātūrāmus.
5. Nūntiī praemiīs animōs nautārum incitāre parābunt.
6. Bonum erit[3] concordiam et auxilium in bellō habēre.
7. Sociī signa et arma ad terram novam portāre mātūrāvērunt.

**B.** 1. Es (*my friend*).
2. Erit (*a farmer*).
3. Erat (*a sailor*).
4. Fuimus (*comrades*).
5. Erunt (*our friends*).

---

[3] In English we add *it*; in Latin no such word is used.

90

*The Stock Exchange in New York is in Roman style, with Corinthian columns. Many banks, too, have the form of ancient temples.*

CHARLES PHELPS CUSHING

**C.** 1. It [3] is bad to owe money.
2. We ought to report the plan of war to the men.
3. Farmers, hasten to increase the supply of grain.
4. It [3] was pleasing to see the courage and harmony of the colonists.

**Vocabulary**

| | |
|---|---|
| ar'ma, –ō'rum, n., plur., *arms, weapons* | (armor) |
| auxi'lium, auxi'lī, n., *aid*; plur., *reinforcements* | (auxiliary) |
| bel'lum, –ī, n., *war* | (belligerent) |
| concor'dia, –ae, f., *harmony* | (concord) |
| dē'beō, dēbē're, dē'buī, *owe, ought* | (debt) |
| mātū'rō, mātūrā're, mātūrā'vī, *hasten* | (maturity) |

### English Word Studies

1. What is meant by large *armaments*? When is a person called *bellicose*? What is an *auxiliary* engine on a sailing ship? Eleven organizations listed in the St. Louis telephone directory are called *Concordia*, six in Milwaukee. Do you know any by that name?

2. Latin phrases in English:

**multum in parvo,** *much in little.*
**de novo,** *anew,* literally, *from a new* (start).
**in memoriam,** *to the memory* (of). Tennyson used this as a title for a poem.

**91**

*A gladiator in the arena. From "Demetrius and the Gladiators."*

# Lesson xix

## SPARTACUS

Spartacus fuit clārus servus, captīvus Rōmānōrum. Sociōs ēvocāvit et ad bellum incitāvit: "Ō sociī, Rōmānī nōn sunt aequī. Puer eram in oppidō meō, et vīta grāta semper erat. Magna erat concordia in patriā nostrā. Populus aequus erat. Silvās magnās et agrōs lātōs
5 amāvī; līber ibi fuī. Vērum amīcum habuī, puerum bonum et grātum. Sed Rōmānī patriam meam vāstāvērunt; mē et amīcum meum ex patriā portāvērunt. Nunc post[1] multōs annōs vir sum et in arēnā pugnō. Hodiē[2] in hōc[3] oppidō virum quem[4] nōn cognōvī[5] occīdī[6] —et erat amīcus meus! Estisne virī? Populum Rōmānum nōn amātis.
10 Iniūriās nōn merēmus. Nōnne nunc hōra est? Ad arma! Pugnāte! Vocāte sociōs ad auxilium! Servōs līberābimus, līberī erimus, ad patriam migrāre mātūrābimus."

---

[1] *after.*  [2] *today.*  [3] *this.*  [4] *whom.*  [5] Perf. of **cognōscō**, *recognize.*  [6] *I killed.*

1. What happened to Spartacus and his boyhood friend?
2. How did the friend die?

READING   Showerman, pp. 72–73; Tappan, pp. 139–140. If you want
to read an interesting novel about Spartacus, read *The
Gladiators*, by Arthur Koestler (New York, Macmillan,
1939).

## Asking Questions

In Latin a question is usually introduced by an interrogative word
—either a pronoun (**quis,** *who?* **quid,** *what?*), or adverb (**ubi,** *where?*
etc.), or the syllable **–ne.** This last is therefore a kind of question
mark at the beginning of a sentence and cannot be translated. It is
never used alone but is always attached to the first word in the sentence. Since it becomes part of the word, the word accent may shift:
īnsulam'ne.[7]

When **nōn** is used in a question, it is put first and **–ne** is attached
to it: **nōnne.**

---

[7] There was a tendency to avoid attaching –ne to a word ending in a
short vowel if the next to the last
syllable was short (see p. 384).

Thus **Corsi'cane** would not be used
but **–ne** would be attached to some
other word in the sentence.

*The Roman Forum as it once was, with the rostra (speakers' platform) at the left,
arch of Septimius Severus, and Senate at the right rear.*

## Conversation: A Geography Lesson

**M. = Magister,** *teacher*     **D. = Discipulī,** *pupils*

**M:** Spectāte, discipulī. **D:** Spectāmus, magister.

**M:** Ubi est Italia? **D:** In Eurōpā Italia est.

**M:** Estne Italia lāta? **D:** Italia longa sed nōn lāta est.

**M:** Īnsulamne vidētis? **D:** Corsicam vidēmus.

5    **M:** Estne Corsica magna īnsula? **D:** Parva, nōn magna īnsula est Corsica.

**M:** Quid in Siciliā vidētis? **D:** Aetnam vidēmus.

**M:** Magnam īnsulam mōnstrō; Britannia est. Colōnī ex Britanniā ad Americam migrāvērunt.

10    **M:** Fuitne Gallia prōvincia? **D:** Gallia fuit prōvincia imperī[8] Rōmānī.

**M:** Nōnne magna fuit glōria Galliae? **D:** Magna fuit glōria Galliae.

**M:** Discipulī, quis oculōs bonōs habet? **Lūcius:** Ego.[9]

15    **M:** Mōnstrā discipulīs Rōmam. **Lūcius:** Rōma in Italiā est.

*Note.* Ask questions and make statements similar to the above, using the map on page 104 or a large wall map.

**Questions**   Answer in Latin.
1. Eurōpane est in Italiā?
2. Estne Italia īnsula?
3. Ubi est Rōma?
4. Estne Italia prōvincia?

**Vocabulary**   ae′quus, –a, –um, *even, just, calm*     (equality)
lā′tus, –a, –um, *wide*     (latitude)
op′pidum, –ī, n., *town*
po′pulus, –ī, m., *people*     (popular)
vē′rus, –a, –um, *true*     (verify)

### English Word Studies

1. What is *popular* government? Use *depopulate* in a sentence. What is meant by the sentence: "I listened to his attacks with *equanimity*"? Give three more derivatives of **aequus.**

2. Give ten derivatives of **nūntiō, portō, probō, spectō,** and **vocō** found by attaching one of the prefixes **ad–, dē–, ex–,** or **in–.**

---

[8] *Empire.*     [9] *I.*

**94**

## VIRGINIA ET VĒRA

Virginia et Vēra sunt duae puellae quae[1] in oppidō nostrō vītam grātam agunt. Estne oppidum in Eurōpā? In Eurōpā nōn est; in Americā est, et puellae Americānae sunt. Nōmen oppidī "Chicago" est. Agisne vītam grātam in tuō oppidō?

Virginia ad Vēram accessit: "Multī virī oppidum nostrum accū- 5 sant. Nōn aequum est. Nōnne oppidum et populum dēfendere dēbēmus? Nōnne in hōc[2] animum nostrum pōnere dēbēmus? Causa nostra aequa est." Vēra respondit: "Quī[3] videt oppidum nostrum id[4] semper dēfendit et laudat. Quī[3] accēdit inimīcus[5] excēdit amīcus."

Quot[6] litterās nōmen "Virginia" habet? Nōmen "Virginia" octō 10 litterās habet; nōmen "Vēra" quattuor habet; habetne quīntam? Littera prīma ambōrum[7] "V" est; littera ultima "a" est. Nōmen "Virginia" longum est; nōmen "Vēra" nōn longum est. Puella Virginia parva est; Vēra magna est, sed Vēra semper Virginiae cēdit. Cēdisne amīcō tuō? Puella parva habet nōmen magnum; puella 15 magna habet nōmen parvum. Estne Vēra vēra? Habitatne Virginia in Virginiā? Estne aequum nōmen "Alta" in puellā nōn altā pōnere? Estne Clāra clāra? "Quid[8] est in nōmine?"[9] poēta rogāvit.

---

[1] *who.*  [3] *he who.*  [5] *unfriendly.*  [7] *both.*  [9] Ablative of **nōmen.**
[2] *on this.*  [4] *it.*  [6] *how many.*  [8] *what.*

*Nomen oppidi Chicago est. The Museum of Science and Industry.*

EGON BERKA

**Questions** 1. What does Virginia think that she and Vera should do?
2. Which of the girls more often has her way?

## Third Conjugation

1. Verbs of the *third conjugation* have the stem vowel –ĕ–. Note the difference of stem vowel in:

*1st Conj. (Long-A Verbs):* Pres. stem **portā–** (from infin. **portāre**)
*2d Conj. (Long-E Verbs):* Pres. stem **docē–** (from infin. **docēre**)
*3d Conj. (Short-E Verbs):* Pres. stem **pōnĕ–** (from infin. **pōnĕre**)

2. The short vowel –ĕ– of the third conjugation changes to –ĭ– in forming the present tense, except in the third person plural, where it becomes –u–. In the first person singular it disappears before –ō–.

| | |
|---|---|
| pōnō, *I place,* etc. | pōnimus |
| pōnis | pōnitis |
| pōnit | ponunt |

3. The endings of the perfect tense are the same as in the first and second conjugations: **posuī**, etc. (see p. 398).

4. The short stem vowel –ĕ– in the third conjugation verbs changes to short –ĭ– before –te in forming the plural imperative: sing., **accēde**; plur., **accēdĭte**, *approach.*

*The Elks Memorial in Chicago has Doric columns and a Roman dome.*

JAMES SAWDERS

**Practice**
1. Conjugate **agō** and **dēfendō** in the present and perfect tenses.
2. Form the present imperative, singular and plural, of the above verbs, and of **vocō** and **videō**.
3. Give the Latin for *he departs, he moves, he hastens, we are defending, you* (plur.) *approach*.

**Exercises A.** 1. Semper, puerī, agite vītam bonam.
2. Colōnī ex agrīs in oppida excessērunt.
3. Equōsne tuōs, Cornēlī, in aquam agis?
4. Agricolae ad oppidum nostrum nōn accēdunt.
5. Ubi praedam pōnitis? In viā praedam pōnimus.
6. Ad īnsulam cessimus et castra dēfendere parāvimus.

**B.** 1. He lived a good life.
2. Is he not living a long life?
3. The slave is-getting-ready to put the grain into the wagon.
4. Ought we not to increase the number of farmers in the fields?

**Vocabulary**  a′gō, a′gere, ē′gī, *drive, do, discuss, live or spend* (time)   (agent)
cau′sa, –ae, f., *cause, reason, case*   (causal)
cē′dō, cē′dere, ces′sī, *move, retreat, yield*   (accede)
  accē′dō, accē′dere, acces′sī, *approach* (w. **ad**)
  excē′dō, excē′dere, exces′sī, *depart*
dēfen′dō, dēfen′dere, dēfen′dī, *defend*   (defendant)
pō′nō, pō′nere, po′suī, *put, place*   (postpone)

## English Word Studies

We have seen that many English nouns and adjectives have preserved their original Latin forms. A great many more have preserved the base of the Latin word. Others again consist of the Latin base plus silent –e. The following are examples:

base: *form, public, sign;* base plus –e: *cause, fortune, fame, cure*

The same rules are illustrated in the following words in which changes in the base have taken place:

base: *letter* (**littera**), *number* (**numerus**), *car* (**carrus**), *clear* (**clārus**); base plus –e: *single* (**singulī**)

Give five other examples from nouns and adjectives already studied.

*Alba Domus. The White House in Washington has Ionic columns.*

# Lesson xxi

## VIR QUĪ PATRIAM REGIT

Estne aequus vir quī[1] patriam nostram regit? Officium virī quī populum regit est patriam semper cōnsiliō et armīs dēfendere et servāre, in bellō virōs ad pugnam ēvocāre. Magnam concordiam in patriā habēre dēbēmus. Bonīs virīs patriam, magnam nostram cūram,
5 mandāre dēbēmus. Bonōs virōs probāmus, malōs accūsāmus. Vir quī populum regit multum agit; vītam dūram agit. Multī virī ad eum[2] accēdunt et litterās mittunt. Eī[3] grātiās agere dēbēmus.

Vir quī patriam regit in albā domō[4] habitat. In quō[5] oppidō habitat? Semperne ibi manet? Quattuor aut octō annōs sed nōn
10 duodecim annōs ibi manet. Tum excēdit et alium virum ad Albam Domum mittimus. Vīdistīne Albam Domum? Multī puerī et puellae eam[6] spectāvērunt. Ūnus ex puerīs[7] fortasse[8] erit vir quī in Albā Domō habitābit. Fortasse tū[9] eris ille[10] vir! Exspectāsne hoc[11]? Sī[12] labōrābis, fortasse hoc praemium, officium nōn parvum, merēbis.
15 Disciplīnā, pretiō fāmae, parā regere patriam. Patria exspectat.

**QUESTIONS**  1. What is the President's duty?
2. Who sees the White House?
3. Answer the questions asked in the story.

---

[1] *who.*   [3] *to him.*   [5] *what.*   [7] *one of the boys.*   [9] *you.*   [11] *this.*
[2] *him.*   [4] *a white house.*   [6] *it.*   [8] *perhaps.*   [10] *that.*   [12] *if.*

## Apposition

1. **Multī virī, amīcī familiae meae, in oppidō sunt,** *Many men, friends of my family, are in the town.*

2. **Nautīs, amīcīs nostrīs, pecūniam dōnāvimus,** *We gave money to the sailors, our friends.*

*Observe* that **amīcī** (1) identifies the subject **virī** and stands in direct relation to it and is therefore in the nominative like it, but **amīcīs** (2) identifies **nautīs**, the indirect object, and is therefore in the dative. No verb is involved. This construction is called *apposition*. A noun in apposition with another noun (or pronoun) is in the same case as the other noun (or pronoun).

**Practice**    Give the Latin for the words in italics: I saw John, my *friend.* Have you heard the story of Spartacus, the *slave?* We lived in England, a large *island.* I told it to Mr. Jones, *my teacher.*

## Hints for Developing "Word Sense"

Few words in any language, except prepositions, etc., have exactly the same meaning at all times. While words, as a rule, have one general meaning, they may have several *shades of meaning*, which depend entirely upon their context, or surroundings. In translating a Latin word, therefore, it is necessary to get its exact meaning (as opposed to its general or "vocabulary" meaning) from its context or setting; for example,

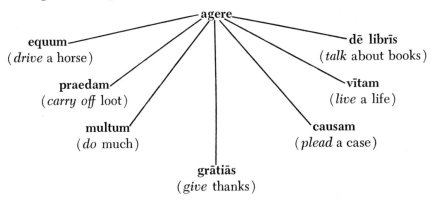

The above are only a few of the meanings of **agō.** When translating do not stick to the meanings given to words in the vocabulary, but figure out one best suited to the context. In this way you will learn to express yourself in good English.

**Exercises** **A.** 1. In Americā, patriā nostrā, semper habitābimus.

2. Amīcōs nostrōs, Lūcium et Mārcum, exspectāmus.

3. Vir aequus, amīcus puerōrum et puellārum, populum regit.

4. Mārcus multum agit. In agrīs equōs agit, in bellō praedam agit, in forō causās agit, amīcō prō [13] cēnā grā-tiās agit, cum [14] amīcīs dē officiīs agit. Vītam bonam agit.

**B.** 1. Did the boys see our friend, the farmer?

2. Our friends, the sailors, have departed.

3. Send aid to our allies, the Roman people.

4. It is the duty of the prisoner, a public slave, to drive the horses.

**Vocabulary** an'nus, –ī, m., *year* (annual)

exspec'tō, exspectā're, exspectā'vī, *look out for, await* [*spectō*]

mit'tō, mit'tere, mī'sī, *let go, send* (admittance)

offi'cium, offi'cī, n., *duty* (official)

re'gō, re'gere, rē'xī, *guide, rule* (regent)

**English Word Studies**

1. Many English verbs preserve merely the Latin base; others add silent –*e:* (1) *defend, laud;* (2) *cede, evoke.*

Give five other examples from verbs that you have studied.

2. Show how *admit* and *emit* get their meanings from **mittō**; then use them in English sentences. Explain by derivation: *demote, deter, invocation, equity.* Give three derivatives of **cēdō**.

---

[13] *for.*                [14] *with.*

*The Capitol at Washington has a Roman dome and Corinthian columns.*

When the original Roman Forum became too small, new fora were built by various emperors. Here are the remains of two, that of Trajan at the left, that of Augustus at the right.

# Lesson xxii

## RŌMĀNĪ

Quondam[1] Rōma, oppidum Italiae, parva erat. Rōmānī, populus firmus, oppidum mūnīvērunt quod arma capere et patriam dēfendere parāvērunt. Victōriīs magnīs patriam servāvērunt et auxērunt. Magna praemia Rōmānī accēpērunt, quod officium fēcērunt. Magnum numerum colōnōrum in aliās terrās mīsērunt. Multās terrās barbarās 5 cēpērunt, prōvinciās fēcērunt et aequē[2] rēxērunt. Barbarī linguam Latīnam accēpērunt. Rōmānī frūmentum ex aliīs terrīs in Italiam portāvērunt. Ad Britanniam, Hispāniam, Āfricam, Graeciam, Asiam nāvigāvērunt et oppida mūnīvērunt.

Nunc Rōma magna et pulchra est. Multī Americānī ad Italiam 10 veniunt et viās antīquās et templa pulchra inveniunt. Mātūrābisne in Italiam venīre et ruīnās Rōmānās invenīre?

**QUESTIONS**   1. Why were the Romans rewarded?
2. What do visitors to Italy see?

**READING**   Grose-Hodge, pp. 25–37.

---

[1] once.          [2] justly.

*Another view of the imperial fora. The shops of the Forum of Trajan are in the center background, to the right is the Forum of Augustus, in the foreground are the three columns of the Temple of Venus in the Forum of Caesar.*

### Present of Third (–iō) and Fourth Conjugation Verbs

In certain forms of a few important verbs of the third conjugation, –ĭ– is inserted before the stem vowel. This occurs in the first person singular of the present tense (which explains the term "–iō verbs") and in the third person plural. But most verbs ending in –iō belong to the *fourth conjugation* and have the stem vowel –ī–. They retain long –ī– throughout their conjugation except where long vowels are regularly shortened (p. 17). Note by contrast that –iō verbs of the third conjugation have short –ĭ– throughout the present tense:

| THIRD CONJUGATION (*I take*, etc.) | | FOURTH CONJUGATION (*I fortify*, etc.) | |
|---|---|---|---|
| capiō | capimus | mūniō | mūnīmus |
| capis | capitis | mūnīs | mūnītis |
| capit | capiunt | mūnit | mūniunt |

The imperative shows similar differences: **cape, capite** [3]; **mūnī, mūnīte.**

The endings of the perfect tense are the same as in the other conjugations: **cēpī, mūnīvī,** etc. (see pp. 399–400).

---

[3] The imperative singular of **faciō** is **fac.**

**Practice**     Conjugate and give all possible meanings of the present and perfect tenses of **accēdō, inveniō, faciō.**

**Exercises**  **A.** 1. Castra mūniunt et virōs ēvocant.
        2. Nōnne aequum est semper amīcōs dēfendere?
        3. In agrīs frūmentum, magnum auxilium, invenīmus.
        4. Ubi estis, puerī et puellae? Venīmus, magister.
        5. Virī singulī praemia accipiunt, quod officium fēcērunt.
        6. In oppidō cibum inveniunt et multam praedam capiunt.

   **B.** 1. We are fortifying the camp.
        2. It is pleasing to find money.
        3. We do not find our friend Marcus.
        4. Marcus is not receiving a reward because he was a bad boy.

*Stamp of British Guiana, with Latin motto: "Damus peti-musaue vicissim," "We give and seek in return."*

**Vocabulary**   ca′piō, ca′pere, cē′pī, *take, seize*          [*captīvus*]
        acci′piō, acci′pere, accē′pī, *receive*
        fa′ciō, fa′cere, fē′cī, *do, make*          (efficient)
        mū′niō, mūnī′re, mūnī′vī, *fortify*          (munitions)
        quod, conj., *because*
        tem′plum, –ī, n., *temple*          (Templar)
        ve′niō, venī′re, vē′nī, *come*          (convene)
        inve′niō, invenī′re, invē′nī, *come upon, find*

### Latin and English Word Formation: Vowel Changes

When a Latin word is compounded with a prefix, short –ă– or short –ĕ– in the root is usually "weakened" to short –ĭ– before a single consonant except –r–. The English derivatives show the same change. Long vowels are not affected. Study the following examples:

From **agō**, Latin **ex-igō, ab-igō, red-igō,** etc.; English *exigency*, etc.
From **habeō**, Latin **pro-hibeō, ex-hibeō,** etc.; English *prohibit, exhibit,* etc.
From **teneō**, Latin **con-tineō, re-tineō,** etc.; English *continent, retinue,* etc.

Illustrate the rule further by compounding **capiō** and **faciō** with **ad–, dē–, ex–,** and **in–.** Give English derivatives of these compounds in further illustration of the rule.

**103**

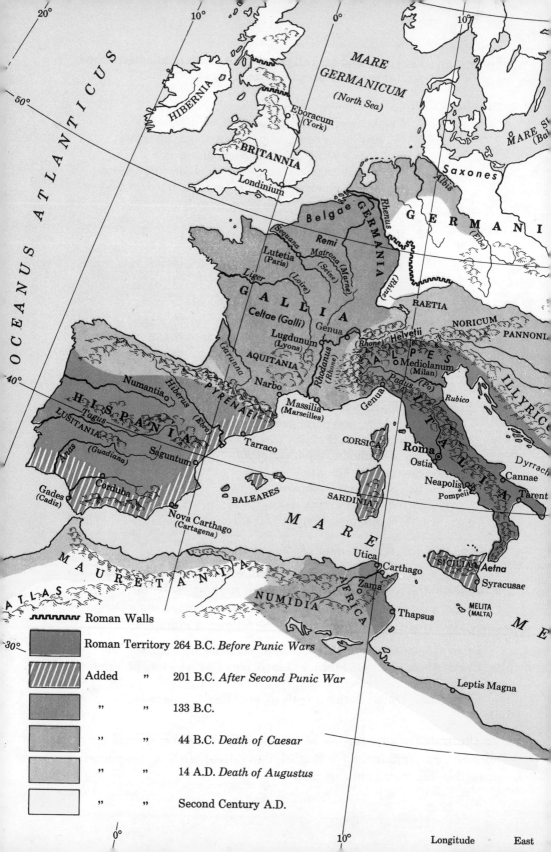

MARE
GERMANICUM
(North Sea)

OCEANUS ATLANTICUS

HIBERNIA

Eboracum
(York)

BRITANNIA

Londinium

Saxones

Albis
(Elbe)

GERMANI

Belgae

GERMANIA

Rhenus

Remi

Sequana
(Seine)

Lutetia
(Paris)

Matrona (Marne)

RAETIA

NORICUM

PANNONI

Liger
(Loire)

GALLIA

Genua

Helvetii

ILLYRICU

Celtae (Galli)

Lugdunum
(Lyons)

(Rhone)

Mediolanum
(Milan)

AQUITANIA

Garumna

Rhodanus
(Rhone)

Padus (Po)

Rubico

Narbo

PYRENAEI

Genua

Massilia
(Marseilles)

HISPANIA

Hiberus (Ebro)

Numantia

CORSICA

Roma

Dyrrach

LUSITANIA

Tagus

Saguntum

Ostia

Cannae

Togus

Anas (Guadiana)

Tarraco

Neapolis

Tarent

Gades
(Cadiz)

Corduba

BALEARES

SARDINIA

Pompeii

Nova Carthago
(Cartagena)

MARE

Utica

SICILIA

Aetna

MAURETANIA

Carthago

Syracusae

Zama

ATLAS

NUMIDIA

AFRICA

MELITA
(MALTA)

ME

Thapsus

Leptis Magna

Roman Walls

Roman Territory 264 B.C. *Before Punic Wars*

Added " 201 B.C. *After Second Punic War*

" " 133 B.C.

" " 44 B.C. *Death of Caesar*

" " 14 A.D. *Death of Augustus*

" " Second Century A.D.

Longitude          East

*Equi carros ducunt. Relief on a sarcophagus (stone coffin) in Rome.*

# *Lesson xxiii*

## AMĪCITIA

Mārcus, amīcus meus, fīlius est vīcīnī [1] nostrī. Nōn in oppidō sed in agrīs habitāmus. Causam amīcitiae nostrae nārrābō.

Mārcus praemium accēpit: equum et carrum. Carrus parvus est et pretium carrī nōn magnum erat. Prīmō [2] equus carrum dūcere nōn
5 voluit.[3] Sed Mārcus equum docuit et disciplīnā multum effēcit. Nunc equus carrum dūcit.

Quōdam diē [4] Mārcus ad casam nostram vēnit et vocāvit: "Ad terminum agrōrum māteriam carrō portābō. Auxilium tuum rogō. Venī."

10 Māteriam in carrō posuimus. Prīmō in viā plānā, tum ad locum altum, terminum agrōrum, Mārcus equum agere mātūrāvit. Ibi puer malus dē viā nōn cessit et equum terruit et ego [5] paene [6] cecidī [7] ex carrō. Sed aequus erat animus Mārcī, quī [8] equum tenuit et mē [9] servāvit. Ad terminum vītae meae nōn vēnī. Nōnne Mārcō, vērō
15 amīcō, grātus esse dēbeō et praemium dōnāre? Perīculum semper amīcōs firmōs efficit.

QUESTIONS    1. Why did the wagon cost little?
              2. Why is the speaker grateful to Marcus?

---

[1] *neighbor.*   [3] *did not want.*   [5] *I.*   [7] *fell.*   [9] Accusative of **ego.**
[2] *at first.*   [4] *one day.*   [6] *almost.*   [8] *who.*

*Ancient statues near the palace of the President of Italy.*

## Word Order

We have seen that the words in a Latin sentence show their connection with one another by means of endings, regardless of position (unlike English). They may therefore be shifted rather freely without obscuring the relationship. The more or less normal order is:

| SUBJECT | PREDICATE |
|---|---|
| noun—*adjective* (*gen., appositive*) | *abl.*—indir. obj.—dir. obj.—*adverb*—verb |

(a) *Remember*, therefore, that:

1. Adjectives usually follow their nouns, but adjectives indicating quantity and size precede: **virī bonī; multī virī.**

2. Possessive adjectives (**meus, tuus,** etc.) follow their nouns, unless emphatic.

3. A genitive often follows its noun.

4. An indirect object often stands before a direct object.

5. A word used to ask a question usually stands first, as in English.

6. The verb generally stands last. Forms of the linking verb are often placed in the middle of a sentence, as in English.

7. For **nōnne,** see p. 93.

(b) *But this normal order is far less regular in Latin than the normal order in English.* The shifted order serves to bring out varying shades of emphasis. This is done also in English, though to a less extent, largely in imitation of the Latin. Emphasis is gained in Latin particularly by:

1. Putting the emphatic words *first* in the sentence: **Magna est glōria Dominī,** also common in English: *Great is the glory of the Lord!*

2. *Separating* the emphatic word from the word to which it belongs: **Magnās puer amīcō grātiās ēgit,** *The boy thanked his friend very much.*

**107**

But sometimes little Ad. runs ahead, or little Ab. lags behind, or Mrs. Verb leads the way. Anything can happen in this family—or in a parade.

*Parade of the Latin sentence.*

**Exercises  A.** 1. Invēnī in viā pecūniam, nōn cēpī.
2. Ubi est terminus agrōrum Mārcī, amīcī nostrī?
3. Ad arma vocā, Mārce, virōs et mūnī loca plāna.
4. Ad locum altum vēnērunt et magnam silvam vīdērunt.
5. Multōs habēre dēbēmus equōs, sed magnum est pretium.
6. Magister tuus concordiam nōn efficit, quod malī sunt puerī.

**B.** 1. Great is the fame of our teacher.
2. Are you coming to our friend's dinner?
3. They are hastening to lead the horses to water.
4. The price of instruction is small, but the rewards are great.

**Vocabulary**  dū'cō, dū'cere,[10] dū'xī, *lead, draw*            (reduce)
effi'ciō, effi'cere, effē'cī, *make (out), bring about*  [*faciō*]
lo'cus, –ī, m., *place*; plur., lo'ca, n.[11]            (local)
pre'tium, pre'tī, n., *price*            (precious)
ter'minus, –ī, m., *end, boundary*            (terminal)

**English Word Studies**

1. Explain by derivation: *location, efficiency, terminate, invention.*

2. Latin phrases in English:

**ex animo,** *from the heart* (sincerely).
**Experientia docet,** *Experience teaches.*
**ad infinitum,** *to infinity,* i.e., without limit.
**ad astra per aspera,** *to the stars through difficulties* (motto of the state of Kansas).

---

[10] The imperative singular is **dūc.**

[11] Note that **locus** changes gender in the plural.

*Election posters and notices of gladiatorial shows on a house front in Pompeii. Lucretius Satrius furnishes twenty pairs of gladiators and his son ten pairs.*

#  Glimpses of Roman Life

### SIGNS OF THE TIMES

Perhaps nothing gives us quite so intimate a glimpse of a civilization as its signs and posters on walls, in windows, on posts, and the like. We are fortunate in being able to catch such a glimpse of Roman life through the signs found at Pompeii, a city near Naples which was buried by a shower of volcanic ashes from Mt. Vesuvius in 79 A.D. For more than two hundred years digging has been going on in the ruins, and hundreds of notices painted or scratched on house walls have been uncovered. Among them are the scribblings of small boys, who over and over practiced writing the alphabet. Sometimes they started a fable, as "Once upon a time a mouse . . ." Sometimes they quoted lines from Virgil and other poets. They and grown-ups too wrote their names over and over again. A kind of "pig Latin" is represented by **anumurb** for **urbānum,** like "eesay" for "see." There are messages to sweethearts; in one, greetings are sent to a girl whom the lover calls his little fish. Another girl is called the queen of Pompeii, evidently meaning the beauty queen. To another, who is unnamed, there is merely the message **Venus es.** Several run like this: **Helena amātur ā Rūfō,** "Helen is loved by Rufus." Perhaps this was written for the sake of teasing, as boys today write "John loves Jennie" or the like on fences or walls. But another tells about a girl who cannot stand a certain boy. Some of

**109**

the messages are not very complimentary: "thief" occurs several times. One reads: **Stronnius nīl scit,** "Stronnius knows nothing." In another, one person says hello to another and adds: **Quid agit tibi dexter ocellus?** "How is your right eye?" Apparently the writer is having some fun about a black eye. The owners of houses tried to keep away idlers by such signs as this: **Ōtiōsīs locus hic nōn est. Discēde, morātor,** "This is no place for idlers. Go away, loafer." Sometimes there are New Year's greetings or "Christmas" greetings (**Iō Sāturnālia**). In some cases record is kept of special events, as a birthday or the arrival of the emperor. One writer indicates that he has a cold. One says he (or she) baked bread on April 19; another that he put up olives on October 16; another tells of setting a hen on April 30. One wall lists daily expenditures, as for cheese, bread, oil, and wine. What appears to be a laundry list mentions a tunic (shirt) and a cloak on April 20, underwear on May 7, two tunics on May 8. No wonder that some unknown wrote: "Wall, I wonder that you have not collapsed from having to bear the tiresome stuff of so many writers."

When we come to formal notices, we find that election posters play a prominent part. These ask support for this man or that because he is deserving or respectable or honest or because he delivers good bread, etc. The supporters include teamsters, tailors, barbers, dyers, and many other groups. One inscription advocates giving away the money in the public treasury.

Another group of notices advertises the shows of gladiators, similar to our prize fights. Besides mentioning the number of matches, they often name other attractions, such as awnings to keep the sun off, sprinklers to keep the dust down, animal fights, athletic contests.

Hotels advertised frequently. One offers a dining room with three couches and all conveniences (**commodīs**). In an apartment house (**īnsula**) shops on the ground floor are offered from July 1, and luxurious (**equestria,** suitable for a rich man) upstairs apartments; "see agent of the owner."

Signs offer rewards for return of lost or stolen articles. On one sign a man says that he found a horse on November 25 and asks the owner to claim it on a farm near the bridge.

**DISCUSSION**  1. What kind of signs are most frequently seen today?
**QUESTIONS**  2. What impressions about us would a foreigner get from such signs?

110

# Unit IV Review

## ENGLISH AND LATIN WORD STUDIES

1. Give prefix and Latin root word from which the following are derived: **excipiō, adigō, ērigō, afficiō;** *allocation, depopulate, exigency, efficient, accessory.*

2. Make Latin words out of **ad–** and **capiō, in–** and **pōnō, ad–** and **teneō, dē–** and **mereō.**

3. The first word in each of the following lines is a Latin word. Pick the correct derivative from the English words which follow it.

| | | | | |
|---|---|---|---|---|
| **pōnō** | pone | pony | exponent | put |
| **mittēmus** | mitten | meet | send | remit |
| **populus** | poplar | population | pope | pop |
| **capit** | cap | cape | decapitate | recipient |
| **dūcō** | conduct | paint | duck | deuce |
| **aequum** | equestrian | equine | equity | equip |

## VOCABULARY

### NOUNS
1. annus
2. arma
3. auxilium
4. bellum
5. causa
6. concordia
7. locus
8. officium
9. oppidum
10. populus
11. pretium
12. templum
13. terminus

### ADJECTIVES
14. aequus
15. lātus
16. vērus

### VERBS
17. accēdō
18. accipiō
19. agō
20. capiō
21. cēdō
22. dēbeō
23. dēfendō
24. dūcō
25. efficiō
26. excēdō
27. exspectō
28. faciō
29. inveniō
30. mātūrō
31. mittō
32. mūniō
33. pōnō
34. regō
35. veniō

### CONJUNCTION
36. quod

*Roman children's tunics of cloth. Found in Egypt, whose dry climate preserved them,
they are now in the Royal Ontario Museum, Toronto.*

## VOCABULARY (English Meanings)

NOUNS
1. *year*
2. *arms*
3. *aid*

4. *war*
5. *cause*
6. *harmony*
7. *place*

8. *duty*
9. *town*
10. *people*
11. *price*

12. *temple*
13. *end*

ADJECTIVES
14. *even, just*

15. *wide*
16. *true*

VERBS
17. *approach*
18. *receive*
19. *drive, do*
20. *take*

21. *move, yield*
22. *owe, ought*
23. *defend*
24. *lead*
25. *bring about*

26. *depart*
27. *await*
28. *do, make*
29. *come upon*
30. *hasten*

31. *send*
32. *fortify*
33. *put*
34. *rule*
35. *come*

CONJUNCTION
36. *because*

## GRAMMAR SUMMARIES

### Questions

| *In Latin* | *In English* |
|---|---|
| 1. Interrogative pronoun or adverb at beginning. | 1. Interrogative pronoun or adverb at beginning; or interrogative form of verb (*Did you go?*). |
| 2. **–ne** attached to first word. | 2. Interrogative form of verb. |

**Word Order**

| *In Latin* | *In English* |
|---|---|
| 1. Free. | 1. Used to show relation of words. |
| 2. Adjectives, except those indicating quantity or size, more often follow. | 2. Adjectives precede. |
| 3. Verb is usually at end. | 3. Verb is after subject. |
| 4. Objects are usually before verb. | 4. Objects follow verb. |

## UNIT PRACTICE AND EXERCISES

**Noun and Adjective Drill**

1. Decline **multum auxilium, populus clārus, concordia vēra.**
2. Give in Latin the singular and plural of the following in the case indicated:

nom.: *my duty*  acc.: *a small price*  abl.: *our friend*
dat.: *a good place*  gen.: *a sacred land*  nom.: *a just man*

*The ruins in ruins. The house whose wall is shown on page 109 was struck by a bomb in 1943. At the left edge of the standing wall, beyond and above the American soldier, one can make out the last two letters of the name Satri, shown in full in the other picture.*

UNITED STATES ARMY

**Verb Drill A.** Decide which form of **sum** translates the English in the first column:

| | | | | |
|---|---|---|---|---|
| *they were* | fuimus | sunt | erant | sumus |
| *you will be* | erō | eris | estis | fuistis |
| *you are* | eris | fuistī | fuistis | es |
| *he was* | erant | erat | erit | fuērunt |
| *we are* | sunt | sumus | estis | erimus |
| *they will be* | erunt | erant | erit | sunt |
| *we were* | erant | erimus | sumus | fuimus |

**B.** Give the third plural of the following verbs in the present, future, and perfect: sum, exspectō, dēbeō, mātūrō, ēvocō.

**C.** 1. Give tense, person, and number, and translate: **regunt, pōnit, erunt, mātūrātis, mīsit, fuit, fēcistī, es, exspectābimus, eris, dūxērunt, invenīmus, veniunt, accēdit, laudābunt.**

2. Give in Latin: *he will be; I fortified; they approached; you* (sing.) *await; we are; they do; they received; you* (plur.) *came; we shall be; they will hasten; they will be; he leads; we are defending; he departed; he takes.*

# Stories

The capitol of Cuba in Havana (left) and that of California at Sacramento resemble the one in Washington.

ARTHUR LANG                    PICTURES INC.

*Pluto Proserpinam ad inferos ducit. Drawn by Willy Pogany.*

*Wall painting from Pompeii with birds, fountains, trees, and flowers.*

# *Lesson xxiv*

## CERĒS ET PRŌSERPINA

Cerēs, dea frūmentī, et fīlia Prōserpina [1] in Siciliā habitāvērunt. Quondam [2] Prōserpina et aliae puellae in agrīs erant. Locum commodum invēnērunt et flōrēs [3] variōs lēgērunt. Ōtium grātum erat; magnum erat studium puellārum.

Plūtō, deus īnferōrum, [4] Prōserpinam vīdit et amāvit. Equōs 5 incitāvit et ad locum accessit ubi puellae erant. Puellae fūgērunt. Prōserpina fugere mātūrāvit, sed Plūtō valuit et eam [5] cēpit, in carrō posuit, ad īnferōs dūxit.

Cerēs nocte [6] ex agrīs vēnit. Fīliam exspectāvit, sed Prōserpina non vēnit. Magna erat cūra deae. Ad multa loca, ad terminōs terrae 10 Cerēs accessit. Ōtium nōn invēnit.

Quod Cerēs Prōserpinam nōn invēnit, in agrīs nōn labōrāvit. Flōrēs nōn erant, frūmentum in agrīs nōn erat. Populus vītam dūram ēgit et deam accūsāvit quod pretium cibī magnum erat. Multī agricolae dīxērunt: 15

"Quid [7] agēmus? In agrīs labōrāmus sed frūmentum nōn habēmus. Deī nōn aequī sunt; officium nōn faciunt."

Iuppiter, quī deōs et virōs regit, iniūriās populī vīdit et deae agrōrum nūntiāvit:

"Prōserpina valet sed Plūtō eam habet. Mercurium nūntium ad 20 īnferōs mittam. Mercurius fīliam tuam ad tē [8] dūcet. Sed nōn semper in terrā Prōserpina manēbit. Ita commodum erit: partem [9] annī in terrā, partem sub terrā aget."

Ita Iuppiter concordiam effēcit. Cerēs fīliam accēpit. Prōserpina partem annī in terrā, partem sub terrā ēgit. Cum [10] lībera in terrā 25 est, multōs flōrēs et magnam cōpiam frūmentī vidēmus, quod Cerēs grāta in agrīs est et magnum est studium deae. Sed cum Prōserpina ad īnferōs excēdit, Cerēs trīstis [11] est, et flōrēs variī nōn sunt.

QUESTIONS   1. What was Proserpina doing when Pluto came?
2. What happened to the flowers after Proserpina left?
3. On what terms did Proserpina go back to her mother?

---

[1] *Proser'pina.*
[2] *once.*
[3] *flowers.*
[4] *those below,* i.e., the ghosts of the dead in Hades.
[5] *her.*
[6] *at night.*
[7] *what.*
[8] *you.*
[9] Accusative singular of **pars.**
[10] *whenever.*
[11] *sad.*

**117**

READING  Hamilton, pp. 57–64 (Mentor ed., pp. 49–54); Sabin, pp. 43–47; Guerber, pp. 183–187, 194–195; Bulfinch, pp. 58–64; Norton and Rushton, pp. 141–145.

## Third Conjugation: Future

The future sign of verbs of the first and second conjugations is –bi– (p. 36). The future sign of verbs of the third and fourth conjugations, however, is –ē–. The –ō verbs of the third conjugation, in forming the future, substitute –ē– for the stem vowel –ĕ–, except in the first singular (–am).[12]

---

*I shall place*, etc.

| | |
|---|---|
| pōnam | pōnēmus |
| pōnēs | pōnētis |
| pōnet | pōnent |

---

[12] The third singular and plural have –ĕ–, according to rule (p. 17).

*Roman children throw bowling balls at toy soldiers.*

**Practice**   1. Give the present of **mittō**, the future of **cēdō**, and the perfect of **dēfendō**.
2. Tell the form of **fūgit, valēbis, efficit, dūcēmus, docēmus, accipitis, mūniunt, migrāvit, agent.**

**Exercises**   **A.** 1. Valēsne, fīlia mea? Valeō.
2. Captīvī in silvās lātās fugiunt.
3. Litterās ad Mārcum, amīcum meum, mittam.
4. Puerī bonī ex studiīs magnam fāmam accipiunt.
5. Puerī ex oppidō nōn excēdent sed puellās dēfendent.
6. Multās hōrās in ōtiō nōn agēmus sed semper labōrābimus.

**B.** 1. They fortify the camp.
2. They will rule the province.
3. Did you approve the shape of the wagon?
4. We shall remain in the town and send a messenger.

**Vocabulary**   com'modus, –a, –um, *suitable, convenient*   (commodious)
de'us, –ī, m., *god*                                                        (deity)
fu'giō, fu'gere, fū'gī, *flee*                                      (fugitive)
ō'tium, ō'tī, n., *leisure*                                          (otiose)
stu'dium, stu'dī, n., *eagerness, interest;* plur., *studies*
                                                                                (studious)
va'leō, valē're, va'luī, *be strong, be well*          (valid)
va'rius, –a, –um, *changing, varying*                   (variety)

### English Word Studies

1. What are *commodities* and why are they so called? Why does the plural of **studium** mean *studies*? Can you explain the word *cereal*? Give three more derivatives of **varius**.

2. Latin phrases in English:

**auxilio ab alto,** *by aid from* (*on*) *high.*
**victoria, non praeda,** *victory, not loot.*
**Montani semper liberi,** *Mountaineers* (*are*) *always free* (motto of the state of West Virginia).

**ex officio,** *out of* (*as a result of*) *one's duty* or *office;* for example, a president of an organization may be a member of a committee *ex officio* (pronounced "offishio" in English) as a result of his office as president.

*Germani Marcum capiunt. Lucius equum incitat.*

# Lesson xxv

## LŪCIUS ET MĀRCUS

Rōmānī cum Germānīs, populō firmō et dūrō, bella perpetua gessērunt. Ōtium semper bellō cēdit, et nunc quoque [1] bella perpetua gerimus. Variae sunt bellōrum causae.

Quondam [2] Rōmānī et Aquītānī, sociī Rōmānōrum, cum Germānīs
5 pugnābant. [3] Germānī pugnam nōn aequē incipiunt, et Rōmānī cum sociīs lātē fugiunt. Lūcius, clārus Aquītānus, ex equō virōs Rōmānōs et Aquītānōs in Germānōs incitāvit. Servus Lūciō clārē nūntiāvit: "Germānī frātrem [4] tuum Mārcum capiunt!" Lūcius frātrem amāvit. Perīculum Mārcī Lūcium magnā cūrā affēcit. Lūcius equum incitāvit,
10 armīs Germānōs terruit, frātrem servāvit, fūgit. Sed equus nōn valuit: Lūcius frātrem sōlum [5] in equō posuit et ad castra Aquītānōrum et Rōmānōrum equum incitāvit. Tum sōlus Germānōs exspectāvit. Multī Germānī accessērunt. Lūcius firmus cēdere incipit, auxilium exspectat—sed auxilium nōn venit—ē vītā excēdit. Mārcus vīdit et
15 equum in Germānōs incitāvit et vītam āmīsit. [6]

Varia et dūra est fortūna bellī et variē virōs afficit, sed glōriam semper laudāmus.

QUESTIONS    1. Who was Marcus' brother?
             2. Who was killed?

---

[1] *too.*    [2] *once.*    [3] *were fighting.*    [4] *brother.*    [5] *alone.*    [6] *lost.*

## Formation of Adverbs

In English, adverbs are usually formed from adjectives by adding the suffix *–ly*: adj., *clear*; adv., *clearly*.

In Latin, adverbs are usually formed from first and second declension adjectives by adding *–ē* to the base:

|  |  |
|---|---|
| *adj.*, **clārus** | **līber** |
| *adv.*, **clārē** | **līberē** |

**Practice**    Form adverbs from **pūblicus, grātus, commodus, aequus.** Give the Latin for *harshly, truly, firmly.*

## Ablative of Accompaniment

As you already know, the means *with which* something is done is expressed by the ablative without a preposition (p. 43): *They fought with arms,* **Armīs pugnāvērunt.** When, however, *with* means *together with* or *along with,* the preposition **cum** is used with the ablative. This expresses *accompaniment*: **Cum servō venit,** *He is coming with the slave.*

*Caution.* When tempted to use **cum** (*with*), be sure that *with* means accompaniment or association. In the following English sentences decide when **cum** should be used and when it should be omitted:

1. Come *with me.*
2. Play *with us,* Jane.
3. John writes *with ink.*
4. Anna is *with the teacher.*
5. George fights *with inkwells.*
6. Play *with these toys,* Grace.

**Virō pugnat.**
(The man is used as a weapon.)

**Cum virō pugnat.**

**Exercises** **A.** 1. Nautae, pūblicē līberāte captīvōs.
2. Nautae terram firmam clārē vidēre incipiunt.
3. Cum populō barbarō bellum perpetuum gerēmus.
4. Armīs templa dēfendent et cum sociīs pugnābunt.
5. Magister dūrus poenā puerōs malōs aequē afficit.
6. In amīcitiā firmā et perpetuā cum sociīs nostrīs manē-bimus.
7. Servus cum magnā cōpiā pecūniae fūgit; nōn ōtium sed cūrās invēnit.

**B.** 1. We shall send the slave with food.
2. They will defend the island with arms.
3. It is not just to carry on war with friends.
4. A bad boy afflicts the family with constant care.
5. The settlers are beginning to flee with (their) families.

Costa Rica stamp issued in honor of the Olympic Games of 1924. Classical buildings are shown. Many countries have issued special stamps for these games, which are held every four years. They originated in ancient Greece.

**Vocabulary**
| | |
|---|---|
| affi'ciō, affi'cere, affē'cī, *affect, afflict with* | [*faciō*] |
| cum, prep. with abl., *with* | |
| dū'rus, –a, –um, *hard, harsh* | (durable) |
| fir'mus, –a, –um, *strong, firm* | (firmness) |
| ge'rō, ge'rere, ges'sī, *carry on* | (belligerent) |
| inci'piō, inci'pere, incē'pī, *take to, begin* | [*capiō*] |
| perpe'tuus, –a, –um, *constant* | (perpetuity) |

### Latin and English Word Formation

The preposition **cum** is often used as a prefix in Latin and English but always in the assimilated forms **com–, con–, col–, cor–, co–.** It usually means *together* rather than *with*.

Define the following words, all formed from verbs which you have studied: *convoke, collaborate, commotion, convene*. What is a political *convention*?

Give five other English words formed by attaching this prefix to Latin verbs, nouns, or adjectives already studied.

*Graecia. The Parthenon Temple crowning the Acropolis Hill at Athens.*

# Lesson xxvi

## VĪTA ANTĪQUA

Poētae multa [1] dē deīs et virīs antīquīs docent. Multās fābulās dē
clārīs Graecīs et Rōmānīs et dē perpetuā glōriā Rōmānōrum ā
magistrō tuō audiēs et ex librīs trahēs. Fortasse studia tua tē [2] ad
Graeciam et Italiam trahent. Ibi templa deōrum et loca clāra vidēbis
dē quibus [3] poētae scrībunt. Tum verba poētārum commodē memoriā 5
tenēbis. Italia multās antīquās ruīnās continet. Multa dē vītā antīquōrum Graecōrum et Rōmānōrum inveniēs et audiēs sī [4] cum amīcīs
ad Italiam nāvigābis et ibi manēbis. Multī Americānī ex Eurōpā
variās rēs [5] Rōmānās portant. Fortasse amīcus tuus rēs Rōmānās
habet et puerīs et puellīs mōnstrāre incipiet. Librī tuī Latīnī multās 10
novās fābulās dē clārīs Rōmānīs continēbunt. Sī puerī tardī nōn erunt,
librōs accipient. Nōnne verba mea puerōs tardōs afficient? Numerum
librōrum tuōrum augēre dēbēs.

----

[1] *many things.*      [2] *you* (accusative).      [3] *which.*      [4] *if.*      [5] *things.*

**123**

*The Department of Justice Building, Washington, has a Latin inscription on the pediment.*

QUESTIONS
1. How will you learn about the Romans?
2. What four things do the ancient poets tell about?

### Future of Third (–iō) and Fourth Conjugation Verbs

Verbs of the fourth conjugation form the future by adding –ē– and the personal endings directly to the present stem. Long –ī– of the stem is shortened, however, since it precedes another vowel. The future of verbs of the third conjugation ending in –iō is the same as that of fourth conjugation verbs; the reason for this is the insertion of –ĭ– (p. 102).

---

| THIRD CONJUGATION | | FOURTH CONJUGATION | |
| --- | --- | --- | --- |
| (*I shall take*, etc.) | | (*I shall fortify*, etc.) | |
| capiam | capiēmus | mūniam | mūniēmus |
| capiēs | capiētis | mūniēs | mūniētis |
| capiet | capient | mūniet | mūnient |

---

Practice
1. Give the future tense of **incipiō** and **audiō**.
2. Give the Latin for *they will affect, we shall hear, you* (plur.) *will receive, they will draw, it will contain*.
3. Tell the form of **inveniētis, audīs, faciam, vidēbunt, parāvistī**.

Exercises  **A.** 1. Carrī magnam cōpiam frūmentī continent.
2. Equī carrōs agricolārum tardē trāxērunt.
3. Equōs in locō lātō et commodō continēbimus.
4. Magister tardōs puerōs poenā pūblicē afficiet.
5. Nautae nostrī ex aquā virōs trahent et servābunt.
6. Colōnī ex agrīs frūmentum portābunt et magnam pecūniam accipient.

**B.** 1. We shall save the people with food.
2. Anna, a good girl, will receive a book.
3. The late boys will not hear the words of the famous man.
4. The boys will not receive a reward, because they are late.

124

**Vocabulary**  au′diō, audī′re, audī′vī, *hear*              (audience)
conti′neō, continē′re, conti′nuī, *hold* (*together*), *contain*
                                                     [*teneō*]
li′ber, li′brī, m., *book*                                  (library)
tar′dus, –a, –um, *slow, late*                     (retard)
tra′hō, tra′here, trā′xī, *draw, drag*        (attraction)
ver′bum, –ī, n., *word*                               (verbal)

## Latin and English Word Formation

Most prefixes are also used as prepositions, but a few are not. **Re–** is used only as a prefix in both Latin and English; it means *back* or *again*. It sometimes has the form **red–**, especially before vowels. Examples: **retineō**, *hold* **back**; **reficiō**, *make* **again**; **redigō**, *drive* **back**.

In English, **re–** is freely used with all sorts of words: *remake, revisit, rehash, refill.*

Give seven examples of the prefix **re–** in English words derived from Latin. Explain *revoke, incipient, refugee, audition.*

*Mosaic floor of about 400 A.D. recently found in Sicily (cf. p. 61). It shows girls dressed in the latest "Bikini" bathing suits. The girl in the center with a laurel wreath on her head and a palm branch in her hand is the winner in some contest—swimming or running—or was it in a beauty contest?*

TIME

## AENĒĀS

The Trojan War was fought over three thousand years ago at Troy, in Asia Minor near the Dardanelles in what is now Turkey. The story of the war is told by the Greek poet Homer in the *Iliad*. Virgil, the Roman poet, tells part of the story in his *Aeneid* and goes on to tell of the Trojan Aeneas, said to be the son of the goddess Venus. After the fall of Troy Aeneas eventually reached Italy and, according to the story, he and his companions were the ancestors of the Romans.

Troiānī cum Graecīs multōs annōs bellum gessērunt. Graecī Troiam occupāvērunt. Aenēās Troiānus arma cēpit et cum multīs virīs oppidum dēfendere mātūrāvit. Sed Venus dea, māter Aenēae,[1] eum[2] in mediō oppidō invēnit et verba fēcit:

5 "Audī sententiam meam. Tenē memoriā familiam tuam. Convocā familiam et amīcōs firmōs et fuge. Novam patriam inveniēs. Cēde fortūnae. Deī Troiam vāstant. Troiānōs poenā dūrā afficient."

[1] Genitive singular.
[2] *him.*

*Aeneas patrem portat et filium parvum ducit. Sculpture on a Roman tomb.*

Cōnsilium Aenēās nōn grātē audīvit sed probāvit. Virōs redūxit 10
et amīcōs convocāvit. Tum ex oppidō patrem [3] portāvit et fīlium
parvum dūxit. Cum multīs servīs et sociīs fūgit. Singulī in locum commodum convēnērunt et ibi castra posuērunt. Māteriam ex silvā
portāvērunt et nāvēs [4] parāvērunt. Tum nāvēs in aquam trāxērunt et
undīs mandāvērunt et migrāvērunt. Ad multās īnsulās et terrās novās 15
vēnērunt sed patriam novam nōn invēnērunt. Vītam dūram ēgērunt.
Īra Iūnōnis,[5] rēgīnae deōrum, hoc [6] effēcit.

In īnsulā Crētā castra posuērunt. Tum in mediō somnō Aenēās
Penātēs [7] vīdit et sententiam audīvit:

"Crēta patria vestra nōn erit. Excēdite, Troiānī. Locus est quem [8] 20
Graecī Hesperiam, aliī Italiam vocant. Ibi terminum cūrārum per-
petuārum inveniētis. Ibi in ōtiō et concordiā habitābitis et magnum
oppidum pōnētis et mūniētis."

Ita Troiānī cōnsilium novum cēpērunt. Castra mōvērunt et ad
Italiam nāvigāvērunt.                                                    25

**QUESTIONS**   1. What did Venus tell Aeneas to do?
2. Whom does Aeneas take with him from Troy?
3. Why didn't Aeneas stay in Crete?

**READING**   Hamilton, pp. 319–321 (Mentor ed., pp. 220–222); Sabin,
pp. 331–333; Gayley, pp. 346–350; Bulfinch, pp. 262–263;
Guerber, pp. 360–364; Norton and Rushton, pp. 14–21.

### Idioms

Every language has expressions that do not make sense or sound
right when they are translated word for word into another language.

---

[3] Accusative singular of **pater**.
[4] Accusative plural of **nāvis**.
[5] *of Juno*.
[6] *this*.
[7] Accusative plural.
[8] *which* (accusative).

*Latin inscription in the Library of
Congress, Washington.*

*Sport scenes in a wall painting at Pompeii—sailing, fishing, swimming, sun-bathing. You could look at your wall all winter and dream of next summer's vacation.*

The French for "How do you do?" literally means "How do you go?" which doesn't sound right to us. Come to think of it, "How do you do?" sounds peculiar to us too when we look at the separate words. It doesn't mean "In what way are you doing something?" And of course a Frenchman considers our expression just as queer as we consider his.

Such expressions are called *idioms*. Every language has hundreds of them. The following are some of the common ones in Latin. Memorize them and put them in your notebook under the heading "Idioms."

1. **grātiās agō**, *thank*, with dat. (literally, *act gratitude*)
2. **grātiam habeō**, *feel grateful*, with dat. (lit., *have gratitude*)
3. **vītam agō**, *live a life* (lit., *act life*)
4. **bellum gerō**, *wage* or *carry on war*
5. **castra pōnō**, *pitch camp* (lit., *place camp*)
6. **viam mūniō**, *build a road* (lit., *fortify a road*; roads were built like walls)
7. **verba faciō**, *speak, make a speech* (lit., *make words*)
8. **memoriā teneō**, *remember* (lit., *hold in memory*)
9. **cōnsilium capiō**, *adopt a plan* (lit., *take a plan*)

**Exercises   A.** 1. Puerōs ex mediā silvā in oppidum redūcam.
2. Rōmānī multās longās viās in Italiā mūnīvērunt.
3. Virī ex multīs terrīs convenient et verba facient.
4. Puerōs singulōs convocābimus et sententiās audiēmus.
5. Magistrō nostrō grātiam habēmus et līberē grātiās agēmus.
6. Pōnite castra, puerī, in agrīs et ibi agite līberam vītam.

**B.** 1. The boys will find water and pitch camp.
   2. We ought to feel grateful to your friends.
   3. We shall remember the teacher's words about duty.
   4. The girls feel grateful and will thank the teacher.

**Vocabulary**  conve′niō, convenī′re, convē′nī, *come together*  [*veniō*]
con′vocō, convocā′re, convocā′vī, *call together*  [*vocō*]
me′dius, –a, –um, *middle, middle of*  (mediator)
redū′cō, redū′cere, redū′xī, *lead back*  [*dūcō*]
senten′tia, –ae, f., *feeling, opinion, motto*  (sentence)

## English Word Studies

A friend is a person whom you know well and treat familiarly. How many English words can you call friends, according to this definition? If you will trace English words back to their Latin roots, you will gain many new friends. For example: A "sentence" in grammar is a single, complete *opinion* or expression. A judicial "sentence" is a judge's *opinion*. A "convention" *comes together* in an "auditorium" to *hear* the speaker. A "mediator" settles disputes by taking

*Mediator and belligerents.*

a *middle* position. A spiritualistic "medium" is supposed to take a *middle* position between the unseen spirit and the "audience" who *hear*. A "studious" person is one who is *eager* to learn. An "alarm" is a call *to arms* (**ad arma**). To "repatriate" a person is to bring him *back* to his *fatherland*. Learn to look carefully at the make-up of every strange English word and you will often detect an old Latin friend in disguise.

What is a *convocation? Verbosity? Durum* wheat?

*Aeneas* is the name of a town in Washington. Three states have towns named *Virgil*. Three have towns named for *Juno*, four for *Venus*. In three states you will find a *Crete*.

The New York telephone directory lists forty-three firms called *Venus*; Minneapolis and other cities have two or more. Why is this a popular name?

**129**

*The Forum at night. The lighted up buildings are the Temple of Faustina (left), the Colosseum (rear), the Arch of Titus, in front of which is the Temple of Vesta, the Temple of Castor.*

## *Lesson xxviii*

**The Story of Lucius**

### FORUM RŌMĀNUM

Quondam puer parvus Lūcius in Italiā habitābat. Dē glōriā patriae multa [1] audiēbat. Magister Lūciō reliquīsque puerīs loca clāra Rōmae mōnstrābat. In medium Forum Rōmānum cum puerīs properābat. In hunc [2] locum populus Rōmānus conveniēbat. Ibi virī
5 amīcōs vidēbant et aedificia [3] pūblica templaque spectābant. Ibi nūntiī populum convocābant et magnās victōriās nūntiābant. Ibi virī clārī in rōstrīs [4] verba pūblicē faciēbant et sententiās dēfendēbant.

Magister multa dē patriā in Forō docēbat. Puerī magistrō magnam grātiam habuērunt, quod Forum amāvērunt. Ē Forō Lūcius re-
10 liquīque puerī cum magistrō in Sacram Viam properābant et tabernās [5] spectābant. Cupitisne [6] plūra [7] dē Lūciō audīre?

---

[1] *many things.*    [3] *buildings.*        [5] *shops.*    [7] *more.*
[2] *this.*            [4] *the rostra* (speakers' platform).    [6] *desire.*

**130**

1. Where did the Romans meet their friends?

2. Why were the boys grateful to their teacher?

### Hints for Reading Latin

As your eyes move across the page, following the order of words, separate the words into groups according to their sense and grammatical relation. Since this grammatical relation is shown by the word endings, not, as in English, by the word order, watch the endings carefully. Each word group, or phrase, should be read and understood as a unit. When you come to the end of the sentence translate in the English word order.

Here are the first four sentences of **Forum Rōmānum** separated into groups of words according to their grammatical relation. Each division represents the words your eye should take in at each stop.

Quondam || puer parvus Lūcius || in Italiā habitābat. || Dē glōriā patriae || multa audiēbat. || Magister || Lūciō reliquīsque puerīs || loca clāra Rōmae || mōnstrābat. || In medium Forum Rōmānum || cum puerīs || properābat.

*The two-thousandth anniversary (1930) of Virgil's birth is honored by this Italian stamp. It has on it a quotation from Virgil about farmers.*

### Imperfect Tense

The Latin *imperfect* tense is called imperfect because it often represents incomplete acts, not because anything is wrong with it. It is formed by adding the tense sign –bā– to the present stem and then attaching the personal endings, which you already know:

| SINGULAR | PLURAL |
|---|---|
| portā**bam**, *I was carrying, did carry, carried* | portā**bāmus**, *we were carrying*, etc. |
| portā**bās**, *you were carrying*, etc. | portā**bātis**, *you were carrying*, etc. |
| portā**bat**, *he, she, it was carrying*, etc. | portā**bant**, *they were carrying*, etc. |

Similarly **docēbam, pōnēbam, mūniēbam, capiēbam.** (For full conjugation see pp. 397–400.) For the imperfect of **sum** (**eram**, etc.) see p. 401.

*Observe* that the personal ending for the first person singular is **–m,** not **–ō** as in the present tense. For the short vowels see p. 17.

### How the Perfect and Imperfect Differ

The imperfect tense always refers to action or being as *repeated, customary,* or *continuous,* like the English progressive past, and must be carefully distinguished from the perfect. In the following sentences the first group would be in the perfect in Latin, the second in the imperfect:

<table>
<tr><td align="center">PERFECT</td><td align="center">IMPERFECT</td></tr>
<tr><td>1. I saw John yesterday.</td><td>1. I saw John frequently.</td></tr>
<tr><td>2. I went to camp last year.</td><td>2. I used to go to camp every year.</td></tr>
<tr><td>3. Did you ever play football?</td><td>3. Did you play football long?</td></tr>
<tr><td>4. The alarm clock rang and I got up.</td><td>4. The alarm clock kept on ringing, but I did not get up.</td></tr>
</table>

Latin has two past tenses: perfect and imperfect; English has six ways of translating them: past, emphatic past, present perfect, progressive past, customary past, repeated past. Notice the difference in the following:

**Vēnī,** *I came* (past), or *I have come* (present perfect), or *I did come* (emphatic past).

The translation will depend on the context, but the first is much more common.

**Veniēbam,** *I was coming* (progressive past), or *I used to come* (customary past), or *I kept on coming* (repeated past).

Sometimes, however, the imperfect is best translated by the simple past; this is especially true of **sum.**

In Latin, the perfect is used much more often than the imperfect. In translating the English past into Latin, use the perfect unless there is a clear reason for using the imperfect.

**Exercises** **A.** 1. Puellae puerīque excessērunt.
2. Properāte, puellae; tardae estis.
3. In viā properābam; ibi amīcum meum vīdī.
4. Mārcus amīcum vocābat sed amīcus nōn vēnit.
5. Multōs equōs in viīs vidēbāmus, sed nunc ubi sunt equī?
6. Multī virī in agrīs habitābant sed nunc ad oppida migrāvērunt.

**B.** 1. Have you received many letters?
2. We were leading the horses to water.
3. We kept-on-waiting but they did not come.
4. Marcus came to dinner but the-rest-of the boys did not come.

**Vocabulary** pro′perō, properā′re, properā′vī, *hasten*
-que, conj., *and* (translated before the word to which it is joined)
re′liquus, –a, –um, *remaining, rest (of)*           (relic)

### English Word Studies

What does the English word *forum* mean? What use of the Roman Forum gave this meaning to our word (see p. 144)? Can you find any organizations or groups today which use the name *Forum*? Arkansas has a town named *Forum*.

How did the *Mediterranean* Sea gets its name?

The English word *deficit* preserves the third person singular present of Latin **dēficiō**.

*Deficit.*

*Ira Neptuni magna est. Neptune drives the winds away from the Trojan ships. A sketch by the painter Rubens.*

# *Lesson xxix*

## AD ITALIAM

In magnīs undīs nāvēs[1] Troiānōrum volvuntur.[2] Sed Troiānī ex mediīs undīs servantur et ad Actium[3] properant; ibi inveniunt Helenum Troiānum, quī terram regēbat. Helenus Troiānōs convocat et verba pauca facit:

5 "Longa est via ad Italiam, ad quam[4] accēdere parātis. Accēdite ad Siciliam et nāvigāte ab Siciliā ad Italiam fīnitimam. Dūrum est semper nāvigāre, sed Fāta viam invenient."

Sententia Helenī grātē accipitur, et Aenēās Helenō grātiās agit. Castra moventur nāvēsque[1] undīs committuntur. "Italiam, Italiam 10 videō!" clāmat nauta et terram mōnstrat. In terrā equī clārē videntur. "Signum proelī sunt equī," dīcit Anchīsēs;[5] "equīs bellum geritur.

---

[1] Nominative plural.    [2] *are tossed.*    [3] *Actium (Ak'shium).*    [4] *which.*
[5] Father of Aeneas; pronounced *Ankī'sēs* in English.

**134**

Proelium committere nōn dēbēmus." Nōn ibi manent sed ad Siciliam
fīnitimam nāvigant. Aetna eōs[6] terret et ab Siciliā fugiunt.

Tum Iūnō, rēgīna deōrum, quae[7] Troiānōs nōn amāvit, ad
Aeolum, quī ventōs regit et continet, venit dīcitque:                 15

"Sī ventī dūrī in nāvēs[8] Troiānōrum mittentur, magnam grātiam
habēbō et magna praemia tibi[9] dōnābō."

Aeolus ventōs in nāvēs mittere mātūrat. Altīs undīs Troiānī terrentur. Arma virīque in undīs sunt. Tum Neptūnus, deus undārum,
ventōs audit et ad locum venit ubi nāvēs sunt. Īra Neptūnī magna  20
est; ventī lātē fugiunt. Paucī Troiānī āmittuntur; reliquī ad terram
fīnitimam veniunt et servantur. Sed in quā[10] terrā sunt? Nōn sciunt.[11]

**QUESTIONS**   1. Where does Helenus tell the Trojans to go?
2. What does Juno ask Aeolus to do?
3. What does Neptune do?

---

[6] *them.*   [7] *who.*   [8] Accusative plural.   [9] *to you.*   [10] *what.*   [11] *know.*

*The Lincoln Memorial in Washington is beautiful in its simplicity. The columns are
Doric; the festoons at the top are frequently seen on Roman buildings.*

PHILIP GENDREAU

READING     Hamilton, pp. 322–323 (Mentor ed., pp. 222–223); Sabin, pp. 334–336; Bulfinch, pp. 264–266; Guerber, pp. 364–366.

## Voice: Active and Passive

When the verb shows that the subject acts, i.e., is doing something, it is in the *active voice:*

**Vir accūsābit,** *The man will accuse.*

When the verb shows that the subject is acted upon, it is in the *passive voice:*

**Vir accūsābitur,** *The man will be accused.*

*Observe* that voice is shown in Latin by endings. The linking verb **sum** has no voice, for it merely indicates existence.

## Progressive and Passive Verb Forms in English

Distinguish in English between active progressive forms and passive verb phrases, both of which use some form of the verb *to be.*

Active (progressive): *He is seeing* (**videt**); *They were calling* (**vocābant**).
Passive: *He is seen* (**vidētur**); *They were being called* (**vocābantur**).

In Latin there is no difficulty about distinguishing active and passive.

Active                  Passive

*He is kicking.*             *He is being kicked.*

**Practice**     Tell which of these verbs are passive: *he called, we were cold, he was laughing, they were found, you are being beaten, he is fighting, they will be scolded, he will praise, you will be invited, it was being written, we were reading, she was sent.*

## Passive Voice of the Four Conjugations

In Latin the passive voice of all conjugations is formed by substituting the passive personal endings for the active: [12]

| ENDINGS | | PRESENT | |
|---|---|---|---|
| –r | –mur | portor, *I am carried* | portāmur, *we are carried* |
| –ris | –minī | portāris, *you are carried* | portāminī, *you are carried* |
| –tur | –ntur | portātur, *he is carried* | portantur,[13] *they are carried* |

Similarly **doceor, pōnor, mūnior, capior** (see pp. 397–400).

### IMPERFECT

portābar, *I was being carried, was carried*

portābāris, *you were being carried, etc.*

portābātur, *he was being carried, etc.*

portābāmur, *we were being carried, etc.*

portābāminī, *you were being carried, etc.*

portābantur, *they were being carried, etc.*

Similarly **docēbar, pōnēbar, mūniēbar, capiēbar,** (see pp. 397–400).

### FUTURE

portābor, *I shall be carried*

portāberis, *you will be carried*

portābitur, *he will be carried*

portābimur, *we shall be carried*

portābiminī, *you will be carried*

portābuntur, *they will be carried*

Similarly **docēbor, pōnar, mūniar, capiar** (see pp. 397–400).

*Observe* that **r** occurs in five of the six passive endings.

**Practice**
1. Conjugate **accipiō** in the present passive, **dēfendō** in the imperfect passive, **inveniō** in the future passive.
2. Translate: *we shall be accused, he is being taught, it is not approved, they were being sent, it will be received, he will be heard, you* (sing.) *are moved, they are ruled, you* (plur.) *will be seen, we are awaited.*

---

[12] But in forms ending in –ō in the active (as **portō** and **portābō**), the passive ending –r *is added to,* not *substituted for,* the active ending. The –ō– becomes short.

[13] For the vowel shortened before –**ntur,** see p. 17.

**Exercises A.** 1. Amā fīnitimum tuum.
2. Reliquī nautae ad prōvinciam mittentur.
3. Rōmānī proelium cum fīnitimīs nunc committunt.
4. Paucī virī in fīnitimīs agrīs oppidīsque vidēbantur.
5. Multa praemia reliquīs puerīs puellīsque dōnābuntur.
6. Captīvī ad oppidum redūcentur et proelium committētur.

**B.** 1. They will find food in the house.
2. Food will be found in the house.
3. Are the-rest-of the boys working in the fields?
4. The-rest-of the men will be sent to the island.

**Vocabulary** commit′tō, commit′tere, commī′sī, *join together, commit, entrust;* proe′lium commit′tō, *begin battle* [*mittō*]
fīni′timus, –a, –um, *neighboring;* fīni′timus, –ī, m., *neighbor*
pau′cī, –ae, –a, *few* (paucity)
proe′lium, proe′lī, n., *battle*

### Latin and English Word Formation

We have seen how Latin and English words are formed from others by the use of prefixes. There are other ways of forming new words. These we shall discuss later. For the present it is sufficient to recognize the roots that words have in common. Note the relationship and review the meanings of the following words which have occurred in the preceding vocabularies:

1. amīcus and amīcitia
2. nāvigō and nauta
3. nūntiō and nūntius
4. capiō and captīvus (a "captive" is one who is *taken*)
5. pugna and pugnō
6. puer and puella
7. habeō and habitō (to "inhabit" a place is to keep on *having* it)

Try to associate new Latin words with those you have already studied, as well as with English derivatives which you find.

Towns named *Neptune* are in New Jersey and Tennessee; *Neptune Beach* is in Florida.

The four cities which have more firms named *Neptune* listed in their telephone directories than other cities are New York (forty-nine), Boston (eleven), Seattle (four), Los Angeles (four). Why is this name popular in these cities?

*Aeneas leaving his ship (right) to meet Dido, all in fifteenth-century costume, as painted by the Italian artist Francesco di Giorgio. In the Portland Museum of Art.*

# Lesson xxx

## AENĒĀS IN ĀFRICĀ EST

Aenēās sociōs convocāvit et verba fēcit:

"In terrā nōn nōtā sumus. Sed deī praesidium nostrum sunt. Deīs vītam committite. Neque terra neque aqua nōs[1] terret. Inveniēmus viam aut faciēmus. Italia nostra erit. Ibi et terminus malōrum nostrō- rum et ōtium perpetuum ā Troiānīs invenientur. Ibi patria erit et 5 nova Troia."

Tum Aenēās cum sociō ūnō ex castrīs excessit. Loca explōrāre mātūrāvit. Venus māter eum[2] vīdit et appellāvit. Nōmen oppidī, quod[3] appellātur Carthāgō et in Āfricā est, et nōmen rēgīnae, quae[4] est Dīdō, Aenēae[5] Venus nūntiat. Via ā deā Aenēae mōnstrātur; 10 Aenēās prōcessit et magnum oppidum vīdit. In mediō oppidō templum erat. Ad templum rēgīna Dīdō cum paucīs sociīs vēnit. Ibi erant reliquī Troiānī quōs[6] undae ab Aenēā[7] sēparāverant.[8]

Dīdō mala Troiānōrum audīvit et dīxit:

"Auxiliō meō aut in Italiam aut in Siciliam commodē veniētis, 15 amīcī. Sed sī in nostrā patriā manēre grātum est, oppidum nostrum vestrum est, et praesidium habēbitis."

Tum magna cēna ā rēgīnā parātur. Aenēās nūntium ad fīlium, quī Iūlus[9] appellātur, mittit; nūntius dīcit:

"Venī ad oppidum, Iūle. Pater tē[10] exspectat." 20

---

[1] *us.*
[2] *him.*
[3] *which.*
[4] *who.*
[5] Dative.
[6] *whom.*
[7] Ablative.
[8] Use the English derivative in the past perfect tense (*had —*).
[9] *Iulus* (*Īyū'lus*)
[10] *you.*

*Aeneas tells his story to Dido and her sister Anna while Cupid, pretending to be Aeneas' son, causes Dido to fall in love with Aeneas.*

Sed in locō Iūlī Venus deum Amōrem [11] mittit. Sed et Aenēās et reliquī Troiānī deum [12] crēdunt esse Iūlum. Tum Amor rēgīnam afficit, et Dīdō Aenēam amāre incipit.

QUESTIONS    1. How does Aeneas find out where he is?
                      2. Whom does he see at the temple?
                      3. What choice does Dido offer the Trojans?

READING    Hamilton, pp. 324–326 (Mentor ed., pp. 223–225); Sabin, pp. 335–336; Guerber, pp. 366–367.

## Transitive and Intransitive Verbs

A *transitive* verb is one which tells what the subject does to the direct object:

**Anna aquam portat,** *Anna is carrying water.*
**Puer virum videt,** *The boy sees the man.*

An *intransitive* verb is one which cannot have a direct object:

**Anna labōrat,** *Anna is working.*
**Puer excēdit,** *The boy departs.*

In English, and generally in Latin, only transitive verbs are used in the passive voice.

---

[11] *Love,* the Roman god Cupid.

[12] **deum . . . Iūlum:** *believe the god to be Iulus.*

## Ablative of Agent

Let us see what happens when the two sentences containing transitive verbs are turned around and the verb becomes passive:

**Aqua ab Annā portātur,** *The water is carried by Anna.*
**Vir ā puerō vidētur,** *The man is seen by the boy.*

*Observe* that in both English and Latin (*a*) the direct object of the active verb becomes the subject of the passive verb; (*b*) the subject of the active verb becomes the object of a preposition (**ā, ab,** *by*), indicating the *agent*.

*Caution.* Distinguish carefully between the ablative of agent and the ablative of means, both of which are often translated with *by*. Remember that *"means" refers to a thing*, while *"agent" refers to a person*. Besides, the ablative of *means* is never used *with* a preposition, but the ablative of *agent* is never used *without* the preposition **ā** (**ab**). This preposition means *by* only when used before a noun referring to a person (or persons) and with a passive verb.

*Pompeian wall painting showing a fight in the amphitheater between Pompeians and visitors from a near-by town—just like a fight between spectators at a modern football game.*

1. **Puella poenā terrētur,** *The girl is scared by punishment* (**means**).
2. **Puella ā puerīs terrētur,** *The girl is scared by the boys* (**agent**).

**Practice** **A.** Tell which expresses means and which agent:
1. I was hit *by a stone.*
2. He was liked *by everybody.*
3. The game will be won *by our team.*
4. This book was bought *by me with my own money.*
5. John will be sent for *by messenger,* Mary *by letter.*
6. The note had been written *by hand* and not *with a typewriter.*

**B.** Change the following from active to passive, or from passive to active, and translate:
1. Vir librum videt.
2. Oppida ā populō reguntur.
3. Puerī verba tua exspectābant.
4. Reliqua pecūnia ab amīcō meō accipiētur.

**C.** Turn back to page 124 and put into the passive **A.** 4, 5, 6.

*Greek air-mail stamps with figures of the winds. Here shown are the North Wind (Boreas), South (Notos), and West (Zephyros). We have noted the tendency to imagine the winds as living creatures in the story and picture on page 134.*

## Agreement

In both English and Latin, when two subjects are connected by *or* (**aut**), *either . . . or* (**aut . . . aut**), *neither . . . nor* (**neque . . . neque**), the verb agrees with the nearer subject: *Neither the boys nor the girl is in the forest,* **Neque puerī neque puella in silvā est.**

**Exercises** **A.** 1. Equus puerum trahit; puer ab equō trahitur.
2. Aut puerī aut virī ad agrōs equōs redūcent.
3. Neque servus neque equus in viīs vidēbitur.
4. Mārcus amīcus [13] vērus ā multīs virīs appellābātur.

---

[13] Observe that the predicate nominative (p. 10) may be used with verbs other than **sum.**

5. Neque praesidium neque auxilium ā sociīs nostrīs mittitur.
6. Multa praemia ā reliquīs puerīs puellīsque grātē accipientur.
7. Magister puerōs puellāsque docēbat; puerī puellaeque ā magistrō docēbantur.

**B.** 1. The girls were scared by the bad boys.
2. The grain is being carried by wagon to the town.
3. The men see few houses; few houses are seen by the men.
4. Neither water nor grain is being carried by the-rest-of the men.

**Vocabulary**  appel'lō, appellā're, appellā'vī, *call*      (appellate)
aut, conj., *or*; aut . . . aut, *either . . . or*
et . . . et, conj., *both . . . and*
ne'que (or nec), conj., *and not, nor*; ne'que . . . ne'que, *neither . . . nor*
praesi'dium, praesi'dī, n., *guard, protection*
rēgī'na, –ae, f., *queen*

## English Word Studies

1. What is meant by taking an *appeal* to a higher court? Why is such a court called an *appellate* court? What is an *appellation*? *Carthage* is a town name in eleven states; *Cartago* is in California.
2. Latin phrases in English:

magnum bonum, *great good.*
via media, *a middle way* or *course.*
consilio et armis, *by counsel and by arms.*
terra firma, *solid earth* (as opposed to water).
In Deo speramus, *In God we trust* (motto of Brown University).
Explain **Elizabeth regina.**

*Terra non firma.*

*The Palatine Hill as seen from Romulus and Remus Square on the Aventine Hill. There is a valley containing the Circus Maximus between the two hills.*

*A model of ancient Rome, with Circus Maximus (left) and Colosseum.*

# ~~~ Glimpses of Roman Life

## THE ETERNAL CITY

The Romans tell us that Rome was founded in 753 B.C. The first settlement was on the Palatine Hill, named after Pales, the goddess of shepherds. This was natural because the first settlers were shepherds. As the city grew, it spread to the near-by hills and the valleys between them. In time it came to be known as the "City of the Seven Hills." These hills are neither high nor extensive. The Palatine is only 142 feet above the level of the Tiber River—about the height of a ten-story building.

Below the Palatine Hill was the valley which came to be known as the Forum. At first a marshy district, it became the market place of Rome, then the chief shopping and business district, and finally the civic center. In its final development it was a rectangular paved space surrounded by temples, law courts, senate house, and other public buildings. At one end was a speakers' platform called the *rostra* because it was ornamented with the beaks of ships (**rōstrum** = beak) captured in a war fought in the fourth century B.C.[1]

The Palatine, because of its nearness to the Forum, became the residential district for statesmen and wealthy people. Hence it was that the first emperors had their homes there. Eventually the whole imperial administration was centered on this hill, and the emperor's buildings covered it completely. So the hill which was named after the protecting goddess of the shepherds who built their rude huts there came to be the site of *palatial* buildings. Thus it happens that our word *palace* is derived from the name of the hill.

Another hill near the Forum, the Capitoline, got its name from the famous temple of Jupiter known as the Capitolium, because it was the "head" (**caput**), or chief temple of that god. From it the Capitol at Washington gets its name, as well as the capitols of our states. The hill also had on it the temple of Juno Moneta. Why the goddess Juno was called Moneta is not certain. In connection with

---

[1] The fourth century B.C. (before Christ) covers 400–301 B.C.; the first, 100–1 B.C. Then comes the first century A.D. (p. 51, note 1).

the temple a mint for coining money was later established, and thus from the word **monēta** we get our words *money* and *mint*.

The streets of Rome were narrow and crooked. In the early days they were unpaved. Only during the last part of the first century B.C. did Rome begin to become beautiful.

In the early days the people of Rome got their water from wells, springs, and the Tiber River, which winds its way along one side of the city in the shape of the letter S. In 312 B.C. Appius Claudius built the first aqueduct, which brought in pure water from springs about seven miles east of Rome. Later, other aqueducts were built, some having their sources nearly forty miles away. There were many street fountains (pp. 8, 176), and eventually public baths and many private houses were piped for running water.

For better administration the Emperor Augustus divided the city into fourteen regions, or wards. One feature of this arrangement was the reorganization and extension of the police and fire department (**vigilēs,** *watchmen*). Previously fire protection had been so poor that private fire companies were organized. These even bought up burning houses at bargain prices and then extinguished the fire.

In early days a wall known as the Servian wall was built around the city. But Rome soon outgrew this. In the third century A.D. Emperor Aurelian built a new wall, which is still standing.

At its height, ancient Rome had a population of more than a million. The modern city has been growing rapidly in recent years, and has now passed this figure. In 1953 it had 1,722,836 people and had once again become the largest city in Italy.

Rome has been an important city for a longer time than any other city in the world. For hundreds of years it was the capital of the great Roman Empire, then it continued its importance as the seat of the Pope, and in recent generations it has become also the capital of one of the leading nations of modern Europe. The name given it in ancient times—"Eternal City" (**urbs aeterna**)—has been justified.

DISCUSSION QUESTIONS

1. What is a civic center? Describe the one in your town, or in a town you have visited, and compare it with that of ancient Rome.
2. Compare the development of Rome and of Washington, D. C.
3. Compare the development of the water supply of Rome with that of some American town.

READING    Showerman, pp. 14–28; Mills, pp. 293–301; Grose-Hodge, pp. 25–37.

# Unit V Review

## LESSONS XXIV–XXX

**ENGLISH WORD STUDIES**

1. What is wrong with this sentence: "This is the first time in a month that I have set foot on *terra cotta*"?

2. Define according to derivation: *relic, digest, Mr., doctor, libel, audio-visual, mediation, retardation.* Look up in the dictionary if necessary.

3. Give prefix and Latin root word from which the following are derived: **redigō, concipiō, attrahō, committō;** *respect, component, incorrigible, exhibit.*

A Roman aqueduct (*see p. 42*) on a French stamp.

**VOCABULARY**

| NOUNS | | | |
|---|---|---|---|
| 1. deus | 3. ōtium | 6. rēgīna | 9. verbum |
| 2. liber | 4. praesidium | 7. sententia | |
| | 5. proelium | 8. studium | |

| ADJECTIVES | | | |
|---|---|---|---|
| 10. commodus | 12. fīnitimus | 15. paucī | 18. tardus |
| 11. dūrus | 13. firmus | 16. perpetuus | 19. varius |
| | 14. medius | 17. reliquus | |

| VERBS | | | |
|---|---|---|---|
| 20. afficiō | 23. committō | 27. fugiō | 31. redūcō |
| 21. appellō | 24. contineō | 28. gerō | 32. trahō |
| 22. audiō | 25. conveniō | 29. incipiō | 33. valeō |
| | 26. convocō | 30. properō | |

| PREPOSITION | | |
|---|---|---|
| | 34. cum | |

| CONJUNCTIONS | | | |
|---|---|---|---|
| 35. aut | 37. et . . . et | 39. neque . . . | 40. -que |
| 36. aut . . . aut | 38. neque | neque | |

*The Gorgas Library at the University of Alabama has Ionic columns.*

## VOCABULARY (English Meanings)

NOUNS
1. god
2. book
3. leisure
4. guard
5. battle
6. queen
7. opinion
8. eagerness
9. word

ADJECTIVES
10. convenient
11. hard
12. neighboring
13. strong
14. middle (of)
15. few
16. constant
17. remaining
18. slow
19. changing

VERBS
20. affect
21. call
22. hear
23. join together, entrust
24. contain
25. come together
26. call together
27. flee
28. carry on
29. begin
30. hasten
31. lead back
32. draw
33. be strong

PREPOSITION
34. with

CONJUNCTIONS
35. or
36. either . . . or
37. both . . . and
38. nor
39. neither . . . nor
40. and

## GRAMMAR SUMMARIES
### Ablative uses

| | *In Latin* | | *In English* |
|---|---|---|---|
| MEANS | 1. Ablative without preposition | 1. | Objective with preposition *with* or *by*. |
| ACCOMPANI-MENT | 2. Ablative with **cum.** | 2. | Objective with preposition *with*. |
| AGENT | 3. Ablative with **ab.** | 3. | Objective with *by*. |

### Past Tenses

| *In Latin* | *In English* |
|---|---|
| 1. Perfect (**vēnī**). | 1. *a.* Past (*I came*). |
| | *b.* Present Perfect (*I have come*). |
| 2. Imperfect (**veniēbam**). | 2. *a.* Progressive past (*I was coming*). |
| | *b.* Customary past (*I used to come*). |
| | *c.* Repeated past (*I kept on coming*). |

*The old capitol at Frankfort, Kentucky, is classical in design.*

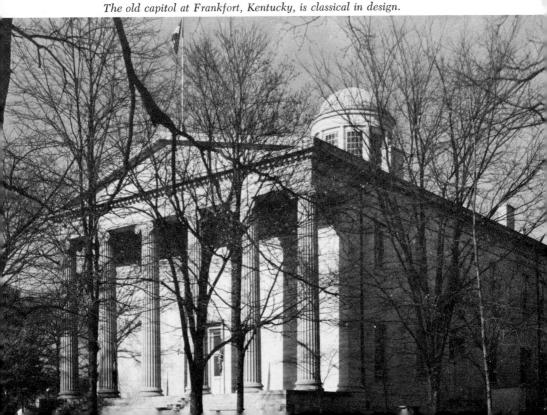

## UNIT PRACTICE AND EXERCISES

**Form Drill**

1. Form and translate adverbs from **lātus, līber,** and **perpetuus.**
2. Conjugate **trahō, incipiō,** and **audiō** in the future, active and passive.
3. Translate: **gerit, geret, incipient, incipiunt, properābō, fugiam, audīris, audiēris, afficiuntur, mittentur, convēnimus, continēbitur, convocābuntur, invenientur.**
4. Give in Latin: *they will hear, they will be heard, I shall see, I shall be seen, he will begin, she will be heard, we shall be called together, it will draw, they will be led back, he was being taught, you* (sing.) *will flee, you* (plur.) *will be affected.*
5. Give the Latin for the following in the singular and plural in the case required: *great interest* (nom.), *a good price* (gen.), *varying opinion* (dat.), *a small guard* (acc.), *a neighboring place* (abl.).

**Sentence Drill**

**A.** Complete and translate:
1. Rēgīna (*by many*) vidēbitur.
2. (*We are called*) amīcī bonī.
3. Multa bella ā Rōmānīs (*were carried on*).
4. Verba magistrī ā paucīs (*are heard*).
5. Puer ex aquā ā virō (*will be dragged*).
6. Patria ā puerīs (*will be saved*).

**B.** Translate:
1. Few find leisure.
2. The men will receive aid.
3. The teacher will praise the girls.
4. The boy scares the horses.
5. Many will hear my words.

**C.** Change the above into the passive (the subject becomes the agent; the direct object becomes the subject) and translate.

## UNIT VI

# *More Stories*

The Temple of Castor and Pollux reflected in the pool of the home of the Vestal Virgins in the Roman Forum.

*Aeneas meets his mother Venus when he lands on African soil. From a tapestry woven
for an Italian cardinal in the seventeenth century, now in the Cleveland Museum of Art.*

# Lesson xxxi

## AENĒĀS ET DĪDŌ

Ad Annam sorōrem[1] Dīdō properāvit: "Anna soror," dīxit, "animus meus miser perīculīs terrētur; Aenēam amō. Quid[2] agam?"

Anna respondit: "Aenēās est bonus et amīcus vir. Prō Troiā pugnāvit sed patriam āmīsit; nunc prō nostrā patriā multōs annōs pugnābit. Populī fīnitimī nōn sunt amīcī. Terminī nostrī ab Aenēā 5 proeliīs dēfendentur."

Aenēās in Āfricā cum rēgīnā mānsit. Dīdō Troiānum per medium oppidum dūxit et eī[3] oppidum mōnstrāvit.

Tum Iuppiter Mercurium nūntium ad Aenēam mīsit. "Annum in hōc[4] locō ēgistī," Mercurius dīxit. "Verba deī memoriā nōn tenēs; 10 properā in Italiam cum sociīs tuīs, ubi fīlius tuus reget. Ibi ōtium habēbis."

Aenēās sociōs convocāvit. Sociī frūmentum in nāvēs[5] portāvērunt. Dīdō Aenēam appellāvit:

"Cūr fugis? Dūrus es; iniūriam facis. Magnum est perīculum 15 nostrum. Ā populīs fīnitimīs agrī nostrī vāstābuntur, oppidum āmittētur. Praesidium nostrum esse dēbēs. In concordiā perpetuā habitābimus."

Aenēās respondit: "Deum Mercurium vīdī. Officium meum est ad Italiam nāvigāre. Dūrum est, sed deus imperat." 20

Aenēās tardē excessit et ad nāvēs vēnit. Sociī convēnērunt et nāvēs in aquam trāxērunt. Tum nāvēs undīs ventīsque commīsērunt. Dīdō misera nāvēs vīdit et sē[6] interfēcit.[7]

Troiānī ad Italiam migrāvērunt et patriam novam invēnērunt. Dīdō vītam āmīsit, Aenēās patriam invēnit. Ita[8] librī poētārum 25 docent.

QUESTIONS    1. What does Mercury tell Aeneas to do?
2. What argument did Dido use to persuade Aeneas to stay in Carthage?

---

[1] Accusative: *sister.*    [3] *to him.*    [5] Accusative plural.    [7] *killed.*
[2] *what.*    [4] *this.*    [6] *herself.*    [8] *so.*

**153**

**READING**      Hamilton, pp. 326–328 (Mentor ed., pp. 225–226); Sabin, pp. 337–338; Gayley, pp. 350–352; Bulfinch, pp. 266–268.

## Words Used as Nouns

A *pronoun* is a word used instead of a noun, as *he* or *she*, which takes the place of the name of some person, or as *that*, which takes the place of the name of a thing.

We have seen that the infinitive form of the verb may be used as a noun, as subject or object (p. 89).

An adjective also may be used as a noun. In Latin the masculine and feminine adjectives refer to persons, the neuter to things. The usage is common in English but is not always applied in the same way as in Latin. It is the same in:

  1. **Bonī laudantur,** *The good* (i.e., *good men*) *are praised.*
  2. **Multum facit,** *He does much.*

*Stamp issued by Italy in honor of Virgil (cf. p. 131), with a quotation from his most famous poem, the Aeneid.*

*Another Italian stamp honoring Virgil. In the quotation from the Aeneid Aeneas is greeting the land promised him by the Fates, the land which is to be his home and his country.*

But it is different in:

  3. **Nostrī veniunt,** *Our* (*men*) *are coming.*
  4. **Multa facit,** *He does many* (*things*).

## Conversation

(See map of the Roman world on pp. 104–105.)

M = Magister               D = Discipulī

M: Spectāte, puerī et puellae. D: Spectāmus, magister.

**154**

*Mercury in modern style at Rockefeller Center, New York, but he still has his familiar symbols: winged hat, winged feet, winged staff with snakes (called caduceus).*

M: Ubi oppida vidētis? D: In Āfricā et in Asiā et in Eurōpā multa oppida vidēmus.

M: In mediā terrā aquam vidētis. Illam[9] aquam "Medi-terrā- neum Mare"[10] vocāmus.     5

M: Ibi est Lūsitānia—vidētisne? D: Vidēmus.

M: Ubi est Hibernia? D: Hibernia est īnsula in Ōceanō Atlan- ticō.

M: Multī virī multōrum populōrum in Eurōpā habitant.

M: Ubi pugnābant Sociī in Bellīs Magnīs? D: Sociī in Galliā 10 pugnābant.

**QUESTIONS**  Answer in Latin.

1. Ubi habitāmus?
2. Nōnne officium nostrum est patriam dēfendere?
3. Ubi est Graecia?

**Exercises  A.** 1. Magna in proeliō fēcit.

2. Nōnne bonum facere dēbēmus?
3. Puer miser in viā librum āmīsit.
4. Vīta ā multīs in bellō āmittētur.
5. Nostrī prō patriā et familiīs patriae pugnābant.
6. Multōs annōs in perīculō ēgimus; nunc ōtium habēmus.

---

[9] *that.*     [10] *Sea.*

**B.** 1. Were the girls being scared by the horses?

2. The people will be called together by the queen.

3. I have entrusted the care of the money to the teacher.

4. The boys saw the danger clearly and fled to the woods.

**Vocabulary**  āmit′tō, āmit′tere, āmī′sī, *let go, lose*      [*mittō*]

mi′ser, mi′sera, mi′serum, *unhappy, poor*      (misery)

perī′culum, –ī, n., *danger*      (perilous)

prō, prep. with abl., *in front of, before, for*

**English Word Studies**

1. As a prefix **prō–** has its prepositional meanings, with the additional one of *forward*. Define the following derivatives of words which you have already studied: *provoke, prospect, produce, proceed.*

What is an *annuity*? Tell which of the following are derived from **līber, lībrī,** and which from **līber, –a, –um:** *liberty, librarian, liberal, liberate.*

2. Latin phrases in English:

**pro patria,** *for (one's) country.*

**pro forma,** *for (as a matter of) form.*

**pro bono publico,** *for the public good.*

*The death of Dido. The goddess of death is cutting off a lock of Dido's hair. From a tapestry in the Cleveland Museum of Art.*

The Sibyl, Aeneas, and Charon in a painting by Van Dyck.

# Lesson xxxii

## AENĒĀS AD ĪNFERŌS [1]

Aenēās fīlius Anchīsae [2] fuit, quī [3] in Siciliā ē vītā excesserat. Tum Anchīsēs in somnō ad fīlium vēnerat et fīlium vocāverat: "Venī, fīlī, ad īnferōs, ubi sum. Sibylla [4] viam nōvit et tē [5] dūcet."

Ita Aenēās in Italiam prōcessit, ubi Sibylla habitābat. Cōnsilium Sibyllae erat: "Sī in silvā rāmum [6] aureum inveniēs, ad īnferōs tē 5 prōdūcam et sine perīculō redūcam." Ita Aenēās in silvam properāvit. Auxiliō Veneris [7] rāmum invēnit et cum Sibyllā ad īnferōs dēscendit. Ibi multa nova vīdit et nōvit.

Tum ad magnam silvam vēnērunt. Ibi erat Dīdō. Aenēās rēgīnam vīdit et appellāvit: "Vērumne nūntius nūntiāvit? Vītamne āmīsistī? 10 Causane fuī? Invītus [8] ex patriā tuā excessī, sed ita deus imperāvit." Sed rēgīna, nunc inimīca, verbīs lacrimīsque Aenēae nōn movētur. Neque Aenēam spectāvit neque respondit sed in silvam fūgit.

---

[1] *The Lower World* (cf. p. 117, n. 4).
[2] *Anchises* (*Ankī'sēs*; gen.).
[3] *who.*
[4] *the Sibyl* (a prophetess).
[5] *you* (acc.).
[6] *branch.*
[7] Genitive of **Venus.**
[8] *unwillingly.*

Aenēās tardē ex silvā excessit et locum vīdit ubi malī poenā affi-
15 ciēbantur. Tum Aenēās Sibyllaque in Ēlysium[9] prōcessērunt. Ibi
animae[10] bonōrum in concordiā vītam agēbant. Iniūriae et bella
aberant. Ibi Anchīsēs erat. Grātus fīlium accēpit et nūntiāvit: "Clārōs
Rōmānōs quī posteā in terrā erunt et glōriam populī tuī mōnstrābō.
Rōmānī malōs superābunt et populōs aequē regent." Aenēās ab
20 Anchīse nōn retinētur et ā Sibyllā in terram redūcitur. Tum loca
commoda in Italiā occupāre mātūrāvit.

**QUESTIONS**  1. What did Aeneas need to go safely into the Lower
World?
2. Whom did he see there?

**READING**  Hamilton, pp. 328–334 (Mentor ed., pp. 226–230); Sabin,
pp. 338–341.

*Mercury, the messenger, is a favorite figure on postage stamps. Here he is on stamps
of Greece, France, Australia, Tripolitania, South Africa, Italy.*

**Past Perfect Active**

The *past perfect* tense (sometimes called pluperfect) refers to an
action that was completed before a certain time in the past: *He
had gone* (before something else happened).

In Latin, the past perfect is formed by adding the tense sign
—erā— to the perfect stem, together with the personal endings of the
imperfect. The tense signs and personal endings together are the
same as the various forms of the imperfect tense of **sum: portāveram,
docueram, fueram,** etc. (For full conjugation see pp. 397–401.)

---

[9] *Ely'sium,* the heaven of the Greeks and Romans.    [10] *souls.*

*Note.* The *future perfect* tense refers to an action completed before a certain time in the future: *He **will have gone*** (before something else will happen). In Latin, it is formed by adding the tense sign –eri– to the perfect stem, together with the personal endings of the present: **portāverō, docuerō, fuerō,** etc. (cf. pp. 397–401).

Neither the past perfect nor the future perfect is of great importance as compared with the perfect.

**Practice**
1. Conjugate in the perfect: **videō, cēdō, efficiō;** in the past perfect: **moveō, incipiō;** in the imperfect: **retineō, prōcēdō.**
2. Tell the form of **āfuimus, prōdūxerat, retinuistī, nōvērunt, prōcesserimus, āmīserātis, docēbās.**

**Exercises A.**
1. Parvī puerī linguam retinēre dēbent.
2. Multī puerī aberant. Nōnne valēbant?
3. Carrī ex silvā vēnerant et ad oppidum tardē prōcēdēbant.
4. Agricolārum fīliī et fīliae multa dē agrīs et equīs nōvērunt.
5. Paucī labōrābant sed reliquī puerī in castrīs semper manēbant.
6. Magister puerōs nōn retinuit, quod fōrmās verbōrum nōn nōverant.
7. Magistrī fīlius multa dē librīs nōvit, sed agrī fīlium agricolae docent.

*The classical architecture of the Pennsylvania Railway Station, Philadelphia (30th Street). What is the style of the columns?*

**B.** 1. We know much about many lands and peoples.
2. We shall see strange lands, towns, and peoples.
3. Marius has fought in Gaul for (his) native land.
4. We are the sons of free (men) and love our native land.
5. The slave deserved a large reward, because he had saved the life of our son.

**Vocabulary**

ab'sum, abes'se, ā'fuī, *be away, be absent*      [*sum*]
fī'lius, fī'lī, m., *son*      [*fīlia*]
inimī'cus, –a, –um, *unfriendly*; as noun, *enemy*      [*amīcus*]
nōs'cō, nōs'cere, nō'vī, *learn*; in perf. tense, "have learned" = *know*
prōcē'dō, prōcē'dere, prōces'sī, *go forward, advance*   [*cēdō*]
prōdū'cō, prōdū'cere, prōdū'xī, *lead out*      [*dūcō*]
reti'neō, retinē're, reti'nuī, *hold (back), keep*      [*teneō*]
si'ne, prep. with abl., *without*      (sinecure)

## Latin and English Word Formation

We have seen that the preposition **in** is used as a prefix (p. 76). There is another prefix **in–**, used chiefly with adjectives and nouns, which has an entirely different meaning and must be carefully distinguished from the former. It is a negative prefix, as in *injustice*. It is assimilated like the other prefix **in–**, as in *il-legal, im-moral, ir-regular*. Define the following derivatives of words which you have already studied:

*immemorial, immaterial, inglorious, ingratitude, illiberal, illiteracy, infirm*

Tell which of the two prefixes (preposition or negative) is used in each of the following:

*inhabit, invalid, invoke, induce, invariable, inequality, inundate, immovable, impecunious*

The prefix **dis–** in English and Latin means *apart*, but sometimes it is purely negative like **in–**. Distinguish carefully from **dē–**. It is either assimilated or left unchanged, as follows:

*dis-inter, dis-locate, dis-arm, dif-fuse, di-vert, di-stant, dis-similar*

Define the first three of these words, derived from words in previous vocabularies.

*Roman boy with ball and dove. Roman girl protecting her dove from a snake. Statues of bronze (left) and marble.*

# Lesson xxxiii

## LŪCIUS PILAM ĀMITTIT

LŪCIUS: Mārce, venī ad nōs.

MĀRCUS: Mēne vocās, Lūcī?

LŪCIUS: Tē vocō. Pilam [1] meam novam āmīsī. Dā [2] nōbīs auxilium. Sī et nōs et tū pilam petēmus nōs eam [3] inveniēmus. Sed sine auxiliō tuō numquam [4] ea ā nōbīs inveniētur.   5

MĀRCUS: Ubi pilam āmīsistī? Quid [5] faciēbās?

LŪCIUS: In herbā āmīsī. Ego et Cornēlius lūdēbāmus. Is pilam nōn āmīsit; ego āmīsī.

MĀRCUS: Invēnī pilam tuam, Lūcī! Cape.

LŪCIUS: Magnam grātiam tibi prō auxiliō tuō habeō, Mārce. 10 Auxilium tuum semper memoriā tenēbō. Nunc tē nōn dīmittēmus: lūde nōbīscum. Dubitāsne? Tē vincam!

MĀRCUS: Grātiās agō; nōn dubitō. Vōbīscum lūdere cupiō. Sed mē nōn vincēs quod integer sum.

LŪCIUS: Cupisne pilā aut armīs lūdere?   15

MĀRCUS: Retinēte arma vestra. Inimīcī nōn sumus. Pilā lūdere cupiō.

---

[1] *ball.*   [2] *give.*   [3] *it.*   [4] *never.*   [5] *what.*

1. Who lost the ball?
2. Who found it?
3. What was the reward?

## How Personal Pronouns Are Used

In English, personal pronouns are used to show the person of the verb: *I am, you are*. In Latin, as we have seen (p. 16), personal endings are used instead. When, however, emphasis or sharp contrast in subjects is desired, the Latin uses the personal pronouns **ego** (*I*) and **tū** (*you*). **Is** and **ea** serve as the personal pronouns of the third person (*he* and *she*). The full declension of these will be given later. Memorize the declensions of **ego** and **tū**: [6]

|  | SINGULAR | PLURAL |
|---|---|---|
| *Nom.* | **ego**, *I* | **nōs**, *we* |
| *Gen.* | **meī**, *of me* | **nostrum**, *of us* |
| *Dat.* | **mihi**, *to (for) me* | **nōbīs**, *to (for) us* |
| *Acc.* | **mē**, *me* | **nōs**, *us* |
| *Abl.* | **mē**, *with (from, etc.) me* | **nōbīs**, *with (from, etc.) us* |

|  | SINGULAR | PLURAL |
|---|---|---|
| *Nom.* | **tū**, *you* | **vōs**, *you* |
| *Gen.* | **tuī**, *of you* | **vestrum**, *of you* |
| *Dat.* | **tibi**, *to (for) you* | **vōbīs**, *to (for) you* |
| *Acc.* | **tē**, *you* | **vōs**, *you* |
| *Abl.* | **tē**, *with (from, etc.) you* | **vōbīs**, *with (from, etc.) you* |

## Possessive Adjectives

The possessive adjectives, **meus**, **noster**, **tuus**, and **vester**, are derived from the bases of their corresponding personal pronouns: **ego** (me–), **nōs** (nostr–), **tū** (tu–), and **vōs** (vestr–).

The possessive adjective follows its noun except when emphatic.

*Caution.* To show possession, use the possessive adjectives **meus**, **tuus**, **noster**, and **vester**, *not* the genitives **meī**, **tuī**, **nostrum**, and **vestrum**.

QUESTION   What is the difference between **tuus** and **vester**?

---

[6] When the preposition **cum** is used with the ablative forms of **ego** and **tū**, it is attached to them: **mēcum**, *with me;* **nōbīscum**, *with us.*

*A gate in the wall of Aurelian at Rome, built in the third century, but the battlements are medieval. The pyramid was an ancient tomb, in imitation of the Egyptian.*

### Personal Pronoun Test

Translate the italicized English words into the proper Latin forms.

1. I shall give *you* a present.
2. *I* criticize *you; you* criticize *me*.
3. *She* is my friend; *he*, my enemy.
4. She showed *us* beautiful flowers.
5. I will show *you* (*sing.*) the house.
6. We'll treat *you* (*plur.*) if you'll treat *us*.
7. He came *to us* and showed *us* many pictures.
8. Come *with us* and we will go *with you* (*plur.*).
9. *He* was mentioned *by me*, but *she* told *me* nothing.
10. *Your* daughter was seen *by us with you* (*sing.*) on the street.

**Exercises  A.**
1. Multa ā tē, amīce, accēpī.
2. Liber tuus ā mē nōn retinēbitur.
3. Cupitisne vidēre nōs, amīcōs vestrōs?
4. Ego sum amīcus tuus; is est inimīcus.
5. Fīlius meus in perīculum mēcum properāre nōn dubitāverat.
6. Ego sum miser sine tē; tū misera es quod tēcum nōn maneō.

**163**

**B.** 1. My words are not being heard by you.
2. We are foreigners; you are Americans.
3. I desire to present the reward to you (*sing.*).
4. Come (*plur.*) with us; we are your friends, not your enemies.

**Vocabulary**  cu′piō, cu′pere, cupī′vī, *desire*                  (cupidity)
dīmit′tō, dīmit′tere, dīmī′sī, *let go, send away*     [*mittō*]
du′bitō, dubitā′re, dubitā′vī, *hesitate, doubt*   (indubitable)
e′go, me′ī, *I*                                       (egoist)
in′teger, –gra, –grum, *untouched, fresh*             (integer)
is, *he, it;* [7] ea, *she, it* [7]
tū, tu′ī, *you*
ves′ter, ves′tra, ves′trum, *your* (referring to two or more persons)

I--- I--- I---
Now let's talk about me for a while.

EGO I ST

### Latin and English Word Formation

We have seen that prefixes are so called because they are attached to the beginnings of words (p. 70). *Suffixes* are attached to the ends of words (**sub**, *under, after;* **fīxus**, *attached*). Like the Latin prefixes, the Latin suffixes play a very important part in the formation of English words.

The Latin suffix –**ia** usually has the form –*y* in English. Give the English forms of the following words found in the preceding vocabularies: **memoria, glōria, familia, iniūria.**

What must be the Latin words from which are derived *colony, luxury, perfidy*?

Some –**ia** nouns drop the –**ia** entirely in English: *concord, vigil, matter* (from **māteria**).

You will find it useful to list suffixes in your notebook, together with many examples of their use in English words.

---

[7] The word *it* is used to translate **is** and **ea** when the noun referred to is masculine or feminine in Latin but its English equivalent is neuter (p. 20).

**164**

*Statuae deorum. An ancient statue of Neptune with his trident and a modern statue by Robert Aitken of Jupiter with his thunderbolt and eagle.*

# Lesson xxxiv

## Q. FABIUS MAXIMUS

Bellō[1] Pūnicō secundō Hannibal virōs suōs cum Rōmānīs pugnāre iubēbat sed Q.[2] Fabius Maximus semper discēdēbat neque in ūnō locō manēbat. Sine victōriīs Hannibal Italiam in prōvinciam redigere nōn poterat.[3]

Maximus perpetuō labōre etiam Tarentum, oppidum Italiae, 5 recēpit. Līvius in hōc[4] oppidō fuerat sed oppidum āmīserat et ad arcem[5] virōs remōverat. Maximus ad portās oppidī virōs prōdūxit et oppidum recēpit; tum is etiam ad arcem prōcessit. Ibi Līvius, superbus quod arcem retinuerat, Fabiō dīxit: "Meā operā[6] Tarentum recēpistī." Fabius respondit: "Certē, Līvī, nam ego recēpī oppidum 10 quod[7] tū āmīsistī."

---

[1] Ablative: in ——.     [3] *was able.*     [5] *citadel* (accusative).     [7] *which.*
[2] Q. = Quīntus.     [4] *this* (ablative).     [6] *effort.*

*Olympia, Washington, has a state capitol in Roman style, like so many other state capitols and the Capitol in Washington, D.C.*

Statuās deōrum ex oppidō Tarentō Maximus nōn remōvit sed, quod deī inimīcī Tarentīnīs erant, Tarentīnōs in oppidō statuās retinēre iussit.

QUESTIONS    1. How did Maximus weaken Hannibal?
                 2. How did Livius help in recovering Tarentum?

### Infinitive Object

1. **Virōs discēdere iussī,** *I ordered the men to go away.*
2. **Mē labōrāre docuistī,** *You taught me to work.*

*Observe* that (1) in English such verbs as *order, teach* (also *wish, forbid,* etc.) have an infinitive as the *object,* often with a noun or pronoun in the accusative, which may be regarded as its *subject*; (2) in Latin, too, certain verbs of similar meaning have the infinitive with its subject in the accusative case.

Exercises   **A.** 1. Māteria ā servīs removēbitur.
                 2. Deus nōs etiam inimīcōs amāre docet.
                 3. Fīliōs nostrōs bonōs librōs semper retinēre docēmus.
                 4. Nōnne bonum est inimīcōs in amīcitiam et concordiam redigere?
                 5. Magister nōs amīcōs nostrōs dīmittere et ā viā discēdere iussit.

166

**B.** 1. It was good to see our friends.
2. Lucius, order the boy to lead out fresh horses.
3. They had hesitated to remove the grain without wagons.
4. The sons of farmers are beginning to go away from the farms (*use* **ager**).

| Vocabulary | | |
|---|---|---|
| disce′dō, disce′dere, disces′sī, *go away, depart* | | [*cēdō*] |
| e′tiam, adv., *also, even* | | |
| iu′beō, iubē′re, ius′sī, *order* | | |
| por′ta, –ae, f., *gate* | | (portal) |
| red′igō, redi′gere, redē′gī, *drive back, reduce* | | [*agō*] |
| remo′veō, removē′re, remō′vī, *remove* | | [*moveō*] |

## Latin and English Word Formation

The Latin suffix –ia usually has the form –*y* in English, as we have seen (p. 164). When it is preceded by –t–, the combination –tia as a general rule has the form –*ce* in English.

Give the English forms of the following words found in the preceding vocabularies: **grātia, sententia.**

What must be the Latin words from which are derived *science, diligence, prudence, absence*?

The *tarantula* (a spider) and the *tarantella* (a dance) both got their names from Tarentum. Look them up in the dictionary.

*Fabius* is the name of towns in three states. Missouri, New York, Ohio, and Wisconsin have towns named *Hannibal*. Pennsylvania has a *Tarentum*.

*In faraway New Zealand the Town Hall at Dunedin is in the familiar Roman style. One touch of ancient Rome makes the whole world kin.*

JAMES SAWDERS

*Venus at the Forge of Vulcan in a painting by Van Dyck.*

# Lesson xxxv

## AENĒĀS ET TURNUS

Troia ā Graecīs capta erat et Aenēās cum paucīs Troiānīs ad Italiam vēnerat et per terrās barbarōrum virōs prōdūxerat. Sed Iūnō inimīca mānsit et contrā Aenēam miserum multōs barbarōs populōs Italiae incitāvit. Ā Turnō Lāvīnia, fīlia rēgis [1] Latīnī, amābātur sed 5 Aenēae [2] dōnāta est. Turnus bellum gerere nōn dubitāvit. Ab Aenēā bellum nōn grātē susceptum est; ad terminum vītae sub armīs esse nōn cupīvit. Sed causa Troiānōrum ā Fātīs suscepta erat. Aenēās etiam ā Graecīs quī in Italiā habitābant beneficium et auxilium accēpit, quod Turnō inimīcī erant. Per multōs diēs bellum gestum 10 est et multa ēgregia exempla virtūtis [3] in proeliīs clārīs prōposita sunt.

---

[1] Genitive singular of **rēx**.   [2] Dative.   [3] *of courage.*

A *floor mosaic from Pompeii. That the Romans were fond of birds is shown by the frequency with which they put them in wall paintings and floor mosaics. Roman literature too tells of pet birds.*

Tandem Turnus sōlus Aenēam sōlum ad pugnam ēvocāvit, quod reliquīs exemplum prōpōnere cupīvit. In locō commodō sub portīs oppidī pugnāvērunt. Nōn longa fuit pugna, quod Venus, māter Aenēae, fīliō ēgregia arma dōnāverat quae [4] deus Vulcānus fēcerat. Fāta iusserant auxilium ad Turnum nōn mittī; [5] itaque Iūnō aberat. 15 Turnī vīta fūgit et Aenēās ad terminum perīculōrum vēnit et ōtium invēnit.

**QUESTIONS**  1. Why did Turnus carry on war with the Trojans?
2. Why did Aeneas defeat Turnus?

**READING**  Hamilton, pp. 335–342 (Mentor ed., pp. 230–235); Sabin, pp. 341–342; Gayley, pp. 367–372; Bulfinch, pp. 290–292.

### Perfect Participle

A *participle* is that form of a verb which is used like an adjective.

The *past participle* in English usually ends in *–ed: carried.* The *perfect (passive) participle* in Latin is declined like the adjective **magnus.** In the first conjugation it is regularly formed by adding **–tus** to the present stem: **portā–tus.** It agrees, like an ordinary adjective, with a noun or pronoun in gender, number, and case: **litterae plicātae,** *the folded letter.* The perfect participle represents an act as having taken place before the time indicated by the main verb.

From now on the perfect participle of each new verb will be given in the vocabularies as the fourth form. The four forms given are called the *principal parts.*

---

[4] *which.*

[5] *to be sent.*

## Perfect Passive Tense

In English, the past passive tense is formed by using the past tense of *to be* (i.e., *was*) as an auxiliary or helping verb with the past participle: *he was carried.*

In Latin, the perfect passive tense is formed by using the *present* tense of **sum** as an auxiliary with the perfect participle: **portātus est.** The participle really modifies the subject and therefore agrees with it in gender, number, and case.

| | | | |
|---|---|---|---|
| **portātus** (–a, –um) | **sum,** *I was, have been carried* | **portātī** (–ae, –a) | **sumus,** *we were, have been carried* |
| | **es,** *you were, have been carried* | | **estis,** *you were, have been carried* |
| | **est,** *he was, has been carried* | | **sunt,** *they were, have been carried* |

Similarly **doctus sum, positus sum, mūnītus sum, captus sum.**
(For full conjugation see pp. 397–400.)

*Note.* In English, the past perfect passive is formed by using the past perfect tense of *to be* (i.e., *had been*) as an auxiliary with the past participle: *he had been carried.*

In Latin, the past perfect passive is formed by using the *imperfect* tense of **sum** (i.e., **eram**) as an auxiliary with the perfect participle: **portātus erat.** (For full conjugation see pp. 397–400.) The future perfect passive is formed by using the *future* tense of **sum** with the perfect participle: **portātus erit.** (For full conjugation see pp. 397–400.)

**Practice**

1. Conjugate in the perfect passive: **trahō, –ere, trāxī, trāctus; videō, –ēre, vīdī, vīsus;** in the past perfect passive: **moveō, –ēre, mōvī, mōtus; agō, –ere, ēgī, āctus.**
2. Translate: *they have been seen; I had been dragged; you have been moved; driven; having been driven.*

**Exercises  A.** 1. Arma carrīs ad castra portāta erant.
2. Causam populī suscipere est officium bonōrum.
3. Equī ab agricolā per silvam ad aquam āctī sunt.
4. Ēgregiumne exemplum amīcitiae memoriā tenētis?
5. Vir ā puerō sub aquam trāctus erat, sed et vir et puer servātī [6] sunt.
6. Ēgregium exemplum beneficī ā magistrō vestrō prōpositum est.

---

[6] Note that the participle is plural because it refers to both **vir** and **puer.**

**B.** 1. He knew much about horses.
2. He was taught by good teachers.
3. The farmer's son had seen few towns.
4. My son presented an excellent example.
5. The rest of the books had been removed by the teacher.

**Vocabulary**  benefi′cium, benefi′cī, n., *kindness*  [*faciō*]
ēgre′gius, –a, –um, *distinguished, excellent*  (egregious)
exem′plum, –ī, n., *example*  (exemplify)
per, prep. with acc., *through*
prōpō′nō, prōpō′nere, prōpo′suī, prōpo′situs, *put forward, offer*  [*pōnō*]
sub, prep., *under, close to*; with acc. after verbs of motion; with abl. after verbs of rest
susci′piō, susci′pere, suscē′pī, suscep′tus, *undertake*  [*capiō*]

*This stamp, in honor of the 75th anniversary of the American Bar Association, an organization of lawyers, is based on a design appearing on a frieze of the United States Supreme Court. The figures are in part of ancient origin; so wisdom is represented by the goddess Minerva with her owl. The other figures represent Justice, Divine Inspiration, and Truth.*

WIDE WORLD

## Latin and English Word Formation

The preposition **sub,** used as a prefix in Latin and English, means *under, up from under:* **sus-tineō** *hold up;* **suc-cēdō,** *come up.* It is regularly assimilated before certain consonants: *suc-ceed, sus-ceptible, suf-fer, sug-gest, sus-pend, sup-port, sur-rogate, sus-tenance,* but *sub-mit, sub-trahend.* We use it freely in English to form new words: *sub-lease, sub-let.*

**Per** usually remains unchanged when used as a prefix.

Explain by derivation the meaning of *permanent, permit, sustain, suspect.* What is meant by being *susceptible* to colds?

Why are iron and steel mills named after *Vulcan*? Why does the name *Vulcan* occur more often in the Pittsburgh telephone directory than that of any other Roman god? What do you infer from the fact that Birmingham, Chicago, Detroit, and New York are the cities in whose telephone directories the name *Vulcan* occurs ten or more times? Birmingham, with thirty-four occurrences, is second only to New York. Michigan, Missouri, West Virginia have towns named *Vulcan.*

*The sons of Niobe being killed by Apollo as their sisters look on. A painting by Richard Wilson in the Museum of Fine Arts, Boston.*

# Lesson xxxvi

## NIOBĒ

Niobē,[1] rēgīna superba, in Graeciā habitābat. Avus erat Iuppiter, quī deōs virōsque rēxit, et hoc[2] superbiam rēgīnae auxit. Niobē erat superba etiam quod septem fīliōs et septem fīliās habuit.

Apollō deus erat fīlius deae Lātōnae, et Diāna erat fīlia. Aliōs 5 līberōs Lātōna nōn habuit.

Sacra[3] Lātōnae ā populō suscipiēbantur. Superba Niobē adfuit et rogāvit:

"Cūr mātrī[4] duōrum līberōrum sacra suscipitis? Hoc nōn permittam. Etiam Niobē dea est; xiv, nōn duōs, līberōs habet. Lātōna 10 glōriam nōn meret—Niobē esse prīma dēbet. Vōbīs līberīsque vestrīs exemplum ēgregium prōpōnō. Sī sententia mea ā vōbīs nōn probata erit, poenā afficiēminī."

Superba verba rēgīnae ā Lātōnā audīta sunt. Fīlium vocāvit et officium permīsit:

15 "Tē iubeō septem fīliōs Niobae interficere."

---

[1] Ni′obē.  [2] this.  [3] sacred rites.  [4] for the mother.

Prīmus fīlius adfuit et interfectus est, tum reliquī. Niobē septem fīliōs nunc per linguam superbam āmīserat, tamen remānsit superba quod fīliae remānsērunt. Itaque Lātōna iussit etiam fīliās septem ēdūcī et ā Diānā interficī. Singulae fīliae ē vītā discessērunt, et Niobē misera in saxum dūrum mūtāta est. Poenā magnā affecta erat. Niobae 20 exemplum memoriā tenēre dēbēmus.

QUESTIONS
1. Give three reasons for Niobe's pride.
2. Who was Diana's brother?
3. Why were Niobe's children killed?

READING
Hamilton, pp. 348–349 (Mentor ed., pp. 238–239); Sabin, pp. 13–15; Gayley, pp. 99–103; Bulfinch, pp. 117–120; Guerber, pp. 93–96.

Practice
1. Conjugate in the perfect passive: āmittō, –ere, āmīsī, āmissus; retineō, –ēre, retinuī, retentus; redigō, –ere, redēgī, redāctus; cupiō, –ere, cupīvī, cupītus; in the past perfect passive: iubeō, –ēre, iussī, iussus; nōscō, –ere, nōvī, nōtus.

2. Tell the form and translate: ēductī sumus, susceptum erat, permissum erit, trāctī estis, mōtus es, āctī erant, vīsae estis, iussae sunt, portātus erō, prōpositum est.

### Present Infinitive Passive

In English, the present infinitive passive is formed by using the auxiliary *to be* with the past participle: *to be seen.*

In Latin, the present infinitive passive is formed by changing the active infinitive ending –**re** to –**rī**, except in the third conjugation:

---

*Active:* portāre, *to carry;*     docēre; mūnīre
*Passive:* portārī, *to be carried;* docērī; mūnīrī

*Note.* In the third conjugation, final –**ĕre** is changed to –**ī:**

    *Active:* pōnere, *to place;*    capere
    *Passive:* pōnī, *to be placed;* capī

---

Practice
Form and translate the present passive infinitive of **videō, agō, trahō, suscipiō, ēdūcō, moveō, appellō,** and **inveniō.**

Exercises
A. 1. Nōnne dūrum est sub aquā remanēre?
2. Equī ex oppidō per agrōs lātōs ēductī erunt.
3. Pecūnia merērī et servārī ā puerīs puellīsque dēbet.

4. Puerī adfuērunt prīmī, quod puellae tardae fuērunt.
5. Tibi vītam līberōrum meōrum permittere nōn dubitāvī.
6. Verbīs bonōrum virōrum semper incitārī et regī dēbēmus.

**B.** 1. We have ordered the boys to be dismissed.
2. The boys are absent, but the girls are present.
3. The men had been ordered to seize the fortified town.
4. The children ought to be called together by the teacher.

**Vocabulary**  ad'sum, ades'se, ad'fuī, adfutū'rus,[5] *be near, be present*

[*sum*]

ēdū'cō, ēdū'cere, ēdū'xī, ēduc'tus, *lead out*   [*dūcō*]

interfi'ciō, interfi'cere, interfē'cī, interfec'tus, *kill*   [*faciō*]

lī'berī, –ō'rum, m., *children*   [*līber*]

permit'tō, permit'tere, permī'sī, permis'sus, *let go through,*
*allow, entrust* (with dat.)   [*mittō*]

prī'mus, –a, –um, *first*   (primary)

rema'neō, remanē're, remān'sī, remānsū'rus,[5] *remain*

[*maneō*]

### English Word Studies

1. The town of *Apollo* is in Pennsylvania; *Diana* is in Tennessee
and West Virginia; *Niobe* is in New York and North Dakota. According
to telephone directories, New York has thirty-three firms named
*Apollo*, St. Louis thirteen, Buffalo six; New York has twenty-four
named *Diana*, Chicago eight, Rochester four, Akron three. Do you
know of any firm or product with these names?

What is a *primary* school? A political *primary*?

The word *education* is often wrongly said to be derived from
**ēdūcere**. As you can see, the derivative of **ēdūcere** would be *eduction*.
*Education* comes from a related word, **ēdūcāre**, *to bring up*. According
to derivation then if you are well educated you are well brought
up.

2. Latin phrases in English:

**Deo gratias,** *thanks to God.*

**per annum,** *by* (*through*) *the year.*

**sub rosa,** *under the rose,* i.e., in concealment.

**Dei gratia,** *by the grace of God* (seen on Canadian coins).

**sic semper tyrannis,** *thus always to tyrants* (motto of the state of
Virginia).

---

[5] A few verbs lack the perfect participle; some of these have the future active
participle in **-ūrus**, which then is used as the fourth principal part.

# ᚛ᚚᚔ Glimpses of Roman Life

## FOOD AND MEALS

The easiest way to give an idea of Roman foods is by listing some important foods which were unknown to the Romans: potatoes, tomatoes, bananas, oranges, sugar, coffee, tea. Butter was rarely used, except externally as a sort of salve or cold cream. Milk and cheese were freely used. Instead of sugar, honey served for sweetening. The extensive use of honey made beekeeping a very important occupation. Wheat bread baked in round loaves (see picture on page 185) was the "staff of life." Cabbage, onions, beans were among the chief vegetables. Apples, pears, grapes, olives were the chief fruits. The **mālum Persicum** (from which our word *peach* is derived) was, as its name shows, originally brought from Persia.

Much use was made of salads of various kinds, as is true in Italy today. Hence one reason for the importance of olive oil. This was used also in cooking, instead of butter, and besides was burned in lamps.

The favorite meat was pork. Various kinds of fowl and birds were eaten, even peacocks by the wealthy classes. Fish and oysters became extremely popular.

Besides milk and water the chief drink of the Romans was wine. There were many grades of native and imported wines. They were usually mixed with water when drunk at meals.

Breakfast was a simple meal, chiefly of bread. In the country, dinner (**cēna**) was at noon, but in the city this was postponed till early evening. Instead there was a luncheon (**prandium**) at midday or somewhat earlier.

The dinner consisted of a course of relishes (lettuce, onions, eggs, oysters, asparagus, etc.), called the **gustus** (*taste*), followed by the chief course (meat, fish, or fowl and vegetables), then the dessert, called the **secunda mēnsa** (*second table*) of fruit, nuts, and sweets. The Latin expression **ab ōvō usque ad māla**, *from eggs to apples*, meaning from beginning to end, shows what the usual relishes and

**175**

desserts were; cf. English *from soup to nuts*. Wine was served with the meal. Tobacco was unknown.

The guests reclined on couches instead of sitting on chairs. There were couches along the three sides of the rectangular table, each with room for three people. As the guests reclined on their left elbows, only their right hands were free. Forks were rarely used. Food was taken up with the fingers or with spoons. Meat was cut up before being served. Though much use was made of the fingers, we may well imagine that people of culture ate quite as daintily as we do who have forks to help us. They had finger bowls and napkins.

**QUESTIONS**   1. Where did we originally get the important foods which the Romans knew nothing about?
2. Name the order of meals and describe a Roman dinner.
3. How would you arrange a Roman banquet in your Latin club or school?

**READING**   Showerman, pp. 124–136; McDaniel, pp. 120–136; Grose-Hodge, pp. 201–205.

*Food shop in Pompeii. As not all houses had running water, the corner fountain was popular.*

# Unit VI Review

## ENGLISH WORD STUDIES

1. Find and use in sentences as many English derivatives as possible from **servō, moveō, dūcō, capiō.** For example: from **servō** is derived *conservation*, used as follows: *The **conservation** of our soil and of our forests is a necessity.*

2. Pick out from the vocabulary below the Latin words from which each of the following is derived: *primitive, permission, beneficiary, exemplary, proposition, librarian, inimical, integration, commiserate, retention, reproduce.*

## VOCABULARY

| NOUNS | 2. exemplum | 4. liber | 6. perīculum |
|---|---|---|---|
| 1. beneficium | 3. fīlius | 5. līberī | 7. porta |

| ADJECTIVES | 9. inimīcus | 11. miser | 13. vester |
|---|---|---|---|
| 8. ēgregius | 10. integer | 12. prīmus | |

| PRONOUNS | 14. ego | 15. is, ea | 16. tū |
|---|---|---|---|

| VERBS | 22. discēdō | 28. permittō | 34. removeō |
|---|---|---|---|
| 17. absum | 23. dubitō | 29. prōcēdō | 35. retineō |
| 18. adsum | 24. ēdūcō | 30. prōdūcō | 36. suscipiō |
| 19. āmittō | 25. interficiō | 31. prōpōnō | |
| 20. cupiō | 26. iubeō | 32. redigō | |
| 21. dīmittō | 27. nōscō | 33. remaneō | |

| ADVERB | 37. etiam | | |
|---|---|---|---|

| PREPOSITIONS | 39. prō | 41. sub | |
|---|---|---|---|
| 38. per | 40. sine | | |

## GRAMMAR SUMMARY

### First Conjugation: Principal Parts

Verbs of the first conjugation generally form the perfect stem by adding –v to the present stem and form the perfect participle by adding –tus to the present stem. Review the following verbs, whose principal parts are regular.

accūsō, amō, appellō, convocō, dōnō, dubitō, ēvocō, exspectō, habitō, incitō, labōrō, laudō, līberō, mandō, mōnstrō, nāvigō, nūntiō, occupō, parō, portō, probō, pugnō, servō, spectō, vāstō, vocō.

## UNIT PRACTICE AND EXERCISES

**Form Drill A.** Give the Latin for *I, me, we, us, with me, with us; you* (as sing. subject and object), *you* (as plur. subject and object), *of you* (sing. and plur.), *with you* (sing. and plur.).

**B.** Give in Latin the singular and plural of *great danger* and *my son* used as subject, used as direct object, and used as indirect object.

**C.** 1. Give the present passive infinitive of **appellō, āmittō, removeō,** and **audiō.**

2. Translate *to undertake, to be undertaken; to order, to be ordered; to lead out, to be led out.*

**D.** Give in six tenses, translating each tense form: 1. the active first singular of **iubeō,** and 2. the passive third plural of **permittō.**

**E.** 1. Translate **fuerant, fuistī, iusserāmus, discessit, remōvī, retinuistis, cupīvimus, ēdūxit, prōpositum est, remōtī sunt, dubitāverō.**

2. Give in Latin *he had been, she has been seen, it has been presented, he has remained, undertaken, it will be entrusted, they have been, we had been sent away.*

## VOCABULARY (English Meanings)

| NOUNS | | | |
|---|---|---|---|
| 1. kindness | 2. example | 4. book | 6. danger |
| | 3. son | 5. children | 7. gate |

| ADJECTIVES | 9. unfriendly | 11. unhappy | 13. your |
|---|---|---|---|
| 8. distinguished | 10. untouched | 12. first | |

| PRONOUNS | 14. I | 15. he, she | 16. you |
|---|---|---|---|

| VERBS | 22. depart | 28. entrust | 34. remove |
|---|---|---|---|
| 17. be away | 23. hesitate | 29. go forward | 35. hold back |
| 18. be present | 24. lead out | 30. lead out | 36. undertake |
| 19. lose | 25. kill | 31. offer | |
| 20. desire | 26. order | 32. reduce | |
| 21. send away | 27. learn | 33. remain | |

| ADVERB | 37. also | | |
|---|---|---|---|

| PREPOSITIONS | 39. for | 41. under |
|---|---|---|
| 38. through | 40. without | |

## A Latin Play

### POST BELLUM

**Persōnae**

Lūcīlia } Rōmānae
Valeria
Zōē, *serva*

Gāius, *frāter Lūcīliae*
Philippus, *servus*

Locus: In ātriō Lūcīliōrum. (*Accēdunt Lūcīlia et Valeria.*)

VALERIA: Victōria est nostra! Multa oppida, multa castra nostrī occupāvērunt.

LŪCĪLIA: Deī bonī sunt!

VALERIA: Caecilius tuus aderit—et meus vir pactus,[1] Arrius.

LŪCĪLIA: Zōē! Zōē! (*Accēdit Zōē.*) Zōē, nova mea ōrnāmenta! 5 (*Exit Zōē.*)

VALERIA: Nova est serva.

LŪCĪLIA: Captīva est. Pater meus eam [2] cum aliā praedā praemīsit.

VALERIA: Parva est—et trīstis.[3] Lacrimās in oculīs vīdī. (*Zōē accēdit. Ōrnāmenta et vestēs pulchrās portat. Lūcīlia et Valeria eam* 10 *nōn vident.*)

LŪCĪLIA: Bellum dūrum est. Zōē patriam et familiam āmīsit. Misera est.

VALERIA: Serva est.

---

[1] *fiancé.*   [2] *her.*   [3] *sad.*

*Scene in a Roman Atrium.*

15    Lūcīlia: Serva nunc est—sed tamen puella misera. Amīca mea erit. Eam amō.

Valeria: Bah! (*Lūcīlia servam videt.*)

Lūcīlia: Ōh, Zōē! (*Zōē ōrnāmenta et vestēs Lūcīliae dat.*) Ecce,[4] Valeria! (*Lūcīlia ōrnāmenta et vestēs Valeriae mōnstrat.*)

20    Valeria: Pulcherrima[5] sunt! Et tū es pulcherrima.

Lūcīlia: Nōn pulchra sum, Valeria. Ecce, lenticulās[6] habeō, multās lenticulās!

Valeria: Quod flāva[7] es lenticulae adsunt. Tū tamen es pulchra.

Lūcīlia: Nōn pulchra, sed misera sum. Caecilius mē nōn amābit.

25    Valeria: Nūgae![8] Certē tē amābit. (*Accēdit Gāius.*)

Gāius: Arrius adest, Valeria.

Valeria: Quid?

Gāius: Arrius, vir pactus tuus, domum vēnit.

Valeria: Quis eum[9] vīdit?

30    Gāius: Ego eum vīdī.

Valeria: Ōh, valē, Lūcīlia! Valē! (*Exit cum Gāiō.*)

Lūcīlia: Beāta[10] est Valeria.

Zōē: Et tū beāta eris, domina.

Lūcīlia: Quid dīcis?

35    Zōē: Serva sum, domina; tū tamen amīca mihi es. Lenticulās cūrābō.

Lūcīlia: Cūrābisne?

Zōē: Remediō occultō.

Lūcīlia: Vērumne dīcis?

40    Zōē: Ego multās lenticulās habēbam; nunc absunt.

Lūcīlia: Ōh, Zōē! Sī lenticulās cūrābis, Caecilius mē amābit!

Zōē: Certē amābit. (*Accēdit Gāius.*)

Gāius: Lūcīlia! Novus servus adest—meus.

Lūcīlia: Novusne servus?

45    Gāius: Puer est—captīvus. Pater eum praemīsit. Iam[11] accessit. Appellātur Philippus.

Zōē: Philippus?

Gāius: Ecce! (*Ad iānuam[12] properat. Accēdit Philippus.*)

Zōē: Philippus est—frāter meus!

50    Philippus: Zōē est—soror mea! (*Lacrimant.*)

Zōē: Ō domina, beāta sum. Deī certē bonī sunt.

Lūcīlia: Familia nostra beātissima Rōmae[13] erit.

---

| | | | |
|---|---|---|---|
| [4] *see!* | [7] *blonde.* | [10] *happy.* | [13] *the happiest in Rome.* |
| [5] *very beautiful.* | [8] *nonsense.* | [11] *already.* | |
| [6] *freckles.* | [9] *him.* | [12] *door.* | |

 UNIT VII

# Games and Gods

*The Temple of Apollo in Pompeii.*

Sleepyhead. A schoolboy, perhaps, at the left, with his lantern, pictured in stone. Below, statue of a young Roman in the Metropolitan Museum of Art.

Rolling hoops and playing leapfrog.

# *Lesson* xxxvii

## LŪDUS

Lūciumne in memoriā habētis? Lūcius reliquīque puerī Rōmānī
ā magistrō in pulchrum Forum Rōmānum ēductī erant. Nunc iterum
dē Lūciō audiētis. Dē lūdō Lūcī nunc agēmus. Lūdus est locus ubi
magister puerōs puellāsque docet. Prīmus lūdus vocātus est "lūdus
litterārum." In Lūcī lūdō puellae ob variās causās nōn erant, et paucī 5
puerī. Rōmānī līberōs in pūblicum lūdum nōn mīsērunt quod lūdī
pūblicī nōn erant. Sed tamen pretium disciplīnae erat parvum. Puerī
pecūniam et praemia ad magistrum portābant. Servī puerōs ad
lūdum ante lūcem [1] dūcēbant et lanternam librōsque portābant.
Nōnne dūrum erat multās hōrās in lūdō agere? Servī in lūdō manē- 10
bant et puerōs ad familiās redūcēbant.

### WHAT ROMAN BOYS STUDIED

Etiam magister servus erat. Litterās et verba et numerōs docuit.
Lingua lūdī erat Latīna, quod puerī Rōmānī erant. Numerōs Lūcius
nōn amāvit. Magister puerīs fōrmās litterārum mōnstrābat. Tum
digitōs puerōrum tenēbat, et litterās faciēbant. Sententiae [2] puerīs ā 15
magistrō mōnstrātae sunt. Exemplum sententiae est: "Ibi semper est
victōria ubi concordia est." Sententiās pulchrās semper amābat
Lūcius et in memoriā tenēbat. Dīligentiā et studiō praemia merēbat.

### BAD LUCK

Tardī discipulī poenā affectī sunt, sed Lūcius semper prīmus vēnit,
quod ad lūdum properāvit neque in viīs remānsit. Sed mala fortūna 20
vēnit. Pecūnia Lūciō permissa erat et ad magistrum portābātur. In
viā pecūniam āmīsit et tardus fuit. Magister puerōs appellāverat, et
reliquī puerī responderant, "Adsum!" Tum magister Lūcium appellāvit. Puerī respondērunt, "Abest!" Tum vēnit Lūcius sine pecūniā
et magister puerīque dē pecūniā āmissā audīvērunt. Magister dūrus 25
Lūcium miserum ā puerīs sublevārī [3] iussit et poenā eum [4] affēcit,
quod pecūniam āmīserat et tardus fuerat.

---

[1] From **lūx.**    [2] *mottoes.*    [3] *to be lifted up.*    [4] *him.*

KONSTANTIN J. KOSTICH

*Pulchrum Forum Romanum. The Arch of Septimius Severus and the Senate at the left; the Temple of Saturn in the center.*

### FOUND!

Magister discipulōs dīmīsit et singulī excessērunt. Lūcius cum servō discessit et pecūniam in viā sub carrō invēnit. Ad lūdum 30 properāvit et magistrō pecūniam dōnāvit. Magister bonō puerō grātiās ēgit et ob dīligentiam laudāvit.

**QUESTION**  What differences are there between your school and that of Lucius?

**Conversation: School**

MAGISTER: Discipulōs appellābō. Anna. ANNA: Adsum.

M: Marīa. MARĪA: Adsum.

M: Mārcus. DISCIPULĪ: Abest.

M: Ubi est Mārcus? D: Ad lūdum nōn vēnit. (Etc.)

5  M: Grātane erat vīta puerōrum Rōmānōrum? D: Nōn grāta erat vīta puerōrum Rōmānōrum, quod puerī Rōmānī ante lūcem in lūdum dūcēbantur.

**184**

M: Ubi puerī Rōmānī labōrābant? D: In lūdō puerī Rōmānī labōrābant.

M: Multīne puerī in lūdō fuērunt? D: Paucī puerī in lūdō 10 fuērunt.

QUESTIONS    Answer in Latin.
1. Ubi nunc estis?
2. Estne grātum in lūdō esse?
3. Pecūniamne tuam āmīsistī?
4. Ubi librum tuum Latīnum āmīsistī?
5. Tardusne in lūdum vēnistī?
6. Semperne tardus in lūdum veniēs?

## How to Study a Latin Paragraph

Do not turn at once to the vocabulary at the end of the book for a word you do not know. Try to read an entire paragraph before you look up a word. There are three good ways to find the meaning of a word without looking it up:

*On the left is a Pompeian wall painting showing a bakery. The round loaves are creased so that they can be broken more easily. Some think that the bread is being given away at this shop. On the right is a modern picture, based on existing remains at Pompeii, which gives a good idea of a Roman shop. In both pictures the boys appear to be hungry.*

1. English derivatives. Nearly every Latin word has at least one English derivative.

2. Related Latin words. If you know the meaning of re– and **dūcō**, you know the meaning of **redūcō**.

3. Sensible guessing.

Use the vocabulary merely to check results. In this way you will save time and learn more Latin. Don't become a vocabulary slave.

### Lazy Latin

The preceding paragraph mentioned *sensible* guessing. Here are some examples of *senseless* guessing that you should avoid—except in fun:

**puer valet,** *a poor valet.*       **Iam satis est,** *I've had enough jam.*
**virī bonī,** *weary and bony.*      **Ubi est porta?** *Where's the porter?*
**ex officiō,** *out of office.*      **Clam iūs petit,** *He asks for clam juice.*
**ante bellum,** *a pretty aunt.*      **Nōn possum comprehendere,** *I didn't catch the 'possum.*

What do these phrases and sentences really mean?

*Italian stamp for Virgil. The scene is in the Lower World, where Anchises is prophesying the glories of Rome to Aeneas.*

**Vocabulary**    **dīligen'tia, –ae,** f., *diligence*      (diligent)
           **lū'dus, –ī,** m., *school*
           **ob,** prep. with acc., (*toward*), *on account of, for*
           **pul'cher, –chra, –chrum,** *beautiful*      (pulchritude)

### English Word Studies

Make a diagram similar to that on p. 99 but substitute seven derivatives of **agere** with their meanings for the seven Latin words.

Find derivatives for the following new words on p. 183: **iterum** (1.2), **lanterna** (1.9), **digitus** (1.15).

Find an English derivative for every word in lines 12–15 of p. 183 except **etiam, erat, et, quod, tum.**

*Puer Romanus a servo ad ludum ducitur.*

# Lesson xxxviii

## LŪDĪ RŌMĀNĪ ET AMERICĀNĪ

Inter lūdōs Rōmānōs et nostrōs similitūdō[1] nōn magna est. In lūdīs Rōmānīs inter puerōs erant nūllae puellae, in nostrīs sunt multae; puerī Rōmānī ad lūdum ā servīs ductī sunt, nōs sōlī aut in carrīs venīmus; magistrī Rōmānī servī erant, nostrī līberī sunt; lingua lūdōrum Rōmānōrum erat Latīna, lingua lūdōrum nostrōrum est 5 Anglica. Ob dīligentiam et studium puerīs Rōmānīs praemia pulchra data sunt, nunc puerī Americānī "A" merent. Tardī discipulī Rōmānī poenā affectī sunt, sed tardī discipulī poenā semper afficiuntur. Ob variās causās vīta discipulōrum nostrōrum grāta est, sed etiam puerī Rōmānī lūdum librōsque amāvērunt. Magna pecūnia lūdīs nostrīs 10 datur et beneficia disciplīnae pūblicae omnēs[2] puerī puellaeque accipiunt. Nōnne est officium pūblicum pecūniam dare et lūdīs auxilium submittere? Rōmānī lūdīs auxilium nōn submīsērunt, neque beneficia disciplīnae pūblicae puerī Rōmānī accēpērunt. Lūdus Rōmānōrum

---

[1] *likeness* (nominative feminine).     [2] *all.*

prīmus lūdus litterārum appellātus est quod ibi magistrī litterās docē-
15 bant. Etiam nostrī lūdī sunt lūdī litterārum.

QUESTIONS    1. How do our schools resemble Roman schools?
                2. How did the boys get to school?

### Principal Parts

The principal parts of the model verbs of the four conjugations
and of **sum** are as follows:

| CONJUGATION | | PRES. INDIC. | PRES. INFIN. | PERF. INDIC. | PERF. PART. |
|---|---|---|---|---|---|
| I | | portō | portāre | portāvī | portātus |
| II | | doceō | docēre | docuī | doctus |
| III | (a) | pōnō | pōnere | posuī | positus |
| | (b) | capiō | capere | cēpī | captus |
| IV | | mūniō | mūnīre | mūnīvī | mūnītus |
| *Irregular Verb* | | sum | esse | fuī | futūrus [3] |

[3] See p. 174, footnote 5.

*The Rotunda of the University of Virginia, used as a library. Thomas Jefferson modeled
it after the Pantheon (see next page). The home he built for himself at Monticello
has a similar design (see page 359). Jefferson was an excellent classical scholar, deeply
interested in the ancient civilization, and helped introduce classical architecture and
other phases of ancient culture in our country.*

JAMES SAWDERS

PHILIP GENDREAU

*The Pantheon at Rome, a temple built in the time of Augustus and rebuilt later.*
*Compare page 88 and the modern buildings on pages 188 and 380.*

### Tense Stems

The many different forms of every Latin verb are built upon only *three stems*. These are obtained from the principal parts as follows:

1. To find the *present stem*, drop –re from the present infinitive active; **portā–**, etc.

2. To find the *perfect stem*, drop –ī from the perfect indicative active: **portāv–**, etc.

3. To find the *participial stem*, drop –us from the perfect participle: **portāt–**, etc.

**QUESTION**  What tenses are formed (*a*) upon the present stem, (*b*) upon the perfect stem, (*c*) with the perfect participle?

**Exercises  A.** 1. Puerōs poenā afficī iussimus.
2. Ob amīcitiam auxilium submīsimus.
3. Castra in locō plānō inter oppidum et silvam erant.
4. Ob multās causās concordia inter līberōs esse dēbet.
5. Officium pūblicum est puerīs puellīsque disciplīnam dare.

**189**

**B.** 1. He has been aroused by the messenger's harsh words.
2. We have furnished reinforcements to the scared provinces.
3. On-account-of the danger we did not desire to sail to Europe.
4. The fields had been destroyed and the town seized by the slaves.

**Vocabulary**   dō,[4] da're, de'dī, da'tus, *give*                    (dative)
in'ter, prep. with acc., *between, among*
submit'tō, –mit'tere, –mī'sī, –mis'sus, *let down, furnish*
                                                          [*mittō*]

### Latin and English Word Formation

As a prefix in Latin and English, **inter–** has its usual meanings. It is rarely assimilated. It is used rather freely in English to form new words: *inter-class, inter-state, inter-scholastic*, etc.

As a prefix **ob–** has the meaning *towards* or *against*. It is regularly assimilated before certain consonants: *oc-cur, of-ficial, o-mission, op-ponent*; but *ob-tain, ob-serve, ob-durate, ob-vious*.

Explain by derivation the meaning of *intercede, opponent, intervene, obvious*. What are *data*?

*Opponent.*

---

[4] **Dō** is irregular in three parts—perfect **dedī**, and ă in **dare** and **datus**. The a is short in all indicative forms except the present tense, second person singular (**dās**), and in the imperative singular (**dā**).

*Pulchra templa deorum. A Roman temple at Baalbek, Lebanon (see p. 75).*

# Lesson xxxix

## TEMPLA DEŌRUM

Silvae erant prīma templa deōrum. Prīmō [1] virī in agrīs habitābant et Nātūram colēbant. Posteā virī quī in oppidīs habitābant
templa pulchra in altīs locīs ad glōriam deōrum pōnēbant. Templa
saepe in altīs locīs posita sunt. Cūr? Quod haec [2] loca caelō fīnitima
erant, in quō deī habitābant.                                              5

"Nātūra est pulchra," hominēs [3] dīxērunt. "Etiam loca sacra ad
quae convenīmus et in quibus deōrum beneficia petimus pulchra esse
dēbent. Deī nōbīs fortūnam bonam dedērunt. Deīs grātiam habēmus
ob frūmentum quō vītam sustinēmus et ob auxilium perpetuum quod
nōbīs submīsērunt."                                                        10

Itaque Graecī et Rōmānī ob beneficia deōrum magna et pulchra
templa faciēbant quae deīs erant grāta. Statua aut deī aut deae
semper in templō pōnēbātur.

In Graeciā et Italiā ruīnae templōrum multōrum et pulchrōrum
videntur. Templum clārum Athēnae, appellātum Parthenōn, ob      15
fōrmam pulchram semper laudātum est. Nōnne fuērunt multa templa

---

[1] *at first.*          [2] *these.*          [3] *men.*

Rōmāna inter pictūrās quās vīdistī? Cūr pictūrās templōrum et Graecōrum et Rōmānōrum, quae in multīs librīs inveniuntur, nōn spectātis? Etiam in actīs diurnīs[4] pictūrās templōrum antīquōrum
20 inveniētis.

In templīs virī auxilium deōrum petēbant. Virī malī quōrum vīta[5] in perīculō erat saepe ad templa fugiēbant, quod neque ex templīs removēbantur neque ibi poenam sustinēbant.

QUESTIONS   1. Where were the first temples? Why?

2. How can we find out what the ancient temples looked like?

### The Relative Pronoun Quī

The English pronouns *who, which, what,* and *that* are called *relative* pronouns because they *relate* or refer to some preceding word, called their *antecedent: The boy who lives next door collects stamps.* The word *boy* is the antecedent of *who.*

There is only one relative pronoun in Latin, declined as follows:

|  | SINGULAR | | | | PLURAL | | |
|  | M. | F. | N. | | M. | F. | N. |
|---|---|---|---|---|---|---|---|
| Nom. | quī | quae | quod | | quī | quae | quae |
| Gen. | cuius | cuius | cuius | | quōrum | quārum | quōrum |
| Dat. | cui | cui | cui | | quibus | quibus | quibus |
| Acc. | quem | quam | quod | | quōs | quās | quae |
| Abl. | quō | quā | quō | | quibus | quibus | quibus |

### English Meanings in Singular and Plural

|  | M., F. | N. |
|---|---|---|
| Nom. | who, which, that | which, that, what |
| Gen. | of whom, whose, of which | of which, whose |
| Dat. | to (for) whom, which | to (for) which |
| Acc. | whom, which, that | which, that, what |
| Abl. | by, etc., whom, which | by, etc., which |

*Observe* that:

1. the following forms are alike in all genders: genitive singular; dative singular; dative and ablative plural;

2. the accusative singular, masculine and feminine, ends in –m, as in English *whom*;

---

[4] *newspapers.*

[5] We use the plural in English; in Latin, the plural means *biographies.*

3. the nominative singular feminine is like the nominative plural feminine and neuter.

## Relative Pronouns as Used in English

*That* as a relative can be used to refer to both persons and things, but *who* always refers to persons and *which* to things. In other words, *which* is the neuter of *who*. *Which* and *that* do not change form to indicate case, while *who* does:

Nom. *who*     Poss. *whose*     Obj. (Acc.) *whom*

## The Relative Pronoun as Used in Latin

When a sentence contains two or more subjects and predicates, the separate parts are called *clauses*. A *relative clause* is introduced by a relative pronoun.

In the following sentences the antecedent and relative are underlined. Give the number and gender of each:

1. *a.* **Puellam terruī; puella abest,** *I scared the girl; the girl is absent.*
   *b.* **Puella quam terruī abest,** *The girl whom I scared is absent.*

2. **Oppidum quod vīdit erat parvum,** *The town which he saw was small.*

3. **Lūdī ex quibus vēnimus erant magnī,** *The schools from which we came were large.*

4. **Virum cui librum dedī vīdistī,** *You saw the man to whom I gave the book.*

5. **Puer cuius librum habeō est amīcus noster,** *The boy whose book I have is our friend.*

*The Temple of Aesculapius, a kind of hospital, as it once was. Shaped like a boat, it was on an island in the Tiber River at Rome. A hospital still stands there.*

*Dancing girls in an ancient relief now in the Louvre, Paris.*

*Observe* that the relative pronoun agrees with its antecedent in gender and number, but that its case depends upon its use in its own clause.

*Note.* The relative may be omitted in English but never in Latin: *The man (whom) I saw,* **Vir** *quem* **vīdī.**

**Practice**   Give in Latin the proper form of the italicized English words:

1. That is not *what* I mean.
2. The boy *whom* I visited is my cousin.
3. I saw the horses *that* were on the road.
4. I know the town *in which* the president was born.
5. Have you seen the girl *to whom* I gave the books?
6. The man *by whom* we were robbed has been arrested.
7. The land *from which* our parents came is beautiful.
8. Have you ever seen the islands *to which* we sailed two years ago?
9. All the men *to whom* we spoke were greatly pleased by your action.
10. All the girls *whom* I have invited have accepted, but one girl *whose* mother is sick may not be able to come.

**Exercises A.** 1. Via quā vēnimus pulchra erat.
2. Vir cui pecūniam permīsī amīcus meus erat.
3. Cūr pecūniam puerō vīsō ā tē in Viā Quīntā nōn dedistī?
4. Librōs quī dē fāmā et fortūnā agunt puerī amant.
5. Cūr nōn fortūnam quam Nātūra vōbīs dedit sustinētis?
6. America ob iniūriās quās accēperat bellum suscipere nōn dubitāvit.

**B.** 1. I saw the boy whose book I lost.
2. The boy whom I saw in the woods is approaching.
3. He endured constant dangers on-account-of (his) enemies.

**Vocabulary**  cūr, interrog. adv., *why*
nātū′ra, –ae, f., *nature*  (natural)
pe′tō, pe′tere, petī′vī, petī′tus, *seek, ask*  (petition)
quī, quae, quod, *who, which, that*
susti′neō, sustinē′re, –ti′nuī, –ten′tus, *hold up, maintain,
  endure*  [*teneō*]

### Word Study: Intensive Prefixes

Most of the Latin prepositions which are used as prefixes in Latin and English may have intensive force, especially **con–, ex–, ob–, per–.** They are then best translated either by an English intensive, as *up* or *out*, or by an adverb, as *completely, thoroughly, deeply.* Thus **commoveō** means to *move greatly,* **permagnus,** *very great,* **obtineō,** to *hold on to,* **concitō,** to *rouse up,* **excipiō,** to *catch, receive;* **cōnservō,** to *save up, preserve;* **complicō,** to *fold up.*

Explain *component, confirmation, evident, elaborate.* What is meant by *conservation* of natural resources? What is a political *conservative*? What is a *contract*?

*Greek temple at Paestum in southern Italy; the American soldiers shown here landed at nearby Salerno in 1943.*

*The interior of the Colosseum as it now is. Formally opened in 80 A.D., it could hold about 50,000 spectators. Awnings over part of the top kept off the sun.*

# *Lesson xl*

## COLOSSĒUM

Lūdōs et pompās populus Rōmānus magnō studiō spectābat. In Italiā, in Āfricā, in Galliā cōnservantur theātra et amphitheātra Rōmānōrum, in quibus lūdī etiam nunc habentur. Nātūra virōrum varia est sed paucī lūdōs nōn amant. Cōnservāsne pictūrās Colossēī
5 Rōmānī quās invenīs?

Captīvī et servī in mediā arēnā pugnāre cōgēbantur. Populus Rōmānus studium lūdōrum numquam intermīsit. Multī captīvī cum magnō animō pugnābant et lībertātem [1] obtinēbant. Multī malī virī etiam prō vītā [2] pugnābant et poenam in arēnā sustinēbant.

10 Quondam duo gladiātōrēs [1] in arēnā Rōmānā pugnābant. Tum inter gladiātōrēs vēnit sine armīs vir bonus aequusque, quī petīvit: "Cūr pugnātis? Proelium intermittite, nam amīcī estis. Malum exemplum prōpōnitis." Gladiātōrēs verbīs nōn permōtī sunt sed virum bonum interfēcērunt. Servī virum ex arēnā trahere incipiēbant. Tum
15 populus īrā permōtus est, quod vir erat Tēlemachus, quī amīcus miserīs semper fuerat et magnam fāmam obtinuerat. Numquam posteā gladiātōrēs in Colossēō pugnāvērunt.

---

[1] Use the English derivative.        [2] See p. 192, note 5.

Scrīptum est:

"Quamdiū[3] stat Colisaeus,[4] stat et[5] Rōma. Quandō[6] cadet Colisaeus, cadet et Rōma. Quandō cadet Rōma, cadet et mundus."[7]  20

QUESTIONS    1. To what use are some ancient theaters put today?
2. What two classes of people fought in the amphitheaters?
3. How long will the world last?

READING    Showerman, pp. 349–351; Davis, pp. 401–406; Mills, pp. 313–316; Grose-Hodge, pp. 224–228.

## Second Conjugation: Principal Parts

The following are verbs already studied, but whose principal parts have not been given in full. Memorize their principal parts:

| | | | |
|---|---|---|---|
| habeō | habēre | habuī | habitus |
| teneō | tenēre | tenuī | tentus |
| contineō | continēre | continuī | contentus |
| augeō | augēre | auxī | auctus |
| maneō | manēre | mānsī | mānsūrus |
| iubeō | iubēre | iussī | iussus |
| moveō | movēre | mōvī | mōtus |
| videō | vidēre | vīdī | vīsus |

*Note.* No general rule can be given for forming the perfect and participial stems of verbs of the second conjugation. Like **habeō**, the most common type, are **dēbeō, mereō, terreō, valeō** (participle, **valitūrus**). **Retineō** is like **contineō**; **removeō**, like **moveō**.

---

[3] *as long as.*     [4] = **Colossēum.**     [5] *also.*     [6] *when.*     [7] *world.*

*The Colosseum as seen from the air. Most of the missing stone was used a few centuries ago to build palaces in Rome.*

*Victoria, the capital of British Columbia, Canada, has a parliament building in the Roman style.*

**Practice**    Give the first singular of **augeō** and the third plural of **videō** in all tenses of the active voice.

### Ablative of Manner

In English, the manner of an action is expressed by an adverb or by a phrase (i.e., a group of words) answering the question *How?* When a phrase is used, a preposition, such as *with*, introduces it.

In Latin, manner is similarly expressed:

1. **Cum studiō labōrat,** *He labors with eagerness (eagerly).*
2. (**Cum**) **magnō studiō labōrat,** *He labors with great eagerness (very eagerly).*

*Note* that when an adjective is used, **cum** may be omitted.

*Caution.* Be careful to distinguish this latest use of "with" from the "with" studied on page 121 under *Caution.* Distinguish the three different uses of "with" in the following sentences:

1. *I shall go **with him with the greatest pleasure.***
2. *We can work **with greater success with this equipment.***
3. ***With my car** I can cover the distance **with you with ease.***

**Exercises  A.** 1. Magnā cūrā silvās nostrās cōnservābimus.
2. Cibō et pecūniā miserōs līberē sustinuimus.
3. Multī puerī ob bellum studia intermīsērunt.
4. Magnā iniūriā tum populus miser regēbātur.
5. Amīcus noster nōn permōtus est sed firmō animō ad oppidum prōcessit.

6. Puer quī prīmum locum obtinuerat cum magnā cūrā studiōque labōrāverat.

**B.** 1. He has been deeply-moved by my words.
2. The teacher carefully taught the boys to save money.
3. The bad boy very carefully removed the teacher's books.

**Vocabulary**  cōnser'vō, –ā're, –ā'vī, –ā'tus, *save, preserve*  [*servō*]
intermit'tō, intermit'tere, –mī'sī, –mis'sus, *let go, stop,*
   *interrupt*  [*mittō*]
obti'neō, obtinē're, obti'nuī, obten'tus, *hold, obtain*  [*teneō*]
permo'veō, permovē're, –mō'vī, –mō'tus, *move (deeply)*
   [*moveō*]

### Interesting English Words

Many English words that seem quite dull and ordinary have very interesting stories locked up within them. The key to these stories is Latin. Use this key and do not lose it. Let us try it now.

The "efficient" person is the one who *accomplishes* (**efficiō**) something—remember this when you hear people talk about "efficiency." A "traction" company is engaged in *drawing* or *hauling* vehicles. What is a "tractor"? What sort of person is a "tractable" person? Politicians should remember that a public "office" is a *duty*. An "office" is also a place where one does his *duty* or *daily work*.

Find the stories in *petition, competition, promotion, demotion, condone, conservative*.

*Competition.*

The English form of **Colosseum** is *Coliseum*. It occurs thirteen times in the San Francisco telephone directory, three in that of New Orleans.

*Verus Romanus. Dentatus refuses the Samnites' bribe.*

# Lesson xli

### VĒRUS RŌMĀNUS

Audīvistīne dē Dentātō? "Quis fuit et quid fēcit?" rogās. Quod Dentātum nōn nōvistī aut memoriā nōn tenēs, tē monēbō.

Dentātus fuit clārus Rōmānus quī variīs modīs inimīca oppida castraque cēpit. Modus eius [1] vītae et ab amīcīs et ab inimīcīs pro-
5 bābātur ac laudābātur, nam Rōmānus bonus erat. Cum [2] officia pūblica intermittēbat, agricola erat atque in agrīs labōrābat.

Samnītēs,[3] quōs Dentātus cēdere coēgerat, magnam pecūniam ad clārum virum mīsērunt. "Pecūnia quam coēgimus est tua. Auxi-lium tuum atque amīcitiam petimus." Tum Dentātus permōtus eōs [4]
10 monuit: "Quod aurum mihi datis? Cōnservāte aurum vestrum. Nam vērus Rōmānus pecūniam obtinēre nōn cupit sed eōs [4] quī aurum habent superāre."

**QUESTIONS**
1. What did Dentatus do when he was not in public service?
2. What is the point of Dentatus' answer to the Samnites?

---

[1] *his.*  [2] *whenever.*  [3] *the Sam'nites.*  [4] *them.*

## Interrogatives

*Interrogative* pronouns and adjectives are used to ask questions.

1. **Pronoun.** In English, the interrogative pronoun *who* refers only to persons, *what* refers only to things.

In Latin, the interrogative pronoun corresponding to *who* and *what* is **quis, quid,** declined as follows:

|      | SINGULAR | | PLURAL | | |
|------|----------|---|--------|---|---|
|      | M., F. | N. | M. | F. | N. |
| Nom. | quis, *who?* | quid, *what?* | quī | quae | quae |
| Gen. | cuius, *whose?* | cuius, *of what?* | quōrum | quārum | quōrum |
| Dat. | cui, *to whom?* | cui, *to what?* | quibus | quibus | quibus |
| Acc. | quem, *whom?* | quid, *what?* | quōs | quās | quae |
| Abl. | quō, *by whom?* | quō, *by what?* | quibus | quibus | quibus |

*Note.* The plural is translated like the singular.

2. **Adjective.** In English, the interrogative pronoun *who* is not used as an adjective; we cannot say, *Who man?* But *what* may be used as an adjective, referring to either persons or things: *What man? What thing?*

In Latin, the interrogative adjective is **quī, quae, quod,** declined like the relative pronoun (p. 192). Compare the interrogative **quis** with the relative **quī** and note differences in the singular.

**Lapsūs Linguae** ("Slips of the Tongue"). Have you ever said, *Who did you see?* Why is *who* incorrect? Give the correct form and translate the sentence into Latin.

**Practice**  **A.** Decline *what comrade? what price?*

**B.** Decide whether the words in italics are pronouns or adjectives, then give the proper Latin form:
1. *Who* were those men?
2. *What* girls came?
3. *What* did he say?
4. *What* towns were destroyed?

*Drugstore run by Cupids in a wall painting at Pompeii. What, no sandwiches or sundaes?*

5. *Whose* book is that?
6. To *whom* shall I give this?
7. To *whom* shall I go?
8. By *whom* (sing.) was he seen?
9. *What* boys do you mean?

**Exercises A.** 1. Quis mē accūsat?
2. Quō modō sociī pecūniam coēgērunt?
3. Quī puer verbīs bonī virī nōn permōtus est?
4. Cui puerō, cui puellae, Nātūra nōn vītam grātam dedit?
5. Ā quō vōs puerī magnā cūrā dē perīculīs monitī erātis?
6. Quid amīcī tuī fēcērunt atque quod praemium accipient?
7. Quod cōnsilium, puellae, ā magistrō vestrō vōbīs datum est?

**B.** 1. Whom did you seek?
2. By what street did you girls come?
3. To whom shall we give the money?
4. In what manner did you obtain the money?

**Vocabulary** atque (ac), conj., *and*
cō'gō, –ere, coē'gī, coāc'tus, (*drive together*), *collect, compel* [*agō*]
mo'dus, –ī, *manner* (mode)
mo'neō, –ē're, mo'nuī, mo'nitus, *remind, warn* (monitor)
nam, conj., *for* (in the sense of "because," introducing a verb)
quis, quid, *who, what*

## English Word Studies

1. What is a *cogent* reason for doing something? What is an *intermission* in a play? Explain the meaning of *modal, model, admonition.*

2. Latin phrases in English:

inter nos, *between us.*
in absentia, *in absence.*
Pax vobiscum, *Peace (be) with you!*
in perpetuum, (*to perpetuity*), *forever.*
sine qua non, *a necessity* (lit., *without which* [*condition it is*] *not* [*possible*]).
cui bono? (lit., *to whom for a good?*) *for whose benefit is it? What good is it?*
Ilium fuit, *Ilium has been* (i.e., *no longer exists*), said of Troy (**Ilium**) after its destruction by the Greeks; now applied to anything that is past.

*In Gallia. Roman aqueduct at Maintenon, France.*

# *Lesson xlii*

**PŪBLIUS MĀRCŌ SAL.**[1]

A letter that might have been sent by a young Roman from Caesar's camp in Gaul in 55 B.C. to a friend in Rome.

Sī valēs, bene est; ego valeō. Magnō studiō litterās tuās lēgī quae cum cūrā scrīptae et plicātae erant.

Dē Galliā rogās ac dē nōbīs cognōscere cupis. Vīta nostra nōn dūra est. Multī captīvī in castrīs iam coāctī sunt. Caesar multās pugnās iam pugnāvit et multa oppida mūnīta cēpit. Mox erit dominus 5 Galliae, et Gallia in prōvinciam redigētur. Sed dominus aequus erit. Tum virōs nostrōs trāns Rhēnum ēdūcet et Germānōs terrēbit. Iam eōs[2] monuit. Modum quō bellum gerit probō. Sententia eius[3] est:

---

[1] For **salūtem dīcit:** *Publius pays his respects to Marcus,* the usual form of greeting in a letter.

[2] *them.*

[3] *his.*

**203**

"Veniō, videō, vincō." Magnus et ēgregius vir est. Fortasse trāns
10 aquam in Britanniam prōcēdēmus, quae est magna īnsula dē quā
nōn ante lēgī aut cognōvī.

Quid Quīntus noster agit? Quae nova officia suscēpit? Cūr nōn
ante scrīpsit? Litterās tuās cum studiō exspectābō. Valē.[4]

QUESTIONS   1. Did Publius have an easy time in Gaul?
                    2. Has Publius seen Germany yet? Britain?

READING     Showerman, pp. 498–499; Davis, pp. 207–209; Johnston, pp.
             315–317.

### Third Conjugation: Principal Parts

Memorize the principal parts of the following verbs already
studied. No rule can be given for the formation of the third and
fourth parts, but in the commonest type the perfect ends in –sī. The
participle always ends in –tus or –sus:

| | | | |
|---|---|---|---|
| 1.  cēdō | cēdere | cessī | cessūrus |
| (Similarly accēdō, discēdō, excēdō, prōcēdō) | | | |
| gerō | gerere | gessī | gestus |
| mittō | mittere | mīsī | missus |
| (Similarly āmittō, committō, dīmittō) | | | |
| dūcō | dūcere | dūxī | ductus |
| (Similarly prōdūcō, redūcō) | | | |
| regō | regere | rēxī | rēctus |
| trahō | trahere | trāxī | trāctus |
| dēfendō | dēfendere | dēfendī | dēfēnsus |
| agō | agere | ēgī | āctus |
| redigō | redigere | redēgī | redāctus |
| nōscō | nōscere | nōvī | nōtus |
| 2.  accipiō | accipere | accēpī | acceptus |
| incipiō | incipere | incēpī | inceptus |
| cupiō | cupere | cupīvī | cupītus |
| faciō | facere | fēcī | factus |
| afficiō | afficere | affēcī | affectus |
| efficiō | efficere | effēcī | effectus |
| fugiō | fugere | fūgī | fugitūrus |

---

[4] *farewell.*

**204**

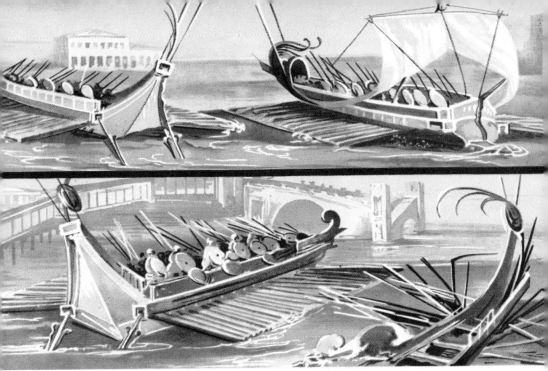

*Fortasse trans aquam in Britanniam procedemus.* This wall painting from Pompeii shows Roman warships in a battle. The soldiers are visible but the rowers are below deck. In the lower panel one of the ships has been overpowered and beached.

*Note.* The change or lengthening of the vowel of the perfect and participial stems may be compared with the change of vowel in English *sing, sang, sung; sit, sat,* etc.

**Practice**   Give the third singular of **mittō** and the first plural of **accipiō** in all tenses of the passive voice.

**Exercises**  **A.** 1. Quid sub aquā scrībit?
2. Captīvī ante portam positī erant.
3. Bella trāns Ōceanum cum victōriā gessimus.
4. Litterae ā tē scrīptae cum cūrā plicātae erant.
5. Litterās quās scrīpsī plicābō et ad amīcum meum mittam.
6. Bonus est dominus noster, quod populum cum concordiā regit.
7. Linguam Latīnam cum studiō legere incipimus; nova verba iam cognōvimus.

**B.** 1. The new words ought always to be learned.
2. I do not know the boy who lives across the street.
3. Marcus, who wrote the letter which you are reading?
4. The poor prisoners had been dragged across the fields.

**205**

**Vocabulary**    **an'te,** adv. and prep. with acc., *before* (of time or place)
        **cognōs'cō, cognōs'cere, cognō'vī, cog'nitus,** *learn*; perf.
          tense, "have learned" = *know*               **[*nōscō*]**
        **do'minus, –ī,** m., *master*              (dominate)
        **iam,** adv., *already*
        **le'gō, le'gere, lē'gī, lēc'tus,** *gather, choose, read*   (legible)
        **pli'cō, –ā're, –ā'vī, –ā'tus,** *fold*      (application)
        **scrī'bō, scrī'bere, scrīp'sī, scrīp'tus,** *write*    (Scripture)
        **trāns,** prep. with acc., *across*

## Latin and English Word Formation

**Ante–** has its regular meaning and form when used as a prefix.
**Trāns–** (or **trā–,** as in **trā-dūcō**) means *through* or *across*.

**Importance of the Verb.** The most important part of speech in
Latin for English derivation is the verb, and the most important part
of the verb is the *perfect participle*. This form is also the most important for Latin word formation. Therefore *learn carefully* the principal parts of every verb.

By associating Latin word and English derivative, you can make
the English help you in your Latin, and *vice versa*. You can often
tell the conjugation or the perfect participle of a Latin verb by the
help of an English derivative. The English word *mandate* shows
that **mandō** has **mandātus** as its perfect participle and is therefore
of the first conjugation. Similarly *migrate, donation, spectator,* etc.
The word *vision* helps one remember that the perfect participle of
**videō** is **vīsus.** Similarly *motion* from **mōtus,** *missive* from **missus,**
*active* from **āctus.** Give the derivatives from **lēctus, nōtus, ductus.**
Explain *election, deposit, complication, domineer.*

In compounds short **–a–** becomes short **–e–** before two consonants (cf. p. 103): **captus, acceptus.** Give two examples each
from compounds of **capiō** and **faciō.**

*Girl with a puppy. A bronze statuette
of the first century* A.D. *in the Metropolitan Museum of New York. The
little Roman girl is calling to someone.*

# ~~~ Glimpses of Roman Life

## ROMAN SCHOOLS

Even before going to school some Roman children learned the alphabet by playing with letters cut out of ivory, as ours do from their blocks. They started to school at about the same age as our children. The schools were quite different, however. They were very small private schools, usually run by slaves for small fees. Work began early in the morning. The children were taken to and from school by slaves called **paedagōgī,** a Greek word which means those who "lead (take) children." They did no teaching but merely kept their children in order. Our word *pedagogue* is derived from this word.

In the elementary school, called the **lūdus litterārum,** the three *R*'s formed the basis of the curriculum. For reading the Romans had to depend at first on the Twelve Tables of the law, the first set of laws that the Romans put in writing. In the third century B.C. a schoolteacher translated the *Odyssey* from Greek for the use of his pupils. Later other works of literature were used.

The pupils wrote on wax tablets, consisting of wooden boards covered with a thin layer of wax. They wrote by scratching the wax with a pointed stylus made of metal or bone. The other end of this was flat for erasing, or rather smoothing over the wax.

The Romans also wrote with pen and ink on papyrus, a kind of paper made out of thin strips of a reed which grew in Egypt. Most books were made by hand out of rolls of this material. But it was expensive, and school children used only the backs of old books and loose sheets for their "scratch paper." Parchment came to be used instead of wax-covered wood for tablets. Eventually a number of these were put together to form a book of our kind, and the papyrus roll went out of fashion.

Arithmetic was complicated by the fact that the Romans did not have the Arabic system of numerals, with its zero, that we use. Multiplication and division were impossible. The Romans had two helps in their arithmetic: an elaborate system of finger counting and the abacus, or counting board, similar to those used as toys by children today and those which you sometimes see in Chinese laundries.

*A wall painting from Pompeii showing Roman writing materials: wax tablets, inkwells, papyrus rolls, etc. In the upper right is a cylindrical box containing a number of papyrus rolls.*

More advanced education prepared boys for the one respected profession in ancient Rome, that of law and public life. Hence the secondary school, called the **schola grammaticī** (*school of the grammarian*), specialized in language, composition, rhetoric, and public speaking. But the course was also a broadly cultural one and included literature, both Greek and Latin. Most educated Romans learned to speak and write Greek fluently.

The college course in the **schola rhētoricī** (*school of the rhetorician*) was still more technical in preparation for a career in which public speaking, whether in a law court or a legislative body, played a very important role. For graduate work students could go to such university centers as Athens or Rhodes and listen to lectures by famous philosophers and professors of rhetoric.

Although the aim of the schools beyond the elementary stage was the narrow one of preparing citizens for public service, the practical Romans felt that a liberal training in literature and philosophy was the best system for their needs.

QUESTIONS   1. What educational advantages do you have that a Roman boy did not have?
2. Compare books and writing material then and now.
3. What sort of education should our government officials have?

READING   Showerman, pp. 194–202; Davis, pp. 191–204; Grose-Hodge, pp. 152–160; Johnston, pp. 85–95; Mills, pp. 323–330.

# Unit VII Review

## LESSONS XXXVII–XLII

### ENGLISH WORD STUDIES

1. Find and use in sentences as many English derivatives as possible from **vocō, videō, mittō,** and **faciō.** Remember the importance of the perfect participle.

2. The first word, printed in boldface type, in each of the following lines is a Latin word. From among the last five words in each line pick the one which is an English derivative of the first word.

| | | | | | |
|---|---|---|---|---|---|
| **dō** | dough | dote | do | dot | dative |
| **moneō** | month | remain | admonition | moan | remind |
| **cōgō** | cog | incognito | cognate | cogency | concoct |
| **petō** | pet | compete | petal | petite | impede |
| **legō** | leg | log | collect | lag | lick |

### VOCABULARY

NOUNS
.1. **dīligentia**
2. **dominus**
3. **lūdus**
4. **modus**
5. **nātūra**

ADJECTIVE
6. **pulcher**

PRONOUNS
7. **quī**
8. **quis**

VERBS
9. **cognōscō**
10. **cōgō**
11. **cōnservō**
12. **dō**
13. **intermittō**
14. **legō**
15. **moneō**
16. **obtineō**
17. **permoveō**
18. **petō**
19. **plicō**
20. **scrībō**
21. **submittō**
22. **sustineō**

ADVERBS
23. **cūr**
24. **iam**

PREPOSITIONS
25. **ante**
26. **inter**
27. **ob**
28. **trāns**

CONJUNCTIONS
29. **atque, ac**
30. **nam**

## VOCABULARY (English Meanings)

| NOUNS | | |
|---|---|---|
| 1. *diligence* | 2. *master* | 4. *manner* |
| | 3. *game, school* | 5. *nature* |

ADJECTIVE

6. *beautiful*

PRONOUNS

7. *who*    8. *who?*

| VERBS | | | |
|---|---|---|---|
| | 12. *give* | 16. *hold, obtain* | 20. *write* |
| 9. *learn* | 13. *stop* | 17. *move deeply* | 21. *furnish* |
| 10. *collect, compel* | 14. *gather, read* | 18. *seek* | 22. *maintain* |
| 11. *save* | 15. *remind, warn* | 19. *fold* | |

ADVERBS

23. *why*    24. *already*

PREPOSITIONS

| | 26. *between, among* | 28. *across* |
|---|---|---|
| 25. *before* | 27. *on account of* | |

CONJUNCTIONS

29. *and*    30. *for*

## UNIT PRACTICE AND EXERCISES

**Principal Parts**

1. Give the four principal parts of the following verbs: **committō, cēdō, dūcō, agō, faciō.**

2. Give in Latin the principal parts of the following verbs: *defend, flee, have, be, see, remain, increase, learn.*

**Form Drill**

1. Give in all tenses the second singular active of **moveō;** the third singular passive of **agō;** the third plural passive of **accipiō.**

2. Decline **quae nātūra, quod signum, quī dominus.**

3. Supply the missing words in the right form and translate:
   a. (*To whom*) librum dabō?
   b. (*What*) librōs lēgistī?
   c. (*Whom*) petis?
   d. (*Who*) litterās scrīpsit?
   e. (*By whom*) litterae scrīptae sunt?

**"With" Ablatives**

Review pages 43, 121, 198, and then decide whether the "with" phrase in each of the following sentences expresses *a.* means, *b.* manner, or *c.* accompaniment:

1. Say it *with flowers.*
2. My uncle farms *with a mule.*
3. I spent the evening *with friends.*
4. We shall talk over matters *with him.*
5. The soloist sang *with deep feeling.*
6. All supported the case *with enthusiasm* and *money.*

# *Advanced Reading*

*The giant Polyphemus (see p. 213) as depicted in the motion picture "Ulysses."*

COURTESY PARAMOUNT PICTURES

*Ulysses pokes fun at Polyphemus. A painting by J. M. W. Turner, the famous English artist (1751–1850).*

*The destruction of the ships of Ulysses as shown in an ancient wall painting found at Rome.*

# *Lesson xliii*

## ULIXĒS

Ulysses (or Odysseus) was a Greek who fought in the Trojan War.
His many wanderings before he returned home to Ithaca, an island west
of Greece, are described by the Greek poet Homer in the *Odyssey*.

Ulixēs, dux Graecus quī in bellō Troiānō pugnāverat, post pācem
ad Ithacam, in quā īnsulā habitāverat, properāvit. Sed multa mala
miser sustinuit nec salūtem invēnit. Cūrīs dūrīs pressus decem annōs
in multīs terrīs ēgit.

Post pācem ā Troiā cum multīs mīlitibus Ulixēs nāvigāverat. Ad 5
terram Lōtophagōrum [1] accessit. Paucī mīlitēs Graecī lōtum ēdē-
runt [2] et amāvērunt; et ducem et sociōs nōn memoriā tenuērunt.
Ulixēs mīlitēs ad nāvēs redūxit.

Tum ad Siciliam ventīs āctus est. In Siciliā habitāvērunt Cyclōpēs,[3] hominēs altī et dūrī quī singulōs oculōs [4] habuērunt. Neque 10
deōrum neque hominum lēgēs timuērunt. Ulixēs cum paucīs hominibus in hōc [5] locō frūmentum petīvit. Magna spēlunca [6] inventa est
quae multum frūmentum continuit. Tum vēnit Cyclōps [7] quī appellātus est Polyphēmus. Ovēs [8] in spēluncam ēgit. Polyphēmus Graecōs
vīdit et rogāvit: "Ā quō locō venītis? Quī hominēs estis? Quid 15
petitis?" Ulixēs respondit: "Nōs Graecī sumus. Ego Nēmō appellor.
Auxilium tuum petimus."

Polyphēmus duōs hominēs cēpit et ēdit; [10] tum somnum cēpit.
Reliquī Graecī sude [11] oculum Polyphēmī pressērunt, quī clāmāvit et
sociōs ēvocāvit. "Quid est?" rogant. "Quis tē vulnerāvit?" Poly- 20
phēmus respondet: "Nēmō mē vulnerāvit." Itaque reliquī Cyclōpēs
discessērunt. Polyphēmus Graecōs petīvit sed nōn invēnit quod sub
ovibus ligātī ex spēluncā excessērunt.[12] Līberātī ad nāvēs properā-
vērunt atque ibi salūtem invēnērunt.

---

[1] *Lotus-eaters.*
[2] *ate the lotus.*
[3] *Cȳclŏ'pēs.*
[4] *one eye apiece.*
[5] *this.*
[6] *cave.*
[7] *Cȳclŏps.*
[8] *sheep.*
[9] *No-man.*
[10] *ate.*
[11] *with a stake.*
[12] This trick still works. In 1940 two
German prisoners escaped from a
Canadian prison camp by clinging to
the under side of a garbage truck.

**213**

1. How long did it take Ulysses to reach home?
2. Why did not the other Cyclopes help Polyphemus?
3. What does the term "lotus-eater" mean when applied to anyone today?

READING   Hamilton, pp. 304, 105–109 (Mentor ed., pp. 211, 81–84); Sabin, pp. 307–312; Gayley, pp. 318–323; Bulfinch, pp, 241–244; Guerber, pp. 337–345; Colum, pp. 156–167.

## Third Declension: Masculine and Feminine Nouns

In nouns of the *third declension* the genitive singular ends in –is; the base is obtained by dropping this ending. All three genders occur in nouns of the third declension; no general rule for gender can be given. The gender, as well as the nominative and genitive singular, must therefore be learned from the vocabulary. Masculine and feminine nouns are declined alike, as follows:

|        | ENDINGS |       | EXAMPLES |          |       |          |
|--------|---------|-------|----------|----------|-------|----------|
|        | SING.   | PLUR. | SING.    | PLUR.    | SING. | PLUR.    |
| *Nom.* | — [13]  | –ēs   | mīles    | mīlitēs  | lēx   | lēgēs    |
| *Gen.* | –is     | –um   | mīlitis  | mīlitum  | lēgis | lēgum    |
| *Dat.* | –ī      | –ibus | mīlitī   | mīlitibus| lēgī  | lēgibus  |
| *Acc.* | –em     | –ēs   | mīlitem  | mīlitēs  | lēgem | lēgēs    |
| *Abl.* | –e      | –ibus | mīlite   | mīlitibus| lēge  | lēgibus  |

*Observe* that the dative and ablative plural are alike; this is true of all declensions. The nominative and accusative plural also are alike in the third declension.

Practice   1. Decline homō magnus, pāx aequa.
2. Tell the form of salūtem, ducum, modum, māteriā, mīlitibus, lēgī, nātūrae, ducem, mīlite.

Exercises A. 1. Sine pāce vīta dūra est.
2. Dux mīlitēs ad pugnam prōdūxit.
3. Ibi valet populus ubi lēgēs valent.
4. Salūs patriae in armīs mīlitum nostrōrum pōnitur.
5. Sine bellō pācem et ōtium et salūtem obtinēre cupimus.
6. Magna est glōria mīlitum quī bellō pressī nōn cessērunt.

---

[13] The ending of the nominative singular varies. When not omitted, it is usually –s; c or g of the base combines with –s to form –x.

**B.** 1. Which boys were absent?

2. "Safety first!" is a good motto on the roads.

3. The general ordered the soldiers to be called-together.

4. Many books sent by boys and girls were received by the soldiers.

**Vocabulary**
clā'mō, –ā're, –ā'vī, –ā'tus, *shout, cry out* (clamor)
dux, du'cis, m., *leader, general* [*dūcō*]
ho'mō, ho'minis, m., *man, human being* (homicide)
lēx, lē'gis, f., *law* (legal)
mī'les, mī'litis, m., *soldier* (military)
pāx, pā'cis, f., *peace* (pacifist)
pre'mō, –ere, pres'sī, pres'sus, *press, press hard* (pressure)
sa'lūs, salū'tis, f., *health, safety* (salutary)

## English Word Studies

1. Explain *illegal, impressive, depression, ducal, militant.* To *salute* a person is to wish him *health,* as we say *"good* morning," not *"bad* morning." To *pay* a person is to *pacify* him. What is a *pacifist?*

Four states have towns named *Ithaca,* best-known being that in New York. Four states have towns named *Ulysses.* Why do you think that iron and steel works in San Francisco, Oakland, and Pittsburgh have the name *Cyclops?*

2. Latin phrases in English:

**lex scripta,** *the written law.*
**pax in bello,** *peace in (the midst of) war.*
**novus homo,** *a new man* (in politics); hence, *an upstart.*
**Dux femina facti,** *A woman (was) leader in (of) the deed.*

*Ulysses enters the cave of Polyphemus. From the motion picture "Ulysses."*

*Chester, England, originally a Roman camp (see p. 218), has an ancient wall.*

# Lesson xliv

## COLŌNĪ

Dē colōnīs quī ē Britanniā ad Americam vēnērunt multa fortasse nōvistī. Patriam relīquērunt et terram novam petīvērunt. Multī antecessērunt, reliquī posteā ad terram petītam trānsportātī sunt. In locīs altīs stetērunt et terram novam grātē spectāvērunt. Etiam puerī
5 puellaeque Rōmānae dē "colōnīs" cognōvērunt.

Mīlitēs ā Rōmānīs in Britanniam trānsportātī sunt et bella ibi gessērunt. Vālla fēcērunt atque viās mūnīvērunt. Tum colōnōs trādūxērunt et colōnīs agrōs captōs et oppida occupāta dedērunt. Per colōnōs in Britanniam trāductōs lingua Latīna et lēgēs Rōmānae
10 Britanniae datae sunt. Semper mīlitēs antecēdunt, tum colōnī veniunt et in pāce salūteque vīvunt.

Rōmānī oppida in Britanniā mūnīvērunt—Londīnium, Eborācum, Lindum; nunc appellantur London, York, Lincoln. Multae ruīnae Rōmānae etiam nunc in Britanniā stant. Quis nōn cupit ad Britan-
15 niam nāvigāre et ibi ruīnās relīctās vidēre?

1. How did the Roman colonists get farms?

2. Are there any traces of Roman buildings in England?

## Fourth Conjugation: Principal Parts

Memorize the principal parts of the following verbs, which have occurred in previous lessons:

| | | | |
|---|---|---|---|
| audiō | audīre | audīvī | audītus |
| veniō | venīre | vēnī | ventūrus |
| conveniō | convenīre | convēnī | conventūrus |
| inveniō | invenīre | invēnī | inventus |

*Finnish stamp with Pax on it, issued at the end of the war with Russia.*

## Numerals: How Lucius Learned to Count

**Ūnus** [1] puer et ūnus puer sunt **duo** puerī; duo ducēs et ūnus dux sunt **trēs** ducēs; duo equī et duo equī sunt **quattuor** equī; trēs carrī et duo carrī sunt **quīnque** carrī; quattuor oppida et duo oppida sunt **sex** oppida; sex mīlitēs et ūnus mīles sunt **septem** mīlitēs; quīnque nautae et trēs nautae sunt **octō** nautae; septem hominēs et duo 5 hominēs sunt **novem** hominēs; sex puellae et quattuor puellae sunt **decem** puellae.

Summary: **ūnus, duo, trēs, quattuor, quīnque, sex, septem, octō, novem, decem.**

QUESTION Quot [2] hominēs sunt quīnque mīlitēs et trēs nautae?

Exercises **A.** 1. Ubi pecūnia quam āmīserās inventa est?

2. Ob quās causās hominēs agrōs relīquērunt?

3. Servī trāns agrōs equōs territōs trādūxērunt.

4. Multī mīlitēs in Eurōpam iam trānsportātī sunt.

5. Nūntium mīsimus ad Marium, quī sine auxiliīs antecesserat.

6. Cum cūrā carrum age; tua fortasse erit vīta quam cōnservābis.

---

[1] one.      [2] *how many.*      **217**

**B.** 1. We ought to work with eagerness.
2. How did you hear about your friend's health?
3. Marius ordered our soldiers to be led-across.
4. Why do you stand in the middle (of the) street?

**Vocabulary**    antecē'dō, –ere, –ces'sī, –cessū'rus, *go before*     [*cēdō*]
fortas'se, adv., *perhaps*
relin'quō, –ere, relī'quī, relīc'tus, *leave (behind), abandon*
                                (relinquish)
stō, stā're, ste'tī, stātū'rus, *stand*          (station)
trādū'cō, –ere, –dū'xī, –duc'tus, *lead across*     [*dūcō*]
trānsportō, –ā're, –ā'vī, –ā'tus, *transport*      [*portō*]

*Stamp of Transjordan (now called Jordan) when it was under British mandate. Roman ruins are shown.*

### The Latin Influence upon English

Latin words have been coming into English continuously from the beginning of our language down to the present moment. Julius Caesar twice invaded Britain, and a century later the Romans conquered the island. For the next four hundred years the Romans ruled Britain, and the language, at least in the towns, came to be Latin. When the Angles and Saxons invaded Britain in the fifth century and gave their name (*Angle-land, Eng-land*) and language to the island, they adopted a number of Latin words. Even before that they had come into contact with the Romans in northern Germany and borrowed some Latin words. So you might say that Latin affected English even before English existed as a separate language.

As the Romans in Britain found it necessary to build many military camps, which developed into towns, the word **castra** is to be found in a number of town names, many of which have been used in our country also. So *Chester* (Pa.), *Ro-chester* (N. Y., Minn.), *Man-chester* (N. H., Ia., N. C.), *Wor-cester* (Mass., pronounced Wŏoster and so spelled in Ohio), *Lan-caster* (Pa.). What other names with these endings can you give?

We have seen a similar evolution in the United States where frontier forts, erected originally as defenses against the Indians, became trading posts, out of which have grown cities such as Fort Dodge (Ia.), Fort Scott (Kan.), and Fort Worth (Tex.).

218

*Plinius et puer.*

# Lesson xlv

## PLĪNIUS ET PUER

Plīnius,[1] cuius facta bona vōbīs fortasse iam ante nōta fuērunt, multās litterās scrīpsit quās etiam nunc legere possumus. Quondam ad oppidum parvum in quō nātus[2] erat vēnit. Ibi inter multōs hominēs stābat et dē salūte familiārum rogābat. Tum amīcum nōtum cum fīliō cernit. Plīnius ā puerō petīvit: "Discipulusne es?" Puer 5 respondit: "Discipulus Mediōlānī[3] sum." Plīnius commōtus rogāvit: "Cūr nōn hīc[4]? Cūr patriam relīquistī?" Puer respondit: "Nōn possum, nam magistrōs nōn habēmus." Tum Plīnius amīcō dīxit:[5] "Verbīs fīlī tuī commōtus sum. Certē lūdum hīc habēre potestis atque dēbētis. Cognōsce cōnsilium meum. Ego nōn līberōs habeō sed 10 tertiam partem pecūniae quam dabitis parātus sum dare."

QUESTIONS   1. Where did Pliny see his friend?
   2. Why did the boy go to school in another town?
   3. What was Pliny's offer?

---

[1] *Pliny.*   [2] *born.*   [3] *at Milan.*   [4] *here.*   [5] From **dīcō.**

*Wall painting from Pompeii showing a girl with curls and a hairnet. What is she planning to write on the tablet with her stylus?*

### Participles Used as Adjectives and Nouns

Perfect participles of many verbs came to be used as simple adjectives, just as in English: **parātus**, "prepared," *ready*; **nōtus**, "known," *familiar*; **certus**, "decided," *sure*. A participle, like any adjective, may be used as a noun: **factum**, "having been done," *deed*.

### Conjugation of *Possum*

**Possum** is a compound of **sum** and is therefore irregular. It has no passive voice. Review the conjugation of **sum. Possum = pot(e) + sum. Pot–** becomes **pos–** before all forms of **sum** which begin with s–. The perfect tenses are regular.

---

PRESENT

| | |
|---|---|
| **possum,** *I can, am able* | **possumus,** *we can, are able* |
| **potes,** *you can, are able* | **potestis,** *you can, are able* |
| **potest,** *he can, is able* | **possunt,** *they can, are able* |
| Imperfect **poteram,** etc., *I could, was able* | Future **poterō,** etc., *I shall be able* |

(For full conjugation see p. 401.)

---

**Practice**
1. Give the form and the meaning of **potuerās, poterātis, potuērunt, possunt, poterit, posse**.
2. Translate *you could, they had been able, we shall be able, he can, they could*.

**Exercises** **A.** 1. Amīcus certus in malā fortūnā cernitur.
2. "Facta, nōn verba" sententia nostra esse dēbet.
3. Linguam Latīnam et legere et scrībere possum.
4. Perīcula vītae bonum hominem commovēre nōn poterunt.
5. Facta virōrum clārōrum semper nōta erunt et laudābuntur.
6. Ante bellum patria nostra nōn parāta erat, nam paucōs mīlitēs habēbāmus.

**B.** 1. Few men can neither read nor write.
2. My motto is: "Always ready." Is it yours?
3. We came across the fields, because the road was not familiar.
4. They had not been able to come on-account-of the bad streets.

*Stamp of Chile with Latin mottoes.*

**Vocabulary**

cer'nō, –ere, crē'vī, crē'tus,
(*separate*), *discern, see* (discretion)
cer'tus, –a, –um, *fixed, sure* [*cernō*]
commo'veō, –ē're, –mō'vī, –mō'tus, *disturb* [*moveō*]
fac'tum, –ī, n., *deed* [*faciō*]
nō'tus, –a, –um, *known, familiar* [*nōscō*]
parā'tus, –a, –um, *prepared, ready* [*parō*]
pos'sum, pos'se, po'tuī, ——, *can, be able* (with infinitive) [*sum*]
ter'tius, –a, –um, *third* (*tertiary*)

## English Word Studies

1. Explain *commotion, certificate, notorious, tertiary*.
2. Latin words and phrases in English:

**erratum** (plur. **errata**), *error*.
**terra incognita**, *an unknown land*.
**Te Deum**, *Thee, God* (*we praise*); the name of a hymn.
**Et tu, Brute**, *you too, Brutus* (said by Caesar on receiving the death-blow from his friend, Brutus).
**de facto**, *from* or *according to fact, actual*; as a **de facto** government, one which is actually in operation, even if not recognized as legal.
Translate **ante bellum**.

*The Arc de Triomphe in Paris is a triumphal arch in Roman style like many others throughout the world.*

# Lesson xlvi

### MARCUS PŪBLIŌ SAL.[1]

An answer to the letter on p. 203.

Adductus litterīs ā tē, Pūblī, in Galliā scrīptīs, respondēbō, nam multa nova sunt. Quid putās? Quīntus noster fīliam tertiam Rūfī in mātrimōnium dūxit! Ego nōn potuī hoc[2] prōvidēre; Quīntus mē nōn cōnsuluit. Tūne hoc prōvīdistī? Tenēsne memoriā puellam, 5 parvam ac timidam? Nōn iam timida est; nunc pulchra est, ā multīs amāta.

Dē Caesaris ducis ēgregiīs victōriīs scrīpsistī. Cum magnō studiō litterās tuās lēgī, nam Gallia semper fuit terra nova et nōn mihi nōta. Paucī nūntiī dē Galliā vēnērunt, quī fugam Gallōrum nūn-10 tiāvērunt. Caesar victōriīs suīs glōriam et fāmam armōrum Rōmā-nōrum auxit et pācem effēcit. Caesarī grātiam habēmus quod prō salūte nostrā pugnāvit. Gallōs in fugam datōs nōn iam timēbimus. Alpēs, quae inter nōs et Gallōs stant, nunc Rōmam ā perīculō dē-

---

[1] See p. 203.   [2] *this.*

fendunt, nam Gallī timidī trāns Alpēs mīlitēs nōn trānsportābunt.
Mīlitēs trāductōs removēre dūrum erit. 15

Sī Caesar mē cōnsulit, librum "Dē Bellō Gallicō" scrībere dēbet.
Sī liber ab eō[3] scrībētur, ā multīs hominibus legētur; etiam post
multōs annōs cum cūrā et dīligentiā legētur.

Litterae tuae nōn longae erant. Cūr longās litterās nōn scrībis?
Multa nova vīdistī atque vidēbis. Valē.[4] 20

QUESTIONS  1.  What girl was pretty?
           2.  Where did Caesar win victories?

**Participles Used as Clauses**

The participle, although not much used in English, is very common in Latin. It often is best translated by a subordinate clause,
introduced in English by *who*, etc., *when* or *after, since* or *because,
although,* and *if*; at other times, by a coördinate clause, i.e., one
connected with the preceding by *and*. The meaning of the Latin
sentence as a whole will always show the exact meaning of the
participle. Always translate the participle *literally* before trying to
expand it into a clause. Note the various translations in the following:

---

[3] *him.*                              [4] *farewell.*

*Looking through the Arch of Septimius Severus, built in 203* A.D., *to the Arch of
Titus, built in 81* A.D.

*A pagan Roman tomb below the Church of St. Peter's at Rome. Modern Rome rests on ancient Rome, literally and figuratively. This may be seen everywhere in Rome but nowhere more strikingly than in this famous church. The discovery of these ruins a few years ago created a sensation.*

| | | |
|---|---|---|
| *Relative* | 1. | **Oppida** *capta* **vīdī,** *I saw the towns* **which had been captured** (literally, *the captured towns*). |
| *Temporal* (time) | 2. | **Convocātī** *ad* **proelium** dūcentur, *After they have been* **called together,** *they will be led to battle* (literally, *having been called together*). |
| *Causal* | 3. | **Territī** nōn prōcessērunt, *Because they were scared, they did not advance* (literally, *having been scared*). |
| *Coördinate* | 4. | **Librum** *lēctum* **tibi dabō,** *I shall read the book and give it to you* (literally, *the book read*). |

*Observe* that (a) the *perfect* participle denotes time *before* that of the leading verb; (b) it agrees like an adjective with a noun or pronoun (sometimes not expressed) in gender, number, and case.

**224**

**Exercises**  **A.** 1. Perīculum prōvīsum nōs nōn terruit.
2. Rōmānī multa oppida occupāta relīquērunt.
3. Monitī vōs dē perīculō cōnsulere nōn poterāmus.
4. Pecūnia, ā mē in viā āmissa, ab amīcō meō inventa est.
5. Malus puer, ab amīcīs monitus, verbīs addūcī nōn iam potest.

**B.** Substitute a participle for the words within parentheses:
1. Quattuor librōs (*after reading them*) accēpī.
2. Liber bonus (*if read*) semper amīcus vērus erit.
3. Numerus librōrum (*which I consulted*) magnus fuit.
4. Multōs librōs lēgī (*because I had been influenced*) ā magistrīs meīs.

**C.** 1. I have read the letter written by my son.
2. I saw the girl who had been scared by you. (*Express in two ways.*)
3. The boys read the book because they had been influenced by the teacher's words.

**Vocabulary**  addū′cō, –ere, addū′xī, adduc′tus, *lead to, influence* [*dūcō*]
cōn′sulō, –ere, –su′luī, –sul′tus, *consult*  (consultation)
fu′ga, –ae, f., *flight;* in fu′gam dō, *put to flight*  [*fugiō*]
nōn iam, adv., *no longer*
prōvi′deō, –ē′re, –vī′dī, –vī′sus, *foresee*  [*videō*]
ti′midus, –a, –um, *timid*  (timidity)

### The Latin Influence upon English (*Cont.*)

In a preceding lesson (p. 218) we saw that a number of Latin words came into English as result of the Roman occupation of Britain. Other examples are *wall* (from **vāllum**), together with place names like *Walton* (*Walltown*); *port* (from **portus**, harbor), together with place names like *Portsmouth*; *street* (from **strāta**); *Lincoln* (from **colōnia**, colony); cf. *Cologne*, the name of a German city which was an ancient Roman colony.

A century and a half after the Angles and Saxons settled in England, Pope Gregory sent missionaries to convert the island to Christianity. As the missionaries spoke Latin, they introduced a number of new Latin words into English, especially words dealing with the Church, as *temple* (**templum**), *disciple* (**discipulus**), *bishop* (**episcopus**).

Explain *cologne, Stratford, antecedent, relic, providence.*

*A Roman relief sculpture showing a circus race.*

# Lesson xlvii

### The Story of Lucius (*Cont.*)

### CIRCUS

Dē "lūdō" in quō magister docēbat lēgistis. Sed erat etiam "lūdus"[1] in quō ōtium agēbātur; nam puerī Rōmānī nōn semper labōrābant sed etiam lūdēbant. Dictum est: "Puerī puerī erunt."

#### "THE PARADE'S COMING"

Fēriae[2] erant. Lūcius, amīcus noster parvus, ad lūdōs pūblicōs 5 in Circō factōs ā servō adductus est. Multī hominēs ad Circum conveniēbant; nam populus lūdōs amābat. Nōn paucī ante lūcem[3] vēnerant. Lūcius et servus loca commoda beneficiō amīcī invēnērunt et exspectāvērunt. Sed quid audiunt? Servus clāmat: "Pompa venit! Pompa venit!" Pompa per Forum et Sacram Viam ad Circum prōcesserat et nunc per portam in Circum prōcēdēbat. In pompā 10 fuērunt deōrum fōrmae, virī, puerī, equī, quadrīgae,[4] aurīgae.[5]

---

[1] See Vocabulary.
[2] *holidays.*
[3] From lūx.

[4] Quattuor equī quī carrum trahunt "quadrīgae" appellantur.
[5] "Aurīgae" sunt virī quī quadrīgās agunt.

## THE CHARIOT RACE: "THEY'RE OFF!"

Pompa per Circum ēducta est; Lūcius cum studiō exspectāvit. Tum sex quadrīgae, ad portam redāctae, signum exspectāvērunt. Signum datum est et equī ā portā missī sunt.

Inter aurīgās fuit Pūblius, quī magnam fāmam ob multās vic- 15 tōriās habuit. Erat amīcus familiae Lūcī nostrī, et Lūcius multa dē Circō ā Pūbliō cognōverat. Nunc Lūcius cum reliquīs Pūblium magnō studiō spectābat.

### PUBLIUS HANDICAPPED AT THE START

Sed Pūblius habuit ūnum equum quī erat novus et timidus et tardus; reliquae quadrīgae antecessērunt. Lūcius magnā cūrā 20 affectus, fortūnam malam amīcī nōn prōvīderat. Sed victōria nōn āmissa erat; nam septem spatia erant.

### TWO CHARIOTS OUT OF THE RACE

In mediō Circō erat longa spīna.[6] Terminī spīnae "mētae" appel- lātī sunt. Magnum erat perīculum aurīgārum ad mētās. Itaque in prīmō spatiō nec prīmus nec secundus aurīga quadrīgās ā mētīs 25 regere potuit. Ēiectī[7] per[8] terram equīs trāctī sunt atque iniūriās accēpērunt. Servī virōs ad spīnam portāvērunt et auxilium dedērunt.

### PUBLIUS STILL LAST

Nunc erant quattuor quadrīgae. Sex spatia restābant, sed Pūblius antecēdere nōn poterat. Quīnque, quattuor spatia restābant. Pūblius ultimus erat. Duo spatia restābant; populus clāmābat et cōnsilium 30 multum Pūbliō dabat sed nōn audiēbātur. Pūblius magnā cūrā equōs regēbat et etiam retinēbat, sed populus nōn cognōverat. Ūnum spatium restābat; Lūcius commōtus lacrimās retinēre nōn potuit. Fortūna inimīca erat.

### "AND THE LAST SHALL BE FIRST!"

Sed quid vidēmus? Pūblius antecēdit! Nōn iam equōs retinet sed 35 incitat. Ūnus equus, "Parātus" appellātus (nam semper parātus erat), integer fuit et properāre incipit. Nōn iam Pūblius erat ultimus; iam tertium, iam secundum locum tenet. Ūnus aurīga ante Pūblium restat. Aequī sunt—deī sunt bonī!— prīmus ad mētam ultimam Pūblius venit et victōriae praemia quae meruit accipit! Et Lūcius—quid 40 faciēbat? Clāmābat: "Iō! Iō! Pūblius! Parātus! Clāra victōria!"

---

[6] *wall.*     [7] *thrown out.*     [8] *over.*

**227**

Nōnne grāta erat vīta puerōrum Rōmānōrum? Sed etiam nunc in circō quadrīgās vidēre potestis; nam circum pompamque ā Rōmānīs accēpimus.

QUESTIONS   1. What was the route of the parade?
                2. How many laps were there in the race?
                3. How many chariots?

Vocabulary  pom'pa, –ae, f., *parade*                (pomp)
            spa'tium, spa'tī, n., *space, time; lap*   (spacious)
            ul'timus, –a, –um, *farthest*        (ultimate)

### English Word Studies

Explain the title of Elgar's march *"Pomp and Circumstance."* What derivative of **circus** shows how **circus** got its meaning? Explain by etymology: *declamation, claim, reclamation, expatiate, ultimatum, delude.*

**Ultima Thūlē** was a phrase the Romans used for the "Farthest North." This explains why the American airbase on Greenland was named Thule. Columbus was inspired by a prophecy of the Roman poet Seneca that new worlds (**novōs orbēs**) would be discovered and Thule would no longer be **Ultima Thūlē.**

*An artist's reconstruction of the Circus Maximus at Rome, in the valley between the Aventine and the Palatine (left). Note the emperor's box.*

*Ulysses finds that his men have been turned into pigs by Circe. From the motion picture "Ulysses."*

# Lesson xlviii

## CIRCĒ

Siciliā relīctā, Ulixēs ad rēgnum Aeolī, rēgis ventōrum, nāvigāvit, quī Ulixī ventōs malōs in saccō ligātōs dedit et dīxit: "Malīs ventīs ligātīs, nōn iam impediēris et in patriā tuā salūtem inveniēs."

Itaque multōs diēs [1] Graecī sine impedīmentō et sine cūrā nāvigāvērunt, ūnō amīcō ventō āctī, reliquīs ligātīs. Iam Ithacam clārē 5 cernunt. Sed nautae dē saccō cūrā affectī sunt quod dē ventīs quī in saccō erant nihil audīverant. "Praemia et pecūnia in saccō sunt," nauta dīxit. "Rēx Ulixēs nautīs quī mala sustinuērunt pecūniam dare dēbet." Itaque, saccō apertō,[2] ventī expedītī Graecōs ad rēgnum Aeolī redēgērunt. Sed nōn iam Aeolus auxilium dat. Ūnam nāvem 10 Graecī nunc habent, reliquīs āmissīs.

Nunc, impedīmentīs relīctīs, ad īnsulam veniunt quam Circē pulchra regēbat. Vīgintī hominēs, ab Ulixe ad rēgīnam missī, pācem praesidiumque lēgum petīvērunt. Ab Eurylochō [3] duce per silvam

---

[1] Accusative plural.
[2] Participle of **aperiō,** *open.*
[3] *Eurylochus* (Ūrĭl'okus).

**229**

5 ad rēgīnam pedibus ductī sunt, quae eōs[4] in animālia[5] vertit.
Eurylochus sōlus in animal nōn versus ad nāvem fūgit et Ulixī
omnia[6] dē sociīs impedītīs nūntiāvit. Ulixēs commōtus cum reliquīs
auxilium sociīs pressīs dare mātūrāvit. In viā Mercurium deum vīsum
cōnsuluit. Mercurius eum[7] monuit et herbam eī[8] dedit. "Hāc[9] herbā,"
20 inquit, "vītam tuam servāre et mīlitēs tuōs expedīre poteris." Ulixēs
rēgīnam iussit sociōs in hominēs vertere. Circē Ulixis verbīs et factīs
territa animālia in hominēs vertit. Rēgīna, quae nōn iam inimīca fuit,
magnam ac bonam cēnam parāvit. Sociīs expedītīs, annum ibi Ulixēs
mānsit et vītam grātam ēgit. Tum ā sociīs adductus discessit.

QUESTIONS: 1. What caused the storm that prevented Ulysses from
reaching Ithaca?
2. How did Ulysses find out what Circe had done to his
men?
3. By what means did he rescue them?

READING Hamilton, pp. 305–306 (Mentor ed., pp. 211–212); Sabin,
pp. 313–315; Gayley, pp. 324–327; Guerber, pp. 347–349;
Colum, pp. 169–173; Bulfinch, pp. 245–247; Norton and
Rushton, pp. 255–258.

## Ablative Absolute

In English, we sometimes say, *Such being the case, there is
nothing I can do.* Because such phrases as "Such being the case" are
used loosely and have no direct connection with either the subject or
the predicate of the sentence, they are said to be in the *nominative
absolute*, i.e., they are *absolutely free* in a grammatical sense from
the rest of the sentence. The phrase quoted above is equivalent to
an adverbial clause: *Since such is the case.*

In Latin, this loose construction is very common, with this difference: the *ablative* is used instead of the nominative. This independent use of the participial phrase is therefore known as the *ablative
absolute*. The perfect participle is most frequently used in this
construction.[10]

In English, there is an active and a passive past participle: *having
sent* (act.), *sent* or *having been sent* (pass.). *In Latin, there is only
a passive perfect participle*. In Latin, therefore, the ablative abso-

---

[4] *them.*
[5] Accusative plural: *animals.*
[6] *everything.*
[7] *him.*

[8] *to him.*
[9] *with this.*
[10] Occasionally a noun, adjective, or
present participle is used.

230

*A Roman ship shown in a mosaic floor at Ostia, the seaport of Rome. The two oars were for steering. Ostia was a busy port, especially on account of the importation of wheat from northern Africa.*

lute with the passive participle is often used where the active participle is used in English. That is one reason why the ablative absolute is more common in Latin than the nominative absolute is in English.

Interpret the participle *literally* before attempting to expand it into a clause beginning with *when, since, after, because, if, although* (see p. 223) or an active participle.

1. *Servō accūsātō* (lit., *the slave having been accused*), **dominus discessit**, *After accusing the slave, the master departed.*

2. *Litterīs nōn missīs* (lit., *the letter not having been sent*), **puer pecūniam nōn accēpit**, *Because he did not send the letter, the boy did not receive the money.*

3. *Oppidīs nostrīs captīs* (lit., *our towns captured*), **bellum gerēmus**, *If our towns are captured, we shall wage war.*

4. *Signō datō* (lit., *the signal having been given*), **dux prōcessit**, *Having given the signal, the general advanced.*

If you *read* Latin, i.e., if you get the meaning directly from the Latin without translating, you may omit the second step of expanding into a clause. In any case you will have to understand whether the ablative absolute expresses time, cause, etc.

**231**

*Caution.* The ablative absolute cannot be used when the noun or pronoun with which the participle agrees forms any part of the main sentence (subject or predicate). Compare the following sentence with those above and note that the ablative absolute construction cannot be used because the participle in this case must agree with the subject:

**Servus accūsātus territus est,** *The slave, having been accused, was terrified.*

**Exercises** **A.** In translating the following sentences, be careful to distinguish the ablative absolute from other uses of the participle.
1. Librō āmissō, puella legere nōn potuit.
2. Dux servōrum, signō datō, equōs ēdūcī iussit.
3. Expedītī ex perīculō Deō grātiam habēre dēbēmus.
4. Rōmānī, castrīs mūnītīs, Gallōs in fugam vertērunt.
5. Librīs lēctīs, puerī magistrum aequō animō exspectāvērunt.
6. Captīvī miserī, tractī ad pedēs rēgis, pācem timidē petēbant.
7. Impedīmentīs in oppidō relīctīs, mīlitēs salūtem petīverant.
8. Hominēs, praedā armīsque impedītī, properāre nōn poterant.

**B.** Translate the words in italics by participles:
1. This boy, *sent* to visit his aunt, lost his way.
2. The boy *having been freed,* everyone was happy.
3. *Having read* the books, we returned them to the library.
4. *After putting* the prisoner in jail, the policeman went home.
5. *After* the money *was given,* the boy was returned to his parents.
6. The boys *having been warned* to stop fighting, the principal went back to his office.

**C.** 1. Having written good letters, the boys will receive rewards.
2. Hindered by bad roads, we have not been able to come on foot.
3. The advice of the teacher having been heard, we shall read the book.
4. After sending a messenger, the king shouted: "My kingdom for (**prō**) a horse!"

**Vocabulary**  li′gō, –ā′re, –ā′vī, –ā′tus, *bind*  (ligament)

pēs, pe′dis, m., *foot*  (pedal)

 expe′diō, –ī′re, expedī′vī, expedī′tus, (lit., *make the foot free*), *set free*

 impedīmen′tum, –ī, n., *hindrance*; plur, *baggage*

 impe′diō, –ī′re, impedī′vī, impedī′tus, (lit., *entangle the feet*), *hinder*

rēx, rē′gis, m., *king*  (regal)

 rēg′num, –ī, n., *royal power, kingdom*

ver′tō, –ere, ver′tī, ver′sus, *turn*  (version)

*Impediment of speech.*

### Latin and English Word Studies

Latin words should not always be studied individually but can often be grouped together by *families,* so to speak. This is much easier, much more useful, and much more interesting. For example, there is the word **pēs,** the father of its family. From it are derived many other words in Latin and in English. **Im-pediō** means to *entangle the feet.* An "impediment" is a *tangle,* something in the way. Transportation is still a big problem with an army; it is no wonder that the Romans, without railroads or motor trucks, called the baggage train of the army **impedīmenta. Ex-pediō** means to get the *foot out* of the tangle; therefore in English an "expedient" is a means of solving a difficulty. To "expedite" matters is to hurry them along by removing obstacles.

You have already become acquainted with several other "families" of words (p. 138). Other words which should be studied in groups are **regō, rēgnum,** and **rēx; dō** and **dōnō; dūcō** and **dux; ager** and **agricola; cōnsulō** and **cōnsilium.** Show how the members of these families are related.

What is the meaning of *ligature, ligament, obligation, pedestrian?* Why was *Aeolus* chosen as the name of a company dealing in ventilators? What do you really mean when you say "I am much *obliged*"?

# ᚙᚙᚙ Glimpses of Roman Life

## AMUSEMENTS AND SPORTS

Roman children had as good times as our children have in playing games. Even the babies had their rattles. Girls had their dolls (p. 235); boys played various kinds of marble games with nuts (p. 22). The phrase **relinquere nucēs** (*to give up nuts*) meant to grow up, but "grown-ups," even the Emperor Augustus, sometimes played such games. Vacation was the time for marble games. The poet Martial says: "Sadly the boy leaves his marbles and is called back to school by the teacher—the Saturnalia [Christmas] vacation is all over."

Other amusements were spinning tops, walking on stilts (p. 57), flying kites, rolling hoops (p. 182), playing with toy wagons (p. 277) and toy soldiers (p. 118), etc. Among their games were blind-man's buff, hide and seek, leapfrog, jacks (p. 15). Ball games, some like our tennis and handball, were favorites, especially for men who played at the large public baths.

For indoor amusement the Romans had a board game which was something like chess or checkers, and another like the many games we have in which as many moves are made on a board as are shown by the throwing of dice (p. 57).

Roman boys and men had their sports—not only swimming, fishing (p. 128), hunting (p. 61), etc., but also athletic contests: running, jumping, throwing the discus, boxing, wrestling, fencing.

The chief amusements for the people as a whole were the circus, the gladiatorial shows, and the theater. The oldest and most popular was the circus with its races, fully described in the "Story of Lucius" (see pictures, pp. 226, 228). The races were the main thing; gradually various side shows and acrobatic exhibitions were added to fill in the time between races. The modern circus is a revival of the ancient, but the chariot races no longer have the same prominence. Even the circus parade which precedes the performance today is bor-rowed from the Romans, who called it a **pompa.**

The circus games were held at public expense on holidays. They took place in the valley between the Palatine and Aventine hills. Originally the people sat on the hillsides; later magnificent stands seating 200,000 people were built. Other circuses were built in Rome and elsewhere, but the original Circus Maximus remained the chief one.

For the interest these games created we may compare our baseball and football games. There were various racing clubs, distinguished by their colors, like our schools and colleges; we are reminded also of the "Red Sox" and "White Sox" of baseball. Drivers were popular heroes and often became rich. Their records and those of the horses were carefully kept. One man is said to have won 3559 races. This recalls the attention given to the number of home runs made by famous baseball players.

The theater was another important place for amusement. In imitation of Greek custom, Roman theaters were semicircular and open to the sky. The actors usually wore masks which indicated what kind of part the actor was playing. Women's parts were played by men. Both comedies and tragedies were given. The most famous writers of comedies were Plautus and Terence, whose plays are still in existence.

The gladiatorial contests were rather late importations from Etruria, the region to the north of Rome. At first they consisted of

*Two rag dolls and a jointed terra cotta doll in the Toronto Museum.*

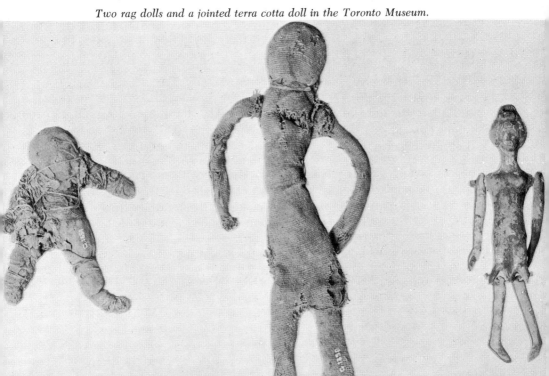

*The baths of Caracalla, Rome, as they once looked. See page 321.*

sword fights between two men—fencing matches with swords instead of foils. Curiously enough, these fights took place at funerals. Later on they became very popular. Fights between men and animals (like the Spanish bullfights) were added, as well as fights between animals. Sometimes very elaborate shows were put on. They were held in open-air amphitheaters. Many Roman towns all over the world had their theaters and amphitheaters. The famous Colosseum at Rome (pp. 196, 197), which had room for 50,000 people, was not built until 80 A.D.

QUESTIONS: 1. What modern sports compare with the circus games of the Romans in popular appeal?
2. In what ways did the Roman theater differ from ours?
3. What were the good and the bad features of the gladiatorial contests?
4. What modern sports have similar features?

READING    Showerman, pp. 308–351; Davis, pp. 374–406; Johnston, chap. IX; Grose-Hodge, pp. 220–228.

# Unit VIII Review

## LESSONS XLIII–XLVIII

### ENGLISH WORD STUDIES

1. Make a sketch map of England (not including Scotland) and indicate on it all the names you can of towns derived from Latin **castra**. Then see how many of these town names are found in the United States and in how many states.

2. The first word in each of the following lines is a Latin word. From among the last five words in each line pick the one which is an English derivative of the first word.

| | | | | | |
|---|---|---|---|---|---|
| **stāre** | status | stair | stare | star | stay |
| **hominī** | homely | home | hominy | homicide | hum |
| **mīles** | mile | militant | mill | millinery | million |
| **premō** | supreme | premises | premonition | express | prime |
| **clāmō** | clam | clamp | clammy | inclement | exclaim |
| **pāx** | pace | packs | Pacific | impact | pass |

### VOCABULARY

NOUNS
1. dux
2. factum
3. fuga
4. homō
5. impedīmentum
6. lēx
7. mīles
8. pāx
9. pēs
10. pompa
11. rēgnum
12. rēx
13. salūs
14. spatium

ADJECTIVES
15. certus
16. nōtus
17. parātus
18. tertius
19. timidus
20. ultimus

VERBS
21. addūcō
22. antecēdō
23. cernō
24. clāmō
25. commoveō
26. cōnsulō
27. expediō
28. impediō
29. ligō
30. possum
31. premō
32. prōvideō
33. relinquō
34. stō
35. trādūcō
36. trānsportō
37. vertō

ADVERBS
38. fortasse
39. nōn iam

Roman theater at Leptis Magna, northern Africa.

## VOCABULARY (English Meanings)

| NOUNS | | | |
|---|---|---|---|
| | 4. *man* | 8. *peace* | 12. *king* |
| 1. *leader* | 5. *hindrance* | 9. *foot* | 13. *health, safety* |
| 2. *deed* | 6. *law* | 10. *parade* | 14. *space* |
| 3. *flight* | 7. *soldier* | 11. *kingdom* | |

| ADJECTIVES | | | |
|---|---|---|---|
| | 16. *known* | 18. *third* | 20. *farthest* |
| 15. *sure* | 17. *prepared* | 19. *timid* | |

| VERBS | | | |
|---|---|---|---|
| | 25. *disturb* | 30. *can* | 35. *lead across* |
| 21. *influence* | 26. *consult* | 31. *press* | 36. *transport* |
| 22. *go before* | 27. *set free* | 32. *foresee* | 37. *turn* |
| 23. *discern* | 28. *hinder* | 33. *leave behind* | |
| 24. *cry out* | 29. *bind* | 34. *stand* | |

| ADVERBS | | |
|---|---|---|
| | 38. *perhaps* | 39. *no longer* |

## GRAMMAR SUMMARY

### Absolute construction

| *In Latin* | *In English* |
|---|---|
| 1. Ablative. | 1. Nominative. |
| 2. Perfect passive participle usually. | 2. Present or past active or passive participle. |
| 3. Construction very common. | 3. Construction much less common. |

## UNIT PRACTICE AND EXERCISES

### Participle Drill

**A.** Substitute a Latin participle in the right gender, number, and case for the words in italics:

1. Puerī (*although they were called*) nōn vēnērunt.
2. Fīliōs virī (*who has been accused*) nōvimus.
3. Perīcula (*if foreseen*) mē nōn terrent.
4. Librum (*after I had read it*) amīcō dōnāvī.
5. Puellae (*because they had been scared*) fūgērunt.

**B.** Translate the ablative absolute in each of the following sentences into good English:

1. **Agrīs vāstātīs,** the people were starving.
2. **Litterīs scrīptīs,** I took a walk.
3. **Auxiliō missō,** they can still win.
4. **Rēgnō āmissō,** he was still king.

*Roman theater at Sabratha, Libya, in nothern Africa, showing the stage with fronts of buildings which served as background, as all the action took place outdoors. One of the finest Roman theaters in existence.*

**Form Drill**

1. Decline rēx magnus, lēx bona.
2. What is the case of **ducum, hominī, mīlitibus, disciplīnae, pācem?**
3. Give in all tenses the third plural of **possum,** translating each tense form.

**Numerals Drill**

1. The teacher assigns a number—"Ūnus," "Duo," "Trēs," etc., to each of ten pupils. The following questions and others like them should be answered by the pupil whose number furnishes the correct answer.

   MAGISTER: Quot (*how many*) sunt trēs et quattuor?
   DISCIPULUS "SEPTEM": Trēs et quattuor sunt septem.
   M.: Quot sunt quattuor et quīnque?
   D. "NOVEM": Quattuor et quīnque sunt novem.
   (A competitive game can be made by having two sets of ten or less and scoring one for the side whose representative answers first.)

2. Give the Latin word for the missing numeral represented by the question mark:

   *a.* III + V = ?   *c.* IV + ? = X   *e.* X − ? = VIII
   *b.* XII ÷ III = ?   *d.* II × V = ?   *f.* VI − I = ?

 UNIT IX

# Myth and History

*This wall painting from Boscoreale, near Pompeii, shows a house front and other details.*

*The ship of the Phaeacians that brought Ulysses home was turned into a rocky island—and here it is, so they say, near the island of Corfu in the Adriatic.*

*Ulysses has himself tied to the mast while he listens to the Sirens. From the motion picture "Ulysses."*

## SĪRĒNĒS ET PHAEĀCIA

Annō in īnsulā quam Circē rēxit āctō, Ulixēs ad Sīrēnēs[1] vēnit. Sīrēnēs corpora avium[2] et capita puellārum habuērunt. Carmina pulchra canēbant, quibus nautae mōtī nāvēs ad saxa vertēbant. Hōc[3] modō vītam āmittēbant.

Sed Ulixēs dē Sīrēnibus ā Circē[4] monitus erat. Perīculō prōvīsō, 5 aurēs[5] sociōrum cērā clausit, sed nōn suās. Iussit manūs[6] pedēsque suōs ad nāvem ligārī. Hōc modō carmina Sīrēnum clārē audīvit neque vītam āmīsit.

Posteā sociī Ulixis interfectī sunt et Ulixēs sōlus ad īnsulam parvam āctus est in quā habitābat rēgīna pulchra cui[7] nōmen erat 10 Calypsō. Rēgīna Ulixem nōn dīmīsit. Itaque Ulixēs ibi octō annōs— longum temporis spatium—remānsit. Sed tum Iuppiter rēgīnam iussit Ulixī nāvem parāre. Hōc factō, Ulixēs expedītus rēgīnam relīquit.

Sed nāvis undīs frācta est ad īnsulam cui[7] nōmen erat Phaeācia.[8] Vulneribus impedītus homō miser vix potuit corpus in silvam fīniti- 15 mam ad flūmen trahere, ubi somnum cēpit.

Interim Nausicaa,[9] rēgis Phaeāciae fīlia, cum aliīs puellīs carrō ad flūmen prōcēdēbat, quod in flūmine vestēs lavāre cupīvit; nam tempus mātrimōnī Nausicaae aderat. Ubi vestēs in flūmine lāvērunt, labōre intermissō, Nausicaa pilam[10] ad reliquās puellās in ōrdine 20 iaciēbat. Sed puella quaedam[11] pilam in flūmen iēcit. Clāmōribus puellārum ab Ulixe audītīs, Ulixēs pilam ex flūmine servāvit. Puellae timidae fugere incipiunt, quod Ulixēs ob mala atque vulnera quae sustinuerat nōn iam pulcher erat. Sed Nausicaa nōn territa ante Ulixem stetit et eī[12] grātiās ēgit. Vestibus plicātīs, ad oppidum in 25 ōrdine prōcessērunt. Ulixēs ab rēge Alcinoō[13] acceptus est, cui factīs clārīs nōtus fuit. Paucōs diēs Ulixēs in Phaeāciā mānsit. Tum Alcinous Ulixem ad patriam Ithacam mīsit. Itaque post vīgintī annōs Ulixēs sōlus sine sociīs ad patriam vēnit.

---

[1] *the Sī'rens.*
[2] *of birds.*
[3] *this* (ablative).
[4] Ablative.
[5] *ears.*

[6] *hands.*
[7] *whose.*
[8] *Phaeacia (Fēā'shia).*
[9] *Nausic'āa.*
[10] *ball.*

[11] *one.*
[12] *to him.*
[13] *Alcinous (Alsin'o-us).*

30    Ulixe in Ithacā vīsō, Neptūnus nāvem in quā Ulixēs trānsportātus
erat ante portum Phaeāciae in saxum vertit. Portus īnsulae hōc [14]
impedīmentō clausus est neque posteā Alcinous et hominēs īnsulae
nāvigāre potuērunt.

QUESTIONS:   1. How did Ulysses manage to hear the Sirens without
                danger?
             2. Why did Nausicaa go to the river?
             3. Why did the girls run away?

READING     Hamilton, pp. 309–311 (Mentor ed., pp. 214–215); Sabin,
            pp. 316–320; Gayley, pp. 328–331; Guerber, pp. 350–353,
            355–357; Colum, pp. 135–142, 174–181; Bulfinch, pp. 251–
            257; Norton and Rushton, pp. 259–262.

## Third Declension: Neuter Nouns

| | ENDINGS | | EXAMPLE | |
|---|---|---|---|---|
| | SINGULAR | PLURAL | SINGULAR | PLURAL |
| Nom. | — | –a | corpus | corpora |
| Gen. | –is | –um | corporis | corporum |
| Dat. | –ī | –ibus | corporī | corporibus |
| Acc. | — | –a | corpus | corpora |
| Abl. | –e | –ibus | corpore | corporibus |

Observe that in the third declension, as in the second, the
nominative and accusative singular of neuter nouns are alike, and
that the nominative and accusative plural both end in –a.

Practice     1. Decline nōmen clārum.
             2. Tell the form of flūminum, capita, tempus, lēgēs, vulnerī,
                nōmine, rēgibus.

Exercises  A. 1. Quae nōmina flūminum Galliae cognōvistis?
             2. Pāce factā, ōrdō in Eurōpā nōn reductus est.
             3. Corpore hominis inventō, puer magistrum vocāvit.
             4. Ob tempus annī frūmentum trānsportāre nōn poterāmus.
             5. Litterae quās fīlia mea scrīpsit nec caput nec pedem
                habent.
             6. Rēx, victōriā barbarōrum territus, mīlitēs trāns flūmen
                trādūxit.

---

[14] this.

**244**

**B.** 1. The river which you see is wide.

2. Horses have large bodies but small heads.

3. (There) were many wounds on the sailor's body.

4. Since the river is closed, grain can no longer be transported.

| Vocabulary | | |
|---|---|---|
| ca′put, ca′pitis, n., *head* | | (capital) |
| clau′dō, –ere, clau′sī, clau′sus, *close* | | (clause) |
| cor′pus, cor′poris, n., *body* | | (corporation) |
| flū′men, flū′minis, n., *river* | | (fluid) |
| nō′men, nō′minis, n., *name* | | (nominate) |
| ōr′dō, ōr′dinis, m., *order, rank* | | (ordinary) |
| tem′pus, tem′poris, n., *time* | | (temporal) |
| vul′nus, vul′neris, n., *wound* | | (vulnerable) |

## English Word Studies

1. Many English words preserve the original Latin forms of the third declension:

| SINGULAR | PLURAL | SINGULAR | PLURAL |
|---|---|---|---|
| *apex* | *apexes* or *apices* | *stamen* | *stamens* or *stamina* (with |
| *appendix* | *appendixes* or *appendices* | | difference of meaning) |
| *genus* | *genera* | *vertex* | *vertexes* or *vertices* |
| *index* | *indexes* or *indices* | | *viscera* (singular rare) |

Nouns with their plurals in –s are *consul*, *ratio*, and many nouns in –**or**: *doctor, actor, factor, labor, victor*, etc.

*Decapitate.*

2. Explain *contemporary, invulnerable, decapitate, capitalism, capital punishment*. What is a *corporation*? What is meant by *incorporated*? State two ways in which *siren* is used today.

3. There is a town named *Calypso* in North Carolina.

*Pensive Penelope.*

# *Lesson 1*

## PĒNELOPĒ

Ulixēs, nāvī et sociīs āmissīs, corpore vulneribus cōnfectō, in patriam pervēnerat. Ad fīnem itineris sed nōn labōrum vēnerat. Et cīvēs et hostēs crēdidērunt Ulixem nōn iam vīvum esse.

Prīmus quī Ulixem vīdit sed nōn cognōvit erat pāstor cuius nōmen 5 erat Eumaeus. Ab Eumaeō Ulixēs nōn pauca dē uxōre Pēnelopē et fīliō Tēlemachō audīvit. Tēlemachus ab īnsulā tum aberat, quod Pēnelopē eum[1] trāns mare ad ultima rēgna cīvitātēsque Graeciae mīserat, in quibus locīs itinera faciēbat et Ulixem petēbat. Per multōs annōs nūllam fāmam dē Ulixe Pēnelopē accēperat. Interim multī ducēs 10 rēgēsque cupiditāte rēgnī Ulixis adductī dē montibus Ithacae et ē fīnitimīs īnsulīs convēnerant et rēgīnam in mātrimōnium petēbant. Cīvēs hōs[2] hostēs ē fīnibus Ithacae sine auxiliō ad montēs redigere nōn poterant. Itaque Pēnelopē, capite submissō, dīxit:

---

[1] *him.*  [2] *these.*

**246**

"Ubi vestem quam faciō cōnfēcerō, nōn iam dubitābō in mātri-mōnium darī."

Itaque exspectāvērunt. Sed cōnsilium Pēnelopae fuit tempus tra-here. Itaque nocte retexēbat [3] vestem quam multā dīligentiā texuerat. Post trēs annōs hominēs cōnsilium Pēnelopae cognōvērunt, et Pēne-lopē accūsāta vestem cōnficere coācta est.

Hōc [4] tempore Ulixēs nāvī ad īnsulam Ithacam trānsportātus est. 20 Eōdem [5] tempore Tēlemachus ā Minervā monitus in patriam prope-rāvit. Ibi ad mare ab Ulixe vīsus atque cognitus est. Ulixēs Tēle-machum ad oppidum antecēdere iussit. Ab Ulixe monitus Tēle-machus neque mātrī neque aliīs dē patre nūntiāvit.

QUESTIONS:  1. Who was Telemachus' father?
2. Why was Telemachus away when Ulysses arrived in Ithaca?
3. How did Penelope deceive the suitors?

READING  Hamilton, pp. 291–292 (Mentor ed., pp. 203–204); Sabin, pp. 320–322; Guerber, pp. 357–359; Colum, pp. 186–187; Bulfinch, p. 189.

## Third Declension: *I*-Stem Nouns

The group of nouns which have –ium instead of –um in the genitive plural are called *i–stem nouns*. In addition to this difference, neuters ending in –e have –ī instead of –e in the ablative singular, and –ia in the nominative and accusative plural. The classes of masculine and feminine i–stem nouns are:

1. Nouns ending in –is having no more syllables in the genitive than in the nominative: cīvis.

2. Nouns of one syllable whose base ends in two consonants: pars (gen. part–is), nox (gen. noct–is).

---

[3] *unwove.*
[4] *at this.*
[5] *at the same.*

JAMES SAWDERS

*The theater of Marcellus at Rome was built in the reign of Augustus.*

|       | SINGULAR | PLURAL | SINGULAR | PLURAL |
|-------|----------|--------|----------|--------|
| *Nom.* | cīvis | cīvēs | mare | maria |
| *Gen.* | cīvis | cīvium | maris | marium |
| *Dat.* | cīvī | cīvibus | marī | maribus |
| *Acc.* | cīvem | cīvēs [6] | mare | maria |
| *Abl.* | cīve | cīvibus | marī | maribus |

**Practice**

1. Decline **nāvis pulchra, iter longum.**
2. Give the singular and plural in Latin in the case required: *high mountain* (gen.), *level sea* (acc.), *small mountains* (dat.), *neighboring enemy* (abl.), *our end* (nom.).

**Exercises** **A.** 1. Ad fīnem itineris longī vēnērunt.

2. Altōs montēs et flūmina alta [7] in Eurōpā vīdī.
3. Bonī cīvēs officia pūblica suscipere nōn dubitant.
4. Parvā nāvī colōnī trāns mare lātum ad Americam migrāvērunt.
5. Ob numerum hostium quī in montibus erant cīvēs in castrīs remānsērunt.

[6] Occasionally –īs is used in the accusative plural.
[7] *deep*, when applied to anything, as a river, below the level of the eye.

*Penelope at her weaving.*
*By Willy Pogany.*

**B.** 1. By whom was a ship seen on a mountain?

2. We have made a long journey but can now see the end.

3. A large number of citizens was called together by the leader.

4. If [8] the sea is closed, the enemy's ships will not be able to transport soldiers.

**Vocabulary**  
*cī′vis, cī′vis,[9] cī′vium, m., *citizen* (civic)

cōnfi′ciō, –ere, –fē′cī, –fec′tus, (*do thoroughly*), *complete, exhaust* (cf. "do up") [*faciō*]

*fī′nis, fī′nis, fī′nium, m., *end*; plur., *borders, territory* (final)

*hos′tis, hos′tis, hos′tium, m., *enemy*,[10] usually plur. (hostile)

i′ter, iti′neris, n., *journey, road, march* (itinerary)

*ma′re, ma′ris, ma′rium, n., *sea* (marine)

*mōns, mon′tis, mon′tium, m., *mountain* (mount)

*nā′vis, nā′vis,[11] nā′vium, f., *ship* (navy)

## English Word Studies

1. Many Latin **i**–stem nouns ending in –**is** are preserved in their original form in English. The original plural in –**es** is pronounced like "ease": *axis, axes; basis, bases.*

Distinguish *axēs* from *axĕs* (plural of *ax*), *basēs* from *basĕs* (plural of *base*).

2. Why is *Penelope* Frocks a suitable name for a firm dealing in women's dresses? A town in Texas is called *Penelope.*

3. Latin phrases in English:

**Tempus fugit,** *Time flies.*

**per capita,** *by heads* or *individuals.*

**me iudice,** *in my judgment* (lit., *I being judge*).

**Fata viam invenient,** *The Fates will find a way.*

**pro tem.** (**pro tempore**), *for the time, temporarily.*

**de jure,** *according to right,* as a **de jure** government; cf. **de facto.**

---

[8] Use ablative absolute.

[9] Nouns marked with an asterisk (*) are i-stem nouns. The genitive plural of such nouns is always given in the lesson vocabularies.

[10] *national enemy,* differing from **inimīcus,** personal enemy.

[11] The ablative singular ends in –ī. A few other masculine and feminine nouns sometimes have this ending.

*Ulysses after he used his old bow against the suitors. From the motion picture "Ulysses."*

# Lesson li

## FĪNIS LABŌRUM

Ulixēs, rēx fortis Ithacae, ad portās oppidī quod rēxerat stābat, ā multīs cīvibus vīsus, sed nōn cognitus, quod vestēs sordidās gerēbat. In oppidum facilī itinere prōcessit. Multōs servōs vīdit ā quibus nōn cognitus est. Canis tamen Ulixis dominum cognōvit et gaudiō[1]
5 affectus ē vītā excessit. Ubi Ulixēs ad rēgīnam adductus est, omnēs procī[2] eum[3] hostem appellāvērunt et discēdere iussērunt. Sed Pēnelopē, quae eum nōn cognōverat, vestibus sordidīs permōta eum manēre iussit et eī[4] cibum dedit.

Pēnelopē vestem cōnfēcerat et nunc tempus aderat quō iūs erat
10 marītum dēligere. Iussit magnum arcum[5] pōnī ante procōs[2] quem Ulixēs clārus ante vīgintī annōs tetenderat. Tum nūntiāvit:

---

[1] *joy.*  [2] *suitors.*  [3] *him.*  [4] *to him.*  [5] *bow.*

"Homō quī arcum Ulixis fortis tendere poterit marītus meus erit;
marītus novus pār Ulixī esse dēbet. Ita iūs est."

Itaque singulī in ōrdine arcum cēpērunt sed tendere nōn potuērunt quod Ulixī parēs nōn fuērunt. Tum Ulixēs arcum petīvit. 15
Omnēs rīsērunt,[6] sed Pēnelopē iussit arcum Ulixī darī. Id[7] quod
reliquī nōn facere poterant—arcum tendere—Ulixī facile erat. Tum
in procōs arcum tendit, quōs in fugam dedit. Tēlemachus et Eumaeus
auxilium dedērunt. Ulixēs omnēs portās oppidī claudī iusserat, ob
quam causam procī ex oppidō ad montēs fugere nōn potuērunt. 20
Salūte petītā, nōn inventā, omnēs interfectī sunt. Hōc[8] modō rēgnum
et uxōrem Ulixēs recēpit et in lībertāte pāceque vītam ēgit. Nōn iam
nāvibus itinera trāns maria faciēbat.

QUESTIONS
1. Why was Ulysses not recognized?
2. Why did everyone laugh when Ulysses asked for the bow?
3. What do we mean when we say of a person, "He cannot bend Ulysses' bow"?

READING
Hamilton, pp. 313–318 (Mentor ed., pp. 216–219); Sabin, pp. 322–323; Colum, pp. 233–254; Bulfinch, pp. 258–261.

## Adjectives of the Third Declension

The adjectives so far studied, such as **magnus, –a, –um** and
**sacer, –cra, –crum,** have been declined like nouns of the first and

---

[6] From **rīdeō.**
[7] *that.*
[8] *this.*

*Libertas. The Statue of Liberty in New York harbor.*

second declensions. Many adjectives, however, belong to the third declension. With the exception of one important class, which will be studied later, almost all adjectives of the third declension are i–stems. They are divided into classes according to the number of forms which are used in the nominative singular to show gender, as follows:

1. **Two endings** [9]—masculine and feminine in –is, neuter in –e: **fortis, forte.**

2. **One ending**—one form for all genders: **pār.**

Adjectives of the third declension have –ī in the ablative singular, –ium in the genitive plural, and –ia in the neuter nominative and accusative plural. Note particularly that the ablative singular, unlike that of most i–stem *nouns*, ends in –ī.

|      | SINGULAR | | PLURAL | |
|------|----------|---------|----------|----------|
|      | M., F.   | N.      | M., F.   | N.       |
| *Nom.* | fortis  | forte   | fortēs   | fortia   |
| *Gen.* | fortis  | fortis  | fortium  | fortium  |
| *Dat.* | fortī   | fortī   | fortibus | fortibus |
| *Acc.* | fortem  | forte   | fortēs [10] | fortia |
| *Abl.* | fortī   | fortī   | fortibus | fortibus |

|      | M., F.   | N.      | M., F.   | N.       |
|------|----------|---------|----------|----------|
| *Nom.* | pār     | pār     | parēs    | paria    |
| *Gen.* | paris   | paris   | parium   | parium   |
| *Dat.* | parī    | parī    | paribus  | paribus  |
| *Acc.* | parem   | pār     | parēs [10] | paria  |
| *Abl.* | parī    | parī    | paribus  | paribus  |

**Practice**

1. Decline **lībertās pār, iter facile.**
2. Give in Latin: *brave boys* (acc.), *brave citizen* (abl.), *all towns* (gen.), *equal right* (acc.), *few enemies* (dat.).

**Exercises A.** 1. Quid est pretium lībertātis?
2. Servus fortibus factīs lībertātem obtinuit.
3. Omnia maria nāvibus hostium clausa erant.
4. In nostrā patriā omnēs cīvēs sunt līberī et parēs.
5. Nōvistīne, amīce bone, hominem quem in nāvī vīdimus?

---

[9] A few adjectives in –er have *three endings* in the nominative singular, one for each gender: **celer, celeris, celere.**

[10] Occasionally –īs is used instead of –ēs (p. 248, footnote 6).

6. Facilī itinere inventō, dux omnēs mīlitēs dē montibus dūcere mātūrāvit.

**B.** 1. All free men love peace.
2. Nature has given us many beautiful (things).
3. We ought not to undertake a long journey now.
4. It will not be easy to defend the freedom of our country on the sea.

**Vocabulary**

| | |
|---|---|
| fa'cilis, fa'cile, (lit., "do-able"), *easy* | [*faciō*] |
| for'tis, for'te, *strong, brave* | (fort) |
| iūs, iū'ris, n., *right* | (jury) |
| līber'tās,[11] lībertā'tis, f., *freedom* | [*līber*] |
| om'nis, om'ne, *all, every* | (omniscient) |
| pār, gen. pa'ris, *equal* | (parity) |
| ten'dō, –ere, teten'dī, ten'tus, *stretch* | (tendon) |

## English Word Studies

A number of English nouns and adjectives preserve the nominative singular, and a few the nominative plural of Latin adjectives of the third declension: *par, pauper, simplex, duplex,* etc.; *September,* etc.; *amanuensis.* Neuter forms occur in *simile, facsimile, insignia* (singular rare), *regalia* (singular rare), *forte* (singular only). The dative plural is seen in *omnibus* (a vehicle *for all*); in the common shortened form *bus* only the ending is left.

---

[11] All nouns ending in –tās are feminine.

*Ancient lighthouses at Alexandria, Egypt, and Dover, England. The former had a statue, like our Statue of Liberty, which too was once used as a lighthouse. See pages 258, 259.*

*Faustulus Romulum et Remum invenit. A painting by the artist P. P. Rubens (1577–1640). Stories of babies nourished by wolves and other animals are still heard.*

METROPOLITAN MUSEUM OF ART

# *Lesson lii*

## RŌMULUS ET REMUS

Silvius Proca, rēx fortis Albānōrum,[1] Numitōrem et Amūlium
fīliōs habuit. Numitōrī rēgnum relīquit, sed Amūlius, Numitōre ē
cīvitāte pulsō, rēxit. Rhēa Silvia, fīlia Numitōris, geminōs,[2] Rōmulum
et Remum, habuit. Amūlius puerōs in Tiberī flūmine pōnī iussit. Sed
5 aqua geminōs in siccō[3] relīquit. Lupa[4] accessit et puerōs aluit.[5]
Posteā Faustulus, pāstor rēgis, puerōs invēnit. Post multōs annōs
Rōmulō et Remō dīxit: "Numitor est avus vester." Adductī pāstōris
verbīs, geminī Amūlium interfēcērunt et Numitōrī, quem Amūlius ē
cīvitāte pepulerat, rēgnum mandāvērunt.
10    Posteā oppidum mūnīvērunt in locō in quō inventī erant, quod dē
nōmine Rōmulī Rōmam appellāvērunt.

Rōmulus Remusque parēs erant, sed Rōmulō nōn facile erat Remō
cēdere. Remō interfectō, Rōmulus sōlus Rōmānōs rēxit et omnibus
iūra dedit.

**QUESTIONS**    1. How was Amulius related to Numitor?
2. To Rhea Silvia?
3. To Remus?

**READING**    Sabin, pp. 100–103.

---

[1] *the Albans.*    [2] *twins.*    [3] *on dry ground.*    [4] *wolf.*    [5] *fed.*

## The Right Word in the Right Place

We have seen from a study of **agō** (p. 99) that a Latin word may have many shades of meaning, which are suggested by the context. In translating, therefore, do not stick to the "vocabulary" meaning of the word but use the one required in good English. Note the varying translation of **magnus** when used with the following nouns:

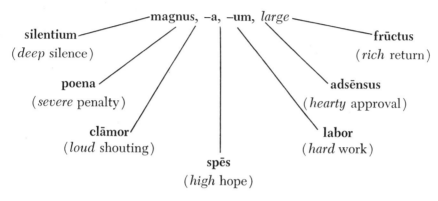

**silentium** (*deep* silence)

**poena** (*severe* penalty)

**clāmor** (*loud* shouting)

magnus, –a, –um, *large*

**spēs** (*high* hope)

**frūctus** (*rich* return)

**adsēnsus** (*hearty* approval)

**labor** (*hard* work)

**Practice**

1. Combine **magnus** with each of the following nouns already studied and translate freely: **perīculum, studium, pecūnia, pretium.**
2. How does **altus** differ when applied to rivers and mountains?
3. Translate **puella pulchra** and **homō pulcher.**

*Roman ruins at Sabratha, in Libya, northern Africa.*

**Exercises A.** 1. Ego aut viam inveniam aut faciam.
2. Dēbēmusne, pāce factā, numerum nāvium augēre?
3. Flūmina omnia Italiae ex montibus ad mare tendunt.
4. Poteruntne hostēs, montibus occupātīs, posteā iter facere?
5. Post multōs annōs Rōmānī iūra cīvitātis omnibus dedērunt.
6. Post oppidum erat mōns altus, in quō fortēs mīlitēs hostium pulsī erant.

**B.** 1. The road stretches through the mountains.
2. Is it not pleasing to all men to see friends?
3. Equal rights of citizenship were given to many Gauls.
4. After a long journey my friend is approaching (**ad**) the end of life.

**Vocabulary**   cī′vitās, cīvitā′tis, f., *citizenship, state*            [*cīvis*]
pel′lō, –ere, pe′pulī, pul′sus, *drive, defeat*            (repulsive)
**post,** prep. with acc., *behind* (of place); *after* (of time)
    post′eā, adv., *afterwards*

### English Word Studies

1. The suffix –**tās** is usually found in nouns formed from adjectives. Its English form is –*ty*, which is to be carefully distinguished from –*y* (p. 164).

What must be the Latin words from which are derived *commodity, integrity, liberty, publicity, timidity, variety*? Note that the letter preceding the ending is usually –*i*–.

*Romulus* and *Remus* are names of towns in Michigan.

2. Latin phrases in English:

**ad fin.** (**ad finem**), *near the end* (of the page).
**P.S.** (**post scriptum**), *written after* (at the end of a letter).

Translate the motto of the University of Texas (supply **est**): **Disciplina praesidium civitatis.** The Los Angeles Public Library bears the inscription **in libris libertas.**

*In Sicilia. The Temple of Juno at Agrigento.*

JAMES SAWDERS

# Lesson liii

## CĪNEĀS ET PYRRHUS

Pyrrhus erat rēx Ēpīrī. Cīneās,[1] quī erat lēgātus in Pyrrhī castrīs et reliquōs lēgātōs amīcitiā et virtūte superābat, cōnsiliīs Pyrrhī nōn probātīs, cum multā lībertāte rēgem monēbat. Quondam Pyrrhus dīxit: "In Italiam prōcēdere et cīvitātem Rōmānam cum celeritāte superāre parō." 5

Cīneās, "Superātīs Rōmānīs," inquit, "quid est tibi in animō[2] facere, rēx fortis?"

"Italiae fīnitima est īnsula Sicilia," inquit rēx, "quam facile erit armīs occupāre."

Tum Cīneās, "Occupātā Siciliā," inquit, "quid posteā faciēs?" 10

Pyrrhus tum respondit: "Posteā trāns mare in Āfricam mīlitēs meōs celerēs trānsportābō et hostēs, quī celeritāte et virtūte mīlitibus meīs nōn parēs sunt, pellam."

Cīneās, "Pulsīs hostibus," inquit, "quid tum faciēs?" "Post haec[3] bella, Cīneā,"[4] inquit Pyrrhus, "pāce cōnfirmātā, vītam in ōtiō agam." 15

---

[1] Cineas (*Sin'eas*).
[2] **quid . . . animō,** *what do you intend?*
[3] *these.*
[4] Vocative.

**257**

*Roman coin showing lighthouse at Messina, Sicily, with statue of Neptune (cf. p. 251).*

Celer Cīneās respondit: "Cūr nōn etiam nunc pācem cōnfirmāre potes atque mēcum in ōtiō vītam agere? Quid tē impedit?"

QUESTIONS
1. What were Pyrrhus' plans?
2. What did Cineas want Pyrrhus to do?
3. What do you think of his argument?
4. What are some of the causes of war?

### Ablative of Respect

Notice the use of the ablative in the following sentences:

1. **Equī et hominēs nōn sunt parēs celeritāte,** *Horses and men are not equal in swiftness.*
2. **Puer erat vir factīs,** *The boy was a man in deeds.*
3. **Numerō, nōn animō superāmur,** *We are surpassed in number, not in courage.*

*Observe* the following points:

1. The ablative expresses the respect in which the meaning of an adjective, a noun, or a verb is true.
2. No preposition is used in Latin, but in English we use a preposition, chiefly *in.*

Exercises  A. 1. Servī cum magnā celeritāte ad flūmen fūgērunt.
2. Omnēs hostēs ē fīnibus nostrīs certē pellēmus.
3. Nōn omnēs puerī dīligentiā et celeritāte parēs sunt.
4. Puer erat celer pede sed studiīs ab omnibus superābātur.
5. Colōnī ex patriā migrant et in variīs terrīs cīvitātem petunt.
6. Pāx et amīcitia cum cīvitātibus fīnitimīs ā Rōmānīs cōnfirmātae sunt.

**B.** 1. We cannot all be swift of foot.
2. Does a horse excel a boy in swiftness?
3. He was king in name, but he did not have a kingdom.
4. (Now that) peace has been established,[5] free citizens will maintain the state.

**Vocabulary**

ce′ler, ce′leris, ce′lere, *swift* (celerity)
cele′ritās, celeritā′tis, f., *swiftness*
cōnfir′mō, –ā′re, –ā′vī, –ā′tus, *make firm, encourage, establish* [*firmus*]
su′perō, –ā′re, –ā′vī, –ā′tus, *overcome, excel* (insuperable)
vir′tūs, virtū′tis, f., *manliness, courage* [*vir*]

### Latin Phrases in English

in omnia paratus, *prepared for all things.*
Dominus providebit, *The Lord will provide.*
Fortes Fortuna adiuvat, *Fortune aids the brave.*
extempore, *without preparation* (lit., *according to the time*).
Arma non servant modum, *Armies do not preserve (show) restraint.*
Virtute et armis, *By courage and by arms* (motto of the state of Mississippi).
Vanitas vanitatum et omnia vanitas, *Vanity of vanities, and all (is) vanity* (from the Vulgate, or Latin translation of the Bible, *Ecclesiastes, I, 2*).
Ense petit placidam sub libertate quietem, *With the sword she seeks quiet peace under liberty* (motto of the state of Massachusetts). President Roosevelt quoted this in 1939 to show the need of arms to preserve peace and liberty.

---

[5] See p. 230.

---

*Libertas. These two Roman coins reveal the Roman idea of liberty. Both figures hold the liberty cap. The word Augusta indicates that the liberty was granted by the emperor. The initials are for senatus consulto, "by decree of the Senate." Compare with the Statue of Liberty on page 251.*

*Atrium in a Roman house.*

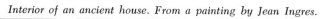

*Interior of an ancient house. From a painting by Jean Ingres.*

# 🌿 Glimpses of Roman Life

## THE HOUSE AND ITS FURNITURE

The Roman town house was different from ours and more like that of southern Europe and Latin America today. It was usually built of concrete covered with stucco. As glass was expensive, there were few windows on the street. The typical house, as found at Pompeii, consisted of two parts, front and rear. The front consisted of a large room, called the atrium, surrounded by small bedrooms. The atrium had an opening in the roof for light and air. The roof sloped down to the opening. Below the opening there was a basin into which the rain fell. This cistern, as we may call it, furnished the soft water for washing, so necessary in a country where most of the water is hard. At the corners of the basin there were often columns extending to the roof.

As the house was built directly on the street, it had no front yard. The heavy front door opened into a hall leading into the atrium. On one side of the hall there might be a small shop, usually rented out to people who did not live in the house. On the other side there was the room of the doorkeeper (iānitor). Very often there was a place for a watchdog. Sometimes a fierce dog was painted on the wall or depicted in mosaic on the floor of the hall.

Opposite the entrance was the study or office (tablīnum) of the master of the house, placed so that he could keep an eye on what was going on. Here he kept his safe. Often there were also upstairs rooms.

The rear of the house surrounded a garden. Because of the columns which ran all around the garden this part was called the peristyle (which means "columns around"). It was often very pretty. Charming fountains and statuary were usually to be seen in the garden. Kitchen, bathroom, dining rooms were in this part of the house. There were often two dining rooms, one on the shady side for summer, the other on the sunny side for winter.

**261**

The walls were covered with elaborate paintings (p. 116, etc.). Rugs and draperies were in common use. The floors were usually made of tile or flagstone, as in Italy today, instead of wood. Chairs were few, and many of them were without backs. On the other hand, there were many couches, used like easy chairs, not only for reading and resting but also at the dinner table (p. 298). There were many kinds of tables and stands, often very beautiful. Many small lamps of bronze or clay were placed everywhere, some on stands, some on large, elaborate candelabra. These burned olive oil. Glass chimneys were unknown. The light was so poor that people went to bed early and got up early. Candles were also used. Portable charcoal heaters were common.

Kitchen utensils and dishes were made of bronze, silver, or earthenware. Those made of earthenware were chiefly red in color and were decorated with engraved lines.

Besides the town houses just described, there were country homes (**vīllae**) which were more elaborate. In Rome there were also apartment houses, called **īnsulae** because they were "islands" surrounded by streets. Most Romans lived in such houses, which were often five or six stories high. They were remarkably like modern apartment houses (p. 294). Many were flimsily built for speculation and were an easy prey for fires.

**DISCUSSION**  1. In what ways did Roman houses differ from ours?
**QUESTIONS**  2. How did the poor lighting facilities affect the daily life of the people?
3. How does climate affect the types of houses?

**READING**  Showerman, pp. 76–88; Mills, pp. 301–309; Johnston, Chap. VI.

*Modern wooden shutters in a Pompeian window. These are restored, but the ashes which covered the originals left a perfect cast which made restoration easy. This house was damaged by bombs in World War II.*

# Unit IX Review

## ENGLISH WORD STUDIES

1. Give the Latin noun suggested by each of the following: *civil, finish, submarine, navigate, corpulent, legislate, nominal, decapitate.*

2. Give the Latin verb suggested by each of the following: *expedite, press, verse, attention, repellent.*

3. Give the Latin adjective suggested by each of the following: *omnipresent, celerity, facilitate, disparity, fortitude.*

4. Find and use in sentences as many English derivatives as possible from **parō, teneō, agō,** and **scrībō.**

5. Make a sketch map of your state and indicate on it all the names you can of towns with classical names.

*Corpulent.*

## VOCABULARY

| NOUNS | | | |
|---|---|---|---|
| 1. caput | 5. corpus | 10. iūs | 15. nōmen |
| 2. celeritās | 6. fīnis | 11. lībertās | 16. ōrdō |
| 3. cīvis | 7. flūmen | 12. mare | 17. tempus |
| 4. cīvitās | 8. hostis | 13. mōns | 18. virtūs |
| | 9. iter | 14. nāvis | 19. vulnus |

| ADJECTIVES | | | |
|---|---|---|---|
| 20. celer | 21. facilis | 23. omnis | |
| | 22. fortis | 24. pār | |

| VERBS | | | |
|---|---|---|---|
| 25. claudō | 26. cōnficiō | 28. pellō | 30. tendō |
| | 27. cōnfirmō | 29. superō | |

ADVERB    31. posteā

PREPOSITION    32. post

*A scene from the motion picture "The Robe," showing a room in a luxurious Roman house. Note the many lamps, the charcoal brazier (at the left), the curtains, the mosaic floor, the walls, the columns, and the costumes.*

## VOCABULARY (English Meanings)

| NOUNS | | | |
|---|---|---|---|
| 1. *head* | 5. *body* | 10. *right* | 15. *name* |
| 2. *swiftness* | 6. *end* | 11. *freedom* | 16. *order* |
| 3. *citizen* | 7. *river* | 12. *sea* | 17. *time* |
| 4. *state* | 8. *enemy* | 13. *mountain* | 18. *courage* |
| | 9. *journey* | 14. *ship* | 19. *wound* |

| ADJECTIVES | | | |
|---|---|---|---|
| 20. *swift* | 21. *easy* | 23. *all* | |
| | 22. *strong, brave* | 24. *equal* | |

| VERBS | | | |
|---|---|---|---|
| 25. *close* | 26. *complete* | 28. *drive* | 30. *stretch* |
| | 27. *make firm* | 29. *overcome* | |

| ADVERB | |
|---|---|
| | 31. *afterwards* |

| PREPOSITION | |
|---|---|
| | 32. *after* |

## GRAMMAR SUMMARY

### Ablative Uses

The ablative case really is a combination of three cases and that is why it has so many different uses.

When an ablative is always used with a preposition we generally do not need a special name for it. One exception is the ablative of agent. The reason is that the preposition **ab** with this ablative cannot be translated in its usual sense of *from* (see p. 70). We also use the name accompaniment for the ablative with **cum**. The reason is to distinguish it from the ablative of means, since both are expressed by *with* in English (see p. 121).

Pay particular attention to the ablatives used without a preposition because the construction differs from English. What are the three ablatives of this class that you have studied?

What ablative have you studied with which a preposition is sometimes used, sometimes not?

What prepositions are used with the ablative?

*This artist's reconstruction of an ancient house is based on existing remains in Pompeii. The view looks through the atrium, with its basin, and the owner's office into the peristyle. Note the balcony at the right, leading into second-story rooms.*

*A silver service from a house in Pompeii, now in the Naples Museum. This beautiful set was found not many years ago. The scenes on the cups represent Cupids in a circus race.*

## UNIT PRACTICE AND EXERCISE

**Form Drill**

1. Decline **dux fortis, lībertās nostra, omnis mīles, rēx magnus, nāvis pulchra.**
2. Give the following in Latin: *a small ship,* in the nom., sing. and plur.; *an easy journey,* in the gen., sing. and plur.; *a good citizen,* in the dat., sing. and plur.; *a brave enemy,* in the acc., sing. and plur.; *the deep sea,* in the abl., sing. and plur.
3. Give the genitive and the accusative, singular and plural, of **tempus, casa, mōns, corpus, fīnis, celeritās, mare, ōrdō, flūmen.**
4. Give in all tenses the third plural active of **impediō;** the first plural passive of **claudō;** the third singular active of **līberō;** the second plural passive of **teneō;** the second singular active of **cōnficiō.**

# UNIT X

# *Gods and History*

*Mercury, messenger of the gods.*

*Two temples in Rome, in the old cattle market, near the Tiber River. During the Middle Ages, both temples, like many others in Rome and elsewhere, were used as Christian churches.*

*The Temple of Caelestis in Dougga, Tunisia, northern Africa.*

# Lesson liv

**The Story of Lucius** (*Cont.*)

## DEĪ

Rōmānī multōs deōs habuērunt. Deōs in omnibus locīs vīdērunt
—in terrā, in agrīs, in frūmentō, in montibus, in silvīs, in undīs maris,
in aquā flūminum, in omnī nātūrā. Nōn omnēs parēs auctōritāte
erant, nam magnī deī erant et parvī deī, deī deaeque. Inter magnōs
deōs prīmus auctōritāte erat Iuppiter, rēx atque pater deōrum 5
hominumque, quī in caelō habitābat et fulmine malōs terrēbat. Iūnō
erat uxor Iovis[1] et rēgīna deōrum. Venus erat pulchra dea amōris.
Mārs, deus bellī, arma pugnāsque amābat. Auctor populī Rōmānī
vocābātur, et fortasse ob hanc[2] causam Rōmānī semper bella gerēbant. Mercurius, celer nūntius deōrum, omnēs celeritāte superābat. 10
Neptūnus erat deus maris, quī equōs in undīs regēbat. Reliquī magnī
deī erant Cerēs, dea frūmentī, Minerva, dea sapientiae, Diāna, dea
silvārum, Vulcānus, deus ignis, Apollō, quī omnia prōvidēbat et
quem hominēs cōnsulēbant, Bacchus, deus vīnī.

### TOO MANY GODS

Lūcius noster nōmina omnium magnōrum deōrum et multōrum 15
parvōrum cognōverat—quod nōn facile erat; nam magnus erat numerus deōrum deārumque. Etiam "terminus agrōrum" deus erat. Concordiam, Victōriam, Salūtem, Pācem, Fortūnam, Virtūtem Rōmānī
deās vocāvērunt, quod sacrae erant et ā Rōmānīs amābantur. Etiam
pecūnia ā Rōmānīs amābātur et dea erat, sed tamen (ita scrībit 20
auctor Rōmānus, Iuvenālis[3]) nōn in templō habitāvit.

Erant etiam deī familiārēs, prīmī quōs Lūcius cognōverat. Lār
familiāris erat deus quī familiam cōnservābat. Penātēs erant deī quī
cibum servābant. Vesta erat dea focī, in quō cibus parābātur. Ad
focum erant parvae fōrmae deōrum. Ibi, omnibus līberīs et familiāri- 25
bus convocātīs, pater Lūcī deīs grātiās agēbat et cibum dōnābat.
Quondam nōn multus cibus erat, sed tamen pater deīs cibum dōnābat. Lūcius ā patre petit: "Cūr cibus deīs ā tē datur? Nōn multum
habēmus." Pater respondit: "Cibō datō, deī hominibus magna
beneficia et longam vītam dabunt."                                           30

---

[1] Genitive singular of **Iuppiter**. [2] *this.* [3] *Jū'venal,* poet of the second century A.D.

**QUESTIONS**  1. Who was Juno's husband?  2. What did the gods do?

**Vocabulary**  auc'tor, auctō'ris, m., *maker, author*  (authorize)
  auctō'ritās, auctōritā'tis, f., *authority, influence*
  familiā'ris, –e, *of the family, friendly*; as noun, m., *friend*
  [*familia*]
  pa'ter, pa'tris, m., *father*  (paternal)

## English Word Studies

Three states have towns named *Juno* but only Florida has a *Jupiter*. One or both appear as names of firms in telephone books of New York, Cincinnati, Columbus, Louisville, etc.

Two states have towns named *Mars*. Many cities, such as Chicago, Newark, Providence, have firms named after *Mars*.

*Mercury* is a town in Texas. As a business name it occurs one hundred thirty-one times in the New York telephone book, fifty-nine in Chicago, fifty-two in Detroit, eleven in Kansas City, etc.

Kentucky, New York, Ohio have towns named *Minerva*. The goddess appears in the telephone directories of Boston, Denver, Philadelphia, etc. Her Greek name *Athena* was given to a town in Oregon.

*Bacchus* is in Utah and *Ceres* in California, New York, Virginia.

*Concordia* is the name of towns in Kansas, Kentucky, and Missouri; nine states have towns named *Victoria*; *Pax* is in West Virginia.

The planets too are named after Roman gods: *Mercury, Venus, Mars, Jupiter, Saturn, Neptune, Pluto. Uranus* is from the Greek.

Iuppiter, rex deorum.          Iuno, regina deorum.

*At the top of this beautiful medal, Jupiter hurls his thunderbolt at the snake-legged Giants. The artist Pistrucci made it to celebrate the victory of the English over Napoleon at Waterloo. In the center, Wellington and Blücher in classical armor are attended by Victory.*

# *Lesson lv*

## SĀTURNUS ET IUPPITER

Auctor et prīmus rēx deōrum Ūranus erat. Hunc fīlius Sāturnus ex rēgnō expulit. Ūranus hīs verbīs Sāturnum monuit: "Tempus auctōritātis tuae nōn longum erit; nam tū ā fīliō tuō expellēris." Hīs verbīs territus Sāturnus omnēs fīliōs in ōrdine dēvorābat. Sed māter illum quem ante[1] reliquōs amābat servāvit. Hic fuit Iuppiter, ad 5 īnsulam Crētam ā mātre missus. Post paucōs annōs hic patrem expulit et rēgnum illīus occupāvit. Sāturnus reliquōs fīliōs reddere coāctus est. Rēgiam[2] in monte Olympō Iuppiter posuit, ex quō in omnēs partēs spectāre poterat. Frātrēs convocāvit. Neptūnō maris rēgnum, Plūtōnī rēgnum īnferōrum[3] permīsit. 10

Sed posteā Gigantēs,[4] fīliī Terrae, cum deīs bellum gessērunt. Illī ad Olympum praecipitēs cucurrērunt sed ā deīs superātī poenīs dūrīs affectī sunt.[5]

QUESTIONS
1. Who was the father of Saturn?
2. Of Jupiter?
3. Who were the sons of Saturn?

---

[1] *more than.*
[2] *palace.*
[3] *of those below,* i.e., the dead.
[4] *the Giants.*

[5] Modern version: in 1941 the Germans and the British fought for the possession of Mt. Olympus.

*A shrine, made of mosaic, in an ancient house at Pompeii. Here statuettes of the Lares, or household gods, were kept.*

**READING**   Hamilton, pp. 80–83 (Mentor ed., pp. 65–67); Sabin, pp. 90–91; Gayley, p. 59; Guerber, pp. 18–20; Norton and Rushton, pp. 119–123.

### The Demonstratives *Hic* and *Ille*

In English, *this* (plur., *these*) and *that* (plur., *those*) are called *demonstratives* because they "point out" persons or objects. They may be used as either adjectives or pronouns; as, ***This** man certainly did not write **that**; **that** could not have been done by **these** boys.*

In Latin, **hic** means *this* (*near* the speaker in place or thought), while **ille** means *that* (*more distant* from the speaker).

|  | SINGULAR | | |  | SINGULAR | | |
|---|---|---|---|---|---|---|---|
|  | M. | F. | N. |  | M. | F. | N. |
| *Nom.* | hic | haec | hoc | *Nom.* | ille | illa | illud |
| *Gen.* | huius | huius | huius | *Gen.* | illīus | illīus | illīus |
| *Dat.* | huic | huic | huic | *Dat.* | illī | illī | illī |
| *Acc.* | hunc | hanc | hoc | *Acc.* | illum | illam | illud |
| *Abl.* | hōc | hāc | hōc | *Abl.* | illō | illā | illō |

Both **hic** and **ille** are declined regularly in the plural, like **bonus** (**hī**, etc., **illī**, etc.), with the exception of the nominative and accusative plural neuter of **hic**, i.e., **haec**. For full declension see p. 395. Note that **hic** and **ille** resemble **quī** in the genitive singular.

From such expressions as *this man, that woman,* etc., the demonstrative adjectives **hic** and **ille** came to be used as a third person pronoun *he, she, it.* The personal pronoun, however, is usually not required in Latin.

### Position of Demonstratives

Demonstrative adjectives regularly precede their nouns in English and Latin: *these boys,* **hī puerī**; *that girl,* **illa puella.** Therefore, when *that* precedes its noun, it is a demonstrative adjective (**ille**); when it follows, it is a relative pronoun (**quī**), equivalent to *who* or *which: The man that I saw was famous,* **Vir *quem*** (not **illum**) **vīdī clārus erat.**

**Exercises A.** 1. Ille erat dux ducum.
2. Hunc cognōvī sed illum ante hoc tempus nōn vīdī.
3. Hī hominēs sunt patris meī amīcī; illī sunt inimīcī.
4. Haec est mea patria; nam ego cīvis Americānus sum.
5. Praeceps in illum virum cucurrī, quod illum nōn vīdī.
6. Māter mea huic hominī grātiam habet, quod hic patrem meum servāvit.

**B.** Supply the right forms of **hic** and **ille** and translate:
1. (*These*) hominēs laudō, (*those*) accūsō.
2. (*This*) flūmen altum est, (*that*) nōn altum est.
3. (*This*) puerī patrem et (*that*) puellae mātrem vīdī.
4. Studia ab (*this*) puerō intermissa sunt, nōn ab (*that*).

**C.** 1. This is my money; that is yours.
2. This boy excels that (one) in (his) studies.
3. What name did the mother give to the boy?
4. When this prisoner has been bound,[6] I shall bind that (one).

**Vocabulary**    cur′rō, –ere, cucur′rī, cursū′rus, *run*          (current)
expel′lō, –ere, ex′pulī, expul′sus, *drive out*          [*pellō*]
hic, haec, hoc, *this*
il′le, il′la, il′lud, *that*
mā′ter, mā′tris, f., *mother*          (maternal)
prae′ceps, gen. **praeci′pitis,** *headlong, steep*          (precipice)

---

[6] Use ablative absolute.

### English Word Studies: The Third Declension

The third declension is very important in Latin because so many words belong to it. More English words are derived from nouns and adjectives of this declension than from any other. The English word is usually derived from the base, not from the nominative. It is therefore doubly important to memorize the genitive, from which the base is obtained. It would be difficult to see that *itinerary* is derived from **iter** if one did not know that the genitive is **itineris.** See how many of the words of the third declension already studied have derivatives from the base. Note the help given for English spelling: *temporal, corporal, military, nominal,* etc.

On the other hand, the English derivative will help you remember the genitive. In the following list of words, a derivative is placed after each; give the genitive: **religiō** (*religion*), **sermō** (*sermon*), **latus** (*lateral*), **rādīx** (*radical*), **orīgō** (*original*), **ēruptiō** (*eruption*), **custōs** (*custody*), **dēns** (*dental*), **mōs** (*moral*).

*Model of the Pantheon in the Metropolitan Museum of Art. This temple, originally built by Agrippa during the reign of Augustus, was rebuilt by the emperor Hadrian in the second century* A.D. *Compare pages 88, 189.*

*Milites Romani. From the motion picture "Quo Vadis."*

# Lesson lvi

## CAEDICIUS FORTIS

Prīmō bellō Pūnicō hostēs locum nātūrā mūnītum occupāverant, et perīculum mīlitum Rōmānōrum magnum erat. Aestās erat, nam Rōmānī semper aestāte, nōn hieme, bella gerēbant. Dux nihil facere poterat. Tribūnus mīlitum Rōmānus cui [1] nōmen Caedicius [2] erat, ad ducem hōc tempore vēnit et sententiam dīxit, locō quōdam [3] mōn- 5 strātō:

"Virōs tuōs servāre poteris sī ad illum locum cccc mīlitēs currere iubēbis. Hostēs, ubi hōs mīlitēs vīderint, proelium committent et hōs omnēs interficient. Dum haec faciunt, facile erit reliquōs mīlitēs ex hōc locō ēdūcere. Haec est sōla via salūtis." 10

"Bonum tuum cōnsilium probō," inquit dux, "sed quis illōs praecipitēs in mortem certam dūcet?"

"Cūr mē nōn mittis? Mors mē nōn terret," respondit tribūnus. Itaque dux tribūnō magnās grātiās ēgit et hunc cum cccc mīlitibus

---

[1] *whose.*     [2] *Caedicius (Sēdish'ius).*     [3] *certain.*

**275**

15 contrā hostēs mīsit. Fortēs illī Rōmānī nihil timuērunt. Neque cessērunt neque fūgērunt sed magnō numerō hostium superātī sunt.
Omnēs aut vītam āmīsērunt aut vulnera accēpērunt. Interim reliquī
mīlitēs Rōmānī integrī salūtem petīvērunt.

   Deī praemium tribūnō ob ēgregium exemplum dōnāvērunt; nam
20 vītam nōn āmīsit. Vulnera multa accēpit sed neque in capite neque
in corde. Illā aestāte hostēs expulsī sunt, et hieme Rōmānī hostēs
nōn iam timuērunt.

QUESTIONS   1. What was Caedicius' suggestion?
             2. What happened to Caedicius?

## Ablative of Time When

   In English, time is expressed with or without the prepositions
*in, on,* etc.: *last summer, in winter.*

   In Latin, the "time when" something happens is expressed by
the ablative, *usually without a preposition.*

   1. **Illō annō in oppidō mānsimus,** *That year we remained in town.*
   2. **Aestāte agrī sunt pulchrī,** *In summer the fields are beautiful.*

*Note.* Compare with the ablative of "place where" (p. 63). Observe that when *at, in,* or *on* denotes *time* instead of *place,* no preposition is used.

*American soldiers enter Rome June 5, 1944, at the Porta Maggiore. On top of the gate
are several aqueducts; below is the tomb of a baker.*

**Exercises A.** 1. Hic puer et aestāte et hieme in agrīs labōrat.
  2. Mīlitēs nostrī, paucī numerō sed corde fortēs, prōvinciam occupāvērunt.
  3. Illā hieme decem librōs lēgī sed hāc aestāte nihil fēcī.
  4. Quīntā hōrā omnēs servī cum magnā celeritāte fūgērunt.
  5. Hōc annō nihil timēmus, quod cōpiam frūmentī habēmus.
  6. Prō Deō et patriā! Haec clāra verba corda virōrum semper incitāvērunt.

**B.** 1. In summer the rivers are not deep.
  2. In that year America had many ships on every sea.
  3. Good citizens love God and do not fear an enemy.
  4. If [4] Marcus is our leader, we shall live in safety this winter.

**Vocabulary**

aes'tās, aestā'tis, f., *summer*
cor, cor'dis, n., *heart* (cordial)
hi'ems, hi'emis, f., *winter*
*mors, mor'tis, mor'tium, f., *death* (mortal)
ni'hil (indeclinable), *nothing* (annihilate)
ti'meō, –ē're, ti'muī, ——, *fear, be afraid* (timid)

*Roman toys in the Toronto Museum.*

### English Word Studies

1. An *excursion* is a *little run out of* town. What is a *current* of water? *Cursive* writing? A *recurrent* illness? *Concurrent* powers of the federal government and the states? *Discord* is *hearts apart; concord, hearts together*. What is a *cordial* welcome? An apple *core*?

2. Latin phrases in English:

**primus inter pares,** *first among his equals.*
**A.D. (anno Domini),** *in the year of our Lord.*
**aut Caesar aut nihil,** *either Caesar or nothing.*
**Alma Mater,** *kindly mother,* applied to a school or college.
**iustitia omnibus,** *justice for all* (motto of the District of Columbia).
**Pater Noster,** *Our Father,* i.e., the Lord's Prayer, which begins with these words.

---

[4] Use ablative absolute, omitting a word for *is.*

*Remains of Roman Carthage, near the modern city of Tunis in northern Africa. Punic Carthage was destroyed by the Romans in the Third Punic War. Years later a Roman colony built a new city.*

JAMES SAWDERS

# Lesson lvii

## CĪVITĀS RŌMĀNA

Duae partēs cīvitātis Rōmānae, Troiānī et Latīnī, contrā perīcula commūnia pugnāvērunt. Ubi cīvitās nova concordiā aucta est, rēgēs populīque fīnitimī praedae cupiditāte adductī partem agrōrum Rōmānōrum vāstābant. Paucī ex amīcīs [1] auxilium Rōmānīs submittē-
5 bant quod perīculīs territī sunt. Sed Rōmānī properābant, parābant, cum hostibus proelia committēbant, lībertātem patriamque commūnem armīs dēfendēbant, mortem nōn timēbant. Dum pāx incerta est,[2] dum eī nē spīrāre quidem [3] sine perīculō possunt, cūram perpetuam nōn remittēbant.

10 Dum haec geruntur,[2] eī Rōmānī quōrum corpora ob annōs nōn iam firma erant sed quī bonō cōnsiliō valēbant dē rē pūblicā [4] cōnsulēbantur et ob aetātem patrēs aut senātōrēs appellābantur.

Prīmō rēgēs erant, quī lībertātem cōnservābant et rem pūblicam augēbant, sed posteā, quod hī superbī fuērunt, Rōmānī fēcērunt
15 cōnsulēs.

Eō tempore corda omnium Rōmānōrum glōriam spērāvērunt. Virī fortēs bella amābant, in castrīs aestāte atque hieme labōrābant, nihil timēbant: virtūs eōrum omnia superāverat. Itaque populus Rōmānus magnum hostium numerum paucīs mīlitibus in fugam dabat, oppida

---

[1] **ex amīcīs = amīcōrum.**
[2] Use the past tense in translating.
[3] **nē . . . quidem,** *not even.*

[4] Translate by the English derivative of this compound noun.

278

nātūrā mūnīta pugnīs capiēbat. Hostibus superātīs et perīculō 20
remōtō, Rōmānī aequē regēbant. Iūra bellī pācisque cōnservābant;
hōc modō auctōritās eōrum cōnfirmāta est. In ultimās partēs mīlitēs
eōrum missī sunt. Lingua Latīna in omnibus terrīs docēbātur. Post
tertium Pūnicum bellum Rōmānī fuērunt dominī omnium terrārum
mariumque. Nunc sine cūrā spīrāre et animōs remittere potuērunt. 25
    Sed tum fortūna, semper incerta, eōs superāvit. Hī pecūniam
imperiumque, nōn iam glōriam spērāvērunt. Superbī, nōn iam aequī
fuērunt; iūra lēgēsque nōn iam cōnservāvērunt.

QUESTIONS    1. What were the two parts of the Roman state?
              2. What did the old men do?
              3. What caused the decay of Rome?

## The Demonstrative Is

|  | SINGULAR |  |  | PLURAL |  |  |
|  | M. | F. | N. | M. | F. | N. |
| --- | --- | --- | --- | --- | --- | --- |
| *Nom.* | is | ea | id | eī (iī) | eae | ea |
| *Gen.* | eius | eius | eius | eōrum | eārum | eōrum |
| *Dat.* | eī | eī | eī | eīs (iīs) | eīs (iīs) | eīs (iīs) |
| *Acc.* | eum | eam | id | eōs | eās | ea |
| *Abl.* | eō | eā | eō | eīs (iīs) | eīs (iīs) | eīs (iīs) |

**Practice**      Decline **ea pars, id longum iter, is vir.**

### How Is Is Used

Instead of pointing, in a forceful way, to a definite person or
thing, as **hic** and **ille** do, **is** usually refers to somebody or something
just mentioned. When used without a noun, it is usually translated
as a personal pronoun, *he, she,* or *it*; therefore, the genitive **eius** may
be translated *his, her, its*, while **eōrum** and **eārum** mean *their*. **Is**
often serves as the antecedent of a relative clause; as **Is quī videt
probat**, *He who sees approves.*

**Exercises**  **A.** 1. Dum spīrō spērō. (*A motto of South Carolina.*)
            2. Is cui librōs dedī eōs nōn remīsit.
            3. Commūne perīculum concordiam facit.
            4. Certa āmittimus dum incerta petimus.
            5. Puellās et eārum mātrem in lūdō vīdī.
            6. Eī puerī quōs aestāte vīdimus erant eius fīliī.
            7. Hostibus pulsīs, disciplīnam nostram nōn remittēmus.

      **B.** 1. Her father and mine are away.
            2. Give him a part of the money.
            3. We shall see him and his mother this summer.
            4. This man is my teacher; that man is her father.

| | | |
|---|---|---|
| **Vocabulary** | commū′nis, −e, *common* | (communistic) |
| | dum, conj., *while* | |
| | incer′tus, −a, −um, *uncertain* | [*cernō*] |
| | is, e′a, id, *this, that; he, she, it* | |
| | *pars, par′tis, par′tium, f., *part* | (partition) |
| | remit′tō, −ere, remī′sī, remis′sus, (lit., *let back*), *relax, send back* | [*mittō*] |
| | spē′rō, −ā′re, −ā′vī, −ā′tus, *hope (for)* | (despair) |
| | spī′rō, −ā′re, −ā′vī, −ā′tus, *breathe* | (inspiration) |

### English Word Studies: The Names of the Months

In early Roman times the year began March 1, and February was the last month. We still use the ancient Roman names of the months. *March* was named after Mars. *April* was the *opening* month (**aperiō**), when the earth seems to open up. *May* is the month when things become *bigger* (**maior**). *June* is Juno's month, *July* was originally called **Quīnctīlis**, the *fifth* month, but was renamed in honor of Julius Caesar after he had the calendar changed to our present system. Similarly *August* was originally **Sextīlis**, the *sixth* month, but was renamed after the Emperor Augustus. *September* was originally the *seventh* month and kept its name even after it later became the ninth; similarly, *October, November, December. January* was named after Janus, the god of beginnings. *February* was the time of purification (**fēbrua**), like the Christian Lent.

*"Main Street" and the Arch of Trajan in Timgad, a Roman town in north Africa.*

# Lesson lviii

## MIDĀS

Midās, nōbilis genere, rēx Phrygiae, multīs oppidīs expugnātīs, magnam auctōritātem habuit. Quondam Sīlēnus, magister deī Bacchī, in agrīs Phrygiae interceptus, ad eum rēgem ductus est. Quod Sīlēnus ab rēge multa beneficia accēpit, Bacchus parātus fuit rēgī dare id quod spērāvit. Midās dīxit: "Sī omnia quae parte corporis meī 5 tetigerō [1] in aurum vertentur, mihi grātum erit."

Hōc factō, omnia commūnia quae rēx tangēbat in aurum vertēbantur. Terram tangit: nōn iam terra est sed aurum. Aquam tangit: eōdem modō in aurum vertitur. Tum grātiās Bacchō prō magnō praemiō ēgit.                                                                   10

Tum rēx cēnam magnam parārī iussit et omnia genera cibōrum in mēnsā pōnī. Haec mēnsa ab eōdem tācta in aurum versa est. Dum magnā celeritāte servī cēnam parant, Midās familiārēs nōbilēs convocāvit. Grātō animō bonam cēnam quae parāta erat spectāvit. Dum cibum capit, cibus in aurum versus est. Vīnum in mēnsā pōnī iussit. 15 Hoc tangit et nōn iam idem est sed in aurum vertitur. Omnibus amīcīs ēgregia cēna grāta fuit sed nōn rēgī. Inter multōs cibōs edere [2] nōn potuit.

Tandem ad Bacchum, auctōrem malōrum, rēx miser prōcēdere mātūrāvit et fīnem supplicī petīvit—nam supplicium et impedīmen- 20 tum, nōn iam praemium erat id quod ā deō accēperat. Bacchus iussit eum in mediō flūmine Pactōlō [3] sē [4] lavāre. Praeceps rēx ad flūmen cucurrit, ubi sē lāvit, sē remīsit, sine cūrā spīrāvit. Arēna [5] flūminis in aurum versa est, et etiam nunc in hōc eōdem flūmine aurum est.

---

[1] From **tangō**.
[2] *eat.*
[3] *Pactō'lus.*
[4] *himself.*
[5] *sand.*

*Silenus holding the infant Bacchus.*

1. Why did Bacchus reward Midas? How?
2. What is meant by the expression used today, "The Midas touch"?
3. What did Mr. Hoover mean in comparing (1940) the gold buried at Fort Knox to that acquired by Midas?

READING  Hamilton, pp. 411–413 (Mentor ed., pp. 278–279); Sabin, pp. 19–21; Gayley, pp. 157–158; Guerber, pp. 177–179; Bulfinch, pp. 52–54.

## The Demonstrative Īdem

The demonstrative **īdem,** meaning *same,* is a compound of **is** and **–dem,** with slight changes for ease of pronunciation:

SINGULAR

|       | M.      | F.      | N.      |
|-------|---------|---------|---------|
| *Nom.* | ĭdem | eădem | ĭdem |
| *Gen.* | eiusdem | eiusdem | eiusdem |
| *Dat.* | eīdem | eīdem | eīdem |
| *Acc.* | eundem | eandem | ĭdem |
| *Abl.* | eōdem | eădem | eōdem |

PLURAL

|       | M.      | F.      | N.      |
|-------|---------|---------|---------|
| *Nom.* | eīdem (īdem) | eaedem | eădem |
| *Gen.* | eōrundem | eārundem | eōrundem |
| *Dat.* | eīsdem (īsdem) | eīsdem (īsdem) | eīsdem (īsdem) |
| *Acc.* | eōsdem | eāsdem | eădem |
| *Abl.* | eīsdem (īsdem) | eīsdem (īsdem) | eīsdem (īsdem) |

Practice  Give the Latin in the singular and plural for *the same body* in the accusative, *the same summer* in the ablative, *the same year* in the genitive, *the same punishment* in the nominative, *the same part* in the dative.

Exercises  A. 1. Eōdem annō lībertās captīvīs data est.
2. Dux eum ad idem supplicium trahī iussit.
3. Dum omnia timēmus, glōriam spērāre nōn possumus.
4. Oppidō expugnātō, Caesar impedīmenta hostium intercēpit.
5. Hic homō nōbilī genere sed nōn magnīs factīs illum superat.
6. Hominēs līberī parēsque esse dēbent, quod eundem Deum habent.

**B.** 1. His punishment scared the rest.
2. He will not send back the same book.
3. When I saw the same boy,[6] I was no longer afraid.
4. Their towns were captured one at a time the same year.

**Vocabulary**  expug′nō, –ā′re, –ā′vī, –ā′tus, (lit., *fight it out*), *capture by assault*   [*pugnō*]
ge′nus, ge′neris, n., *birth, kind*   (generation)
ĭ′dem, e′ădem, ĭ′dem, *same*   (identity)
interci′piō, –ere, –cē′pī, –cep′tus, *intercept*   [*capiō*]
nō′bilis, –e, (lit., "know-able"), *noble*   [*nōscō*]
suppli′cium, suppli′cī, n., *punishment*   [*plicō*]
tan′gō, –ere, te′tigī, tāc′tus, *touch*   (tangent)

## English Word Studies

1. Explain the word *community*. **Supplicium** literally mean *folding* (or bending) *down* for punishment. Explain *supplication*.
2. Latin phrases in English:

**ibid.** (**ibidem**), *in the same place.*
**id.** (**idem**), *the same* (i.e., as mentioned above).
**quid pro quo**, *something for something* ("tit for tat").
**Homo proponit, sed Deus disponit**, *Man proposes, but God disposes.*
Explain **semper idem, genus homo.**

---

[6] Use ablative absolute.

*Tile roof at Herculaneum, nineteen centuries old, just like those made today.*

*Horatius at the bridge.*

# Lesson lix

## HORĀTIUS

Nunc in locīs commodīs sedēbimus et legēmus dē Horātiō,[1] virō fortī nōbilīque genere. Sī haec fābula, nōn tibi nōta, tē dēlectābit,[2] tū ipse lege eandem sorōribus frātribusque tuīs parvīs (sī frātrēs sorōrēsque habēs), quī circum tē sedēbunt et cum magnō studiō
5 audient.

Tarquiniī,[3] ā Rōmānīs pulsī, ā Porsenā,[4] rēge Etrūscōrum, auxilium petīvērunt. Itaque Porsena ipse cum multīs mīlitibus Rōmam[5] vēnit. Rōmānī, dē salūte commūnī incertī, territī sunt, quod magna erat potestās Etrūscōrum magnumque Porsenae nōmen. Rōmānī quī
10 agrōs colēbant in oppidum migrāvērunt; portās clausērunt et oppidum ipsum praesidiīs dēfendērunt. Pars urbis Tiberī flūmine mūnīta est. Pōns sublicius[6] iter hostibus dabat, sed ēgregius vir prohibuit, Horātius Coclēs,[7] illō cognōmine appellātus quod in proeliō oculum āmīserat. Is, extrēmā pontis parte occupātā, mīlitēs hostium sōlus
15 sine auxiliō intercēpit et sustinuit et Rōmānōs quī fugiēbant pontem

---

[1] *Horatius (Horā'shius).*
[2] Translate by the present: *pleases.*
[3] *the Tar'quins,* Etruscan rulers of Rome in the sixth century B.C.
[4] *Por'sena.*
[5] *to Rome.*
[6] *made of piles.*
[7] *Cŏ'clēs* ("One-Eye").

**284**

frangere iussit. Ipsa audācia hostēs terruit. Ponte frāctō, armīs impedītus, praeceps in Tiberim dēsiluit et per multa tēla integer ad Rōmānōs trānāvit. Eius virtūte oppidum nōn expugnātum est. Grāta ob factum clārum eius cīvitās fuit. Multī agrī eī pūblicē datī sunt, quōs ad terminum vītae coluit. Exemplum virtūtis ab eō prōpositum 20 Rōmānī semper memoriā retinuērunt.

QUESTIONS 1. Why did Porsena come to Rome?
     2. How was he prevented from entering the city?
     3. How did Cocles get his name?
     4. Is the destruction of bridges important in wars today?

READING Mills, pp. 67–68; Macaulay's *Lays of Ancient Rome*, "Horatius."

## The Intensive in English and Latin

In English, compound pronouns are formed by joining -*self* to *my, your, him, her, it* and the plural -*selves* to *our, your, them.* These compounds may be used in an intensive or emphatic sense; as, *I saw the man myself.*

In Latin, the pronoun **ipse** is a compound of **is** and the intensive ending **–pse**, and therefore has purely intensive force: **Ipse hominem vīdī,** *I saw the man myself.* Note that **ipse** may be used alone in the nominative to emphasize an omitted subject. It is declined like **ille** (p. 272), except in the neuter nominative and accusative singular.

|  | SINGULAR | | |
| --- | --- | --- | --- |
|  | M. | F. | N. |
| *Nom.* | ipse | ipsa | ipsum |
| *Gen.* | ipsīus | ipsīus | ipsīus |
| *Dat.* | ipsī | ipsī | ipsī |
| *Acc.* | ipsum | ipsam | ipsum |
| *Abl.* | ipsō | ipsā | ipsō |

(The plural is regular.)

Practice Translate **frātris ipsīus, suppliciō ipsō, partēs ipsae, hic cīvis ipse, illārum nāvium ipsārum, sorōrī meae ipsī, eiusdem generis, eōrundem auctōrum.**

Exercises **A.**1. Nōnne idem ipsī cernitis, puerī?
     2. Quae officia soror vestra ipsa suscipiet?
     3. Deī quōs Rōmānī colēbant multī erant.
     4. Quis est puer ille quī cum sorōre meā sedet?

5. Ille homō agricola appellātur quod agrōs colit.
6. Frātrēs et sorōrēs eiusdem familiae paria iūra habēre dēbent.

**B.** 1. These (men) are standing; those are sitting.
2. These letters were written by the king himself.
3. We ourselves shall get much money in a few years.
4. The same winter they saw and heard him themselves.

**Vocabulary**

co'lō, –ere, co'luī, cul'tus, *till, inhabit, worship* (cultivate)
frā'ter, frā'tris, m., *brother* (fraternal)
ip'se, ip'sa, ip'sum, *self, very*
se'deō, –ē're, sē'dī, sessū'rus, *sit* (session)
so'ror, sorō'ris, f., *sister* (sorority)

### English Word Studies: The Norman-French Influence

We saw in earlier lessons (pp. 218, 225) how Latin words were introduced into English at its very beginning. A very important period of influence followed the Norman conquest of England (1066). The language of the Normans was an old form of French, itself descended from Latin. In the course of a few centuries, the English language underwent striking changes and adopted many French (Latin) words. These sometimes show marked variations from the original spelling. Especially common is the change of one vowel to two. Because so many words were borrowed from old French, which was more like Latin than modern French is, English words are often more like Latin in form and meaning than French words are.

Look up the Latin originals of *captain, vizor, homage, duke, peer, treason.* See Scott's *Ivanhoe,* Chap. I, for *pork, beef,* etc. Explain *cult, culture, agriculture, degenerate, infinite, sediment.*

*A silver mirror from Pompeii.*

In Graecia. Olympia as it was in ancient times.

JAMES SAWDERS

# Lesson lx

## CICERŌ ET TĪRŌ

Cicerō et Tīrō fuērunt Rōmānī clārī, alter maximus [1] ōrātor tōtīus Italiae, alter servus fīdus.[2] Posteā Cicerō eum līberāvit. Quod Tīrō dīligentiā sapientiāque Cicerōnī magnum auxilium dabat, Cicerō eum tōtō corde amābat. Neuter sine alterō ūllum iter facere cupiēbat.

Cicerō cum Tīrōne in Graeciā fuerat. Ubi ille in Italiam revertit, 5 Tīrō sōlus in Graeciā relīctus est quod aeger [3] fuit. Cicerō ad eum trēs litterās in itinere ūnō diē [4] scrīpsit. Inter alia haec ipsa scrīpsit:

"Variē litterīs tuīs affectus sum, prīmā parte territus, alterā cōnfirmātus. Hōc tempore tē [5] neque marī neque itinerī committere dēbēs. Medicus tuus bonus est, ut [6] scrībis et ego audiō; sed eum nōn 10 probō; nam iūs [7] nōn dēbet stomachō [8] aegrō darī. Ad illum et ad Lysōnem [9] scrīpsī. Lysōnis nostrī neglegentiam nōn probō, qui, litterīs ā mē acceptīs, ipse nūllās remīsit. Sed Lysō Graecus est et omnium Graecōrum magna est neglegentia. In nūllā rē [10] properāre dēbēs.

"Curium [11] iussī omnem pecūniam tibi dare quam cupis. Sī medicō 15 pecūniam dabis, dīligentia eius augēbitur. Magna sunt tua in mē officia; [12] omnia superāveris, sī, ut spērō, salūtem tuam cōnfirmātam

---

[1] *greatest.*
[2] *faithful.*
[3] *sick.*
[4] Ablative.

[5] *yourself.*
[6] *as.*
[7] *soup.*
[8] Use the English derivative.

[9] Tiro was staying at Lyso's house.
[10] *thing.*
[11] *Cu'rius*, a banker.
[12] *services.*

**287**

vīderō. Ante, dum magnā dīligentiā mihi auxilium dās,[13] nōn salūtem tuam cōnfirmāre potuistī; nunc tē nihil impedit. Omnia dēpōne; salūs
20 sōla in animō tuō esse dēbet."

Nōnne dominī bonī illīs temporibus Eurōpam colēbant? Sed aliī malī erant. Omnī aetāte et in omnibus terrīs bonī et malī hominēs fuērunt et sunt et semper erunt.

QUESTIONS    1. What was Tiro's relation to Cicero?
2. To whom did Cicero write about Tiro's illness?
3. Use a remark in this letter as a basis for discussion of national and racial prejudices.

### Declension of Ūnus

The numeral ūnus and the other words in the vocabulary of this lesson are irregular only in the genitive and dative singular of all genders. In these cases they are declined like **ipse** (p. 285), in all others like **magnus**. If you need help in declining them, see p. 394. Like **hic, ille,** and **is,** these adjectives are emphatic and therefore precede their nouns.

Practice    1. Decline in the singular **alius tuus frāter.**
2. Give the Latin for the following in the genitive and dative singular: *neither sister, the whole town, the other leader, no winter, safety alone, one citizen.*

---

[13] In English the past tense is used.

*Another charming painting from the wall of a house in Pompeii.*

## Words Often Confused

1. **alius** = *another,* one of a group of *three or more.*
   **alter** = *the other,* i.e., *of two* and no more.

2. **tōtus** = *whole,* i.e., no part missing, not capable of being divided.
   **omnis** (singular) = *every.*
   **omnēs** (plural) = *all,* i.e., a complete collection of units or parts.

3. **nūllus** = *not any, no*—always an adjective.
   **nihil** = *not a thing, nothing*—always an indeclinable noun.
   **nēmō** [14] = *no man, no one*—always a noun.

**Exercise**   **A.** 1. Rēx neutrī fīliō rēgnum committet.
2. Cōnsilia alterius ducis alterī nōn erant grāta.
3. Sorōrēs meae agrōs montēsque tōtīus īnsulae vīdērunt.
4. Is homō ipse ab aliīs accūsātus est sed ab aliīs dēfēnsus est.
5. Quīnque amīcī eius iam discessērunt et is sōlus nunc manet.
6. Accēpistīne ipse ūlla praemia prō meritīs tuīs? (*See p. 154.*) Nūlla accēpī neque ūlla exspectō.

**B.** 1. Every man in our whole country ought to work.
2. To one sister I shall give money, to the other this book.
3. Have you seen my mother and sister? I have seen neither.
4. My brother spent part of that same summer alone in the woods.

**Vocabulary** [15] a′lius, a′lia, a′liud,[16] *other, another*   (alias)
   (a′lius . . . a′lius, *one . . . another;* a′liī . . . a′liī, *some . . . others*)
   al′ter, al′tera, al′terum,[17] *the other* (of two)   (alternate)
   (al′ter . . . al′ter, *the one . . . the other*)
   neu′ter, neu′tra, neu′trum, *neither* (of two)   (neutral)
   nūl′lus, nūl′la, nūl′lum, *no, none*   (nullify)
   sō′lus, sō′la, sō′lum, *alone, only*   (solitary)
   tō′tus, tō′ta, tō′tum, *whole*   (total)
   ūl′lus, ūl′la, ūl′lum, *any*
   ū′nus, ū′na, ū′num, *one*   (unit)

*Remember* that the above adjectives except **alter** [17] have **–īus** in the genitive and **–ī** in the dative singular of all genders (p. 288).

---

[14] See p. 332.
[15] **Uter**, *which* (of two), and **uterque**, *each, both,* are likewise irregular and belong to this group but are comparatively unimportant.
[16] Note that the neuter nominative and accusative singular end in **–d**, not **–m** (cf. **ille**).
[17] The genitive singular of **alter** ends in **–īus** (short **–ī**).

*Ancient Herculaneum as it looks today. A street with shops, house fronts, and second-story porch. Note the pavement made of stones of irregular shape.*

### English Word Studies: Spelling

Latin words are often very helpful in fixing the spelling of English words in your mind. In this lesson we shall consider words in which a double consonant occurs.

If the Latin word has a double consonant, it is usually preserved in English, except at the end of a word: *terror,* but *deter* (from **terreō**); *carriage,* but *car* (**carrus**); *rebelled,* but *rebel* (**bellum**); *remitted,* but *remit* (**remittō**). *Letter* has two *t*'s and *literal* only one because the spelling of Latin **littera** varied.

Many prefixes bring about the doubling of consonants by assimilation. The most important are **ad–, con–, in–, ob–, ex–,** and **sub–**. If you will analyze the English word, you can often tell whether the consonant is to be doubled: **con–** and **modus** form **commodus;** prefix **ad–** and you get the English derivative *ac-com-modate* with two *c*'s and two *m*'s. Similarly *commend* has two *m*'s; *re-com-mend* has two *m*'s but only one *c* because **re–** cannot be assimilated. Other examples of doubling through assimilation are *im-material, ac-celerate, suf-ficient, ef-ficient* (but *de-ficient,* for **dē–** is not assimilated).

Find five more examples of doubling of consonants as a result of assimilation.

**290**

*Altar at Pompeii showing a sacrifice. The priest always covered his head.*

# ⤳ Glimpses of Roman Life

## ROMAN RELIGION

In the oldest form of the Roman religion there was a god or spirit for almost everything—even for the hinges of the door. Essentially this was a religion of the family. The worship came to center about the household god known as the Lar (plural, Lārēs). Other household gods of importance were Vesta, goddess of the hearth, the Penates, gods of the food supply, and the Genius, or guardian spirit of the head of the house. This family worship remained the most vital part of Roman religion.

There were many other gods. In course of time, as Greek influence increased, some of these were identified with the chief Greek gods: Jupiter with Zeus, Mars with Ares, etc. These gods all had their special functions: Neptune was god of the sea, Ceres was the goddess of grain, etc.

The identification of the Greek and Roman gods illustrates a common practice among the Romans, that of borrowing gods from other people. First they borrowed from their neighbors, later from people farther away. So in the course of time various religions were introduced from Egypt, Asia Minor, and Persia.

Among the Romans there was a direct connection between religion and the state. Temples were built and restored by the government, and the priests, including the **pontifex maximus,** or chief priest, were government officials.

One important feature of the official religion was the attempt to determine the will of the gods in various ways. The duty of those priests who were called augurs was to determine whether a certain important act (such as a military expedition) would be successful. This they did by watching the flight of birds. Certain movements were supposed to indicate success; others, failure. Another practice, borrowed from the Etruscans, was to sacrifice animals and examine their entrails in order to discover the will of the gods. These two methods were official and were used before important matters were undertaken. Many intelligent Romans lost faith in these practices, but kept them up in order to influence the more ignorant classes. Private persons also resorted to numerous unofficial fortunetellers, such as astrologers, as superstitious people do today.

With so many gods to worship, the Romans naturally had many holidays. Some of these were celebrated with amusements as well as religious observances, as is true of our holidays today. The amusements about which you have read (p. 234) developed in this way.

**QUESTIONS**
1. What part did family worship play in Roman life?
2. What two religious practices of the Romans seem absurd to us?
3. To what extent is astrology practiced today?
4. In what countries today is religion directly connected with the state?

**READING**
Showerman, pp. 280 ff.; Hamilton, pp. 21–51 (Mentor ed., pp. 24–45); Tappan, pp. 65–67; Johnston, pp. 395–404; Grose-Hodge, pp. 166–178.

JAMES SAWDERS

*Ceres on top of the Board of Trade, a Chicago skyscraper.*

# Unit X Review

## LESSONS LIV–LX

### ENGLISH WORD STUDIES

1. Give the Latin words suggested by the derivatives: *cordial, partial, sedentary, fraternity, inspiration, cult, generation, sorority, cursive, remiss, maternal, intercept.*

*Intercept.*

2. Find and use in sentences as many derivatives as possible from **trahō, audiō,** and **premō.**

### VOCABULARY

| NOUNS | | | |
|---|---|---|---|
| 1. aestās | 4. cor | 8. māter | 12. pater |
| 2. auctor | 5. frāter | 9. mors | 13. soror |
| 3. auctōritās | 6. genus | 10. nihil | 14. supplicium |
| | 7. hiems | 11. pars | |

| ADJECTIVES | | | |
|---|---|---|---|
| 15. alius | 18. familiāris | 22. nūllus | 26. ūllus |
| 16. alter | 19. incertus | 23. praeceps | 27. ūnus |
| 17. commūnis | 20. neuter | 24. sōlus | |
| | 21. nōbilis | 25. tōtus | |

| PRONOUNS | | | |
|---|---|---|---|
| 28. hic | 29. īdem | 31. ipse | |
| | 30. ille | 32. is | |

| VERBS | | | |
|---|---|---|---|
| 33. colō | 35. expellō | 38. remittō | 41. spīrō |
| 34. currō | 36. expugnō | 39. sedeō | 42. tangō |
| | 37. intercipiō | 40. spērō | 43. timeō |

| CONJUNCTION | |
|---|---|
| | 44. dum |

*Believe it or not, this is a model of an ancient apartment house at Ostia, near Rome, modern though it looks. A good part of the building still stands.*

## VOCABULARY (English Meanings)

NOUNS
1. *summer*
2. *author*
3. *authority*
4. *heart*
5. *brother*
6. *birth, kind*
7. *winter*
8. *mother*
9. *death*
10. *nothing*
11. *part*
12. *father*
13. *sister*
14. *punishment*

ADJECTIVES
15. *other, another*
16. *the other*
17. *common*
18. *friendly*
19. *uncertain*
20. *neither*
21. *noble*
22. *no, none*
23. *steep*
24. *alone*
25. *whole*
26. *any*
27. *one*

PRONOUNS
28. *this*
29. *same*
30. *that*
31. *-self*
32. *this, that*

VERBS
33. *till, worship*
34. *run*
35. *drive out*
36. *capture by assault*
37. *intercept*
38. *relax, send back*
39. *sit*
40. *hope*
41. *breathe*
42. *touch*
43. *fear*

CONJUNCTION 44. *while*

*Ostia in Chicago. One of its ancient columns on Chicago's lake front.*

"To market, to market, to sell a fat goose." That would seem to indicate what's going on in this sculpture found at Ostia.

The Roman emperor Constantine and his court watching a show. A sculptured relief in Constantinople (named after Constantine), now called Istanbul, Turkey.

JAMES SAWDERS

## GRAMMAR SUMMARY

**Case Uses**

|  | *In Latin* The ablative with— | *In English* The objective with— |
|---|---|---|
| PLACE | 1. Preposition **in**. | 1. Preposition *in*. |
| MEANS | 2. No preposition. | 2. Preposition *with* or *by*. |
| ACCOMPANIMENT | 3. Preposition **cum**. | 3. Preposition *with*. |
| AGENT | 4. Preposition **ab**. | 4. Preposition *by*. |
| MANNER | 5. No preposition or preposition **cum**. | 5. Preposition *with*, etc. |
| RESPECT | 6. No preposition. | 6. Preposition *in*. |
| TIME | 7. No preposition. | 7. No preposition or preposition *at, in,* or *on*. |

## UNIT PRACTICE AND EXERCISES

**Form Drill A.** Make **hic, ille,** and **īdem** agree as demonstrative adjectives with the following nouns in the case required, as follows:

**māteriae** (gen.): **huius, illīus, eiusdem māteriae**

| | | |
|---|---|---|
| aestāte | frātrēs (nom.) | patris |
| capita (nom.) | mortium | pretium (acc.) |
| cor (acc.) | partī | sorōrem |

**B.** Supply the correct form of **is** in the following sentences and translate:

1. (*Him, her, it*) vīdī.
2. (*By him, by her*) ēvocātus sum.
3. Fīlium (*his, her*) docēbō.
4. Nōvistīne (*their*) patrem?
5. Hunc librum (*to him, to her, to them*) mandābō.

**C.** Decline **nūlla māter, alius auctor.**

# Famous Romans

*"Consummation of Empire," a painting in which Thomas Cole depicted his vision of the Roman Empire at the height of its glory.*

COURTESY OF THE NEW YORK HISTORICAL SOCIETY, NEW YORK CITY

*Garden dining room in Pompeii, with built-in couches (now covered with glass as a protection). Cushions were put on top.*

*Garden scene in a house in Pompeii. The growing plants reproduce ancient species.*

# Lesson lxi

## QUĪNTUS CICERŌ ET POMPŌNIA

Pompōnius Atticus erat firmus amīcus M. Cicerōnis. Pompōnia,
soror Atticī, erat uxor Quīntī, frātris M. Cicerōnis. Sed inter Pompōniam Quīntumque nōn semper concordia erat. Ūna gravis causa
inter aliās erat haec, quod apud [1] Quīntum auctōritās Stātī [2] valēbat,
quem domō [3] expellere nūllō modō potuit. Pompōnia aliēnae auctōri- 5
tātī cēdere nōn cupīvit. Neuter alterī cēdere potuit; neuter alterum
movēre potuit. Cicerō Pompōniam accūsāvit, Atticus Quīntum.
Cicerō ad Atticum hōc modō scrīpsit:
"Frātrem meum vīdī. Tōtus sermō inter nōs dē tē et sorōre tuā
fuit. Verba eius nōn inimīca fuērunt. Tum ad Pompōniam contendi- 10
mus. Quīntus eī amīcā vōce dīxit: 'Pompōnia, tū rogā mulierēs ad
cēnam, ego puerōs rogātūrus sum.' (Hī puerī erant fīliī Cicerōnis et
frātris eius.) Sed illa, audientibus nōbīs, 'Ego ipsa sum,' inquit, 'in
hōc locō hospita.' Hoc dīxit quod īdem Stātius cēnam parārī iusserat.
Tum Quīntus, 'Audīsne?' inquit mihi, 'haec semper sustinēre cōgor.' 15
Dīcēs: 'Haec vōx nihil est.' Sed magnum [4] est; verbīs dūrīs atque animō
aliēnō eius oppressus et commōtus sum. Ad cēnam illa nōn adfuit;
Quīntus ad eam sedentem sōlam cibum mīsit; illa remīsit. Grave
vulnus Quīntus accēpit neque ipse ūllam iniūriam fēcit. Cupiēns eam
plācāre nōn potuit. Gravibus cūrīs opprimor. Quid factūrī sumus? 20
Contendere dēbēmus inter sorōrem tuam et frātrem meum pācem
efficere."

QUESTIONS    1. Who was Atticus' brother-in-law?
                 2. Of whom was Pomponia jealous?

### Present Participle

In English, the *present active participle* ends in *–ing: I saw your
brother reading a book.* In Latin, it is formed by adding *–ns* to the
present stem. It is declined like a third declension adjective of one
ending (cf. **pār**, p. 252), with the base ending in *–nt–*: **portāns,
portantis.** For full declension see p. 394.

*Note.* 1. The ablative singular ending is regularly *–e*, but *–ī* is used
whenever the participle is used simply as an adjective. 2. In verbs of the
fourth conjugation, and *–iō* verbs of the third, *–ie–* appears throughout,

---

[1] *with.*      [2] *Statius* (*Stā'shius*), a freedman of Quintus.

[3] *from the house.*
[4] *it is a serious thing.*

*The Shedd Aquarium in Chicago is in the plain Doric style.*

JAMES SAWDERS

forming the base –ient–, as **audiēns, audientis; capiēns, capientis**. 3. **Sum** has no present participle in common use; that of **possum** is **potēns**.

The present participle modifies a noun or pronoun. Like the present infinitive, it represents an act as happening at the time indicated by the main verb.

The present participle cannot be used with the verb **sum** to form a progressive tense, as is done in English with *be* (p. 136). Latin has no present passive participle.

### Future Active Participle

Latin, unlike English, has a future active participle, as we have already seen in the principal parts of some verbs. In most verbs it is formed by dropping the –us of the perfect participle and adding –ūrus: **portātūrus**, *going to carry*; **factūrus**, *going to make*. It is declined like **magnus**. Note that we have to use a phrase to translate it. It is often used with the verb **sum**.

**Practice**   Form and translate the participles of **nāvigō, obtineō**, and **prōdūcō** in the present and future.

**Exercises   A.** 1.  Rōmānīs tardē prōcēdentibus, barbarī fūgērunt.
2.  Duo puerī pugnantēs ā magistrō captī sunt.
3.  Hieme nūllōs agricolās in agrīs labōrantēs vidēmus.

4. Cūr in hōc locō sine frātribus tuīs remānsūrus es?
5. Hī puerī, suppliciō gravī affectī, ā magistrō expulsī sunt.
6. Vōcēs amīcōrum rogantium auxilium ā nōbīs audītae sunt.
7. Oppressī in aliēnō locō, hostēs cum impedīmentīs ad montēs contentūrī sunt.

**B.** (*Instead of clauses, use participles wherever possible.*)
1. The arms given to the other soldiers are heavy.
2. The number of (those) approaching is not large.
3. He was going to fold the letter which he had written.
4. He was accused by you (while he was) defending the public cause.

**Vocabulary**
aliē'nus, –a, –um, *another's, unfavorable* [*alius*]
conten'dō, –ere, –ten'dī, –tentū'rus, *struggle, hasten* [*tendō*]
gra'vis, –e, *heavy, severe* (gravitation)
op'primō, –ere, oppres'sī, oppres'sus, *overcome, surprise* [*premō*]
ro'gō, –ā're, –ā'vī, –ā'tus, *ask* (interrogative)
vōx, vō'cis, f., *voice, remark* [*vocō*]

### English Word Studies

1. What is a *neutral*? An *alien*? What is meant by the statement in the Declaration of Independence "that all men . . . are endowed by their Creator with certain *unalienable* [usually misquoted *inalienable*] rights; that among these are life, liberty, and the pursuit of happiness"?

2. Latin phrases in English:

inter alia, *among other things.*
ipso facto, *by the fact itself, thereby.*
in loco parentis, *in place of a parent.*
una voce, *with one voice, unanimously.*
**Vox populi vox Dei,** *The voice of the people (is) the voice of God.*
obiter dictum, *(something) said by the way* (**ob iter**), *incidentally.*
**Timeo Danaos et dona ferentes,** *I fear the Greeks even when they bring gifts* (Virgil). For the events that led to this remark see page 77.
Explain **in toto, vox humana.**

*Seal of Hunter College, New York, with Latin motto and head of Minerva. Explain the motto.*

*Insignia of the Order of the Cincinnati (p. 305). At the left, three senators present a
sword to Cincinnatus; at the right, he returns to his plow.*

# *Lesson lxii*

## CINCINNĀTUS

Hostēs Minucium,[1] ducem Rōmānum, et mīlitēs eius in locō aliēnō
magnā vī premēbant. Ubi id nūntiātum est, omnēs Rōmānī timentēs
vim hostium cupīvērunt Cincinnātum [2] dictātōrem facere, quod is
sōlus Rōmam ā perīculō nōn levī prohibēre et cīvitātem servāre
5 poterat. Ille trāns Tiberim eō tempore agrum parvum colēbat. Nūntiī
missī eum in agrō labōrantem invēnērunt et cōnstitērunt. Salūte [3]
datā acceptāque, Cincinnātus uxōrem parāre togam iussisse dīcitur;
nam nōn oportēbat [4] sine togā nūntiōs audīre.

Hī nūntiī eum dictātōrem appellant et dīcunt: "Mīlitēs nostrī ab
10 hostibus premuntur et cīvēs terrentur. Perīculum nostrum nōn leve
est. Hostēs nōn cōnsistent sed mox ad portās nostrās ipsās venient.
Auxilium tuum rogāmus." Itaque Cincinnātus, vōcibus eōrum adductus, contrā hostēs contendit. Rōmānī, tēlīs iactīs, hostēs opprī-
munt et castra expugnant. Minuciō servātō, Cincinnātus dīcitur
15 hostēs sub iugum [5] mīsisse. Tum, nūllīs hostibus prohibentibus,
mīlitēs ad urbem redūxit et triumphāvit. Ductī sunt in pompā ante

---

[1] *Minucius (Minū'shius).*
[2] *Cincinnātus (Sinsinā'tus).*
[3] *greeting.*

[4] *it was not proper.*
[5] *under the yoke,* i.e., an arch of
spears. This act signified surrender.

eum ducēs hostium, capta arma ostenta sunt; post eum mīlitēs vēnē- runt praedam gravem portantēs. Et haec omnia Cincinnātus magnā celeritāte gessit: dictātūrā in [6] sex mēnsēs acceptā, sextō decimō diē [7] ad agrōs discessit, nōn iam dictātor sed triumphāns agricola. Eōdem 20 mēnse agricola et dictātor et iterum agricola fuit.

**QUESTIONS**   1. Where was Cincinnatus' farm?
2. Who was with him when the messengers came?
3. How long did he stay away from his farm?

**READING**   Mills, pp. 77–79.

## Perfect Active Infinitive

The *perfect active infinitive* is formed by adding –isse to the perfect stem: **portāvisse**, *to have carried*; **docuisse**, etc. It represents an act as having happened before the time indicated by the main verb.

---

[6] *for.*                              [7] *sixteenth day.*

*The capitol of North Carolina at Raleigh, built in 1831–33, with Doric columns and Roman dome.*

WAYNE ANDREWS

*Prisoners being brought to a Roman camp.*

*Review* infinitive used as subject and object (pp. 89, 90); infinitive with subject in the accusative as in English (p. 166).

**Practice**  Form the perfect active infinitive of **dīmittō, intercipiō, videō, expediō.**

**Exercises A.** 1. Ostendite omnibus bonum exemplum.
2. Vim prohibēre et pācem cōnservāre est nōbile.
3. Rēgis fīlia librum scrīpsisse sine auxiliō dīcitur.
4. Quis dīxit: "Dā mihi lībertātem aut dā mihi mortem"?
5. Rōmānī paucās nāvēs ad Britanniam mīsisse dīcuntur.
6. Mīlitēs cōnsistentēs arma levia cum magnā vī iēcisse dīcuntur.
7. Homō malus mē cōnsistere iussit et omnem meam pecūniam dare.

**B.** 1. We cannot breathe under water.
2. I saw your father folding a letter.
3. That king is said to have tilled the fields himself.
4. Those men are said to have come together in a strange land.

**Vocabulary**

cōnsis'tō, –ere, cōn'stitī, cōnstitū'rus, *stand still, stop* [*stō*]
dī'cō, –ere, dī'xī, dic'tus,[8] *say, tell* (diction)
ia'ciō, –ere, iē'cī, iac'tus, *throw* (projectile)
le'vis, –e, *light* (in weight) (levity)
*mēn'sis, mēn'sis, mēn'sium, m., *month* (semester)
osten'dō, –ere, osten'dī, osten'tus, (*stretch out*), *show*
[*tendō*]
prohi'beō, –ē're, –hi'buī, –hi'bitus, *prevent, keep from*
[*habeō*]
*vīs, — [9], f., *force, violence*; plur. vī'rēs, vī'rium, *strength*
(vim)

## Latin and English Word Studies

1. The suffix **–or** is added to the stem of the past participle and therefore is preceded by **t** or **s**; it indicates the doer of an action: **monitor** (*one who warns*), **scrīptor** (*one who writes*), **inventor** (*one who finds*). It is used in English in the same way.

A different suffix **–or** is added to the present base of a verb; it usually indicates a state of being or condition: **timor, amor, terror.** It is used in English.

Find five English words which are formed by adding one of these **–or** suffixes to the stems of verbs that you have studied. Explain *eject, injection, reject, ostentation, prohibition.*

*Eject.*

2. The city of *Cincinnati* was named from the Society of the Cincinnati, formed by army officers at the end of the Revolutionary War. Why do you suppose the Society took that name? What does its motto mean: **Omnia reliquit servare rem publicam?** There is also a town named *Cincinnatus* (N.Y.).

---

[8] The imperative singular is **dīc.**

[9] Genitive and dative singular rarely found (see p. 393).

*Horace's famous line on the entrance gate of Arlington National Cemetery, Arlington, Va., near Washington, where many illustrious heroes are buried.*

# Lesson lxiii

## BELLA

Quae sunt causae bellī? Variī auctōrēs ostendērunt multās esse causās. Multa bella ob iniūriās gesta esse vidēmus. Haec bella iūsta fuērunt. Multī populī pugnant quod putant auctōritātem imperiumque vī bellōque augērī posse. Hī cupiunt patriam esse nūllī secundam.
5 Sī superantur, omnia saepe āmittunt; sī superant, aliēnās terrās occupant, quās in fōrmam prōvinciārum redigunt. Putāsne bella huius generis iūsta esse? Multī dīcunt omnia bella iūsta esse, aliī putant nūlla esse iūsta. Quid dē hōc putās? Possuntne bella prohibērī? Nōvimus aliōs prō lībertāte, aliōs prō glōriā bella gessisse. Quae
10 fuērunt causae bellōrum Americānōrum?

Horātius,[1] poēta Rōmānus, scrībit dulce esse prō patriā vītam āmittere. Sī patria in perīculō est, nōnne putās mūnus nostrum esse eam dēfendere? Scīmus nōn levēs esse labōrēs mīlitum, gravia eōs

---

[1] *Horace.* The exact words of his famous phrase are: **Dulce et decōrum est prō patriā morī.**

accipere vulnera, multōs ad mortem mittī; etiam scīmus eōs nōn
dubitāre omnēs labōrēs prō patriā grātō animō suscipere et sustinēre. 15
Prō hīs mūneribus praemia aequa eīs solvere nōn possumus. Sed
praemia nōn exspectant; spērant cīvēs facta sua memoriā tentūrōs
esse et aliōs semper parātōs futūrōs esse patriam dēfendere. Hōc
modō praemia solvere possumus.

Bellane ūllō tempore cōnstitūra sunt? Quis scit? Sed spērāmus 20
parvō spatiō temporis nōn iam bella futūra esse; spērāmus omnēs
hominēs aliōrum iūra cōnservātūrōs esse. Tum bella nōn iam erunt,
et sine bellīs pāx perpetua et amīcitia cōnfirmābuntur.

QUESTIONS  1. Which wars were just?
2. What do soldiers hope for?
3. What are your answers to the questions asked in the text?

## Perfect Passive and Future Active Infinitive

1. The *perfect passive infinitive* is a compound tense, formed by
using the perfect participle with the present infinitive **esse: portātus
esse,** *to have been carried;* **doctus esse** (cf. perfect passive indicative:
**portātus sum**).

2. The *future active infinitive* is a compound tense, formed by
using the future active participle with the present infinitive **esse:
portātūrus esse,** *to be going to carry;* **doctūrus esse.**

In both tenses the participle agrees with the subject of **esse:
Spērō eam haec factūram esse,** *I hope that she will do these things.*

3. There was no future passive infinitive in common use in Latin.

*Learn* the infinitives, active and passive, of the model verbs
(pp. 396–400) and **sum** (p. 401).

Practice  Form and translate the infinitives, active and passive,
of **iaciō, solvō,** and **prohibeō.**

## Infinitive with Verbs of Saying, etc.

In English, after verbs of *saying, thinking, knowing, hearing,*
etc., if the words are not quoted directly, we use a clause often introduced by *that: He says (that) the boys are coming.* But sometimes
we use the infinitive: *The boys are said to be coming; I know him to
be a good man; I heard him say this; I believe this to be true.*

In Latin, the infinitive is *always* used with such words: **Dīcit
puerōs venīre.** Note that **puerōs** is in the accusative because it is the
subject of an infinitive (p. 166). No introductory word is used.

### Direct and Indirect Statement

1. **Dīxit, "Puerī veniunt,"** *He said, "The boys are coming."*
2. **Dīxit puerōs venīre,** *He said that the boys were coming.*

In the first sentence the exact words of the speaker are given, as shown by the use of quotation marks. Such a sentence is called a *direct statement*. In the second sentence the exact words are not given. Such a sentence is called an *indirect statement*. Indirect statements, with verbs in the infinitive and their subjects in the accusative, are used as objects of verbs of *saying, thinking, knowing, hearing,* etc.

*Who* or *Whom?* Explain how a knowledge of indirect statement in Latin will enable one to use *who* and *whom* correctly, as follows:

1. *Mr. Smith is a man **who**, I believe, **is** honest.*
2. *Mr. Smith is a man **whom** I believe **to be** honest.*

**Exercises  A.** 1. Dīcunt, "Cīvis iūstus lībertātem amat."
2. Cīvis iūstus lībertātem amāre dīcitur.
3. Dīcunt cīvem iūstum lībertātem amāre.
4. Putāmus nostra mūnera futūra esse levia.
5. Nōs omnēs scīmus in spatiō vītae esse cūrās et labōrēs.
6. Putāsne hunc pecūniam dēbitam solvisse aut solūtūrum esse?
7. Putō pecūniam ab illō nōn solūtam esse.
8. Putō, Mārce, illum hominem futūrum esse prīmum aut secundum ōrdine.

*The tomb of Augustus as it once was. Augustus (emperor from 27 B.C. to 14 A.D.) was responsible for the pax Romana, which lasted two centuries. How many wars have we had since 1776?*

**B.** Translate the words in italics:
1. I know *him to be* wise.
2. I know the *signal was given.*
3. I believe the *men have been led across* the river.
4. They say the *wagon was drawn* by mules.
5. I hear that your *sister will live* in Detroit.

**C.** 1. Galba said, "My father is a soldier."
2. We all know that his father is brave.
3. I think that Galba himself will be a soldier.
4. I hear that Galba's brother was a sailor and was not scared by the sea.
5. He himself said, "I am going to be a soldier, for my father is a soldier."

**Vocabulary**

| | | |
|---|---|---|
| iūs′tus, –a, –um, *just* | | *[iūs]* |
| la′bor, labō′ris, m., *work, hardship* | | *[labōrō]* |
| mū′nus, mū′neris, n., *duty, service, gift* | | (munificent) |
| pu′tō, –ā′re, –ā′vī, –ā′tus, *think* | | (reputation) |
| sci′ō, scī′re, scī′vī, scī′tus, *know* | | (science) |
| secun′dus –a, –um, *second* | | (secondary) |
| sol′vō, –ere, sol′vī, solū′tus, *loosen, pay* | | (solution) |

*Italian stamp issued for Horace's two-thousandth birthday (1935) quotes his line on patriotism.*

LIRE **POSTE ITALIANE**
2,55 DVLCE ET DECORVM EST PRO PATRIA MORI
+1,00
BIMILLENARIO ORAZIANO

**English Word Studies: Spelling**

The base of the Latin present participle is **–ant, –ent,** or **–ient,** according to the conjugation (p. 299). This is used as a suffix in English, with the same meaning as the participial ending *–ing.*

A common mistake in the spelling of English words is due to the confusion of *–ant* and *–ent.* Reference to the Latin helps:

1. All English words derived from the first conjugation follow the Latin spelling with an *–a–*: *expectant, emigrant.*
2. Most English words that are derived from the other conjugations follow the Latin spelling with an *–e–*: *regent, agent, efficient, expedient.*
3. But some words have an *–a–*: *tenant, defendant.*

Give eight English words with suffix *–ant* or *–ent* derived from Latin words previously studied. Explain *laboratory, omniscient, solvent, absolve, remunerate.*

**309**

*Shakespeare's Coriolanus as presented at the Phoenix theater in New York in 1954.
Here Coriolanus' mother is pleading with him.*

## Lesson lxiv

### CORIOLĀNUS

Mārcius, nōbilis Rōmānus, Coriolōs,[1] oppidum Volscōrum,[2] ex-
pugnāverat. Ob hoc mūnus "Coriolānus" appellātus est.

Post bellum ob variās causās plēbs īrā ācrī permōta Coriolānum
accūsāvit, clāmāns eum esse hostem. Coriolānus, perīculum īnstāre
5 sentiēns, fūgit ad Volscōs quōs ipse superāverat. Volscī dīcuntur eum
benignē [3] accēpisse, nam sēnsērunt eum esse ducem fortem ac iūstum
et Rōmam nōn iam amāre. Etiam spērāvērunt eum contrā Rōmānōs
pugnātūrum esse.

---

[1] *Corï'olī.*     [2] *Volsci (Vol'sī).*     [3] *kindly.*

Mox Coriolānus, dux ā Volscīs lēctus, ad urbem Rōmam contendit, omnia in itinere vāstāns. Rōmānī, castrīs eius ad urbem 10 positīs, bellō īnstantī territī sunt. Lēgātī dē pāce ad Coriolānum missī sunt sed ubi pervēnērunt ab eō remissī sunt. "Mātrem eius ad eum mittēmus," putāvērunt Rōmānī; "sī cūra urbis cor eius nōn tanget, amōre mātris ille certē tangētur, et fīnem labōrum nostrōrum inveniēmus." Itaque māter et uxor Coriolānī cum duōbus parvīs fīliīs 15 ad castra hostium pervēnērunt.

Coriolānus, verbīs ācribus mātris permōtus et lacrimīs omnium tāctus, dīcitur clāmāvisse: "Quid fēcistī, māter? Tū sōla Rōmam servāvistī sed mē vīcistī." Tum iussit Volscōs discēdere. Rōma lacrimīs, nōn armīs servāta erat. Coriolānī facta semper in memoriā 20 omnium haerēbunt.

QUESTIONS   1. How did Coriolanus get his name?
               2. Where did he go when exiled?
               3. Why did he spare Rome?

READING    Mills, pp. 74–77.

*Doric porch on the D'Evereux mansion built in Natchez, Miss., in 1840.*

### How Indicative and Infinitive Differ in Tense

1. *It was thought that he was present.*
2. *He was thought to be present.*

In the first sentence, the verb in the subordinate clause is in the past indicative. In the second sentence, the infinitive *to be* refers to the same time but is in the present tense. The tenses of the indicative are determined by their *relation to present time,* but the tenses of the infinitive are determined by their *relation to the verbs on which they depend.* This is true in Latin as in English; remember it in translating a Latin infinitive into an English "that" clause.

Why is it wrong to say: "I would have liked to have seen"?

### How the Tenses of the Infinitive Differ

1. The present infinitive represents time or action as *going on,* from the standpoint of the introductory verb:

**Dīcit** ⎫ eōs vocāre, *He* { *says* / *said* } *(that) they* { *are* / *were* } *calling.*
**Dīxit** ⎭

(Change **vocāre** to **vocārī** and translate.)

2. The future infinitive represents an act that will occur *later,* from the standpoint of the introductory verb:

**Dīcit** ⎫ eōs vocātūrōs esse, *He* { *says* / *said* } *(that) they* { *will* / *would* } *call.*
**Dīxit** ⎭

3. The perfect infinitive represents time or action as *completed before* that of the introductory verb:

**Dīcit** ⎫ eōs vocāvisse, *He* { *says* / *said* } *(that) they* { *have* / *had* } *called.*
**Dīxit** ⎭

(Change **vocāvisse** to **vocātōs esse** and translate.)

*Note* that the participle in the compound forms of the infinitive must agree with its subject (see 2 above).

**Exercises** **A.** 1. Omnēs sēnsimus perīculum īnstāre.
    2. Puer nōn clāmāre potuit, quod vōx haesit.
    3. Quis dīxit socium meum sine frātre pervēnisse?
    4. Servī spērāvērunt labōrem futūrum esse facilem.
    5. Omnēs puerī certē sciunt Columbum ad Americam pervēnisse.
    6. Rōmānī dīcēbant Caesarem esse fortem ducem nec superātum esse.

7. (*a*) Omnēs scīmus puerōs Americānōs esse ācrēs et fortēs. (*b*) *Substitute* scīvimus *for* scīmus *in* (*a*) *and translate.*

**B.** Translate the words which are in italics:
1. He knew *me to be* his friend.
2. He knew that *I was working* hard.
3. We saw that *we would* not *arrive* in time.
4. He said that his *son was being taught* by new methods.
5. We hear that your *father has been sent* to Europe on a secret mission.

**C.** 1. Who said that we would not come?
2. We can prove that our cause is just.
3. My mother wrote that the islands were beautiful.
4. The boy thought that (his) father had been saved.
5. The general says that the soldiers of the provinces were brave.

*Italian stamp honoring Horace's two-thousandth birthday (cf. p. 309). The quotation from his Odes welcomes the return of spring: the snow disappears, the grass returns to the fields, the leaves to the trees. This poem was a favorite of Thomas Jefferson's.*

**Vocabulary**

ā′cer, ā′cris, ā′cre,[4] *sharp, keen* (acid)
hae′reō, –ē′re, hae′sī, hae′sus, *stick* (adhesive)
īn′stō, –ā′re, īn′stitī, ——, *threaten* [*stō*]
perve′niō, –ī′re, –vē′nī, –ventū′rus, (*come through*), *arrive* [*veniō*]
sen′tiō, –ī′re, sēn′sī, sēn′sus, *feel, realize* (sense)
sī, conj., *if*

**English Word Studies**

By addition of the suffix –**ia** (p. 164) to the base of the present participle, a suffix –**antia** or –**entia** is formed which becomes –*ance*, –*ence*, –*ancy*, or –*ency* in English (cf. the change of –*tia* to –*ce* [p. 167]: **scientia**, *science*). The difficulty in spelling is again removed by reference to the Latin (cf. p. 309).

Give eight English nouns with this suffix derived from Latin words previously studied. Explain *coherence, sensitive, consensus, intangible, dissension, inherent.*

---

[4] Cf. p. 252, footnote 9.

*The Vestal Virgins perform their rites in preparation for a sacrifice. From "Quo Vadis."*

# Lesson lxv

## The Story of Lucius (*Cont.*)

### VIRGINĒS VESTĀLĒS

Etiam cīvitās focum Vestae habuit. Templum Vestae in Forō urbis Rōmae stābat. Ibi sex puellae, Virginēs Vestālēs appellātae, ignem perpetuum Vestae semper servābant. Magna erat glōria Vestālium, et maximē ā populō Rōmānō amābantur. Eīs in viīs urbis 5 vīsīs, omnēs cōnstitērunt atque dē viā cessērunt. Facile erat eās cognōscere, quod omnēs semper albās vestēs gessērunt, neque ūlla alia mulier vestem eiusdem generis gessit. In Circō loca ēgregia eīs dabantur. Sed dūrum fuit supplicium Vestālis quae mala fuit: ea vīva sub terrā posita est.

Iūlia, soror Lūcī, Vestālis erat et multa dē vītā Vestālium dīcēbat. 10
Cum reliquīs Vestālibus in Ātriō[1] Vestae ad templum habitāvit sed
saepe patrem et mātrem et frātrēs vidēbat. Dīxit vītam Vestālium
grātam esse sed labōrem numquam facilem esse: eās omnia magnā
cūrā dīligentiāque facere cōgī. Dīxit Vestālēs ligna[2] in focō eōdem
modō semper pōnere et omnia certīs hōrīs in ōrdine facere. Itaque 15
spatium disciplīnae longum erat. Puellae sex annōrum, ā patribus
mātribusque Vestae datae, prīmōs decem annōs discipulae ēgērunt,
tum decem annōs in officiīs ēgērunt et posteā parvās puellās docuērunt. Tamen post trīgintā annōs lībertās eīs data est et eae ad
amīcōs familiāsque redīre[3] potuērunt, sed multae in Ātriō Vestae 20
mānsērunt. Sex sōlae Vestālēs in Ātriō ūnō tempore habitāvērunt.

[1] *ā'trium, house.*      [2] *wood.*      [3] Infinitive of **red-eō**, *go back.*

*Courtyard of the home of the Vestal Virgins in the Roman Forum, near the Temple of
Vesta. On the side are the statues of the chief Vestals (cf. p. 5). At the left, the tall
Basilica of Maxentius, now often used for outdoor symphony concerts; at the right,
a church built into the Temple of Venus and Rome.*

JAMES SAWDERS

# MISFORTUNE

Quondam Iūlia, aquam sacram portāns, vīdit aliam Vestālem ante portam sedentem lacrimantemque et ad eam cucurrit. Causā petītā, illa respondet, vōce haerente: "Sīvī [4] ignem sacrum exstinguī; labōre 25 cōnfecta, somnō oppressa sum." Iūlia, corde malā fortūnā amīcae tāctō, tamen illī nūllum cōnsilium dare potuit. Itaque illa pontificī omnia dīxit, et hic eam verberāvit—nihil aliud facere potuit, quod ita lēgēs iussērunt.

## RIGHT OR WRONG

Hōc audītō, Lūcius ācrī vōce respondit illam miseram nōn me-30 rēre ob lassitūdinem poenā afficī et ōtium habēre dēbēre, sed eius soror, Iūlia, quae aliam sententiam habuit, respondit: "Etiam amīca mea ipsa quae verberāta est sentit supplicium aequum fuisse. Mūnera nostra gravia sunt. Sī multā cūrā mūnera nōn efficiēmus, perīculum grave īnstābit. Itaque poena neglegentiae ācris esse dēbet. Sī ego 35 ignem exstinguī sinam [5] (quod spērō numquam futūrum esse), gravem poenam, etiam mortis, solvere dēbēbō."

**QUESTIONS**
1. How would you explain the origin of the custom of keeping the sacred fire burning?
2. How many Vestals were there, including those in training?

**READING**  If you want to know more about the Vestals, read the fascinating novel, *The Unwilling Vestal*, by Edward Lucas White.

**Vocabulary**  num′quam, adv., *never*
respon′deō, –ē′re, respon′dī, respōn′sus, *answer* (response)
ta′men, adv., *nevertheless*
*urbs, ur′bis, ur′bium, f., *city*  (suburban)

## English Word Studies

1. What is an *urban* community? What are the *suburbs* of a city? What is meant by an *urbane* person? What is a *correspondent*? Explain the difference between *adhesion* and *cohesion*.

2. *Vesta* as the name of a firm is found in the telephone directories of Atlanta, Cincinnati, Houston, etc. Why is it suitable for the name of a battery?

---

[4] *I let.*  [5] From sinō: *I let.*

*Spareribs for the lady's dinner. A de luxe Roman butcher shop, with easy chair and footstool. The customer is watching the butcher closely. Cleaver and chopping block look very modern. From a sculptured relief in Dresden.*

# ꙮ Glimpses of Roman Life

## HOW THE ROMAN MADE HIS LIVING

In early days nearly every Roman was a farmer and even later farming remained the chief occupation of the Romans, as it once was of Americans. It is not surprising therefore that Cincinnatus left his plow to lead the Romans in war and on its successful completion returned to his farm. In the early days many a war was won by the "embattled farmers." Nor is it surprising that farming was considered the foundation of Roman life, as it is of American life, and that the Roman character, like ours, was largely determined by it.

At first farms were small and were worked by the owner and his family. The increased use of slave labor led to increase in the size of farms and to a change in the attitude toward farming.

Industry was not so highly developed among the Romans as among us. There were no large factories. Much of the work was done by hand either at home or in small shops. The spinning of thread and its weaving into cloth were often done at home. Even the Emperor Augustus wore clothing made by slaves under his wife's direction. There were carpenters, workers in metal, masons and bricklayers, makers of tools, wagonmakers, brickmakers, and so on. There were no huge factories for the manufacture of automobiles, telephones, railroad equipment, and hundreds of other articles because they had not been invented. The making of bricks and pottery came nearest to being industry in the modern sense.

*Believe it or not, this is an ancient Roman scene in spite of the very modern wicker chair.*

The free workers were members of what may be called unions, whose chief purposes were to bring the members together for good fellowship and to provide burials for the members who died. Many slaves, too, came to be employed in industry.

The shops were very small—there were no department stores or chain stores. Usually a small room at the front of a private residence was used as a shop. The wares were often displayed outside. Sometimes the shopkeepers cluttered up the sidewalks and streets so much that traffic was interfered with until some strict official prevented this practice—even as today.

Such were the occupations of the poorer classes. Rich men invested their money in wholesale trade, real estate, loans, government contracts, and foreign trade. The professions, with the exception of law and public life, were not well developed. Doctors and teachers were usually slaves or freedmen, i.e., former slaves. Law and politics were largely reserved for the upper classes.

**DISCUSSION**
**QUESTIONS**

1. What are the chief professions today?
2. What percentage of our people today are engaged in farming? In industry?
3. Have you seen goods displayed on sidewalks? Is this permitted by law?

**READING**

Showerman, pp. 225–252; Johnston, pp. 328–355; Grose-Hodge, pp. 206–219.

# Unit XI Review

## LESSONS LXI–LXV

### ENGLISH WORD STUDIES

1. Explain the following and give the Latin words from which they are derived: *omnipotent, alienate, vocal, expulsive, oppressive, diction, ostensible, prohibit.*

2. Find and use in sentences as many English derivatives as possible from **dīcō** and **putō**.

3. The first word in each of the following lines is a Latin word. From among the last five words in each line pick the one which is an English derivative of the first word.

| | | | | | |
|---|---|---|---|---|---|
| **scit** | skit | sky | sigh | scientific | sit |
| **tangō** | tangerine | tang | intangible | tango | tactics |
| **putātus** | putty | put | repute | potato | pot |
| **dīcere** | contradict | dixie | dice | decree | decent |
| **gravia** | graft | graveyard | gravity | engrave | gray |

### VOCABULARY

|  |  |  |  |
|---|---|---|---|
| NOUNS | 2. **mēnsis** | 4. **urbs** | 6. **vōx** |
| 1. **labor** | 3. **mūnus** | 5. **vīs** | |

|  |  |  |  |
|---|---|---|---|
| ADJECTIVES | 8. **aliēnus** | 10. **iūstus** | 12. **secundus** |
| 7. **ācer** | 9. **gravis** | 11. **levis** | |

|  |  |  |  |
|---|---|---|---|
| VERBS | 17. **iaciō** | 22. **prohibeō** | 27. **sentiō** |
| 13. **cōnsistō** | 18. **īnstō** | 23. **putō** | 28. **solvō** |
| 14. **contendō** | 19. **opprimō** | 24. **respondeō** | |
| 15. **dīcō** | 20. **ostendō** | 25. **rogō** | |
| 16. **haereō** | 21. **perveniō** | 26. **sciō** | |

|  |  |  |
|---|---|---|
| ADVERBS | 29. **numquam** | 30. **tamen** |

CONJUNCTION  31. **sī**

*Greenwood Plantation, a home in the classical style at St. Francisville, La., built in 1830.*

## VOCABULARY (English Meanings)

| NOUNS | | | |
|---|---|---|---|
| 1. *work* | 2. *month* | 4. *city* | 6. *voice* |
| | 3. *duty, service* | 5. *force* | |

| ADJECTIVES | | | |
|---|---|---|---|
| 7. *sharp, keen* | 8. *another's* | 10. *just* | 12. *second* |
| | 9. *heavy, severe* | 11. *light* | |

| VERBS | | | |
|---|---|---|---|
| 13. *stop* | 17. *throw* | 22. *prevent* | 27. *feel, realize* |
| 14. *struggle, hasten* | 18. *threaten* | 23. *think* | 28. *loosen, pay* |
| 15. *say, tell* | 19. *overcome* | 24. *answer* | |
| 16. *stick* | 20. *show* | 25. *ask* | |
| | 21. *arrive* | 26. *know* | |

| ADVERBS | | |
|---|---|---|
| | 29. *never* | 30. *nevertheless* |

| CONJUNCTION | |
|---|---|
| | 31. *if* |

320

*The Bank of England in London wears a Roman dress.*

*Pennsylvania Station, New York, resembles the ancient baths of Caracalla shown on page 236.*

## GRAMMAR SUMMARIES
### Participles

<table>
<tr><td>In Latin</td><td>In English</td></tr>
</table>

| *In Latin* | *In English* |
|---|---|
| 1. Present active (**portāns**). | 1. Present (*carrying*). |
| 2. No present passive. | 2. Present passive (*being carried*). |
| 3. No perfect active. | 3. Past active (*having carried*). |
| 4. Perfect passive (**portātus**). | 4. Past passive (*having been carried*). |
| 5. Future active (**portātūrus**). | 5. No future active. |

### Indirect Statement

| *In Latin* | *In English* |
|---|---|
| 1. No conjunction is used. | 1. "That" is frequently used. |
| 2. The subject is in the accusative. | 2. The subject is in the nominative. |
| 3. The verb is in the infinitive. | 3. The verb is in the indicative. |

## UNIT PRACTICE AND EXERCISES

**Form Drill**
1. Decline **vōx ipsa, nūllus pēs.**
2. Give in all tenses the third plural active of **timeō;** the third singular passive of **remittō.**
3. Form the participles, active and passive, of **regō, iaciō, sciō,** and **respondeō.**
4. Form the infinitives, active and passive, of **sentiō, intercipiō, ostendō,** and **mōnstrō.**

**Exercises   A.** Translate the words in italics. Be careful to make the participle agree with its noun in gender, number, and case:
1. *Running* water is usually fresh.
2. We saw the boys *dragging* a big sled.
3. They heard the sound of men *approaching*.
4. Are they *going to remain*?
5. She was *going to say* something.
6. He forgot to mail the letter *after he had folded* it.
7. *When he had heard these words,* he felt encouraged.

**B.** Complete in Latin these indirect statements and translate:
1. Sciō (*the boys read*) librōs.
2. Spērō (*the boys will read*) librōs.
3. Putō (*the boys have read*) librōs.
4. Dīxit (*the books were being read*) ā puerīs.
5. Dīxit (*the books had been read*) ā puerīs.

# UNIT XII

# *More Myth and History*

Note the books, writing materials, costumes, and wall decoration in this scene from
"The Robe."

20TH CENTURY-FOX

*The Roman aqueduct in Segovia, Spain. The white stripes in the street are caused by the sun shining through the arches. Spain became Roman very early (see map, p. 104).*

*The Roman theater at Mérida, Spain. Look at the map (p. 104) and pick out the countries which are represented by Roman ruins illustrated in this book.*

# Lesson lxvi

## QUATTUOR AETĀTĒS

Antīquī dīxērunt prīmam aetātem esse auream. Sāturnus erat rēx deōrum hominumque. Illō tempore poenae lēgēsque aberant, quod omnēs hominēs iūstī erant. Nūllae nāvēs in marī erant, nec trāns mare lātum hominēs nāvigābant. Bellum numquam erat nec mīlitēs et arma. In ōtiō vītam hominēs agēbant, nam omnēs terrae concordiā 5 et pāce ligātae sunt. Hominēs in agrīs nōn labōrābant; terra nōn culta ipsa frūmentum et omnia ūtilia dabat. Urbēs nōn erant. Neque hiems neque aestās erat: semper erat vēr. Flūmina lactis[1] et vīnī erant. Quod omnēs agrī commūnēs erant, terminī agrōrum nōn erant. Aliēnōs agrōs hominēs nōn cupiēbant. 10

Sāturnō expulsō, Iuppiter rēx erat. Nunc incipit secunda aetās, quae ex argentō est, dūrior quam prīma, grātior tamen quam tertia. Tum aestās et hiems esse incipiunt; quattuor sunt spatia annī. Tum prīmum in agrīs labōrāre hominēs incipiunt.

Tertia aetās ex aere[2] erat. Dūrior erat quam secunda. 15

Quārta aetās, quae ex ferrō est, dūrissima omnium est. Poenae gravissimae statuuntur, sed hominēs interficiunt et rapiunt. Nautae in omnī marī ad ultima loca nāvigant et ūtilia petunt quae in variīs terrīs continentur. Bellīs numquam intermissīs, hominēs terrās aliēnās vincere mātūrant. Nihil sacrum est; omnia rapiuntur. Hominēs in 20 agrīs labōrant; nam labor omnia vincit.

Haec dīcunt auctōrēs clārissimī Rōmānī dē quattuor aetātibus. Vergilius[3] putābat iterum aetātem auream futūram esse. Etiam nunc multī putant vītam semper grātiōrem futūram esse. Putātisne condiciōnem fortūnamque populī Rōmānī meliōrem[4] fuisse quam condi- 25 ciōnem nostram? Quō modō statuistis hanc sententiam vēriōrem esse? Quae erit condiciō hominum post mīlle annōs? Quis hoc prōvidēre potest? Aliī dīcunt: "Tempora mūtantur, et nōs mūtāmur in illīs." Aliī respondent hominēs semper eōsdem fuisse et futūrōs esse. Quae est sententia vestra? Possuntne fortasse ambae[5] sententiae vērae 30 esse?

---

[1] of milk.    [2] of bronze.    [3] Virgil.    [4] better.    [5] both.

1. Why did not men work in the Golden Age?
2. When did they begin?
3. When did crime begin?

## Comparison of Adjectives

Adjectives change form to show *degree*. This is called *comparison*. There are three degrees: *positive, comparative, superlative*. The positive is the simple form of the adjective; the others indicate a greater degree. To *compare* an adjective is to give the three degrees.

In English, the comparative is formed by adding –*er* (–*r*) to the positive: *high-er, brave-r.* The superlative is formed by adding –*est* (–*st*) to the positive: *high-est, brave-st.* But adjectives of more than one syllable are often compared by the use of *more* and *most: more skillful, most skillful.*

In Latin, the comparative is formed by adding –*ior* (m. and f.), –*ius* (n.) to the base of the positive, and the superlative is formed by adding –*issimus, –a, –um*:

| POSITIVE | COMPARATIVE | SUPERLATIVE |
|---|---|---|
| altus, –a, –um, *high* (base, **alt–**) | altior, altius, *higher* | altissimus, –a, –um, *highest* |
| fortis, –e, *brave* (base, **fort–**) | fortior, fortius, *braver* | fortissimus, –a, –um, *bravest* |

*Hints for Translating.* The comparative may also often be translated *more, too, rather*; the superlative, *most, very, exceedingly*: ūtilior, *more useful*; altissimus, *very high*.

## Declension of the Comparative

Adjectives are declined as follows in the comparative:

| | SINGULAR | | PLURAL | |
|---|---|---|---|---|
| | **M., F.** | **N.** | **M., F.** | **N.** |
| *Nom.* | altior | altius | altiōrēs | altiōra |
| *Gen.* | altiōris | altiōris | altiōrum | altiōrum |
| *Dat.* | altiōrī | altiōrī | altiōribus | altiōribus |
| *Acc.* | altiōrem | altius | altiōrēs | altiōra |
| *Abl.* | altiōre | altiōre | altiōribus | altiōribus |

*Observe* that, while comparatives are declined like adjectives of the third declension, they do not have –ī in the abl. sing., –ium in the gen. plur., or –ia in the nom. and acc. plur. neuter, i.e., comparatives are not i–stems.

Remember that in Latin when **quam** is used, the two things compared are in the same case, but in English *than* is usually followed by the nominative because a verb is understood: **Fortiōrem virum quam illum nōn vīdī,** *A braver man than he (is) I have not seen.*

**Practice**  1. Compare **grātus, nōbilis, clārus, levis, longus.**
2. Decline **tardus** in the comparative.
3. Decline **supplicium iūstius.**

**Exercises  A.** 1. Novissimum librum ad frātrem meum mittere statuī.
2. Quid est ūtilius et grātius quam librōs bonōs semper legere?
3. Eī duo itinera ostendimus—alterum facile, alterum longius et incertius.
4. Condiciōnēs pācis dūrissimae ab hostibus victīs semper esse habentur.
5. Gallī vīribus corporis Rōmānōs superābant sed nōn erant fortiōrēs virī.
6. Homō dē viīs mē rogāvit; ego respondī hanc esse plāniōrem quam illam.

*Labor omnia vincit.*

*Tablet with Greek spelling exercise, styli, inkwell, wax tablets.*

**B.** 1. Nothing is more useful than water.
2. Why are not the rivers of Italy very long?
3. Does peace have nobler victories than war?
4. I know that that river is swift but not very wide.
5. More severe terms of peace than these will be determined (upon).

**Vocabulary**

ae′tās, aetā′tis, f., *age* (eternal)
condi′ciō, condiciō′nis, f., *condition, terms* (conditional)
quam, conj., *than*
ra′piō, –ere, ra′puī, rap′tus, *carry off* (rapacious)
sta′tuō, –ere, sta′tuī, statū′tus, (*make stand*), *establish,*
*determine* [*stō*]
ū′tilis, –e, *useful* (utility)
vin′cō, –ere, vī′cī, vic′tus, *conquer* (invincible)

## English Word Studies

It is important to distinguish different words that came from the same stem. "Plain" and "plane" both come from **plānus**, *level*. A "plain" is a *level* field; a "plain" person is not above the average *level* in appearance, etc. A "plane" is a *level* surface (hence "plane" geometry); it is also a tool which makes surfaces *level*. "Plane" is therefore used in a more literal sense than "plain."

Take **corpus**: a "corpse" is a dead *body*; a "corps" (pronounced "core") is a *body* of men forming part of an army. The former is literal, the latter, figurative. A "corporation" is a *body* of men united for commercial or other purposes. A "corpuscle" is a little *body* in the blood. "Corporal" punishment is punishment inflicted upon the *body*, i.e., a whipping; but something "corporeal" has a *body*, i.e., it is not imaginary. Similarly, a "principal" is the *leading* person in a school; a "principle" is a *leading* rule.

In accordance with the above suggestions explain *statue* and *statute*; *urban* and *urbane*; *sensory* and *sentiment*; *respiration* and *inspiration*.

*Saturnus* occurs twice in the Buffalo telephone directory.

**328**

# *Lesson lxvii*

## BAUCIS ET PHILĒMŌN

Iuppiter et Mercurius per Phrygiam, quae in Asiā est, iter fēcērunt, sed nēmō in tōtā illā gente eōs cognōvit. Omnēs eōs esse hominēs
humilēs iūdicāvērunt. Ad mīlle casās accessērunt; nam locum somnō
aptum petīvērunt. Sed omnēs, hīs vīsīs, casās celeriter clausērunt.
In tōtā regiōne ācriter repulsī sunt. Tamen ūna casa, parva et 5
humilis, eōs nōn reppulit. Ibi Baucis et Philēmōn[1] multōs annōs
ēgerant. Condiciōne humilī nōn affectī, paupertātem leviter et
fortiter sustinuērunt. Duo tōta domus[2] fuērunt, et dominī et servī
ipsī; nam nūllōs servōs habuērunt.

Cēnam humilem Baucis magnā dīligentiā et celeritāte parāvit; 10
numquam celerius labōrāverat. Tum, omnibus īnstrūctīs, deōs ad

---

[1] *Baucis (Bau'sis), Philē'mon.*          [2] *household* (predicate nominative).

*Jupiter and Mercury are welcomed by Philemon and Baucis. A painting by P. Gyselaer.*

cēnam vocāvit. Mēnsa, nōn pulchra sed ūtilis, paucīs sed bonīs cibīs
īnstrūcta erat. Vīnum sūmunt, sed semper crātēr [3] vīnum continēbat.
Tum Philēmōn et Baucis, ad mēnsam sedentēs, clārē sēnsērunt deōs
15 adesse. Tum Iuppiter, "Deī sumus," inquit. "Tōtam hanc gentem
poenam solūtūram esse statuimus, quod nēmō nōbīs auxilium dedit,
sed vestra vīta servābitur. Ad montem prōcēdēmus." Itaque Baucis
et Philēmōn, hāc ōrātiōne permōtī, ad montem tardē prōcessērunt.
Ibi cōnstitērunt et vīdērunt tōtam regiōnem sub aquā esse, casam
20 suam sōlam manēre. Dum spectant, casa eōrum in pulchrum
templum vertitur.

Tum Iuppiter, "Quid cupitis?" inquit; "id quod petitis dōnābō."
Philēmōn, uxōre cōnsultā, respondit: "Nūllum mūnus nōbīs grātius
aptiusque est quam esse sacerdōtēs [4] illīus templī et ē vītā eōdem
25 tempore excēdere, quod in concordiā multōs annōs ēgimus." Hoc
mūnus Iuppiter eīs permīsit.

Post multōs annōs, Philēmōn et uxor, aetāte gravēs, ante sacrum
templum stābant. Corpora eōrum in arborēs [5] tardē vertuntur; vōcēs
haerent; nōn iam spīrant. Neuter ante alterum ē vītā excessit. Multōs
30 annōs hae duae arborēs ante templum stābant.

QUESTIONS    1. What was Jupiter looking for?
                 2. Why did it take so long to find it?
                 3. How did Philemon find out that his guests were gods?

READING    Hamilton, pp. 150–153 (Mentor ed., pp. 111–113); Sabin,
                 pp. 83–84; Gayley, pp. 77–80; Guerber, pp. 43–44; Bulfinch,
                 pp. 54–57.

## Formation of Adverbs

1. Adverbs formed from adjectives of the first and second declensions are explained on page 121.

2. Adverbs formed from adjectives of the third declension, as
a rule, add –iter to the base; as, adj., **fortis**, adv., **fortiter**; adj., **ācer**,
adv., **ācriter**.

The comparison of adverbs is very similar to that of adjectives:

| POSITIVE | COMPARATIVE | SUPERLATIVE |
|---|---|---|
| altē | altius | altissimē |
| fortiter | fortius | fortissimē |

---

[3] *bowl.*      [4] *priests.*      [5] *trees.*

Note that in the comparative degree the adverb always has the same form as the neuter accusative singular of the comparative adjective.

**Practice**    Form and compare adverbs from the following adjectives already studied: **longus, ūtilis, levis, clārus, firmus, gravis, vērus.**

**Exercises**    **A.** 1. Sciō hoc flūmen esse longius quam illud.
2. Pater meus omnia iūstē et celeriter iūdicat.
3. Hī mīlitēs, ē castrīs ēductī, ad pugnam ā duce īnstruuntur.
4. Tardius pervēnimus quod reliquī puerī celerius cucurrērunt.
5. Nostrī fortissimē pugnāvērunt sed ab hostibus repulsī sunt.
6. Puerī magistrō librum dedērunt, et ille ōrātiōne aptā respondit.

*Roman porch on a home in Athens, Ga., built in 1855.*

**B.** 1. We shall breathe more easily.
2. No one approves a very long speech.
3. We certainly hope that peace has been established.
4. The battle was sharply fought, but few men received severe wounds.

**Vocabulary**

ap′tus, –a, –um, *fit, suitable*                                  (adapt)

*gēns, gen′tis, gen′tium, f., *people, nation*          [*genus*]

hu′milis, –e, *low, humble*                                  (humility)

īn′struō, –ere, īnstrū′xī, īnstrūc′tus, *arrange, provide*
[*struō, arrange*]

iū′dicō, –ā′re, –ā′vī, –ā′tus, *judge*                    (judicial)

nē′mō, dat. nē′minī, acc. nē′minem (no other forms),
*no one*                                                         [*homō*]

ōrā′tiō, ōrātiō′nis, f., *speech*                          (orator)

re′giō, regiō′nis, f., *region*                              [*regō*]

repel′lō, –ere, rep′pulī, repul′sus, *drive back, repulse*
[*pellō*]

Model of a racing chariot made in the Libbey High School, Toledo, Ohio, Mrs. P. Emerson Burton, teacher.

### English Word Studies: The Suffix –iō

In Latin the suffix –iō is added to verb stems, usually to that of the past participle. As this generally ends in –t or –s, words of this origin are likely to end in –tiō or –siō. The suffix indicates an act or the result of an act: ōrātiō is the act of speaking, or the result, i.e., a speech. Nouns with this suffix have –iōnis in the genitive. Therefore the base ends in **n**. The English form of the suffix, which is very common, is –ion (–tion, –sion): region, oration, session. It often has the force of the suffix –ing.

Give and define ten English words with the suffix –ion derived from Latin verbs which you have studied. Look up the origin and meaning of *gentle, gentile, genteel, jaunty*.

*At the left, door of the memorial to the Wright brothers at Kitty Hawk, N. C., honoring their first airplane flight in 1904. It depicts earlier attempts at flying; Icarus is on the right half of the door, in the second panel from the top. At the right, statue of Icarus made in 1951 by Helene Sardeau.*

# Lesson lxviii

### DAEDALUS ET ĪCARUS

In īnsulā magnā Crētā Mīnōs[1] fuit rēx. Daedalus[2] cum fīliō parvō Īcarō[2] ibi captīvus fuit. Fugere nōn potuit quod mare prohibuit. "Neque per terram," inquit, "neque per mare fugere possum, sed caelum certē nōn clausum est. Illā viā difficillimā prōcēdēmus." Itaque ālās parāvit, simillimās ālīs vērīs avium.[3] Partēs ālārum cērā 5 ligāvit. Īcarus ad patrem stābat, ālās levissimās tangēbat, opus patris impediēbat. Tandem fīnis labōris difficilis aderat; ālae parātae erant. Daedalus tempus aptum esse iūdicāvit. Tum ālās corporī fīlī iūnxit et eum hīs verbīs ācriter monuit:

---

[1] *Mī'nos* (nom. sing.).  [2] *Daedalus (Dĕd'alus), Ic'arus.*  [3] *of birds.*

**333**

10    "In mediō caelō prōcēdēmus; nam, sī humilius volābimus,[4] undae
ālās graviōrēs facient; sī altius volābimus, ignis ālās ūret[5] et in
mare cadēs."

Tum omnēs partēs ālārum fīliō ostendit et omnia in ōrdine expli-
cāvit. Perīculum esse sēnsit et fīliō timuit, quī patrī dissimillimus
15 erat. Ālīs īnstrūctus antecessit et fīlium post volāre iussit.

Agricolae territī ex agrīs eōs vīdērunt; multī putāvērunt eōs deōs
aut deīs similēs esse. Celerrimē pater fīliusque āera[6] ālīs pepulērunt.[7]
Multās regiōnēs multāsque gentēs relīquērunt. Tum puer nōn iam
timidus patrem ducem relīquit. Ōrātiōnem patris memoriā nōn
20 tenuit et altius volāvit quod iūdicāvit nihil accidere posse. Sed multa
accidērunt: celeriter sōl cēram solvit; nōn iam ālae haesērunt. Praeceps puer miser in mare cecidit; frūstrā[8] nōmen patris clāmāvit. Ab
illō posteā hoc mare nōmen[9] accēpit.

Interim pater, nōn iam pater, in omnibus regiōnibus fīlium
25 petīvit, nōmen fīlī clāmāvit. Tandem ālās propriās Īcarī in undīs vīdit
sed corpus eius numquam invēnit.

Tum ipse ad Siciliam pervēnit et ibi multōs annōs ēgit. Sed fābula
ab aliīs dicta huic dissimilis est: scrībunt eum in Italiam volāvisse et
ibi in templō ālās posuisse. Hōc modō deīs prō salūte grātiās ēgit.

30    Prīmus omnium hominum Daedalus, Nātūrā victā, per caelum
lātum volāvit, sī auctōrēs Graecī et Rōmānī vērum dīxērunt. Nunc
multī hominēs facile volant, sed nēmō ālīs propriīs. Nāvibus ālās
iūnximus.

QUESTIONS    1. In what way did Icarus disobey his father?
             2. Where did Daedalus land?
             3. Explain why Oregon has the motto **Alis volat propriis.**

READING      Hamilton, pp. 192–194 (Mentor ed., pp. 139–140); Sabin,
             pp. 260–261; Gayley, pp. 246–248; Guerber, pp. 253–255;
             Bulfinch, pp. 161–163; Norton and Rushton, pp. 126–129.

### Comparison of –er Adjectives and Their Adverbs

The superlative of all adjectives ending in –er is formed by
adding –rimus, –a, –um to the nominative singular masculine of the
positive:

---

[4] *fly.*
[5] *will burn.*
[6] Accusative singular: *air.*
[7] From **pellō**: *beat.*
[8] *in vain.*
[9] The Icarian Sea.

| POSITIVE | COMPARATIVE | SUPERLATIVE |
|---|---|---|
| līber, lībera, līberum | līberior, līberius | līberrimus, –a, –um |
| ācer, ācris, ācre | ācrior, ācrius | ācerrimus, –a, –um |
| celer, celeris, celere | celerior, celerius | celerrimus, –a, –um |

The corresponding adverbs are formed as follows:

| POSITIVE | COMPARATIVE | SUPERLATIVE |
|---|---|---|
| lībere | līberius | līberrimē |
| ācriter | ācrius | ācerrimē |
| celeriter | celerius | celerrimē |

**Practice**  Compare **miser, pulcher, altus**. Form and compare the corresponding adverbs. Decline **illa līberior patria**.

### Adjectives with Superlative in –limus

The superlative of five adjectives ending in –lis is formed by adding –limus, –a, –um to the base of the positive:

| POSITIVE | COMPARATIVE | SUPERLATIVE |
|---|---|---|
| facilis, –e | facilior, facilius | facillimus, –a, –um |
| difficilis, –e | difficilior, difficilius | difficillimus, –a, –um |
| similis, –e | similior, similius | simillimus, –a, –um |
| dissimilis, –e | dissimilior, dissimilius | dissimillimus, –a, –um |
| humilis, –e | humilior, humilius | humillimus, –a, –um |

*Note.* The superlative of other –lis adjectives, such as **nōbilis, –e, ūtilis, –e**, etc., is formed regularly—i.e., by adding –issimus to the base of the positive: **nōbil–issimus, –a, –um**.

The adverb of **facilis** is **facile**. The adverbs formed from the other adjectives in the preceding list are formed regularly.

In the superlative the corresponding adverbs end in –ē: **facil-limē**.

### Dative with Adjectives

1. **Hic liber est similis illī**, *This book is similar to that.*
2. **Ille homō est frātrī meō inimīcus**, *That man is unfriendly to my brother.*

*Observe* that the dative is often used with Latin adjectives whose English equivalents are followed by *to*. The following have already been studied: **amīcus, inimīcus, similis, dissimilis, aptus, grātus.**

**Exercises A.** 1. Hic equus similior meō est quam ille.
2. Rōmānōrum deī dissimillimī nostrō Deō erant.
3. Ille liber difficillimus est, nam pauca clārē explicat.
4. Humilis homō nec altē cadere nec graviter potest.
5. Nihil est nōbīs ūtilius quam bonus liber; nam est nōbilissimus amīcōrum.

**B.** 1. This region is fit for (to) some settlers, but not for others.
2. As the bad men approached, the boys ran more quickly.
3. The places in which our soldiers fell are most sacred.
4. The teacher in a very beautiful speech unfolded the life of Caesar.

**Vocabulary**    ca'dō, –ere, ce'cidī, cāsū'rus, *fall*                    (casualty)
ac'cidō, –ere, ac'cidī, ——, *fall to, befall, happen* (with dat.)
diffi'cilis, –e, *difficult*                                            [*facilis*]
ex'plicō, –ā're, –ā'vī, –ā'tus, *unfold, explain*        [*plicō*]
fa'cile, adv., *easily*                                                  [*facilis*]
iun'gō, –ere, iūn'xī, iūnc'tus, *join* (*to*)             (junction)
pro'prius, –a, –um, (*one's*) *own*                          (propriety)
si'milis, –e, *like*                                                  (similarity)
    dissi'milis, –e, *unlike*

### English Word Studies

1. Explain *accident, coincidence, proprietor, inexplicable, decadent*. What is meant by the *assimilation* of the foreign population in our country?

2. Lawyers use so many Latin phrases daily that they must be familiar with Latin. A few such phrases are:

**subpoena,** a summons to court *under penalty* for failure to attend.
**in propria persona,** *in one's own person* (not through some one else).
**ex post facto,** *resulting after the fact*; as a law which makes punishable acts committed before its passage.
**in forma pauperis,** *in the form* (or *manner*) *of a poor man*; to sue as a poor man and so avoid the costs of the suit.

Look through the court records and legal items in the newspapers for other Latin phrases.

*Elephanti maximi—the first tanks. From the motion picture "Scipio Africanus."*

# Lesson lxix

## PYRRHUS ET EIUS VICTŌRIA

Rōmānī, quī erant optimī mīlitēs, gentēs quae proximae urbī erant vīcerant et in ulteriōrēs partēs Italiae pervēnerant; summā virtūte contrā maiōrem numerum hostium in extrēmīs ac difficillimīs regiōnibus Italiae pugnāverant. Posteā bellum novī generis, dissimile aliīs, cum Pyrrhō, rēge maximō Ēpīrī, gessērunt.    5

Pyrrhus in Italiam īnferiōrem ā Tarentīnīs, gente pessimā, vocātus erat, quī eō tempore cum Rōmānīs pugnābant. Is in Italiam mīlitēs trānsportāvit et elephantōrum auxiliō Rōmānōs fortiter pugnantēs reppulit, quod Rōmānī elephantōs maximōs nōn ante vīsōs timuērunt. Peius [1] tamen Pyrrhō victōrī quam victīs Rōmānīs accidit, nam 10 plūrimī Pyrrhī mīlitēs cecidērunt. Pyrrhus, ubi plūrima corpora Rōmānōrum interfectōrum in fronte vulnera habēre vīdit, haec verba fēcit: "Bene Rōmānī pugnāvērunt. Cum tālibus [2] mīlitibus tōtus orbis [3] facillimē ā mē vincī potest!" Familiāribus dē victōriā agentibus dīxit:

---

[1] *a worse thing.*    [2] *such.*    [3] *world.*

15 "Sī iterum eōdem modō vīcerō, nūllōs mīlitēs in Ēpīrum redūcam."
Nam hanc victōriam nōn ūtilem esse iūdicāvit quod plūrēs mīlitēs
āmīserat.

QUESTIONS 1. What was the cause of Pyrrhus' victories?
2. What is a "Pyrrhic victory"?

READING Mills, pp. 102–105.

## Irregular Adjectives Compared

In English, some adjectives in common use are compared irregularly, such as *good, better, best; bad, worse, worst.*

In Latin, the following adjectives, among others, are compared irregularly and should be memorized:

| POSITIVE | COMPARATIVE | SUPERLATIVE |
|---|---|---|
| bonus, –a, –um (*good*) | melior, melius (*better*) | optimus, –a, –um (*best*) |
| malus, –a, –um (*bad*) | peior, peius (*worse*) | pessimus, –a, –um (*worst*) |
| magnus, –a, –um (*large*) | maior, maius (*larger*) | maximus, –a, –um (*largest*) |
| parvus, –a, –um (*small*) | minor, minus (*smaller*) | minimus, –a, –um (*smallest*) |
| multus, –a, –um (*much*) | ——, plūs [4] (*more*) | plūrimus, –a, –um (*most*) |

*Exercise.* Find English derivatives of the above forms.

*Note* that adverbs formed from the above adjectives are compared, in general, according to the rule (p. 330); exceptions used in this book are noted in the vocabularies.

**Extrēmus** and **Summus.** In English we sometimes have to use nouns to translate adjectives like **extrēmus** and **summus: in extrēmā ōrātiōne,** *at the end of the speech;* **summus mōns,** *top of the mountain* (cf. **reliquī mīlitēs,** *rest of the soldiers;* **in mediō flūmine,** *in the middle of the river*). When used in this way, the adjective usually precedes its noun.

**Exercises** **A.** 1. Puerī ad īnferiōrem partem flūminis iter facient.
2. Optimī cīvēs patriam semper optimē dēfendent.

---

[4] Gen. **plūris;** there is no masculine and feminine singular, and no dative in any gender; the plural is **plūrēs, plūra,** gen. **plūrium,** etc. See p. 394.

3. Summus mōns ā nōbīs facillimē occupātus est.
4. Pessimī hominēs in ultimās regiōnēs mittī dēbent.
5. Hī septem puerī territī sunt quod perīculum maximum esse sēnsērunt.
6. Agricolae quī meliōrēs agrōs habent maiōrem cōpiam frūmentī habēbunt.
7. Nōnne spērās proximum mēnsem nōn futūrum esse dūriōrem quam hunc?

**B.** 1. The smallest boy is not the worst.
2. Can a horse run more swiftly than a man?
3. The smaller man fought more bravely than the larger.
4. We shall do this very quickly and well without your aid.

**Vocabulary**

| | |
|---|---|
| bĕ'nĕ, adv., *well* | [*bonus*] |
| extrē'mus, –a, –um, *farthest, last, end of* | (extremist) |
| īnfe'rior, īnfe'rius, *lower* | (inferiority) |
| pro'ximus, –a, –um, *nearest, next* (with dat.) | (proximity) |
| sum'mus, –a, –um, *highest, top of* | (summit) |
| ulte'rior, ulte'rius, *farther* | (ulterior) |

*Jupiter prophesies Roman greatness in a quotation from Virgil's Aeneid on an Italian stamp.*

## English Word Studies

1. A number of English words preserve the forms of the comparative and superlative of Latin irregular adjectives: *major* (cf. *mayor*), *maximum, minor, minus, minimum, plus, inferior, superior, ulterior, prior, anterior, posterior, interior, exterior, junior, senior.*

What is the difference between a *majority* and a *plurality* vote? Between a *majority* and a *minority* report?

2. Latin phrases in English:

**excelsior,** *higher* (motto of the state of New York).

**esse quam videri,** *to be rather than to seem* (*to be*) (motto of the state of North Carolina).

**e pluribus unum,** *one* (*country*) *out of many* (*states*) (motto of the United States, found on its coins).

Translate the motto of Oklahoma (also of the University of Illinois and the American Federation of Labor): **Labor omnia vincit.**

*Fabricius before Pyrrhus. A painting by a Dutch artist of the seventeenth century.*

# Lesson lxx

## PYRRHUS ET FABRICIUS

Fabricius,[1] quī erat īnferior genere quam aliī Rōmānī, tamen ab omnibus amātus est quod optimus fortissimusque mīles erat. Neque amīcōs neque inimīcōs suōs fallēbat. Praemia numquam sūmēbat. Itaque Rōmānī cīvitātis suae salūtem eī crēdidērunt et eum inter
5 aliōs lēgātōs ad Pyrrhum mīsērunt.

Multa quae dē Fabriciō et eius summā honestāte Pyrrhus audīverat vēra esse crēdidit. Itaque hunc lēgātum in castrīs suīs cōnspectum bene accēpit. Ad extrēmum eī dīxit: "Cūr nōn in Ēpīrum mēcum venīs et ibi manēs? Tibi quārtam rēgnī meī partem tribuam."
10 Sed Fabricius respondit sē neque partem rēgnī sibi tribuī cupere neque sūmptūrum esse.

---

[1] *Fabricius* (Fabrish'ius).

Proximō annō Fabricius contrā Pyrrhum pugnāvit. Medicus rēgis mediā nocte ad eum vēnit et dīxit sē prō praemiō Pyrrhum interfectūrum esse. Fabricius, quī nēminem fefellerat, respondit sē nūllum praemium prōpōnere et iussit hunc ligātum ad dominum redūcī 15 et Pyrrhō omnia dīcī. Ubi rēx medicum ligātum cōnspexit, maximē mōtus dīxit: "Ille est Fabricius quī nōn facilius ab honestāte quam sōl ā cursū [2] suō āvertī potest!"

QUESTIONS
1. Why did the Romans have so much confidence in Fabricius?
2. What offer did Pyrrhus make to Fabricius?
3. What reason did Pyrrhus have for being grateful to Fabricius?

### Reflexive Pronouns

In English, as we have seen (p. 285), the emphatic pronouns *myself, ourselves,* etc., correspond to Latin **ipse:** *I myself saw him,* **Ipse eum vīdī.** There is also a *reflexive* use of these same English pronouns as objects of verbs or prepositions to refer to the subject of the verb: *I saw myself.*

In Latin, the personal pronouns of the first and second persons may be used reflexively, but in the third person Latin has a special reflexive pronoun, **suī,** declined alike in the singular and plural:

| | | | |
|---|---|---|---|
| *Gen.* **suī,** | *of himself, herself, itself, themselves* | | |
| *Dat.* **sibi,** | *to* " " " " | | |
| *Acc.* **sē** (**sēsē**), | " " " " | | |
| *Abl.* **sē** (**sēsē**), | *with (from,* etc.) " " " " | | |

QUESTION   Why do reflexive pronouns have no nominative?

### Use of Reflexive Pronouns

(ego) **mē rogō,** *I ask myself*          (nōs) **nōs rogāmus,** *we ask ourselves*
(tū) **tē rogās,** *you ask yourself*      (vōs) **vōs rogātis,** *you ask yourselves*
(is) **sē rogat,** *he asks himself*       (eī) **sē rogant,** *they ask themselves*

**Practice**   Give in all tenses the first singular of **līberō;** the second plural of **fallō;** the third singular of **interficiō,** using the proper reflexive pronoun with each.

---

[2] Ablative: *course.*

*Pyrrhus at left. At right, Navy medal of honor. Minerva, representing the United States, holds the fasces, Roman symbol of lawful government, and wards off Discord armed with snakes.*

### Reflexive Adjectives

Corresponding to **meus, tuus, noster,** and **vester,** derived from **ego, tū, nōs,** and **vōs,** there is the reflexive adjective **suus, –a, –um,** *his own, her own, its own, their own,* derived from **suī.**

*Caution.* Remember that **suus** *always refers to the subject of the verb.* When *his, her,* etc., do not refer to the subject, then **eius,** etc., must be used (p. 279). Note the difference in the following:

1. **Patrem eius vīdī,** *I saw his father.*
2. **Patrem suum vīdit,** *He saw his father.*

**Exercises A.** 1. Frāter eius mātrem suam fefellit et posteā sē interfēcit.
2. Tū tē ipsum fallere semper potuistī sed mē numquam fefellistī.
3. Crēditisne Deum mare terramque prō sē aut prō nōbīs fēcisse?
4. Mūnera pūblica optimīs, nōn pessimīs, hominibus tribuī dēbent.
5. Puerum currentem vīdī, sed ille crēdidit sē ā mē nōn vīsum esse.
6. Arma sūmēmus et nōs fortiter dēfendēmus contrā pessimōs hostēs.

**B.** Translate the words in italics:

1. We saw *his* brother.
2. You will see *their* friends.
3. The girl loved *her* mother.
4. He wasted *his* money and *theirs*.
5. They will defend *themselves* and *us*.

**C.** 1. He says that he himself has four brothers.
2. We always praise ourselves and blame others.
3. Entrust yourselves and all your (possessions) to us.
4. The leader of the enemy, having caught sight of us, killed himself.

**Vocabulary**

cōnspi′ciō, –ere, –spe′xī, –spec′tus, *catch sight of, see*
[*spectō*]

con′trā, prep. with acc., *against*

crē′dō, –ere, crē′didī, crē′ditus, *believe, entrust* (with dat.)
(credible)

fal′lō, –ere, fefel′lī, fal′sus, *deceive* (fallacy)

lēgā′tus, –ī, m., *envoy* [*lēgō, appoint*]

su′ī, reflex. pron., *of himself*, etc. (suicide)

sū′mō, –ere, sūmp′sī, sūmp′tus, *take* (assumption)

su′us, –a, –um, reflex. adj., *his own*, etc.

tri′buō, –ere, tri′buī, tribū′tus, *grant* (contribute)

## English Word Studies

In the fourteenth century there began a great revival of interest in the ancient Latin and Greek authors. This revival is known as the *Renaissance* (from **re-nāscor**, *to be born again*). Beginning in Italy, it spread over western Europe and reached England in the sixteenth century. Ever since then many new words have been added to English from Latin and Greek. These new words are easily distinguished by their similarity to the Latin originals. Over ninety per cent of the words in Caesar and Cicero have English derivatives.

One result of the introduction of new words directly from the Latin was the formation of a number of *doublets*, words derived at different periods from the same Latin word and having different meanings. Note the following (the earlier form precedes): *sample, example* (**exemplum**); *feat, fact* (**factum**); *Mr., master* (**magister**); *loyal, legal* (**lēx**); *mayor, major* (**maior**); *chance, cadence* (**cadō**). There is one set of *quintuplets* in English: *dais, desk, dish, disk, discus,* all from **discus.** Cf. p. 332 for a *quadruplet.*

Show how the above doublets got their meanings from the original Latin meaning.

# Lesson lxxi

## RĒGULUS

Contrā Carthāginiēnsēs arma ā Rōmānīs sūmpta erant.[1] Rēgulus, dux Rōmānōrum, imperiō acceptō, ad Āfricam nāvigāvit et hostēs superāvit. Multa mīlia captīvōrum in Italiam mīsit sed ipse, opere difficilī nōn perfectō, in Āfricā remānsit. Contrā trēs Carthāginiēn-
5 sium ducēs pugnāns victor fuit. Hostēs ā Rōmānīs pressī pācem petī-vērunt. Quam[2] Rēgulus dīxit sē dūrissimīs condiciōnibus datūrum esse. Itaque Carthāginiēnsēs auxilium ā Lacedaemoniīs[3] petīvērunt. Dux quī ā Lacedaemoniīs missus erat cum quattuor mīlibus mīlitum et centum elephantīs contrā Rōmānōs prōcessit. Rōmānīs victīs,
10 Rēgulus captus est.

Rēgulus in Āfricā mānsit sed quīntō annō Carthāginiēnsēs superātī eum ad urbem Rōmam mīsērunt. Eum iussērunt pācem ā Rōmānīs obtinēre et permūtātiōnem captīvōrum facere. Is dīxit, pāce nōn factā, sē ad eōs reversūrum esse. Illī crēdidērunt eum sē trādi-
15 tūrum esse.

Itaque Rēgulus in Italiam pervēnit. Ductus in senātum Rōmānum dīxit sē esse captīvum, nōn iam Rōmānum. Itaque etiam uxōrem, quae eum cōnspexerat et ad eum cucurrerat, ā sē remōvit. Dīxit hostēs, frāctōs multīs proeliīs, spem[4] nūllam nisi[5] in pāce habēre;
20 nōn esse ūtile multa mīlia captīvōrum prō sē ūnō, aetāte cōnfectō, hostibus reddī. "Captīvōs Rōmānōs aurō emere nōn dēbēmus," ex-plicat; "nam virtūs eōrum āmissa est, nec vēra virtūs aurō emī potest." Senātus hōc cōnsiliō numquam ante datō permōtus pācem cum hosti-bus nōn fēcit. Itaque Rēgulus, opere perfectō, Carthāginiēnsēs nōn
25 fefellit sed in Āfricam revertit et sē Carthāginiēnsibus trādidit,[6] ā quibus omnibus suppliciīs interfectus est. Posteā Rōmānī eī honōrēs tribuērunt.

---

[1] First Punic or Carthaginian War, 264–241 B.C. (cf. pp. 165, 275, 351). These wars were for the supremacy of the world. Carthage was in north-ern Africa, near present-day Tunis.

[2] In Latin, a relative is often used at the beginning of a sentence to con-nect with the preceding sentence. In English, a demonstrative is used in-stead.

[3] *the Spartans.*

[4] *hope.*

[5] *except.*

[6] In 1944 an American prisoner was sent by the Germans to the American lines to ask for blood plasma after giving his word that he would return, which he did.

Haec prīmō bellō Pūnicō accidērunt. Posteā Rōmānī, pāce frāctā, duo alia bella cum eīsdem hostibus gessērunt et imperium suum maximē auxērunt.

QUESTIONS    1. Why did Regulus remain in Africa?
            2. What caused his later defeat?
            3. Why did he urge the Romans not to make peace?

READING    Mills, pp. 140–142.

## Declension of *Duo* and *Trēs*

The numbers from 4 to 100 are indeclinable in Latin. For **ūnus** see p. 288. **Duo,** *two,* and **trēs,** *three,* are declined as follows:

|  | M. | F. | N. | M., F. | N. |
|---|---|---|---|---|---|
| *Nom.* | duo | duae | duo | trēs | tria |
| *Gen.* | duōrum | duārum | duōrum | trium | trium |
| *Dat.* | duōbus | duābus | duōbus | tribus | tribus |
| *Acc.* | duōs | duās | duo | trēs | tria |
| *Abl.* | duōbus | duābus | duōbus | tribus | tribus |

## Declension and Use of *Mīlle*

**Mīlle,** when used of one thousand, is usually an indeclinable adjective (like **centum**): **mīlle hominēs.** When used of two or more thousands, it is a neuter plural **i**–stem noun (cf. **mare,** p. 248). The word used with the plural forms of **mīlle** must be in the genitive: **duo mīlia hominum** (lit., *two thousands of men*), *two thousand men.*

|  | SINGULAR | PLURAL |
|---|---|---|
| *Nom.* | mīlle | mīlia |
| *Gen.* | mīlle | mīlium |
| *Dat.* | mīlle | mīlibus |
| *Acc.* | mīlle | mīlia |
| *Abl.* | mīlle | mīlibus |

**Practice**    Give in Latin: *two boys, one hundred children, one thousand citizens, two thousand sailors, three thousand soldiers.*

**Exercises**  **A.** 1. Nāvī frāctā, omnēs certē interficientur.
            2. Duōs optimōs librōs ēmī quōs hāc aestāte legam.
            3. Mīlle nautās cum tribus ducibus in maria ultima mīsimus.

4. Centum mīlia agricolārum, agrīs suīs relīctīs, ad oppida contendērunt.

5. Post duās pugnās hostēs cōnfectī nōn iam vim nostram sustinuērunt.

**B.** 1. Anna was third in rank, but her brother was fifth.
2. Three men were killed, and two received wounds.
3. The lower part of this river is between two nations.
4. All the boys easily completed the work in three hours.

**Vocabulary**

cen′tum, indeclinable adj., *hundred*      (centennial)
e′mō, –ere, ē′mī, ēmp′tus, *take, buy*      (redemption)
fran′gō, –ere, frē′gī, frāc′tus, *break*      (fraction)
impe′rium, impe′rī, n., *command, power*      (imperial)
mīl′le, plur., mī′lia, *thousand*      (millennium)
o′pus, o′peris, n., *work*      (operate)
perfi′ciō, –ere, –fē′cī, –fec′tus, *finish*      [*faciō*]
trā′dō, –ere, trā′didī, trā′ditus, *give* or *hand over, surrender*      [*dō*]

## English Word Studies

1. Much difficulty is caused in English spelling by silent or weakly sounded letters. This difficulty is often solved by referring to the Latin original: *labor·a·tory, rep·e·tition, lib·r·ary, sep·a·rate, auxil·i·ary, compar·a·tive, de·b·t, rei·g·n, recei·p·t.* The Latin original often helps in other difficulties: *con·s·ensus, a·nn·uity, defi·c·it, acce·l·erate.*

Define the above words and give their Latin originals.

2. Much confusion is caused in English by the combinations *ei* and *ie*. Remember that the derivatives of compounds of **capiō** have *ei,* as *receive.*

3. Why is a *fraction* so called? Explain *fracture, exemption.* Explain *treason* and *tradition,* which are doublets, derived from **trādō.** What is *credit* as used in business? What is a *creed*?

*Treason.*

# ❧ Glimpses of Roman Life

## ROMAN SOCIAL AND ECONOMIC CONDITIONS

It is interesting to us to learn that the Romans, like ourselves, had periods of business panics and depressions. We can comfort ourselves with the thought that such depressions will disappear as they did in the past.

From time to time the common people of Rome, who were very poor, suffered from lack of food when the wheat crop failed, as happens even today. At one such time the senate, which was the ruling body, obtained a large amount of wheat and was planning to give it away to the poor. It was in connection with this plan that the plebeians were angry at Coriolanus, as we have already read (p. 310). He advised the senate not to give the wheat free and criticized the plebeians sharply. All this happened in the fifth century B.C.—over twenty-four hundred years ago.

In the time of the Gracchi (second century B.C.) economic conditions became especially bad. The rich nobles had acquired large farms by taking over public lands and by forcing out the poor small farmers. These wandered over Italy with their families and many settled in Rome, where they had a hard time. They could not obtain work on the large farms because these were worked by slave labor. Tiberius Gracchus planned to force the large landowners to sell all but 500 acres of their lands at a reasonable price. He then intended to cut this land up into small farms to be rented at a low cost to the poor. He felt that the men who fought for their country had as much right to a home as the wild beasts in the forests.

After Tiberius' death in a riot Gaius tried to carry out his brother's policies. In addition, he used the unemployed to build roads, stored large amounts of wheat to avoid shortages, gave relief to the poor by selling wheat well below cost, and established colonies. But he, too, met death in a riot. All of his measures have been tried in modern times. The poverty and unrest in southern Italy today is caused in part by the existence of large estates, though progress is being made in dividing them up into small farms.

*The Colosseum by night.*

The problem of dividing up the big estates and of furnishing relief by cheap or free wheat continued to bother Roman leaders for another century after the death of the Gracchi. Julius Caesar, a popular leader who favored such measures, made himself a dictator and established government by emperors. Under his successor, Augustus, a great peace was established which brought prosperity and better living conditions for two hundred years. But the people paid for these advantages by a loss of their liberties and privileges: free speech, political rights, individual liberties of various sorts were gradually reduced.

**DISCUSSION QUESTIONS**

1. Discuss the policy of the Gracchi in giving public lands and wheat to the poor and using the unemployed in building roads. Give some modern parallels.

2. In what European countries has a program of social and economic reform such as that of the Gracchi led to dictatorship?

3. How can we get a maximum of social reform without abandoning important liberties?

348

# Unit XII Review

## LESSONS LXVI–LXXI

## VOCABULARY

| NOUNS | 3. gēns | 6. mīlle | 9. ōrātiō |
|---|---|---|---|
| 1. aetās | 4. imperium | 7. nēmō | 10. regiō |
| 2. condiciō | 5. lēgātus | 8. opus | |

| ADJECTIVES | 14. dissimilis | 18. proprius | 22. suus |
|---|---|---|---|
| 11. aptus | 15. extrēmus | 19. proximus | 23. ulterior |
| 12. centum | 16. humilis | 20. similis | 24. ūtilis |
| 13. difficilis | 17. īnferior | 21. summus | |

| PRONOUN | 25. suī |
|---|---|

| VERBS | 30. emō | 35. iūdicō | 40. statuō |
|---|---|---|---|
| 26. accidō | 31. explicō | 36. iungō | 41. sūmō |
| 27. cadō | 32. fallō | 37. perficiō | 42. trādō |
| 28. cōnspiciō | 33. frangō | 38. rapiō | 43. tribuō |
| 29. crēdō | 34. īnstruō | 39. repellō | 44. vincō |

| ADVERBS | 45. bene | 46. facile |
|---|---|---|

| PREPOSITION | 47. contrā |
|---|---|

| CONJUNCTION | 48. quam |
|---|---|

## ENGLISH WORD STUDIES

1. Give the Latin words suggested by the following English derivatives:

*accident, appropriate, conditional, conspicuous, credible, fallacious, instructive, opera, proximity, rapture, regional, redemptive, repulsive*

2. From the following French numerals obtain the Latin numbers from which they are derived and rearrange in the proper sequence:

*trois, sept, un, cinq, quatre, dix, huit, neuf, deux, six*

3. Find and use in sentences as many English derivatives as possible from **nāvigō, doceō, vincō, sūmō.**

4. Complete each of the following sentences as in this sample: **Perficiō** is to *perfection* as **incipiō** is to *inception.*

a. **Emō** is to *redemption* as    ?    is to *repulsion.*
b. *Creditor* is to **crēdō** as *instructor* is to    ?.
c. **Ūtilis** is to *utility* as    ?    is to *humility.*
d. *Statute* is to **statuō** as *institute* is to    ?.
e. *Consistency* is to **cōnsistō** as    ?    is to **currō.**

## VOCABULARY (English Meanings)

| NOUNS | 3. *nation* | 6. *thousand* | 9. *speech* |
|---|---|---|---|
| 1. *age* | 4. *command* | 7. *no one* | 10. *region* |
| 2. *condition* | 5. *envoy* | 8. *work* | |

| ADJECTIVES | 14. *unlike* | 18. *one's own* | 22. *his own* |
|---|---|---|---|
| 11. *suitable* | 15. *farthest, end of* | 19. *next* | 23. *farther* |
| 12. *hundred* | 16. *low, humble* | 20. *like* | 24. *useful* |
| 13. *difficult* | 17. *lower* | 21. *highest, top of* | |

PRONOUN    25. *of himself*

| VERBS | 30. *buy* | 35. *judge* | 40. *establish* |
|---|---|---|---|
| 26. *happen* | 31. *unfold* | 36. *join* | 41. *take* |
| 27. *fall* | 32. *deceive* | 37. *finish* | 42. *give over* |
| 28. *catch sight of* | 33. *break* | 38. *carry off* | 43. *grant* |
| 29. *believe* | 34. *arrange, provide* | 39. *drive back* | 44. *conquer* |

ADVERBS    45. *well*    46. *easily*

PREPOSITION    47. *against*

CONJUNCTION    48. *than*

## UNIT PRACTICE AND EXERCISES

**Comparison** 1. Compare **aptus, celer, levis, iūstus.** Form and compare adverbs from **certus, ācer, humilis.**

2. Decline **ūtilior liber** and **melior aetās** in the singular.

3. Give in Latin in the singular and plural in the case indicated: *a most beautiful region* (nom.); *a worse time* (acc.); *a rather long journey* (dat.); *the smallest part* (abl.); *a larger ship* (gen.).

**Reflexive Forms** Give in Latin: *he deceives him and himself; they praise them and themselves; they will ask their friends and hers; he accuses himself, we praise him; she will see her father.*

350

# Men Who Made Rome Great

*A modern painting showing the destruction of Carthage by Scipio the Younger in 146 B.C.*

JAMES SAWDERS

*A triumphal procession in the motion picture "Quo Vadis."*

*The triumph of Caesar in a painting by Mantegna (fifteenth century).*

IMP·IVLIO·CAESARI
OB·GALLIAM·DEVICT
MILITARI·POTENCIA
TRIVMPHVS
DECRETVS·INVIDIA
SPRETA·SVPERATA

# *Lesson lxxii*

## The Story of Lucius (*Cont.*)

### CAESARIS TRIUMPHUS

Quondam pater Lūcī ā Forō revertit et dīxit triumphum Caesaris futūrum esse et posteā magnōs lūdōs. C.[1] Iūlius Caesar tum erat maximus Rōmānōrum. Galliam, Alexandrīam, Pontum, Āfricam vīcerat. Decem annōs in Galliā ēgerat atque, multīs mīlibus hostium repulsīs, illam regiōnem in prōvinciam Rōmānam redēgerat. Pom- 5 peius,[2] cum Caesare prō summā potestāte contendēns, in fugam datus erat. Sed nōn satis fuerat: Caesar in Aegyptum prōcesserat et, Alexandrīnīs[3] pulsīs, Cleopātrae nōmen rēgīnae Aegyptiōrum dederat. Postquam in Asiā rēgem Pontī celeriter vīcit, ex eius rēgnō nōtās illās litterās mīserat in quibus erant sōla verba, "Vēnī, vīdī, 10 vīcī." Nunc, hōc opere perfectō, futūrī erant quattuor triumphī, quod Caesar dē bellīs reverterat, cui summa potestās ā deīs commissa est.

### WAITING

Lūcius numquam triumphum vīderat et dē eō multa rogāvit. Pater eī dīxit triumphum esse similem pompae in Circō habitae et Caesarem per Circum et Sacram Viam ad Capitōlium prōcessūrum 15 esse. Lūcius permōtus vix exspectāre poterat. Sed omnia ad eum quī exspectat veniunt; tempus triumphōrum aderat. Prīmus et clārissimus triumphus Caesaris erat Gallicus. Loca emī nōn potuērunt sed pater Lūcī familiāris Caesaris erat et optima loca obtinuit. Postquam Caesar in Campō Mārtiō[4] mīlitēs īnstrūxit et ex praedā eīs 20 praemia tribuit, pompa tardē prōcēdere incipit.

### "HERE THEY COME!"

Post longum tempus (ut[5] Lūcius exīstimāvit) pompa aderat. Prīmī fuērunt cōnsulēs et senātōrēs, post quōs vēnērunt cornicinēs,[6] quī Lūciō grātissimī fuērunt. Tum cōnspexit titulōs[7] ducum oppidōrumque captōrum cum fōrmīs exemplīsque[8] oppidōrum. Dē 25 nōminibus nōn nōtīs multa rogāvit: "Quī sunt Aquītānī? Quī sunt

---

[1] **C. = Gāius.**
[2] *Pompey.*
[3] *the people of Alexandria.*
[4] *Campus Martius (Mar'shius)*, a park in Rome.
[5] *as.*
[6] *buglers.*
[7] *placards* (with names of towns, etc.).
[8] *models* (of wood, etc.).

Belgae?" Pater respondit: "Gallia est omnis dīvīsa [9] in partēs trēs; quārum ūnam incolunt Belgae, aliam Aquītānī, tertiam eī quī ipsōrum linguā Celtae, nostrā Gallī appellantur. Hōrum omnium fortis-
30 simī sunt Belgae." "Quī sunt Helvētiī?" [10] "Helvētiī statuērunt per prōvinciam nostram iter facere quod maiōrēs fīnēs habēre cupīvērunt, sed ā Caesare prohibitī sunt." "Quis est Ariovistus?" "Ariovistus erat superbus rēx Germānōrum, ā Caesare ex Galliā expulsus." "Quī sunt Germānī?" "Maxima pars Germānōrum trāns Rhēnum flūmen in-
35 colunt. [11] Etiam trāns Rhēnum Caesar mīlitēs suōs trādūxit et cum Germānīs contendit." "Quid est Britannia?" "Britannia est extrēma īnsula, ā barbarīs culta; etiam eam Caesar attigit. Sed nōn ante centum annōs nostra erit."

### HAIL! THE CONQUERING HERO COMES!

Posteā Lūcius cōnspexit arma captōrum prīncipum et prīncipēs
40 ipsōs ligātōs, inter quōs erat Vercingetorīx. [12] Nunc populus maximē clāmat. "Quis est ille?" rogat Lūcius. Pater respondet: "Ille est ultimus dux Gallōrum, quī victōs Gallōs ad bellum permōvit, sed Caesarī trāditus est. Postquam pompa Capitōlium attigit, ille interficiētur." Nunc clāmōrēs audiuntur: "Caesar adest! Caesar adest!"
45 Currus imperātōris, quattuor equīs trāctus, cernitur. Caesar ipse togam pictam [13] gerit et scēptrum tenet. In currū [14] stat servus corōnam super Caesaris caput tenēns. Sed subitō [15] omnēs terrentur: axe frāctō, Caesar paene [16] ē currū iactus est. Hic sōlus nōn commōtus est. Dum cōnstitit ac novum currum exspectat, Lūcium cōn-
50 spicit et eum rogat: "Tū, quis es?" Lūcius respondet: "Ego sum Lūcius Iūlius. Patrem meum nōvistī. Mīles erō et multās gentēs vincam." Caesar rīdēns eius caput tetigit et dīxit: "Satis bene incipis. Exīstimō tē imperātōrem futūrum esse." Pompa intermissa rūrsus [17] prōcēdit, et nunc mīlitēs Caesaris accēdunt, clāmantēs, "Iō
55 triumphe! [18] Iō triumphe!" Etiam carmina canunt. Inter alia Lūcius haec audit:
"Ecce [19] Caesar nunc triumphat quī subēgit Galliās."
Itaque omnēs discēdunt, Lūciō clāmānte, "Iō triumphe! Iō triumphe!"

[9] From **dividō**. Use derivative.
[10] *Helvetians (Helvē'shians)*.
[11] A plural verb may be used when the subject is grammatically singular but refers to more than one.
[12] *Vercingetorix (Versinjet'orix)*.
[13] *embroidered* (with gold).
[14] Ablative.
[15] *suddenly*.
[16] *almost*.
[17] *again*.
[18] Exclamation: *Triumph!*
[19] *look*.

1. What was a triumph?
2. What two kings did Caesar defeat?
3. Who came first in the parade and who last?

## Stop! Look! Think!

The words in the following groups closely resemble one another in form or sound and must be carefully distinguished. See the Latin-English Vocabulary.

| | | |
|---|---|---|
| accēdō, accidō | cīvis, cīvitās | ob, ab |
| aetās, aestās | gēns, genus | pars, pār |
| alius, alter, altus | ibi, ubi | pōnō, possum |
| cadō, cēdō | liber, līber, līberī | vīs, vir |

**Vocabulary**  attin′gō, –ere, at′tigī, attāc′tus, *touch, reach*  [*tangō*]
exīs′timō, –ā′re, –ā′vī, –ā′tus, *think*  [*aestimō, estimate*]
in′colō, –ere, inco′luī, incul′tus, *live, inhabit*  [*colō*]
post′quam, conj., *after*  [*post + quam*]
potes′tās, potestā′tis, f., *power*  [*possum*]
sa′tis, adv. and indeclinable adj., *enough*  (satisfaction)
su′per, prep. with acc., *over, above*  [*superō*]

## English Word Studies

1. Most of the names of our states are Indian, but several of them are of Latin origin or form. Vermont means *green mountain* (**viridis mōns**), Pennsylvania is *Penn's woods* (**silva**), Virginia is the *maiden's* land (named after Queen Elizabeth I, the virgin queen), Florida is the *flowery* land (**flōs, flōris**), Colorado is the land of the *colored* or *red* river, Montana is *mountainous* (**mōns**), Nevada is the land of *snow* (**nix, nivis**), and Rhode Island is said to be named after the Greek island of Rhodes, meaning *rose*. New Jersey means "New Caesarea," named after the island of Jersey, one of many places named in honor of one of the Caesars. The titles *Kaiser* and *Czar* also come from Caesar.

Names whose endings only are Latin are Carolina (Charles II), Georgia (George II), Louisiana (Louis XIV), and Indiana.

2. Explain *conjunction, adjunct, infallible, repellent, distraction*.

3. Our word *capitol*, used of a statehouse and of the seat of the United States Congress, is derived from **Capitōlium**. The word *Capitol* occurs as the name of a business one hundred and thirty-nine times in the Washington telephone directory, sixty-one in Indianapolis, twenty-six in Baltimore, etc. Do you know of any firms by this name? A town in Montana has the name *Capitol*.

*An ancient statue of Marius in a museum in Rome. Here Marius is shown wearing the toga of the peaceful orator, not the uniform of a conquering general.*

# Lesson lxxiii

## MARIUS

C. Marius, vir humilis generis, ob ēgregiam virtūtem cōnsul ā Rōmānīs factus est. Plūrimī cīvēs exīstimāvērunt eum esse maximum imperātōrem aetātis suae.

Iugurthā,[1] rēge Numidiae, quae terra in Āfricā est, victō, Marius
5 bellum contrā Cimbrōs et Teutonēs[2] suscēpit. Hī, quī extrēmōs fīnēs Germāniae incoluerant, Cimbrīs sē iūnxerant. Multōs mēnsēs hae duae gentēs novās terrās petīverant et prōvinciam Rōmānam attigerant. Tribus ducibus Rōmānīs ā barbarīs repulsīs, Marius mīlitēs trēs annōs exercuit. Posteā Teutonēs sub Alpibus proeliō superāvit
10 ac super centum mīlia interfēcit.

Cimbrī autem nihil dē victōriā Rōmānōrum audīverant et per lēgātōs praemissōs sibi et Teutonibus agrōs petīvērunt. Marius rīdēns, "Illī tenent," inquit, "semperque tenēbunt terram ā[3] nōbīs acceptam." Proximō annō is cum mīlitibus bene exercitīs contrā eōs
15 pugnāvit. Nec minor erat pugna cum uxōribus eōrum quam cum virīs. Illae quae supererant sē līberōsque suōs interfēcērunt.

Multōs annōs Rōmānī hōs barbarōs īnstantēs timuerant sed post hanc victōriam Alpēs Rōmam ā perīculō prohibēbant.

---

[1] *Jugur'tha.*   [2] *Cimbri (Sim'brī), Teu'tons.*   [3] *from.*

Postquam Rōmānī intellēxērunt necesse[4] esse bellum cum Mi- thridāte[5] gerere, hoc negōtium Sullae commīsērunt. Sed postquam 20 Sulla ex urbe discessit, Marius, quī ipse cupīvit hoc negōtium super omnia suscipere, summam potestātem obtinuit. Posteā Sulla cum mīlitibus quōs circum sē habuit Marium in fugam dedit. Mīlitibus praemissīs, paucōs mēnsēs Rōmae[6] mānsit. Postquam autem Sulla ad bellum discessit, Marius Rōmam vāstāvit.                                    25

Quattuor annōs Sulla cum Mithridāte bellum gessit. Post mortem Marī in Italiam revertit. Omnēs hostēs prae sē agēns, circum multa oppida mīlitēs suōs dūxit. Dictātor factus, multa mīlia cīvium interficī iussit. Amīcus eum monuit: "Nōnne intellegis hoc satis esse? Sī omnēs interficiēs, et nēmō supererit, quōrum cīvium dictātor eris?" 30

QUESTIONS
1. What was the cause of the war with the Cimbri and Teutons?
2. Which did Marius defeat first? Where?
3. What was the cause of the quarrel between Marius and Sulla?
4. Give some examples of men in modern times who, like Marius, rose to high positions from humble beginnings.

READING     Mills, pp. 215–221; 223–231.

### Accusative of Extent

Duōs annōs remānsit, *He remained two years.*
Flūmen decem pedēs altum est, *The river is ten feet deep.*

*Observe* that

1. duōs annōs answers the question, *How long?*
2. decem pedēs answers the question, *How much?*
3. both express *extent* by the accusative;
4. the English and Latin constructions are identical and are not to be confused with the direct object.

### Post, Posteā, and Postquam

The conjunction postquam, meaning *after*, must be distinguished carefully from the adverb posteā, meaning *afterwards*, and the preposition post, meaning *after* (or *behind*). Examine the following:

---

[4] *necessary* (indeclinable).     [5] *Mithridā'tēs.*     [6] *at Rome.*

1. **Post hunc mēnsem plūrēs librōs legam**, *After this month I shall read more books.*

2. **Posteā multōs librōs lēgī**, *Afterwards I read many books.*

3. **Postquam opus perfēcī, multōs librōs lēgī**, *After I finished the work, I read many books.*

*Observe* that

1. the addition of **quam** to **post** makes **postquam** a conjunction, which is followed by a verb, usually in the perfect indicative;

2. **posteā** [7] means literally *after that*, i.e., *afterwards*;

3. the real difficulty is not in Latin but in the English use of *after*, as both a conjunction and a preposition.

*Postquam* vīdit quod *post* sē erat quīnque mīlia pedum cucurrit.

**Exercises**

**A.** 1. Illī hominēs multōs mēnsēs sē exercuērunt.
2. Exīstimō hunc montem esse mīlle pedēs altum.
3. Ego exīstimō nōs in illō locō duōs annōs remānsisse.
4. Super tria mīlia Germānōrum, pāce factā, Rōmānīs sēsē iūnxērunt.
5. Postquam hostēs ā mīlitibus praemissīs victī sunt, paucī superfuērunt.
6. Postquam mīlitēs servōs cōnspexērunt, eōs circum viās prae sē ēgērunt.
7. Quis cōnspexit nautās nāvigantēs "plānīs" [8] (in locō nāvium) super caput?

**B.** 1. In summer we hasten to the fields.
2. The greater part of the winter we remain in town.
3. After the boy fell into the river, his sister ran shouting to her mother.
4. My brother will arrive next year and remain with me [9] the whole summer.
5. We understand that you have been training yourselves for many months.

---

[7] Sometimes **post** is used as an adverb like **posteā**.

[8] i.e., "airplanes."

[9] See p. 162, footnote.

**Vocabulary**  au'tem, conj. (never first word), *however*
cir'cum, prep. with acc., *around*
exer'ceō, –ē're, exer'cuī, exer'citus, *keep busy, train*
(exercise)
intel'legō, –ere, –lē'xī, –lēc'tus, *understand*  (intellect)
negō'tium, negō'tī, n., *business*  [ōtium]
prae, prep. with abl., *before, in front of*
praemit'tō, –ere, –mī'sī, –mis'sus, *send ahead*  [mittō]
super'sum, –es'se, super'fuī, superfutū'rus, *be left (over),*
*survive*  [sum]

## Latin and English Word Formation

Ne– is sometimes used as a negative prefix in Latin: **nēmō**
(**ne–homō**), **negōtium** (**ne–ōtium**), **neuter** (**ne–uter**), **nūllus** (**ne–
ūllus**). We do the same thing in English with *no: nothing, none*
(*no-one*), *neither* (*no-either*).

**Circum, contrā, prae,** and **super** have their usual meanings when
used as prefixes in Latin and English. In English **prae** becomes *pre–*,
as *pre–pare, pre–fix*; **contrā** sometimes retains its form, sometimes
becomes *counter–*, as *contra–dict, counter–act*. **Super** sometimes
becomes *sur–* in English, in which form it must be distinguished from
assimilated **sub**: *surplus, surmount* (**super**), but *surreptitious* (**sub**).

Find ten English words with these prefixes, compounded with
Latin words which you have studied. Explain *intelligence, super-
visor, surplus, precedent.*

*Monticello, Virginia, the home of Thomas Jefferson, which he designed himself,
following ancient models in the Doric columns and the Roman dome.*

Another wall painting from Pompeii. The man at the bottom is taking life easy while the leopard is working hard to get a square meal.

# Lesson lxxiv

## GRACCHĪ

Ti. et C. Gracchī Scīpiōnis Āfricānī nepōtēs [1] erant. Dīligentiā Cornēliae mātris puerī doctī sunt. Cornēlia crēdidit eōs certē summam potestātem obtentūrōs esse. Quondam hospita, domō Cornēliae petītā, ōrnāmenta sua pulcherrima manū prae sē tenēns ostendēbat. Tum Cornēlia līberōs suōs, quī cāsū aderant, manū tetigit atque hospitae dēmōnstrāns dīxit: "Haec sunt mea ōrnāmenta!"

Tiberius iam vir plēbī amīcus erat. Tribūnus plēbis factus [2] populō agrōs dare cupiēbat. Hī agrī pūblicī erant sed multōs annōs ā nōbilibus occupātī erant, quī dīxērunt sē eōs nōn redditūrōs esse. Tamen Tiberius populō eōs reddidit. Tum senātus convocātus dē Tiberiō cōnsuluit. Multī eum dēspicientēs interficere cupīvērunt. Tiberiō accēdente, Scīpiō Nāsīca,[3] senātor, clāmāvit: "Venīte mēcum sī reī [4] pūblicae salūtem cupitis." Tum ille et aliī quī circum eum stābant, Tiberium, impetū factō, interfēcērunt.

---

[1] grandsons.    [2] 133 B.C.    [3] Nasī'ca.    [4] Genitive of **rēs**.

*A model of part of ancient Rome, showing the round Colosseum at the top left, the Circus Maximus in the center, and the Palatine Hill at the right.*

Posteā in somnō Gāius vīdit frātrem suum, quī dīxit: "Cūr dubitās, 15 Gāī? Tū, quī superes, hoc negōtium perficere et vītam tuam populō dare dēbēs." Itaque Gāius opus Tiberī sē perfectūrum esse statuit neque eius cōnsilia dēsertūrum. Tribūnus factus plēbī frūmentum dabat et cīvitātem omnibus quī Italiam incolēbant. Mīlitēs autem exercēre nōn potuit et intellēxit sē sine exercitū nihil efficere posse; 20 sine praesidiō fugere coāctus interfectus est.

Itaque senātus mortem Gracchōrum effēcit. Sed cōnsilia hōrum mānsērunt, et Rōmānī multōs annōs eōs memoriā tenuērunt.

**QUESTIONS**     1. Who was the grandfather of Gaius Gracchus?
                  2. Who was the teacher of Tiberius Gracchus?
                  3. What was the political policy of Gaius?

**READING**     Mills, pp. 199–208.

### Fourth Declension

As we have seen, the first decension is the *A*–declension, the second is the *O*–declension, the third is the consonant and *I*–declension. These three, especially the third, are the most important. A few nouns belong to the *fourth declension*, which is the *U*–declension. Most of these nouns are derived from verbs.

*The Declension Family. Little 1 says "A," 2 says "O," big 3 says "I," and a lot of other letters, tiny 4 says "U."*

*A bakery in Herculaneum which specialized in cakes. In the rear room, the baking dishes hang on the wall. In the front are the mills for grinding the grain; for the bakers ground their own grain. One of the mills has lost its upper millstone; the other has only a small piece left.*

| | ENDINGS | | EXAMPLE | |
|---|---|---|---|---|
| | SING. | PLUR. | SING. | PLUR. |
| *Nom.* | –us | –ūs | cāsus | cāsūs |
| *Gen.* | –ūs | –uum | cāsūs | cāsuum |
| *Dat.* | –uī | –ibus | cāsuī | cāsibus |
| *Acc.* | –um | –ūs | cāsum | cāsūs |
| *Abl.* | –ū | –ibus | cāsū | cāsibus |

*Gender.* Most nouns of the fourth declension in –**us** are masculine; the only feminines in this book are **manus** and **domus**.

**Practice**

1. Decline **exercitus noster, hic impetus fortis.**
2. Name the case or cases of each of the following words: **senātū, impetum, manibus, ōrātiōne, domuī, exercituum, condiciōnibus.**

**Exercises A.** 1. Quid manū tuā tenēs?
2. Paucī cūrās cāsūsque vītae leviter dēspicere possunt.
3. Exercitus noster impetum in (*on*) ōrdinēs Gallōrum fēcit.
4. Omnēs cīvēs in suīs propriīs domibus ā barbarīs interfectī sunt.
5. Maiōrēs gentēs iūra minōrum populōrum dēspicere nōn dēbent.
6. Postquam cāsus ducī nūntiātus est, ille mortem suā manū petīvit.

**B.** 1. I determined to move into another house next month.
    2. I found a suitable house and approached it.
    3. The house was deserted; I could see nothing.
    4. I touched a body with my hand and cried out.

| **Vocabulary** | | |
|---|---|---|
| cā′sus, –ūs, m., *fall, chance, accident* | [*cadō*] |
| dēmōns′trō, –ā′re, –ā′vī, –ā′tus, *show* | [*mōnstrō*] |
| dē′serō, –ere, dēse′ruī, dēser′tus, *desert* | (desertion) |
| dēspi′ciō, –ere, dēspe′xī, dēspec′tus, *look down on, despise* | [*spectō*] |
| do′mus, –ūs,[5] f., *house, home* | (domestic) |
| exer′citus, –ūs, m., (*trained*) *army* | [*exerceō*] |
| im′petus, –ūs, m., *attack* | [*petō*] |
| ma′nus, –ūs, f., *hand* | (manual) |
| red′dō, –ere, red′didī, red′ditus, *give back* | [*dō*] |
| senā′tus, –ūs, m., *senate* | (senatorial) |

## English Word Studies

In two earlier lessons (pp. 97, 100) we saw that many English words are simply the base of a Latin noun, adjective, or verb, or the base plus silent –*e*. A great many such words are derived from the Latin words in this book. A few are *par, facile, prime, just, cede, part*. In the case of verbs, the base of the present indicative, present participle, or perfect participle, or of all three, may furnish an English word: *convene, convenient, convent; remove, remote; agent, act*.

As previously noted, there are sometimes changes in the base, such as the dropping of one of two final consonants, as in *remit, expel*, and particularly the addition of a vowel to the main vowel of the word, as in the following: *p·e·ace mo·u·nt, re·i·gn, rema·i·n. Cont·a·in, ret·a·in*, etc., are from the compounds of **teneō**.

Find ten more words illustrating these principles. Explain *domestic, manual labor, manicure, despicable, impetuous*.

*Manicure.*

---

[5] Usually has abl. sing. **domō** and acc. plur. **domōs** (p. 393).

*Scipio crowns an African king. From the motion picture "Scipio Africanus."*

# Lesson lxxv

## SCĪPIŌ

P. Cornēlius Scīpiō patrem, quī impetū hostium graviter vulnerātus erat, servāvit.[1] Post pugnam Cannēnsem,[2] in quā Rōmānī interclūsī et gravissimē victī sunt, omnibus probantibus, Scīpiōnī, puerō vīgintī annōrum, summum imperium datum est. Ille spem
5 salūtis Rōmānīs reddidit. Postquam sex annōs in Italiā exercituī praefuit, Rōmānī eum exercituī Hispānō praefēcērunt. Ille urbem Carthāginem Novam diē quō vēnit expugnāvit; ita celer erat. Quīntō annō exercitūs hostium ex Hispāniā expulit. Dēmōnstrāverat cīvibus suīs Carthāginiēnsēs vincī posse. Neque aurum rapuerat neque
10 miserīs nocuerat.

Hispāniā victā, hic prīnceps in Āfricam prōcēdere mātūrāvit et ibi Carthāginiēnsēs victōriīs terruit. Tum senātus Carthāginiēnsium Hannibalem ad patriam vocāvit. Sed Scīpiō eum Zamae[3] vīcit, et

---

[1] Second Punic War (218–201 B.C.), greatest of the three wars against Carthage.

[2] *of Cannae (Căn'ē).* The Carthaginian plan of encirclement used in this battle was imitated by the Germans in their conquest of Poland in 1939 and in Belgium and France

in 1940; the American army used it with great success in the Ruhr district of Germany in 1945.

[3] *at Zama* (202 B.C.), in Tunisia, territory fought over by our soldiers in 1943. There is a town in Mississippi named *Zama*.

ille, clārissimus et maximus omnium ducum quī contrā Rōmānōs pugnāvērunt, ex patriā suā fūgit. Scīpiō ob hanc victōriam Āfricānus 15 appellātus est. Nōn iam Hannibal, cuius nōmen līberōs Rōmānōrum terruerat, īnstābat.

Multae rēs dē Scīpiōne Āfricānō trāduntur. Quondam, dum exercituī praeest, ille ad oppidum mūnītum in quō erant multī mīlitēs interclūsī exercitum addūxit. Scīpiō exīstimābat oppidum capī posse, 20 sed paucī eandem spem habuērunt. Cāsū ūnus ē mīlitibus hominem ligātum, quī alterī mīlitī nocuerat, ad eum trāxit et rogāvit: "Quō diē locōque iubēs hunc hominem ad tē ad supplicium venīre?" Tum Scīpiō manum ad oppidum ipsum tetendit et iussit eum hominem in illō oppidō tertiō diē esse. Ita rēs facta est; tertiō diē, impetū 25 ācriter factō, oppidum expugnātum est eōdemque diē ibi ille suppliciō hominem affēcit.

Saepe ante prīmam lūcem hic prīnceps populī Rōmānī domum relinquēbat et in Capitōlium veniēbat et ibi sōlus multās hōrās sedēbat. Aliī putāvērunt Scīpiōnem, deīs dēspectīs, hanc rem ad speciem 30 facere; aliī autem crēdidērunt eum dē salūte cīvitātis deum cōnsulere.

QUESTIONS
1. How old was Scipio when he went to Spain?
2. Why was Scipio called Africanus?
3. What explanations were given of Scipio's visits to the temple?

*Romulus and Remus on an Italian stamp. This ancient bronze wolf is now, as it was in ancient times, on the Capitoline Hill in Rome, where, as Cicero tells us, it was damaged by lightning. You can see where the lightning struck on the left hind leg. The original twins disappeared, and the present ones were added in the fifteenth century.*

**Fifth Declension**

The last of the noun declensions includes comparatively few words. **Rēs** and **diēs**, however, occur constantly and should be memorized. Other nouns of the *fifth declension,* as a rule, have no plural; all are feminine except **diēs**, which is usually masculine.

| | ENDINGS | | EXAMPLES | | | |
|---|---|---|---|---|---|---|
| | SING. | PLUR. | SING. | PLUR. | SING. | PLUR. |
| *Nom.* | –ēs | –ēs | diēs | diēs | rēs | rēs |
| *Gen.* | –ēī or –ĕī | –ērum | diēī | diērum | reī | rērum |
| *Dat.* | –ēī or –ĕī | –ēbus | diēī | diēbus | reī | rēbus |
| *Acc.* | –em | –ēs | diem | diēs | rem | rēs |
| *Abl.* | –ē | –ēbus | diē | diēbus | rē | rēbus |

*Observe* that –e– appears in every ending, for this is the *E*– declension. In **diēs** it is long in the genitive and dative singular, though it precedes a vowel (p. 384).

**Practice**

1. Decline **rēs similis** and **ūna spēs.**
2. Give each of the following in the form indicated: **diēs proximus** (abl. plur.); **prīnceps noster** (acc. sing.); **speciēs nova** (dat. sing.); **impetus maior** (acc. plur.); **manus pulchra** (gen. plur.); **melior lūx** (abl. sing.).

**Lazy Latin**

"Get your facts first" is a good rule for doing almost anything. So get your facts about the words and their forms in a Latin phrase or sentence before you jump to conclusions—or you will find you have missed the mark. You can have some fun with "Lazy Latin" but you will not learn anything from it except to be careful. Can you correct these mistranslations?

**de jure,** *the jury.*  
**sine die,** *die in sin.*  
**bona fide,** *skinny dog.*  
**et tu Brute,** *ate two brutes.*  
**prima facie,** *first-class face.*  

**homo sapiens,** *a sappy man.*  
**lux ex oriente,** *oriental soap.*  
**genus homo,** *the man is a genius.*  
**argumentum ad hominem,** *argument over hominy.*

**Exercises A.** 1. Amīcus certus in rē incertā cernitur.
2. Speciēs illōrum barbarōrum mē puerum terrēbat.
3. Virum quī huic operī praefuit illī urbī praeficiam.
4. Memoria diēī bene āctī est per sē satis magnum praemium.
5. Dēmōnstrāvī illum prīncipem nocuisse senātuī populōque Rōmānō.
6. Lēgātus Rōmānus dīxit exercitum suum domibus nōn nocitūrum esse.
7. Quid significant (*mean*) hae litterae, in signīs Rōmānīs vīsae, "S P Q R"? Rogā magistrum tuum sī nōn nōvistī.

**B.** 1. Most (men) are deceived by the appearance of things.
2. Show him your new books; he will not do harm to them.
3. By chance I heard our leader say that there was hope of peace.
4. We put a general in charge of affairs; he desired to send grain to Europe.

**Vocabulary**

di′ēs, diē′ī, m., *day* (diary)
interclū′dō, –ere, –clū′sī, clū′sus, *cut off* [*claudō*]
lūx, lū′cis, f., *light* (translucent)
no′ceō, –ē′re, no′cuī, nocitū′rus, *do harm* (*to*) (with dat.) (innocent)
praefi′ciō, –ere, –fē′cī, –fec′tus, *put in charge of* (with acc. and dat.) [*faciō*]
prae′sum, –es′se, prae′fuī, praefutū′rus, *be in charge of* (with dat.) [*sum*]
prīn′ceps, prīn′cipis, m., *leader* [*prīmus + capiō*]
rēs, re′ī, f., *thing, matter, affair* (real)
spe′ciēs, speciē′ī, f., *appearance* [*speciō*]
spēs, spe′ī, f., *hope* [*spērō*]

### English Word Studies

1. English words which preserve the forms of the Latin fourth declension are: *census, consensus, impetus, prospectus, status, apparatus* (plural *apparatuses* or *apparatus*; the latter preserves the Latin plural). Note that *consensus* (from **sentiō**) is spelled with an –s– but *census* (from **cēnseō**) with a –c–. An ablative form of this declension is seen in *impromptu*.

The fifth declension is represented by *rabies, series, species*. The last two are used in the plural with no change of form (as in Latin).

The accusative singular is represented by *requiem*, the ablative singular by *specie*, and the ablative plural by *rebus*.

A.M., ante merīdiem, *before midday*; P.M., post merīdiem, *after midday*; M., merīdiēs, *midday*, come from the fifth declension.

2. Latin phrases in English:

**bona fide,** *in good faith.*
**casus belli,** *an occasion for war.*
**prima facie,** *on the first face* (*of it*); as *prima facie* evidence.
**in statu quo,** *in the situation in which* (*it was before*); **status quo,** *the situation in which* (*it was before*).
**sine die,** *without a day* (*being set*); used of adjournment for an indefinite period by a parliamentary body.
Explain **per diem, post mortem, sui generis.**

*The Roman senate house—with the three windows—as it now is ( cf. p. 93).*

# *Lesson lxxvi*

## CATŌ ET SCĪPIŌ

M. Catō, vir humilī genere, ad summōs honōrēs per sē ascenderat. Hic Scīpiōnī, virō nōbilissimā familiā, inimīcus erat et eum dēspexit. Itaque familiārem suum Petīlium iussit in senātū petere et explōrāre ratiōnēs pecūniae praedaeque captae in bellō cum Antiochō[1] ā Scīpiōne gestō. Hōc modō senātum in duās partēs dīvīsit, ūnam quae  5 Scīpiōnī nocēre cupiēbat, alteram quae eum prīncipem maximae virtūtis esse crēdēbat. Tum Scīpiō, cuius īra ex speciē gravī frontis clārē cernī poterat, librum prae sē tenuit et dīxit:

"In hōc librō ratiōnēs scrīptae sunt omnis pecūniae omniumque rērum quās accēpī. Hic est diēs quō mihi in animō erat[2] ratiōnēs 10 apud vōs legere atque explicāre. Nunc autem, quod Petīlius eās explōrāre et mihi imperāre cupit, apud vōs eās nōn explicābō."

Hōc dictō, librum suīs propriīs manibus dīscidit.[3]

---

[1] *Antī'ochus,* a Syrian king.    [2] **mihi . . . erat,** *I intended.*    [3] *tore in pieces.*

**QUESTIONS**
1. In what respect were Cato and Scipio unlike?
2. Why did Scipio tear the book in pieces?
3. According to this story, what is the wrong way to get a person to do something?
4. What other Romans besides Cato rose to high positions from humble origins?

### Genitive and Ablative of Description

1. **virī magnae virtūtis,** *men of great courage.*
2. **spatium decem pedum,** *a space of ten feet.*
3. **hominēs inimīcō animō,** *men with* (or *of*) *an unfriendly spirit.*

*Observe* that in English we may say *men **of*** or ***with*** *an unfriendly spirit.* Both are descriptive. Note also that description is similarly expressed in Latin, i.e., either by the genitive or the ablative, but only when modified by an adjective.

While the *genitive* and the *ablative of description* are translated alike, Latin uses the genitive chiefly for *permanent* qualities, such as measure and number (see 2) and the ablative for *temporary* qualities, such as personal appearance.

*A charming home in Wisconsin on Lake Michigan in a modified Pompeian style. The wall paintings represent the gods Neptune and Venus.*

WALTER H. MAYER

**Exercises** **A.** 1. Lēgātus Gallōrum fuit vir clārissimō genere.
2. "Dīvide et imperā" erat cōnsilium Rōmānōrum.
3. Ille erat puer magnā grātiā apud familiārēs suōs.
4. Hāc aestāte ascendam montem decem mīlium pedum
5. Eum montem sōlī virī maximae virtūtis explōrāvērunt.
6. Frontem huius montis ascendere nōn poterō, quod ea est praeceps et difficillima.

**B.** 1. The general was a man of great influence.
2. Do you desire to climb a mountain which has never been explored?
3. We know that Italy is divided from Gaul by very high mountains.
4. After a journey of two days, we arrived at ( **ad** ) a very beautiful city.

**Vocabulary**  a′pud, prep. with acc., *among*
ascen′dō, –ere, ascen′dī, ascēn′sus, *climb* (*up*), *ascend*
  [*scandō, climb*]
dī′vidō, –ere, dīvī′sī, dīvī′sus, *divide*   (division)
explō′rō, –ā′re, –ā′vī, –ā′tus, *investigate, explore*
  [*plōrō, call out*]
*frōns, fron′tis, fron′tium, f., *forehead, front*   (frontal)
im′perō, –ā′re, –ā′vī, –ā′tus, *command* (with dat. of person)   [*imperium*]
ra′tiō, ratiō′nis, f., *account, reason*   (rational)

## Latin and English Word Formation

The suffixes –ilis and –bilis are added to verb .stems to form adjectives. They indicate what *can be done:* **facilis** is "doable," *easy.* The suffix –ilis usually becomes –ile in English: *facile, fertile.* The more common suffix –bilis becomes –ble, –able, –ible in English: *noble, credible, terrible, amiable, visible, comparable.*

Several suffixes meaning *pertaining to* are added to nouns and adjectives to form adjectives: –āris (English –ar), –ārius (–ary), –ānus (–an, –ane), –icus (–ic). Examples of their use in Latin and English are: **familiāris, frūmentārius, Rōmānus, pūblicus;** *singular, ordinary, human, humane, generic.*

The suffix –tūdō (English –tude) is added to adjective stems to form nouns and means *state of being;* **magnitūdō,** *magnitude.*

Find fifteen other examples of these suffixes in English words derived from Latin words already studied.

Four states have towns named *Cato* and *Scipio.*

*Wearers of the toga represented in this beautiful relief from the Altar of Peace erected in Rome during the reign of Augustus.*

# Lesson lxxvii

**The Story of Lucius** (*Concluded*)

## CĪVIS NOVUS ITER FACIT

Iam Lūcius aetātem quīndecim annōrum attigerat. Nunc pater eius dīxit eum dēbēre proximīs Līberālibus [1] togam praetextam dēpōnere et virīlem togam sūmere. Hōc tempore plūrimī puerī Rōmānī togās praetextās dēpōnēbant. (Puerī Rōmānī togās praetextās gerēbant, sed virī tōtās albās gerēbant. Brācae,[2] quae ā virīs nunc 5 geruntur, ā barbarīs, nōn ā Rōmānīs, illīs diēbus gerēbantur.)

### THE NEW CITIZEN

Līberālia aderant. Multī amīcī convēnērunt. Lūcius, postquam mōrem antīquum servāns togam praetextam ante Larēs posuit, novam virīlem togam sūmpsit. Omnēs familiārēs cum eō ad Forum pedibus prōcessērunt, et posteā ad Capitōlium, ubi nōmen eius in 10 numerō cīvium scrīptum est. Nunc poterat dīcere, "Cīvis Rōmānus

---

[1] The *Liberalia*, a festival held March 17.      [2] *trousers.*

sum!" Tum omnēs cum Lūciō domum [3] revertērunt, ubi optima cēna parāta erat. Multī cibī dē ultimīs terrīs portātī erant, aliī dē Graeciā, aliī dē Asiā, aliī dē Āfricā. Amīcī cēnam variō sermōne in noctem
15 prōdūxērunt et cum Lūciō dē officiīs cīvium, dē bellō et pāce, dē negōtiīs, dē multīs aliīs rēbus ēgērunt. Lūcius nunc intellēxit mūnera et officia cīvis Rōmānī.

### THE JOURNEY

Paulō [4] post Lūcius, iam vir, cum patre iter fēcit. Itaque per portam Capēnam [5] ex urbe discessērunt. Raedā ibi inventā, in Appiā
20 Viā prōcessērunt. Sepulchrīs ad viam cōnspectīs, Lūcius dīxit: "Pater, cūr sepulchra ad viās pōnuntur? Hoc numquam intellegere potuī." Pater respondit: "Hōc modō omnēs ea vidēre possunt." Lūcius dīxit sē nocte inter sepulchra iter facere nōn cupere.

### GOOD ROADS AND GREAT MEN

Quod iter facile et commodum erat, Lūcius dīxit: "Nōnne exīsti-
25 mās Appiam Viam optimam omnium esse?" Pater respondit: "Omnēs nostrae viae optimae sunt. Ob eam causam hostēs vīcimus, fīnēs lātiōrēs parāvimus, potestātem patriae nostrae auximus, et nunc

---

[3] As in English, "place to which" is expressed without a preposition with **domum**: *home.*

[4] *shortly.*

[5] A gate in the wall of Rome.

*The capitol in Caracas, Venezuela, is classical in design.*

gentēs regimus. Aliī pictūrās pulchriōrēs pingunt,[6] aliī ōrant[7] causās melius, sed nōs regimus populōs." "Etiam apud nōs causae optimē ōrantur," respondit Lūcius. "Quis melior ōrātor fuit aut est aut erit 30 quam Cicerō? Hic ōrātor etiam cōnsul fuit et populum Rōmānum rēxit. Ego eum ōrātiōnem habentem in Forō audīvī et eius ōrātiōnēs in lūdō lēgī." "Lēgistīne ōrātiōnēs in Catilīnam, illum quī cīvitātem vī opprimere statuit?" "Illās et aliās lēgī. In prīmā dīxit dē Catilīnā: 'Ō tempora! Ō mōrēs! Senātus haec intellegit, cōnsul videt; hic tamen 35 vīvit.'" "Optimē!" dīxit pater. "In secundā, sī memoria mē nōn fallit, dīxit, postquam Catilīna ex urbe discessit: 'Abiit,[8] excessit, ēvāsit,[9] ērūpit!'[10] Ex Cicerōnis linguā fluēbat ōrātiō dulcior quam mel."

### SCENES BY THE WAY

Tum altōs et pulchrōs arcūs[11] aquaeductūs[12] cernunt, quī optimam aquam dē montibus in urbem dūcit. Pater Lūciō dīxit prīmum 40 aquaeductum ab Appiō factum esse. Appius fuit ille quī Appiam Viam mūnīvit. Ita prōcēdunt, nunc agrōs et vīllās, montēs silvāsque spectantēs, nunc hominēs in viā ipsā, quōrum aliī pedibus prōcēdēbant, aliī aut equō aut raedā aut lectīcā[13] ferēbantur.[14]

### EPILOGUE

Nōn iam vīvunt Lūcius et eius amīcī, nōn iam vīvunt Caesar et 45 Cicerō, prīncipēs summae auctōritātis, sed lingua eōrum vīvit, vīvunt eōrum dicta et facta, lēgēs et mōrēs, glōria et fāma. Haec omnia in eōrum librīs inveniuntur. Eīs quī itinera parva per illōs librōs faciunt Rōmānī ipsī vīvere videntur.

**QUESTIONS**
1. What do you think of the idea of having a ceremony when a boy or girl becomes a citizen?
2. Is it done in your community?
3. Why were the Roman cemeteries along the main highways?

**Vocabulary**
dēpō'nō, –ere, dēpo'suī, dēpo'situs, *put* or *lay aside* [*pōnō*]
mōs, mō'ris, m., *custom*  (moral)
*nox, noc'tis, noc'tium, f., *night*  (nocturnal)
vī'vō, –ere, vī'xī, vīc'tus, *live*  (vivid)

**Synonyms**

We rarely find a word in any language which has exactly the same meaning as another word. Words which have almost the same

---

[6] *paint.*
[7] *plead.*
[8] *he has gone away.*
[9] Ēvādō, ēvāsus—derivative?
[10] Ērumpō, ēruptus—derivative?
[11] Accusative plural.
[12] Genitive singular.
[13] *litter.*
[14] *were carried.*

meaning are called *synonyms*. **Homō** and **vir** both mean *man*, but **homō** sometimes means any *human being*; **vir**, a *"he-man,"* or *hero*.

The following synonyms have occurred in previous lessons:

1. **ante** = *before* (of time and place), adverb or preposition (with accusative).

   **prae** = *before* (of place only), preposition (with ablative).

2. **terra** = *land* (as opposed to water), also some particular *land* or *country*.

   **fīnēs** = *borders,* hence a *land* or *country* with reference to its boundaries.

   **patria** = *fatherland,* the *land* of one's birth.

3. **dux** [**dūcō**] = *a leader* in any field, but often in a military sense.

   **prīnceps** [**prīmus** + **capiō**] = the *first* or *chief* man in a group—usually nonmilitary.

4. **videō** = *see,* the most common word.
   **cernō** = *see clearly.*
   **cōnspiciō** = *catch sight of.*
   **spectō,** *look at.*

5. **labor** = *hard work, toil, suffering.*
   **opus** = usually *a piece of work.*
   **negōtium** = *lack of leisure* [**ōtium**], *business.*

6. **potestās** = *power* in general.
   **auctōritās** = *influence.*
   **rēgnum** = *royal power.*
   **imperium** = *military power, command.*

*Stamp of Barbados, British colony in the West Indies, showing Britannia holding Neptune's trident and driving his sea horses over the waves.*

### English Word Studies

As Latin synonyms differ, so do their English derivatives (though not always in the same way). Distinguish *antecedent* and *precedent*; *duke* and *prince*; *vision* and *discernment*; *visible* and *conspicuous*; *laborer* and *operator*; *labor, opera,* and *negotiation*; *power* and *authority*; *royal* and *imperial*.

Towns named *Cicero* are in Illinois, Indiana, and New York.

# ~~~~ Glimpses of Roman Life

## THE ROMAN CITIZEN

According to tradition, Rome was founded in 753 B.C. April 21 is still celebrated in Italy as the birthday of Rome. The first rulers were kings, but the last king was driven out in 509 B.C. because he was a tyrant. The new government was headed by two consuls of equal power, one to be a check on the other. Their term of office was limited to a year. The Roman historian Livy sees the origin of Roman liberty in this restriction. But this government was not democratic, for it was in the control of a small group of noble families called patricians. For two hundred years the common people (plebs or plebeians) struggled for equality and justice and gradually won most of the rights of their more fortunate fellow citizens. At first they could not hold office and did not even have fair trials in court. Their struggle for democracy and liberty is of great interest to us in this country. First they secured the right to elect special officials, called tribunes, who could veto the acts of the patrician officials. Then they obtained a set of written laws, called the Twelve Tables, which served as a kind of constitution or bill of rights. In 326 B.C. imprisonment and slavery for debt were abolished. This step Livy calls a second beginning of liberty for the plebeians. In 287 B.C. the plebeians succeeded in establishing the principle that a vote of the plebs should have the authority of law. Such a vote was called a "plebiscitum," from which we get our word *plebiscite*. In these ways a fairly democratic form of government was assured for some time.

While these struggles were going on inside the country, wars were being fought and the Roman empire was being formed. The heroic deeds of Horatius, Cincinnatus, Fabricius, Regulus, Scipio, and many others accounted for Roman success and developed the Roman virtues of courage, honesty, organizing ability, patriotism, devotion to family, strict justice, plain living, and the determination to see things through and never to give up. From all this grew the great system of Roman law and government, one of the greatest of our inheritances from Rome. For the Romans organized law and government on a large scale. Their success in this may be compared to the organization of industry during the last hundred years. Europe and Latin America still use Roman law. Even the English common law, the basis of our own, owes much to the law of the Romans. It has been said that Roman law is "a basic platform on which we can build a united world."

No wonder then that the possession of Roman citizenship was highly prized and that the people said with pride "Civis Romanus sum." This citizenship, bestowed in a solemn ceremony, brought the protection of Roman law everywhere in the world. It also brought the responsibility of protecting the Roman state against its enemies. So today citizenship in any country brings both advantages and duties.

"It is clear that the spirit of '76 had a most diversified origin. . . . In listing the 'founding fathers,' it is not enough to include merely American patriots of the caliber of Jefferson, Franklin, and the Adamses. . . . Demosthenes and Aristotle, Brutus, Cicero, and Tacitus belong there, as do many others of similar stamp and influence. . . . Not less than the Washingtons and the Lees, these ancient heroes helped to found the independent American commonwealth."[1]

**DISCUSSION QUESTIONS**

1. The Romans had two consuls as a check on each other. What system of "checks and balances" do we have in our government?
2. The restriction of the consulship to one year was regarded as the origin of Roman liberty. Have we any similar restriction for our highest officials?
3. What is the "Bill of Rights"?
4. Are persons sometimes imprisoned for debt today? Have there been changes in our laws on the subject in the last one hundred years?
5. What are some of the privileges and duties of citizenship today?

---

[1] Charles F. Mullet in the *Classical Journal*, xxxv (1939), 104.

*Seal of the United States, with mottoes. The mottoes at right are based on Virgil: God "has smiled on our undertakings," "a new series of generations." Look for the seal on a dollar bill.*

HARRIS & EWING

# Unit XIII Review

## ENGLISH WORD STUDIES

1. Give the Latin words and prefixes suggested by the following English derivatives: *ascendancy, casualty, circumnavigate, demonstration, familiarity, indivisible, innocuous, intellectual, lucid, opponent, preview, subjunctive, superscription, transcend, virtue.*

2. Find and use in sentences as many English derivatives as possible from **pōnō, veniō,** and **pellō.**

*Italian stamp quoting Horace, with a picture of Rome and the Colosseum.*

## VOCABULARY

| NOUNS | | | |
|---|---|---|---|
| 1. cāsus | 5. frōns | 10. negōtium | 15. rēs |
| 2. diēs | 6. impetus | 11. nox | 16. senātus |
| 3. domus | 7. lūx | 12. potestās | 17. speciēs |
| 4. exercitus | 8. manus | 13. prīnceps | 18. spēs |
| | 9. mōs | 14. ratiō | |

| VERBS | | | |
|---|---|---|---|
| 19. ascendō | 24. dēspiciō | 30. incolō | 36. praesum |
| 20. attingō | 25. dīvidō | 31. intellegō | 37. reddō |
| 21. dēmōnstrō | 26. exerceō | 32. interclūdō | 38. supersum |
| 22. dēpōnō | 27. exīstimō | 33. noceō | 39. vīvō |
| 23. dēserō | 28. explōrō | 34. praeficiō | |
| | 29. imperō | 35. praemittō | |

| CONJUNCTIONS | 40. autem | 41. postquam |
|---|---|---|

| ADVERB | 42. satis |
|---|---|

| PREPOSITIONS | 44. circum | 46. super |
|---|---|---|
| 43. apud | 45. prae | |

## VOCABULARY (English Meanings)

NOUNS
1. chance
2. day
3. home
4. army
5. front
6. attack
7. light
8. hand
9. custom
10. business
11. night
12. power
13. first man
14. account
15. thing
16. senate
17. appearance
18. hope

VERBS
19. ascend
20. reach
21. show
22. lay aside
23. desert
24. look down on
25. divide
26. train
27. think
28. explore
29. command
30. inhabit
31. understand
32. cut off
33. do harm to
34. put in charge
35. send ahead
36. be in charge of
37. give back
38. be left over
39. live

CONJUNCTIONS
40. however
41. after

ADVERB
42. enough

PREPOSITIONS
43. among
44. around
45. in front of
46. above

## GRAMMAR SUMMARY

### Accusative with *Ad* or *In*

When *to* implies literally *motion toward* a place or person, we have seen that the accusative with **ad** or **in** is used. This is true after the following "motion" verbs, previously studied:

**accēdō, cēdō, contendō, dūcō, fugiō, mātūrō, mittō, moveō, nāvigō, portō, prōcēdō, prōdūcō, properō, redigō, redūcō, trānsportō, veniō.**

### Dative of Indirect Object

When *to* does not imply actual motion but indicates the person *to whom* something is given, told, shown, etc., the dative is used. The following verbs, already studied, are transitive and may have an accusative as the *direct object* and a dative as the *indirect object*:

**committō, dīcō, dō, dōnō, iungō, mandō, mōnstrō, nūntiō, ostendō, permittō, prōpōnō, reddō, relinquō, respondeō, submittō, trādō, tribuō.**

Some of these verbs have as the direct object either a neuter pronoun or an infinitive: **dīcō, respondeō, nūntiō.**

With some other verbs the dative is regularly used: **noceō.**

*The Roman theater at Trieste, Italy, was built in the second century* A.D. *and was excavated in 1938. It is surrounded by modern buildings.*

## UNIT PRACTICE AND EXERCISES

**Form Drill**
1. Decline **senātus noster, diēs longior.**
2. Give the genitive and accusative singular and the genitive plural of:

     **id negōtium, haec potestās, illa nox, impetus fortis, īdem prīnceps, quae ratiō, rēs ipsa, cāsus peior, domus ūlla.**
3. Give in all tenses the third singular active of **noceō;** the third plural passive of **dēpōnō;** the first plural active of **imperō;** the third plural passive of **dēspiciō;** the second singular active of **audiō.**
4. Identify by giving voice, tense, and when possible, mood, person, and number:

     **praemīsit, exīstimābō, incoluisse, exercērī, interclūdēns, dēserunt, redde, dēmōnstrāte, explōrārī, dīvidī, imperāns, superestis, praeerimus, praeficiēmus, ascendam, vīvite, dīvīsus, interclūdentur, intellēctum est, permissūrus.**

*The Low Memorial Library of Columbia University, New York, resembles
the Pantheon (p. 189; cf. too p. 188).*

*A house in Ionic style at Milan, Ohio, built about 1828.*

## A Latin Play

## IN BRITANNIĀ

### Persōnae

Dīvicus ⎫
Cocurō ⎬ Britannī
Osbus ⎪
Caractō ⎭
Aliī Britannī

Brigida, *fīlia Dīvicī*
Sulpicius Rūfus, *Rōmānus*
Antōnia, *uxor Rūfī*
Medicus
Servī et Servae

Locus: In tabernā Dīvicī, in Britanniā. (*Aliī Britannī dormiunt, aliī bibunt.*)

Cocurō: Brigida! Vīnum!

Brigida: Ecce! (*Vīnum Cocurōnī dat.*)

Cocurō: Vīnum Rōmānum est. Vīnum Rōmānum amō—nōn autem Rōmānōs.

Osbus: Rōmānōs nōn ōdī.[1] Per Rōmānōs viae bonae, castra 5 mūnīta, multī mercātōrēs, melior cibus in Britanniā nunc sunt.

Cocurō: Rōmānī autem nōn sunt Britannī. Sī hīc[2] manēbunt, Britannia erit Rōmāna.

Dīvicus: Rōmāna erat mulier quae quondam Brigidam meam servāvit. 10

Brigida: Bene dīcit. Graviter aegra eram. Mulier Rōmāna servum suum, medicum doctum, ad mē mīsit. Ille mē cūrāvit.

Osbus: Quis erat illa mulier?

Brigida: Antōnia.

Dīvicus: Uxor Sulpicī Rūfī est, cuius vīlla est proxima. 15

Brigida: Benignī sunt.

Cocurō: Rōmānīs nōn cōnfīdō. Medicīs nōn cōnfīdō.

Osbus: Nōn paucī Rōmānī puellās nostrās in mātrimōnium dūcunt. Cavē,[3] Brigida!

Dīvicus: Brigida Caractōnī spōnsa est. 20

Cocurō: Vir fortis est—et Britannus.

Osbus: Etiam Rōmānī fortēs sunt. Mīlitēs Rōmānī Britannōs ab hostibus dēfendunt.

Cocurō: Britannī sē dēfendere possunt. (*Clāmōrēs audiuntur.*)

---

[1] *I do not hate.*  [2] *here.*  [3] *beware.*

25  BRIGIDA: Pater! Clāmōrem audiō! Quid est?

(*Accēdit Caractō cum aliīs Britannīs. In tabernam dūcunt Sulpicium Rūfum et Antōniam, cum servīs eōrum.*)

CARACTŌ: Ecce, Dīvice! Nōnne clārī sunt captīvī?
DĪVICUS: Caractō! Quid ēgistī?
30  CARACTŌ: Hī Rōmānī in viā iter faciēbant. Magnam pecūniam habent. Itaque nōs illōs cēpimus.
BRIGIDA: Caractō! Latrō es!
CARACTŌ: Latrō? Minimē! Rōmānī fīnēs Britannōrum occupāvērunt. Omnia quae habent sunt nostra.
35  SULPICIUS: Latrō pessime, quid cupis?
ANTŌNIA: Ecce ōrnāmenta mea! Omnia tua erunt, sī nōs dīmittēs.
CARACTŌ: Ōrnāmenta nōn cupiō; plūs cupiō.
SULPICIUS: Plūs? Quid dīcis?
CARACTŌ: Pecūniam habēs. Ubi nūntiābitur familiae tuae amīcīs-
40 que tuīs vōs captōs esse, illī prō vōbīs magnum praemium dabunt.
BRIGIDA: Caractō! Hī Rōmānī sunt fīnitimī nostrī et amīcī. Hic vir est Sulpicius Rūfus. Haec mulier, Antōnia, mē quondam servāvit. Ecce—ille servus est medicus quī mē cūrāvit!
CARACTŌ: Omnēs Rōmānī hostēs Britannōrum sunt.
45  ALIĪ BRITANNĪ: Hostēs sunt!
OSBUS: Caractō! Mīlitēs Rōmānī venient. Vōs capient.
DĪVICUS: Caractō! Nisi [4] hōs Rōmānōs līberābis, Brigida uxor tua nōn erit.
CARACTŌ: Quid? Brigida mihi spōnsa est.
50  DĪVICUS: Nōn iam tibi spōnsa est.
BRIGIDA: Uxor latrōnis nōn erō.
BRITANNĪ: Caractō! Praeda magna erit!
ALIĪ BRITANNĪ: Caractō! Mīlitēs Rōmānī mox aderunt!
SULPICIUS: Mīlitēs Rōmānī latrōnēs interficiunt.
55  ANTŌNIA: Vōbīs nōn nocuimus. Nōs dīmitte!
BRIGIDA: Eōs dīmitte!
CARACTŌ: Prō tē, Brigida—illōs dīmittō. Discēdite omnēs!
ANTŌNIA: Tibi grātiās agimus, Brigida!

(*Discēdunt Rōmānī et Britannī et servī et servae.*)

60  DĪVICUS: Fortis vir es, Caractō—nimis [5] autem audāx.
CARACTŌ: Brigida mē retinēbit, mē docēbit, domina mea erit.

---

[4] *unless.*                    [5] *too* (with **audāx**).

# *Appendix*

## PRONUNCIATION [1]

### Vowels

In Latin, as English, the *vowels* are *a, e, i, o, u.*[2]

At one time the English vowels were pronounced like the Latin, but the pronunciation of English has changed greatly. In French, Spanish, Italian, German, and other languages, which also have adopted the Latin alphabet, the vowels are still pronounced very much as in Latin.

Each of the Latin vowels may be pronounced long or short, the difference being one of *time*. This is called *quantity*. There is also a difference of *sound* between the long and the short vowels, except **a**. This is called *quality*. The pronunciation is approximately as follows:

| LONG | SHORT | LONG AND SHORT AS IN |
|---|---|---|
| ā as in *father* | a as first *a* in *aha* | *Martha* (ā, ă) |
| ē as in *they* or *a* in *late* | e as in *let* | *lateness* (ē, ĕ) |
| ī as in *police* or *ea* in *seat* | i as in *sit* | *seasick* (ī, ĭ) |
| ō as in *note* | o as in *for* | *phonograph* (ō, ŏ) |
| ū as in *rule* or *oo* in *fool* | u as in *full* | *two-footed* (ū, ŭ) |

In this book long vowels are regularly marked –; short vowels are usually unmarked, but ˘ is sometimes used.

*Caution.* It is very important to distinguish the *sounds* of the long and short vowels. To confuse ī and ĭ, or ē and ĕ in Latin is as bad a mistake as for a person to say, *I heard the din in the hall*, when he meant the "dean," or *I forgot the debt*, when he meant the "date."

The English equivalents of **e** and **o** are only approximate. Avoid pronouncing ŏ like *o* in *not* or in *note*.

### Quantity of Vowels

The quantity (and quality) of vowels must be learned as part of the word. There are, however, a few general rules:

---

[1] The best way to learn correct pronunciation is by careful imitation of the teacher; the rules are given for reference.

[2] In English sometimes also *y*, as in *by*, but not in *yes*.

1. A vowel is usually short before another vowel or **h** (because **h** is weakly sounded).

2. A vowel is short before **nt, nd,** and final **m** and **t**.

### Diphthongs

The first three of the following *diphthongs* (two vowels making one sound) are the ones most commonly used:

**ae** like *ai* in *aisle*    **eu** like *eh–oo* (pronounced quickly)
**au** like *ou* in *out*    **ui** like *oo–ee* (pronounced quickly); only in
**oe** like *oi* in *oil*            **cui** and **huic**
**ei** like *ei* in *freight*

### Consonants

All letters other than vowels and diphthongs are *consonants*.

The Latin consonants have, generally speaking, the same sounds as in English. The following differences, however, should be noted:

**b** before **s** or **t** has the sound of **p.**
**c** is always hard as in *cat*, never soft as in *city.*
**g** is always hard as in *go*, never soft as in *gem.*
**i** (consonant) has the sound of **y** in *year*. (**i** is a consonant between vowels and at the beginning of a word before a vowel.)
**s** always has the sound of *s* in *sin*; never of *s* in *these.*
**t** always has the sound of *t* in *ten*; never of *t* in *motion.*
**v** has the sound of **w** in *will.*
**x** has the sound of *x* in *extra.*
      (**ch** = **k; ph** = **p; th** = **t**)

Doubled consonants are pronounced separately: **an–nus.**

In both English and Latin the combination **qu** forms a single consonant and the **u** is not a vowel here.

### English Pronunciation of Latin

The above method of pronunciation is the ancient Roman method. It should be remembered, however, that Latin words which have become thoroughly English should be pronounced as English words; for example in *terra firma*, the *i* is pronounced as in *firm*, not as in *miracle*; in *alumni*, the *i* is pronounced as in *mile.*

### Syllables

Every Latin word has as many syllables as it has vowels or diphthongs: **vir–tū–te, proe–li–um.**

A single consonant between two vowels or diphthongs is pronounced with the second: **fi–li–us, a–git.** Compound words are divided into their component parts and are exceptions to this rule: **ad–es.**

When two or more consonants occur between vowels or diphthongs, the division is made before the last consonant: **por–tus, vīnc–tī, an–nus**. An exception to this rule occurs whenever a mute (**p, b, t, d, c, g**) is followed by a liquid (**l, r**), in which case the mute combines with the liquid and both are pronounced with the second vowel: **pū–bli–cus, cas–tra**.

The next to the last syllable of a word is called the *penult* (Latin **paene**, *almost*; **ultima**, *last*); the one before the penult (i.e., the third from the end) is called the *antepenult*.

### Quantity of Syllables

Some syllables of course take longer to pronounce than others just as some vowels are longer than others.

1. A syllable is *naturally* long if it contains a long vowel or a diphthong: **fā–mae**.

2. A syllable is long *by position* if it contains a short vowel followed by two or more consonants or the double consonant **x** (= **cs**): **sil–vīs, por–tō**.

*Note.* Exception is made in the case of a mute followed by a liquid (see above). **H** is so weakly sounded that it does not help make a syllable long.

*Caution.* Distinguish carefully between long syllable and long vowel; in **ĕxĕmplum** the first two syllables are long, though the vowels are short.

### Accent

The accented syllable of a word is the one that is pronounced with more stress or emphasis than the others; so in the word **an'swer**, the accent is on the first syllable. In Latin the accent is easily learned according to fixed rules:

1. Words of two syllables are accented on the first: **frā'ter**.

2. Words of three or more syllables are accented on the penult if it is long, otherwise on the antepenult: **lēgā'tus, exem'plum; dī'cĕre, si'milis**. Note that the accented syllable is not necessarily long.

### BASIC GRAMMATICAL TERMS

The material here given may be reviewed in connection with the Lessons. For the use of those who prefer to review basic grammar before taking up the Lessons, a number of explanations are given here which will also be found in the body of the book. Teachers can easily devise English exercises for drill with classes which need it. Or the sentences on these pages may be used for that purpose.

### The Sentence. Subject and Predicate

A *sentence* is a group of words which completely express a thought. Every sentence consists of two parts—the *subject*, about which something is said, and the *predicate*, which says something about the subject: *The sailor* (subject) *saved the girl* (predicate), **Nauta puellam servāvit.**

A subject or predicate is said to be *modified* by those words which affect or limit its meaning.

### Parts of Speech

The words of a language are divided, according to their use, into eight classes called *parts of speech*. These are:

| | | | |
|---|---|---|---|
| Nouns | Adjectives | Adverbs | Conjunctions |
| Pronouns | Verbs | Prepositions | Interjections |

### Nouns

A *noun* (from Latin **nōmen**, *name*) is a word that names a person, place, or thing: *Anna*, **Anna;** *island*, **īnsula;** *letter*, **littera.**

Nouns may be classified as:

1. *Common* (applied to any one of a group): *city*, **urbs;** *girl*, **puella.**

2. *Proper* (applied to a particular one of a group): *Rome*, **Rōma;** *Julia*, **Iūlia.**

*Note.* Proper nouns always begin with a capital letter.

### Pronouns

A *pronoun* (Latin **prō**, *for*; **nōmen**, *name*) is a word used instead of a noun. The noun whose place is taken by a pronoun is called an *antecedent* (Latin **ante**, *before*; **cēdō**, *go*).

1. *Personal* pronouns distinguish the three persons: the person speaking (*I*, **ego;** *we*, **nōs**—first person), the person spoken to (*you*, **tū**, **vōs**—second person), the person or thing spoken of (*he*, **is;** *she*, **ea;** *it*, **id;** *they*, **eī**—third person).

2. *Interrogative* pronouns are used to ask questions: *who*, **quis;** *wh.. what*, **quid.**

3. *Relative* pronouns relate to a preceding (antecedent) word and join to it a dependent clause: *who*, **quī;** *which, what, that*, **quod.**

4. *Demonstrative* pronouns point out persons or objects definitely—often accompanied with a gesture: *this*, **hic;** *that*, **ille;** *these*, **hī;** *those*, **illī.**

### Adjectives

An *adjective* is a word used to describe a noun or pronoun or to limit its meaning:

1. *Descriptive* adjectives are either *common* or *proper: good*, **bonus;** *Roman*, **Rōmānus.** Proper adjectives begin with a capital letter.

2. *Limiting* adjectives can be divided into six groups:

    *a. Article—definite* (*the*), *indefinite* (*a, an*). There is no word in Latin for "the" or "a."

    *b. Numerals—cardinals* (*one, two, three*, etc., **ūnus, duo, trēs**, etc.), *ordinals* (*first, second, third*, etc., **prīmus, secundus, tertius,** etc.)

    *c. Possessive* adjectives (formed from personal pronouns): *my, mine,* **meus;** *our, ours,* **noster;** *your, yours,* **tuus, vester;** *his, her, its,* **eius;** *their, theirs,* **eōrum.**

When interrogative, relative, and demonstrative pronouns are used as adjectives, they are called respectively:

    *d. Interrogative* adjectives: ***what street? quae* via?**

    *e. Relative* adjectives: *He spent a year in Italy, in **which** country he saw many beautiful things,* **Annum in Italiā ēgit, in *quā* terrā multa pulchra vīdit.**

    *f. Demonstrative* adjectives: ***that road, illa* via.**

In English, the demonstrative adjectives are the only ones that have different forms in the singular and plural: *this, these; that, those.*

## Verbs

A *verb* is a word that tells what a subject does or is: *He **fought**,* **Pugnāvit;** *He **is** good,* **Bonus est.**

1. According to use, verbs are either *transitive* or *intransitive.*

    *a.* A *transitive* verb is one which tells what a person or thing does to another person or thing: *Anna **is carrying** water,* **Anna aquam *portat*.**

    *b.* An *intransitive* verb is one whose action is limited to the subject: *Anna **is working**,* **Anna labōrat.**

Contrast "set" (transitive) with "sit" (intransitive), and "lay" (transitive) with "lie" (intransitive).

2. Intransitive verbs are either *complete* or *linking* (copulative).

    *a.* A *complete* verb is one which is complete in meaning without an object or other word: *He **sails**,* **Nāvigat.**

    *b.* A *linking* verb is one which links a noun or adjective to the subject: *They **are** good,* **Bonī sunt.**

The chief linking verbs in English are *be, appear, seem, become, feel, look, taste, smell.*

3. An *auxiliary* verb (Latin **auxilium,** *help*) is one used in the conjugation of other verbs: *I **am** learning;* ***Did** you see? They **have** given.*

## Adverbs

An *adverb* is a word used to modify the meaning of a verb, adjective, or other adverb: *He is working now, Nunc* labōrat.

## Prepositions

A *preposition* is a word used to show the relation of a noun or pronoun, called its *object*, to some word in the sentence: *He sails to the island,* **Ad** īnsulam nāvigat.

## Conjunctions

A *conjunction* is a word used to join words, phrases (p. 391), and clauses (p. 391). Conjunctions may be classified according to their use as:

1. *Coördinate,* connecting words or sentences of equal rank (*and,* et; *but,* sed; *or,* aut; *nor,* neque).

2. *Subordinate,* connecting a subordinate clause of a sentence with the principal clause (*if,* sī; *while,* dum; *because,* quod, etc.).

3. *Correlative,* used in pairs (*both . . . and,* et . . . et; *neither . . . nor,* neque . . . neque, etc.).

## Interjections

An *interjection* is a word used to show emotion. It has no direct relation to any other word in the sentence: *O! Alas! Ah! Oh!*

## Inflection

The change of form which words undergo to indicate differences in their use is called *inflection: boy—boys,* **puer—puerī;** *see, saw, seen,* **videō, vīdī, vīsus.** The inflection of nouns, pronouns, and adjectives is called *declension.* They are declined to indicate change in number and case, and sometimes gender. Personal pronouns also indicate person.

## Number

A noun or pronoun is *singular* when it refers to one person or thing: *girl,* **puella;** *house,* **casa;** *mouse,* **mūs;** *tooth,* **dēns.** It is *plural* when it refers to more than one: *girls,* **puellae;** *houses,* **casae;** *mice,* **mūrēs;** *teeth,* **dentēs.**

## Gender

*Gender* is a distinction in the form of words corresponding to a distinction of sex. It is shown by change of word, by change of ending, or by use of a prefix: *father—mother,* **pater—māter;** *master—mistress,* **dominus—domina;** *he-goat—she-goat.* The first words given in each group are *masculine,* the second are *feminine.* Most nouns in English have no gender and are therefore *neuter* ("neither" masculine nor feminine).

388

## Case

*Case* is a change in the form of a noun, pronoun, or adjective to show its use in the sentence: *She* (subject) *is here,* **Ea adest;** *I saw her* (object), **Eam vīdī.**

### Subject and Object

1. The *subject* of a verb is that about which something is said (p. 386).

2. The *direct object* is that which is directly affected by the action indicated in the transitive active verb: *Anna carries water,* **Anna aquam portat.** The term object is also applied to a word dependent upon a preposition.

### Names and Uses of the Cases

1. *Nominative.* A noun or pronoun used as the subject of a verb is in the *nominative* case: *The farmer calls,* **Agricola vocat.**

2. *Accusative (Objective).* A noun or pronoun used as the object of a verb or preposition is in the *accusative* (or *objective*) case: *I sent a book to him,* **Ad eum librum mīsī.**

3. *Dative.* The noun or pronoun that indicates to or for whom the direct object is given, shown, or told is called the *indirect object* and is put in the *dative* case: *I gave him a book,* **Eī librum dedī.**

4. *Genitive (Possessive).* Possession is expressed by the *genitive* (or *possessive*) case: *the boy's book,* **puerī liber.**

### Conjugation

The inflection of verbs is called *conjugation.* Verbs are conjugated by putting together their various forms that indicate *person, number, tense, voice,* and *mood.*

### Person and Number

A verb must agree with its subject in person and number: *The girl is good,* **Puella est bona;** *The girls are good,* **Puellae sunt bonae.**

### Tense

*Tense* means time. There are six tenses:

1. The *present* represents an act as taking place now: *He goes.*

2. The *past* represents an act as having already taken place: *He went yesterday.*

3. The *future* represents an act that will occur later: *He will go tomorrow.*

4. The *present perfect* represents an act as completed, but from the point of view of the present: *He has just gone.*

5. The *past perfect* represents an act as completed at some definite time in the past: *He **had gone*** (before something else occurred).

6. The *future perfect* represents an act as completed at or before some definite time in the future: *He **will have gone*** (before something else will occur).

### Progressive and Emphatic Verb Forms

1. *Progressive* (time or action continuous; used with some form of the auxiliary "be"): *They **are studying**, they **were studying**, they **will be studying**, they **have been studying**, they **had been studying**, they **will have been studying**.*

2. *Emphatic* (with some form of the auxiliary "do," used only in the present and past):

    1. Used in questions: ***Do** (**did**) you **know** this?*
    2. Negative: *I **do** (**did**) not **know** it.*
    3. Emphatic: *I **do** (**did**) **believe** it.*

### Voice

A transitive verb is in the *active voice* when it represents the subject as the doer or agent: *Anna loves Clara*, **Anna Clāram** *amat.*

A transitive verb is in the *passive voice* when it represents the subject as the receiver of the action: *Clara **is loved**,* **Clāra** *amātur.*

*Note.* Intransitive verbs are used only in the active voice in English.

### Mood

1. The *indicative mood* is used to state a fact or to ask a question: *Rome **is** a great city*, **Rōma** *est* magna urbs; *Where **is** Anna?* **Ubi** *est* **Anna?**

2. The *imperative* mood is used to express commands: ***Look** at the waves, **Spectā** undās.*

### Infinitive

The *infinitive* is a verbal noun. It is a form of the verb to which *to* is usually prefixed in English: ***to** go, **to** sing.* It has tense and voice, but not person, number, or mood.

### Participle

The *participle* is a verbal adjective. As an adjective it modifies a noun or pronoun: *a **losing** fight.* As a verb it may have an object or adverbial modifiers: ***losing** his balance, he fell off.* It has four forms in English:

| ACTIVE | · PASSIVE |
|---|---|
| *Present: seeing* | *being seen* |
| *Past:   having seen* | *seen, having been seen* |

*Roman relief sculpture, showing the Roman fondness for balanced arrangement.*

## Phrases

A *phrase* is a group of words without subject and predicate.

One important kind of phrase is the *prepositional phrase*, that is, a preposition together with its object: *in great danger*, **in magnō perīculō.**

## Clauses

A *clause*, like a phrase, is a part of a sentence but differs from a phrase in having a subject and a predicate.

Clauses are classified as:

1. *Principal,* the leading or independent statement in a sentence: ***The girl** whom you saw on the street **is my sister,** Puella* quam in viā vīdistī *soror mea est.*

2. *Subordinate,* a dependent statement modifying some word in the principal clause: *The girl **whom you saw on the street** is my sister,* Puella *quam in viā vīdistī* soror mea est.

## Sentences

1. A *simple sentence* contains one principal clause: *My friend, the farmer, has many horses,* **Amīcus meus, agricola, multōs equōs habet.**

2. A *compound sentence* contains two or more principal clauses connected by a coördinate conjunction, such as "and," "but," etc.: *My friend, the farmer, has many horses, but I have not seen them,* **Amīcus meus, agricola, multōs equōs habet, sed eōs nōn vīdī.**

3. A *complex sentence* contains one principal clause to which one or more subordinate clauses are joined by subordinate conjunctions or by relative or interrogative pronouns: *My friend, the farmer, has many horses which I have not seen,* **Amīcus meus, agricola, multōs equōs habet quōs nōn vīdī.**

## BASIC FORMS

### Nouns

#### First Declension (46) [1]

| | SINGULAR | PLURAL |
|---|---|---|
| NOM. | via | viae |
| GEN. | viae | viārum |
| DAT. | viae | viīs |
| ACC. | viam | viās |
| ABL. | viā | viīs |
| (VOC.) | | |

#### Second Declension (46)

| | SINGULAR | PLURAL |
|---|---|---|
| NOM. | servus | servī |
| GEN. | servī | servōrum |
| DAT. | servō | servīs |
| ACC. | servum | servōs |
| ABL. | servō | servīs |
| | (serve) | |

#### Second Declension (72, 78)

| | SING. | PLUR. | SING. | PLUR. | SING. | PLUR. |
|---|---|---|---|---|---|---|
| NOM. | ager | agrī | puer | puerī | signum | signa |
| GEN. | agrī | agrōrum | puerī | puerōrum | signī | signōrum |
| DAT. | agrō | agrīs | puerō | puerīs | signō | signīs |
| ACC. | agrum | agrōs | puerum | puerōs | signum | signa |
| ABL. | agrō | agrīs | puerō | puerīs | signō | signīs |

#### Third Declension (214, 244)

| | SING. | PLUR. | SING. | PLUR. | SING. | PLUR. |
|---|---|---|---|---|---|---|
| NOM. | mīles | mīlitēs | lēx | lēgēs | corpus | corpora |
| GEN. | mīlitis | mīlitum | lēgis | lēgum | corporis | corporum |
| DAT. | mīlitī | mīlitibus | lēgī | lēgibus | corporī | corporibus |
| ACC. | mīlitem | mīlitēs | lēgem | lēgēs | corpus | corpora |
| ABL. | mīlite | mīlitibus | lēge | lēgibus | corpore | corporibus |

#### Third Declension I-Stems (247)

| | SINGULAR | PLURAL | SINGULAR | PLURAL |
|---|---|---|---|---|
| NOM. | cīvis | cīvēs | mare | maria |
| GEN. | cīvis | cīvium | maris | marium |
| DAT. | cīvī | cīvibus | marī | maribus |
| ACC. | cīvem | cīvēs (–īs) | mare | maria |
| ABL. | cīve | cīvibus | marī | maribus |

#### Fourth Declension (361)

| | SING. | PLUR. |
|---|---|---|
| NOM. | cāsus | cāsūs |
| GEN. | cāsūs | cāsuum |
| DAT. | cāsuī | cāsibus |
| ACC. | cāsum | cāsūs |
| ABL. | cāsū | cāsibus |

#### Fifth Declension (366)

| | SING. | PLUR. | SING. | PLUR. |
|---|---|---|---|---|
| NOM. | diēs | diēs | rēs | rēs |
| GEN. | diēī | diērum | reī | rērum |
| DAT. | diēī | diēbus | reī | rēbus |
| ACC. | diem | diēs | rem | rēs |
| ABL. | diē | diēbus | rē | rēbus |

[1] The numbers in parentheses refer to the pages on which these forms are discussed.

## Irregular Nouns (305, 332, 363)

|  | SING. | PLUR. | SING. | SING. | PLUR. |
|---|---|---|---|---|---|
| NOM. | vīs | vīrēs | nēmō | domus | domūs |
| GEN. | —— | vīrium | (nūllīus) | domūs (–ī) | domuum (–ōrum) |
| DAT. | —— | vīribus | nēminī | domuī (–ō) | domibus |
| ACC. | vim | vīrēs (–īs) | nēminem | domum | domōs (–ūs) |
| ABL. | vī | vīribus | (nūllō) | domō (–ū) | domibus |
| (LOC.) |  |  |  | (domī) |  |

# Adjectives and Adverbs

## First and Second Declensions (46, 72, 78)

|  | SINGULAR M. | F. | N. | PLURAL M. | F. | N. |
|---|---|---|---|---|---|---|
| NOM. | magnus | magna | magnum | magnī | magnae | magna |
| GEN. | magnī | magnae | magnī | magnōrum | magnārum | magnōrum |
| DAT. | magnō | magnae | magnō | magnīs | magnīs | magnīs |
| ACC. | magnum | magnam | magnum | magnōs | magnās | magna |
| ABL. | magnō | magnā | magnō | magnīs | magnīs | magnīs |
| (VOC.) | (magne) |  |  |  |  |  |

|  | SINGULAR |  |  | SINGULAR |  |  |
|---|---|---|---|---|---|---|
| NOM. | līber | lībera | līberum | noster | nostra | nostrum |
| GEN. | līberī | līberae | līberī | nostrī | nostrae | nostrī |
| DAT. | līberō | līberae | līberō | nostrō | nostrae | nostrō |
| ACC. | līberum | līberam | līberum | nostrum | nostram | nostrum |
| ABL. | līberō | līberā | līberō | nostrō | nostrā | nostrō |

Plural, līberī, līberae, lībera, etc.  Plural, nostrī, –ae, –a, etc.

## Third Declension (251)

### THREE ENDINGS

|  | SINGULAR M. | F. | N. | PLURAL M. | F. | N. |
|---|---|---|---|---|---|---|
| NOM. | ācer | ācris | ācre | ācrēs | ācrēs | ācria |
| GEN. | ācris | ācris | ācris | ācrium | ācrium | ācrium |
| DAT. | ācrī | ācrī | ācrī | ācribus | ācribus | ācribus |
| ACC. | ācrem | ācrem | ācre | ācrēs (–īs) | ācrēs (–īs) | ācria |
| ABL. | ācrī | ācrī | ācrī | ācribus | ācribus | ācribus |

### TWO ENDINGS / ONE ENDING

|  | SINGULAR M.F. | N. | PLURAL M.F. | N. | SINGULAR M.F. | N. | PLURAL M.F. | N. |
|---|---|---|---|---|---|---|---|---|
| NOM. | fortis | forte | fortēs | fortia | pār | pār | parēs | paria |
| GEN. | fortis | fortis | fortium | fortium | paris | paris | parium | parium |
| DAT. | fortī | fortī | fortibus | fortibus | parī | parī | paribus | paribus |
| ACC. | fortem | forte | fortēs (–īs) | fortia | parem | pār | parēs (–īs) | paria |
| ABL. | fortī | fortī | fortibus | fortibus | parī | parī | paribus | paribus |

## Present Participle (299)

| | SINGULAR | | PLURAL | |
|---|---|---|---|---|
| | M.F. | N. | M.F. | N. |
| NOM. | portāns | portāns | portantēs | portantia |
| GEN. | portantis | portantis | portantium | portantium |
| DAT. | portantī | portantī | portantibus | portantibus |
| ACC. | portantem | portāns | portantēs (–īs) | portantia |
| ABL. | portante (–ī) | portante (–ī) | portantibus | portantibus |

## Numerals (288, 345)

| | M. | F. | N. | M.F. | N. |
|---|---|---|---|---|---|
| NOM. | ūnus | ūna | ūnum | trēs | tria |
| GEN. | ūnīus | ūnīus | ūnīus | trium | trium |
| DAT. | ūnī | ūnī | ūnī | tribus | tribus |
| ACC. | ūnum | ūnam | ūnum | trēs | tria |
| ABL. | ūnō | ūnā | ūnō | tribus | tribus |

| | M. | F. | N. | M.F.N. (adj.) | N. (noun) |
|---|---|---|---|---|---|
| NOM. | duo | duae | duo | mīlle | mīlia |
| GEN. | duōrum | duārum | duōrum | mīlle | mīlium |
| DAT. | duōbus | duābus | duōbus | mīlle | mīlibus |
| ACC. | duōs | duās | duo | mīlle | mīlia |
| ABL. | duōbus | duābus | duōbus | mīlle | mīlibus |

Alius has aliud in the nom. and acc. sing. neuter; plural regular

## Comparison of Regular Adjectives and Adverbs (326, 334, 335)

| POSITIVE | | COMPARATIVE | | SUPERLATIVE | |
|---|---|---|---|---|---|
| ADJ. | ADV. | ADJ. | ADV. | ADJ. | ADV. |
| altus | altē | altior | altius | altissimus | altissimē |
| fortis | fortiter | fortior | fortius | fortissimus | fortissimē |
| līber | līberē | līberior | līberius | līberrimus | līberrimē |
| ācer | ācriter | ācrior | ācrius | ācerrimus | ācerrimē |
| facilis | facile | facilior | facilius | facillimus | facillimē |

## Comparison of Irregular Adjectives (338)

| POSITIVE | COMPARATIVE | SUPERLATIVE |
|---|---|---|
| bonus, –a, –um | melior, –ius | optimus, –a, –um |
| malus, –a, –um | peior, –ius | pessimus, –a, –um |
| magnus, –a, –um | maior, –ius | maximus, –a, –um |
| parvus, –a, –um | minor, –us | minimus, –a, –um |
| multus, –a, –um | ——, plūs | plūrimus, –a, –um |

## Declension of Comparatives (326, 338)

| | SINGULAR | | PLURAL | | SINGULAR | PLURAL | |
|---|---|---|---|---|---|---|---|
| | M.F. | N. | M.F. | N. | N.[1] | M.F. | N. |
| NOM. | altior | altius | altiōrēs | altiōra | plūs | plūrēs | plūra |
| GEN. | altiōris | altiōris | altiōrum | altiōrum | plūris | plūrium | plūrium |
| DAT. | altiōrī | altiōrī | altiōribus | altiōribus | —— | plūribus | plūribus |
| ACC. | altiōrem | altius | altiōrēs | altiōra | plūs | plūrēs | plūra |
| ABL. | altiōre | altiōre | altiōribus | altiōribus | plūre | plūribus | plūribus |

[1] Plūs has no masculine or feminine singular.

## Pronouns

### *Personal (162)*

|  | SING. | PLUR. | SING. | PLUR. | M. | F. | N. |
|---|---|---|---|---|---|---|---|
| NOM. | ego | nōs | tū | vōs | is | ea | id |
| GEN. | meī | nostrum (nostrī) | tuī | vestrum (–trī) | (For declension | | |
| DAT. | mihi | nōbīs | tibi | vōbīs | see next page— | | |
| ACC. | mē | nōs | tē | vōs | demonstrative is) | | |
| ABL. | mē | nōbīs | tē | vōbīs | | | |

### *Reflexive (341)*

|  | FIRST PERSON | SECOND PERSON | THIRD PERSON SING. AND PLUR. |
|---|---|---|---|
| GEN. | meī | tuī | suī |
| DAT. | (declined | (declined | sibi |
| ACC. | like **ego**) | like **tū**) | sē (sēsē) |
| ABL. | | | sē (sēsē) |

Reflexives are not used in the nominative and have no nominative form.

### *Demonstrative (272, 279, 282, 285)*

|  | SINGULAR | | | PLURAL | | |
|---|---|---|---|---|---|---|
|  | M. | F. | N. | M. | F. | N. |
| NOM. | hic | haec | hoc | hī | hae | haec |
| GEN. | huius | huius | huius | hōrum | hārum | hōrum |
| DAT. | huic | huic | huic | hīs | hīs | hīs |
| ACC. | hunc | hanc | hoc | hōs | hās | haec |
| ABL. | hōc | hāc | hōc | hīs | hīs | hīs |
| NOM. | is | ea | id | eī (iī) | eae | ea |
| GEN. | eius | eius | eius | eōrum | eārum | eōrum |
| DAT. | eī | eī | eī | eīs (iīs) | eīs (iīs) | eīs (iīs) |
| ACC. | eum | eam | id | eōs | eās | ea |
| ABL. | eō | eā | eō | eīs (iīs) | eīs (iīs) | eīs (iīs) |

|  | SINGULAR | | | PLURAL | | |
|---|---|---|---|---|---|---|
|  | M. | F. | N. | M. | F. | N. |
| NOM. | īdem | eadem | idem | eīdem (īdem) | eaedem | eadem |
| GEN. | eiusdem | eiusdem | eiusdem | eōrundem | eārundem | eōrundem |
| DAT. | eīdem | eīdem | eīdem | eīsdem (īsdem) | eīsdem (īsdem) | eīsdem (īsdem) |
| ACC. | eundem | eandem | idem | eōsdem | eāsdem | eadem |
| ABL. | eōdem | eādem | eōdem | eīsdem (īsdem) | eīsdem (īsdem) | eīsdem (īsdem) |

|  | SINGULAR | | | SINGULAR | | |
|---|---|---|---|---|---|---|
|  | M. | F. | N. | M. | F. | N. |
| NOM. | ille | illa | illud | ipse | ipsa | ipsum |
| GEN. | illīus | illīus | illīus | ipsīus | ipsīus | ipsīus |
| DAT. | illī | illī | illī | ipsī | ipsī | ipsī |
| ACC. | illum | illam | illud | ipsum | ipsam | ipsum |
| ABL. | illō | illā | illō | ipsō | ipsā | ipsō |

(Plural regular like **magnus**)　　　　(Plural regular)

## Relative (192)

|  | SINGULAR | | | PLURAL | | |
| | M. | F. | N. | M. | F. | N. |
|---|---|---|---|---|---|---|
| NOM. | quī | quae | quod | quī | quae | quae |
| GEN. | cuius | cuius | cuius | quōrum | quārum | quōrum |
| DAT. | cui | cui | cui | quibus | quibus | quibus |
| ACC. | quem | quam | quod | quōs | quās | quae |
| ABL. | quō | quā | quō | quibus | quibus | quibus |

## Interrogative (201)

| | SINGULAR | |
| | M.F. | N. |
|---|---|---|
| NOM. | quis | quid |
| GEN. | cuius | cuius |
| DAT. | cui | cui |
| ACC. | quem | quid |
| ABL. | quō | quō |

Plural of interrogative like that of relative. Interrogative adjective **quī** declined like relative **quī**.

## Verbs

### First Conjugation

PRINCIPAL PARTS: **portō, portāre, portāvī, portātus**

| ACTIVE | PASSIVE |
|---|---|

#### INDICATIVE

**PRESENT** *I carry,* etc.    *I am carried,* etc.
(15, 137)

| portō | portāmus | portor | portāmur |
| portās | portātis | portāris (−re) | portāminī |
| portat | portant | portātur | portantur |

**IMPERFECT** *I was carrying,* etc.    *I was (being) carried,* etc.
(131, 137)

| portābam | portābāmus | portābar | portābāmur |
| portābās | portābātis | portābāris (−re) | portābāminī |
| portābat | portābant | portābātur | portābantur |

**FUTURE** *I shall carry,* etc.    *I shall be carried,* etc.
(36, 137)

| portābō | portābimus | portābor | portābimur |
| portābis | portābitis | portāberis (−re) | portābiminī |
| portābit | portābunt | portābitur | portābuntur |

**PERFECT** *I carried, have carried,* etc.    *I was carried, have been carried,* etc.
(66, 170)

| portāvī | portāvimus | portātus { sum | portātī { sumus |
| portāvistī | portāvistis | (−a, −um) { es | (−ae, −a) { estis |
| portāvit | portāvērunt (−ēre) | est | sunt |

**PAST** *I had carried,* etc.    *I had been carried,* etc.
**PERFECT** portāveram portāverāmus

| (158, 170) | portāverās | portāverātis | portātus { eram | portātī { erāmus |
| | portāverat | portāverant | (−a, −um) { erās | (−ae, −a) { erātis |
| | | | erat | erant |

|  | ACTIVE | | PASSIVE | |
|---|---|---|---|---|

| | ACTIVE | | PASSIVE | |
|---|---|---|---|---|

FUTURE    *I shall have carried*, etc.      *I shall have been carried*, etc.

|  |  |
|---|---|
| FUTURE | *I shall have carried*, etc. |
| PERFECT | portāverō    portāverimus |
| (159, 170) | portāveris    portāveritis |
| | portāverit    portāverint |

*I shall have been carried*, etc.

portātus (−a, −um) $\begin{cases} \text{erō} \\ \text{eris} \\ \text{erit} \end{cases}$ portātī (−ae, −a) $\begin{cases} \text{erimus} \\ \text{eritis} \\ \text{erunt} \end{cases}$

### INFINITIVE (16, 173, 303, 307)

PRESENT    portāre, *to carry*      portārī, *to be carried*

PERFECT    portāvisse, *to have carried*      portātus esse, *to have been carried*

FUTURE    portātūrus esse, *to be going to carry*

### PARTICIPLE (169, 299, 300)

PRESENT    portāns, *carrying*

PERFECT                        portātus, *(having been) carried*

FUTURE    portātūrus, *going to carry*

### IMPERATIVE (48)

PRESENT    *carry*
          portā      portāte

## *Second Conjugation*

### PRINCIPAL PARTS: doceō, docēre, docuī, doctus

#### INDICATIVE

| | | | | |
|---|---|---|---|---|
| PRESENT | doceō | docēmus | doceor | docēmur |
| (59, 137) | docēs | docētis | docēris (−re) | docēminī |
| | docet | docent | docētur | docentur |
| IMPERFECT | docēbam | docēbāmus | docēbar | docēbāmur |
| (131, 137) | docēbās | docēbātis | docēbāris (−re) | docēbāminī |
| | docēbat | docēbant | docēbātur | docēbantur |
| FUTURE | docēbō | docēbimus | docēbor | docēbimur |
| (59, 137) | docēbis | docēbitis | docēberis (−re) | docēbiminī |
| | docēbit | docēbunt | docēbitur | docēbuntur |

PERFECT (66, 170)

| docuī | docuimus |
|---|---|
| docuistī | docuistis |
| docuit | docuērunt (−ēre) |

doctus (−a, −um) $\begin{cases} \text{sum} \\ \text{es} \\ \text{est} \end{cases}$ doctī (−ae, −a) $\begin{cases} \text{sumus} \\ \text{estis} \\ \text{sunt} \end{cases}$

PAST PERFECT (158, 170)

| docueram | docuerāmus |
|---|---|
| docuerās | docuerātis |
| docuerat | docuerant |

doctus (−a, −um) $\begin{cases} \text{eram} \\ \text{erās} \\ \text{erat} \end{cases}$ doctī (−ae, −a) $\begin{cases} \text{erāmus} \\ \text{erātis} \\ \text{erant} \end{cases}$

FUTURE PERFECT (159, 170)

| docuerō | docuerimus |
|---|---|
| docueris | docueritis |
| docuerit | docuerint |

doctus (−a, −um) $\begin{cases} \text{erō} \\ \text{eris} \\ \text{erit} \end{cases}$ doctī (−ae, −a) $\begin{cases} \text{erimus} \\ \text{eritis} \\ \text{erunt} \end{cases}$

|            | ACTIVE            | PASSIVE      |
|------------|-------------------|--------------|

## INFINITIVE (173, 303, 307)

| PRESENT | docēre | docērī |
|---------|--------|--------|
| PERFECT | docuisse | doctus esse |
| FUTURE | doctūrus esse | |

## PARTICIPLE (169, 299, 300)

| PRESENT | docēns | |
|---------|--------|--------|
| PERFECT | | doctus |
| FUTURE | doctūrus | |

## IMPERATIVE (48)

| PRESENT | docē | docēte |
|---------|------|--------|

### Third Conjugation

PRINCIPAL PARTS: **pōnō, pōnĕre, posuī, positus**

#### INDICATIVE

| PRESENT (96, 137) | pōnō | pōnimus | pōnor | pōnimur |
|---|---|---|---|---|
| | pōnis | pōnitis | pōneris (–re) | pōniminī |
| | pōnit | pōnunt | pōnitur | pōnuntur |

| IMPERFECT (131, 137) | pōnēbam | pōnēbāmus | pōnēbar | pōnēbāmur |
|---|---|---|---|---|
| | pōnēbās | pōnēbātis | pōnēbāris (–re) | pōnēbāminī |
| | pōnēbat | pōnēbant | pōnēbātur | pōnēbantur |

| FUTURE (118, 137) | pōnam | pōnēmus | pōnar | pōnēmur |
|---|---|---|---|---|
| | pōnēs | pōnētis | pōnēris (–re) | pōnēminī |
| | pōnet | pōnent | pōnētur | pōnentur |

| PERFECT (96, 170) | posuī | posuimus | positus (–a, –um) { sum / es / est } | positī (–ae, –a) { sumus / estis / sunt } |
|---|---|---|---|---|
| | posuistī | posuistis | | |
| | posuit | posuērunt (–ēre) | | |

| PAST PERFECT (158, 170) | posueram | posuerāmus | positus (–a, –um) { eram / erās / erat } | positī (–ae, –a) { erāmus / erātis / erant } |
|---|---|---|---|---|
| | posuerās | posuerātis | | |
| | posuerat | posuerant | | |

| FUTURE PERFECT (159, 170) | posuerō | posuerimus | positus (–a, –um) { erō / eris / erit } | positī ( ae, a) { erimus / eritis / erunt } |
|---|---|---|---|---|
| | posueris | posueritis | | |
| | posuerit | posuerint | | |

## INFINITIVE (96, 173, 303, 307)

| PRESENT | pōnere | pōnī |
|---------|--------|------|
| PERFECT | posuisse | positus esse |
| FUTURE | positūrus esse | |

|  | ACTIVE |  | PASSIVE |  |
|---|---|---|---|---|

### PARTICIPLE (169, 299, 300)

| PRESENT | pōnēns |  |  |
|---|---|---|---|
| PERFECT |  | positus |  |
| FUTURE | positūrus |  |  |

### IMPERATIVE (102)

| PRESENT | pōne | pōnite |
|---|---|---|

## Fourth Conjugation

PRINCIPAL PARTS: **mūniō, mūnīre, mūnīvī, mūnītus**

### INDICATIVE

| PRESENT | mūniō | mūnīmus | mūnior | mūnīmur |
|---|---|---|---|---|
| (102, 137) | mūnīs | mūnītis | mūnīris (–re) | mūnīminī |
|  | mūnit | mūniunt | mūnītur | mūniuntur |

| IMPERFECT | mūniēbam | mūniēbāmus | mūniēbar | mūniēbāmur |
|---|---|---|---|---|
| (131, 137) | mūniēbās | mūniēbātis | mūniēbāris (–re) | mūniēbāminī |
|  | mūniēbat | mūniēbant | mūniēbātur | mūniēbantur |

| FUTURE | mūniam | mūniēmus | mūniar | mūniēmur |
|---|---|---|---|---|
| (124, 137) | mūniēs | mūniētis | mūniēris (–re) | mūniēminī |
|  | mūniet | mūnient | mūniētur | mūnientur |

| PERFECT | mūnīvī | mūnīvimus | mūnītus (–a, –um) { sum es est | mūnītī (–ae, –a) { sumus estis sunt |
|---|---|---|---|---|
| (102, 170) | mūnīvistī | mūnīvistis |  |  |
|  | mūnīvit | mūnīvērunt (–ēre) |  |  |

| PAST | mūnīveram | mūnīverāmus | mūnītus (–a, –um) { eram erās erat | mūnītī (–ae, –a) { erāmus erātis erant |
|---|---|---|---|---|
| PERFECT | mūnīverās | mūnīverātis |  |  |
| (158, 170) | mūnīverat | mūnīverant |  |  |

| FUTURE | mūnīverō | mūnīverimus | mūnītus (–a, –um) { erō eris erit | mūnītī (–ae, –a) { erimus eritis erunt |
|---|---|---|---|---|
| PERFECT | mūnīveris | mūnīveritis |  |  |
| (159, 170) | mūnīverit | mūnīverint |  |  |

### INFINITIVE (173, 303, 307)

| PRESENT | mūnīre | mūnīrī |
|---|---|---|
| PERFECT | mūnīvisse | mūnītus esse |
| FUTURE | mūnītūrus esse |  |

### PARTICIPLE (169, 299, 300)

| PRESENT | mūniēns |  |
|---|---|---|
| PERFECT |  | mūnītus |
| FUTURE | mūnītūrus |  |

### IMPERATIVE (102)

| PRESENT | mūnī | mūnīte |
|---|---|---|

|        ACTIVE        |              |          PASSIVE        |              |

## Third Conjugation –iō Verbs

PRINCIPAL PARTS: **capiō, capĕre, cēpī, captus**

### INDICATIVE

| PRESENT | capiō | capimus | capior | capimur |
|---|---|---|---|---|
| (102, 137) | capis | capitis | caperis (–re) | capiminī |
|  | capit | capiunt | capitur | capiuntur |

| IMPERFECT | capiēbam, etc. |  | capiēbar, etc. |  |
|---|---|---|---|---|
| (131, 137) |  |  |  |  |

| FUTURE | capiam | capiēmus | capiar | capiēmur |
|---|---|---|---|---|
| (124, 137) | capiēs | capiētis | capiēris (–re) | capiēminī |
|  | capiet | capient | capiētur | capientur |

| PERFECT | cēpī, etc. |  | captus sum, etc. |  |
|---|---|---|---|---|
| (102, 170) |  |  |  |  |

| PAST PERFECT | cēperam, etc. |  | captus eram, etc. |  |
|---|---|---|---|---|
| (158, 170) |  |  |  |  |

| FUTURE PERFECT | cēperō, etc. |  | captus erō, etc. |  |
|---|---|---|---|---|
| (159, 170) |  |  |  |  |

### INFINITIVE (173, 303, 307)

| PRESENT | capere | capī |
|---|---|---|
| PERFECT | cēpisse | captus esse |
| FUTURE | captūrus esse |  |

### PARTICIPLE (169, 299, 300)

| PRESENT | capiēns |  |
|---|---|---|
| PERFECT |  | captus |
| FUTURE | captūrus |  |

### IMPERATIVE (102)

| PRESENT | cape | capite |
|---|---|---|

**400**

# Irregular Verbs

PRINCIPAL PARTS: **sum, esse, fuī, futūrus**

### INDICATIVE

| PRESENT (75) | *I am, you are, etc.* | |
|---|---|---|
| | sum | sumus |
| | es | estis |
| | est | sunt |

| IMPERFECT (131) | *I was, etc.* | |
|---|---|---|
| | eram | erāmus |
| | erās | erātis |
| | erat | erant |

| FUTURE (89) | *I shall be, etc.* | |
|---|---|---|
| | erō | erimus |
| | eris | eritis |
| | erit | erunt |

| PERFECT (89) | *I was, etc.* | |
|---|---|---|
| | fuī | fuimus |
| | fuistī | fuistis |
| | fuit | fuērunt (–ēre) |

| PAST PERFECT (158) | *I had been, etc.* | |
|---|---|---|
| | fueram | fuerāmus |
| | fuerās | fuerātis |
| | fuerat | fuerant |

| FUTURE PERFECT (159) | *I shall have been, etc.* | |
|---|---|---|
| | fuerō | fuerimus |
| | fueris | fueritis |
| | fuerit | fuerint |

### INFINITIVE (173, 303, 307)

| PRESENT | esse, *to be* |
|---|---|
| PERFECT | fuisse, *to have been* |
| FUTURE | futūrus esse, *to be going to be* |

### PARTICIPLE (300)

| FUTURE | futūrus, *going to be* |
|---|---|

### IMPERATIVE

| PRESENT | *be* | |
|---|---|---|
| | es | este |

---

PRINCIPAL PARTS: **possum, posse, potuī, ——**

### INDICATIVE (220)

| PRESENT | *I am able, I can, etc.* | |
|---|---|---|
| | possum | possumus |
| | potes | potestis |
| | potest | possunt |

| IMPERFECT | *I was able, I could, etc.* |
|---|---|
| | poteram, etc. |

| FUTURE | *I shall be able, etc.* |
|---|---|
| | poterō, etc. |

| PERFECT | *I was able, I could, etc.* |
|---|---|
| | potuī, etc. |

| PAST PERFECT | *I had been able, etc.* |
|---|---|
| | potueram, etc. |

| FUTURE PERFECT | *I shall have been able* |
|---|---|
| | potuerō, etc. |

### INFINITIVE (221, 303)

| PRESENT | posse, *to be able* |
|---|---|
| PERFECT | potuisse, *to have been able* |
| FUTURE | —— |

### PARTICIPLE (299)

| PRESENT | potēns, (*adj.*), *powerful* |
|---|---|

## BASIC SYNTAX

### Agreement

1. *Adjectives.* Adjectives and participles agree in number, gender, and case with the nouns which they modify (13, 169).

2. *Adjectives as Nouns.* Sometimes adjectives are used as nouns (154).

3. *Verbs.* Verbs agree in person and number with their subjects (24).

   *Note.* When two subjects are connected by **aut, aut . . . aut, neque . . . neque,** the verb agrees with the nearer subject (142).

4. *Relative Pronoun.* The relative pronoun agrees in gender and number with its antecedent but its case depends upon its use in its own clause (194).

5. *Appositives.* Appositives agree in case (99).

### Noun Syntax

**Nominative**   1. *Subject.* The subject of a verb is in the nominative (10).

2. *Predicate.* A noun or adjective used in the predicate after a linking verb (*is, are, seem,* etc.) to complete its meaning is in the nominative (10).

**Genitive**   1. *Possession.* Possession is expressed by the genitive (33).

2. *Description.* The genitive, if modified by an adjective, may be used to describe a person or thing (369).

**Dative**   1. *Indirect Object.* The indirect object of a verb is in the dative. It is used with verbs of *giving, reporting, telling,* etc. (38).

2. *With Special Verbs.* The dative is used with a few intransitive verbs, such as **noceō** (378).

3. *With Adjectives.* The dative is used with certain adjectives, as **amīcus, pār, similis,** and their opposites (335).

**Accusative**   1. *Direct Object.* The direct object of a transitive verb is in the accusative (22).

2. *Extent.* Extent of time or space is expressed by the accusative (357).

3. *Place to Which.* The accusative with **ad** (*to*) or **in** (*into*) expresses "place to which" (76).

4. *Subject of Infinitive.* The subject of an infinitive is in the accusative (166).

5. *With Prepositions.* The accusative is used with the prepositions **ad, ante, apud, circum, contrā, inter, ob, per, post, super,** and **trāns;** also with **in** and **sub** when they show the direction toward which a thing moves.

**Ablative**    1. *From Which.* The ablative with **ab, dē,** or **ex** expresses "place from which" (70).

2. *Agent.* The ablative with **ā** or **ab** is used with a passive verb to show the person by whom something is done (141).

3. *Accompaniment.* The ablative with **cum** expresses accompaniment (121).

4. *Manner.* The ablative of manner with **cum** describes how something is done. **Cum** may be omitted, as a rule, only if an adjective is used with the noun (198).

5. *Means.* The means by which a thing is done is expressed by the ablative without a preposition (43).

6. *Description.* The ablative without a preposition is used (like the genitive) to describe a person or thing (369).

7. *Place Where.* The ablative with **in** expresses "place where" (63).

8. *Time When.* "Time when" is expressed by the ablative without a preposition (276).

9. *Respect.* The ablative without a preposition is used to tell in what respect the statement applies (258).

10. *Absolute.* A noun in the ablative used with a participle, adjective, or other noun in the same case and having no grammatical connection with any other word in its clause is called an ablative absolute (230).

11. *With Prepositions.* The ablative is used with the prepositions **ab, cum, dē, ex, prae, prō, sine;** also with **in** and **sub** when they indicate place where.

**Vocative**    The *vocative* is used in addressing a person (69).

## Verb Syntax

**Tenses**    1. *Imperfect. Repeated, customary,* or *continuous* action in the past is expressed by the imperfect (132).

2. *Perfect.* An action completed in the past is expressed by the perfect. It is translated by the English past, occasionally by the present perfect (66, 132).

**Participles**    1. The tenses of the participle (present, perfect, future) indicate time *present, past,* or *future* from the standpoint of the main verb (169, 300).

2. Perfect participles are often used as simple adjectives and, like adjectives, may be used as nouns (220).

3. The Latin participle is often a *one-word substitute* for a subordinate clause in English introduced by *who* or *which, when* or *after, since* or *because, although,* and *if* (223).

**403**

**Infinitive**     1. The infinitive is a verbal indeclinable neuter noun, and as such it may be used as the subject of a verb (89).

2. With many verbs the infinitive may be used as a direct object, like other nouns (90).

3. Certain verbs such as **iubeō** and **doceō** have an infinitive as object, often with a noun or pronoun subject in the accusative (166).

4. Statements that convey indirectly the thoughts or words of another, used as the objects of verbs of *saying, thinking, knowing, hearing, perceiving,* etc., require subjects in the accusative and verbs in the infinitive (307).

*Boy putting a monkey through his tricks. From a Pompeian wall painting.*

## BOOKS FOR REFERENCE

### I. Books for Special Assignments (referred to in the lessons)

Bulfinch, Thomas, *The Age of Fable* (Everyman's Library). E. P. Dutton and Company, New York, 1910.

Colum, Padraic, *The Adventures of Odysseus and the Tale of Troy*. The Macmillan Company, New York, 1927.

Davis, William Stearns, *A Day in Old Rome*. Allyn and Bacon, Boston, 1925.

Gayley, Charles Mills, *Classic Myths in English Literature and Art*. Ginn and Company, Boston, 1911.

Grose-Hodge, Humfrey, *Roman Panorama, a Background for Today*. Cambridge University Press, 1944.

Guerber, H. A., *Myths of Greece and Rome*. American Book Company, New York, 1921.

Johnston, Harold W., *The Private Life of the Romans*. Scott, Foresman and Company, Chicago, 1932. New edition in press.

Mills, Dorothy, *The Book of the Ancient Romans*. G. P. Putnam's Sons, New York, 1927.

Norton, Dan S., and Rushton, Peters, *Classical Myths in English Literature*, Rinehart and Company, New York, 1952.

Sabin, Frances E., *Classical Myths That Live Today*. Silver Burdett Company, New York, 1940.

Showerman, Grant, *Rome and the Romans*. The Macmillan Company, New York, 1931.

Tappan, Eva March, *The Story of the Roman People*. Houghton Mifflin Company, Boston, 1910.

### II. Novels and Other Books for Historical Background

Carcopino, J., *Daily Life in Ancient Rome*. Yale University Press, New Haven, 1940.

Cowles, J. D., *Our Little Roman Cousin of Long Ago*. L. C. Page and Company, Boston, 1913.

Hall, Jennie, *Buried Cities*. The Macmillan Company, New York, 1922.

Lawrence, Isabelle, *The Gift of the Golden Cup*. Bobbs-Merrill Company, Indianapolis, 1946.

Snedeker, Caroline D., *Forgotten Daughter*. Doubleday and Company, New York, 1933.

Stobart, J. C., *The Grandeur That Was Rome*, third edition by F. N. Pryce. Appleton-Century-Crofts, New York, 1934.

White, Edward Lucas, *Andivius Hedulio*. E. P. Dutton and Company, New York, 1921.

White, Edward Lucas, *The Unwilling Vestal*. E. P. Dutton and Company, New York, 1918.

## THE STAR-SPANGLED BANNER

Tr. F. A. Geyser

Ōh, potestne cernī, praefulgente diē,
    Salūtātum signum circā noctis adventum?
Lātī clāv(ī) et stēllae, dēcertant(e) aciē,
    Glōriōsē cingunt oppidī mūnīmentum!
Iaculumque rubēns, globus sūrsum rumpēns
Per noctem mōnstrant vexillum fulgēns.
    Stēllātumne vexillum volāns tegit nōs,
    Patriam līberam fortiumque domōs?
      (For "America" see page 6)

## GOD BLESS AMERICA

Irving Berlin. Tr. by the Virgil class of Central High School, St. Paul (Florence E. Baber, teacher).

Dum nimbī cōgunt
    Trāns maria,
Iūrēmus fidem
    Līberae terrae;
Grātiam habeāmus
    Patriae pulchrae,
Dum nōs cantāmus
    Sollemnī prece.

Deus Americam
    Benedīcat,
Illam servet et dūcat
    Per noctem cum lūce altā;
Dē montibus ad campōs,
    Ad maria undīs albīs,
Deus Americam
    Benedīcat.

## ADESTE FIDĒLĒS [1]

Adeste, fidēlēs,
    Laetī triumphantēs;
Venīte, venīte in Bethlehem;
    Nātum vidēte
    Rēgem angelōrum;
Venīte adōrēmus, venīte adōrēmus,
Venīte adōrēmus Dominum.

Cantet nunc "Iō!"
    Chorus angelōrum;
Cantet nunc aula caelestium:
    "Glōria, glōria
    In excelsīs Deō!"
Venīte, etc.

Ergō quī nātus
    Diē hodiernā,
Iēsū, tibi sit glōria;
    Patris aeternī
    Verbum carō factum!
Venīte, etc.

---

[1] Sung to the tune of the Portuguese Hymn, "O Come, All Ye Faithful."

# GAUDEAMUS IGITUR

Student Song

1. Gau-de - a - mus i - gi-tur, Iu - ve -nes dum su - mus; Post iu-cun-dam iu-ven-tu-tem, Post mo-les-tam se-nec-tu-tem, Nos ha-be-bit hu - mus, Nos ha-be-bit hu - mus.

2. Vi-vat a-ca-de-mi-a, Vi-vant pro-fes-so - res, Vi-vat mem-brum quod-li - bet, Vi-vant mem-bra quae-li - bet, Sem-per sint in flo - re, Sem-per sint in flo - re.

3. Vi-vat et res pu-bli-ca Et qui il-lam re - git; Vi-vat nos-tra ci-vi-tas; Vi-vat haec so-da-li-tas Quae nos huc col-le - git, Quae nos huc col-le - git.

# INTEGER VITAE

Horace, Odes I. 22 (ca. 25 b.c.)          Dr. F. F. Flemming, ca. 1811

1. In - te - ger vi - tae sce - le - ris - que
2. Si - ve per Syr - tes i - ter aes - tu -
3. Nam - que me sil - va lu - pus in Sa -

pu - rus Non e - get Mau - ris ia - cu - lis ne -
o - sas, Si - ve fac - tu - rus per in - hos - pi -
bi - na, Dum me - am can - to La - la - gen et

qu(e) ar - cu Nec ve - ne - na - tis gra - vi - da sa -
ta - lem Cau - ca - sum vel quae lo - ca fa - bu -
ul - tra Ter - mi - num cu - ris va - gor ex - pe -

git - tis, Fus - ce, pha - re - tra,
lo - sus Lam - bit Hy - das - pes.
di - tis, Fu - git in - er - mem.

# *Vocabulary*

## LATIN–ENGLISH

Proper names are not included unless they are spelled differently in English or are difficult to pronounce in English. Their English pronunciation is indicated by a simple system. The vowels are as follows: ā as in *hate,* ă as in *hat,* ē as in *feed,* ĕ as in *fed,* ī as in *bite,* ĭ as in *bit,* ō as in *hope,* ŏ as in *hop,* ū as in *cute,* ŭ as in *cut.* In the ending *ēs* the *s* is soft as in *rose.* When the accented syllable ends in a consonant, the vowel is short; otherwise it is long.

## A

**ā, ab,** *prep. w. abl.,* from, away from, by
**absum, abesse, āfuī, āfutūrus,** be away, be absent
**ac,** *see* **atque**
**accēdō, –ere, accessī, accessūrus,** approach
**accidō, –ere, accidī, —,** fall to, befall, happen ( *w. dat.* )
**accipiō, –ere, accēpī, acceptus,** receive
**accūsō, –āre, –āvī, –ātus,** blame, accuse
**ācer, ācris, ācre,** sharp, keen
**ācriter,** *adv.,* sharply
**ad,** *prep. w. acc.,* to, toward, for, near
**addūcō, –ere, addūxī, adductus,** lead to, influence
**adsum, –esse, adfuī, adfutūrus,** be near, be present
**aeger, aegra, aegrum,** sick
**Aegyptiī, –ōrum,** *m. pl.,* the Egyptians
**Aegyptus, –ī,** *f.,* Egypt
**Aenēās, –ae,** *m.,* Aeneas (Enē'as)
**Aeolus, –ī,** *m.,* Aeolus (E'olus)
**aequē,** *adv.,* justly
**aequus, –a, –um,** even, just, calm
**aestās, aestātis,** *f.,* summer
**aetās, aetātis,** *f.,* age
**Aetna, –ae,** *f.,* (Mt.) Etna
**afficiō, –ere, affēcī, affectus,** affect, afflict with
**Āfricānus, –ī,** *m.,* Africā'nus
**ager, agrī,** *m.,* field, farm, country
**agō, –ere, ēgī, āctus,** drive, do, treat, discuss, live *or* spend ( *of time* ); **grātiās agō,** thank
**agricola, –ae,** *m.,* farmer
**āla, –ae,** *f.,* wing
**albus, –a, –um,** white
**aliēnus, –a, –um,** another's, unfavorable
**alius, alia, aliud,** other, another; **alius . . . alius,** one . . . another; **aliī . . . aliī,** some . . . others

**Alpēs, –ium,** *f. pl.,* the Alps
**altē,** *adv.,* high, far
**alter, altera, alterum,** the other ( *of two* ); **alter . . . alter,** the one . . . the other
**altus, –a, –um,** high, tall, deep
**Americānus, –a, –um,** American; **Americānus, –ī,** *m.,* an American
**amīcitia, –ae,** *f.,* friendship
**amīcus, –a, –um,** friendly; **amīcus, –ī,** *m.,* **amīca, –ae,** *f.,* friend
**āmittō, –ere, āmīsī, āmissus,** let go, lose
**amō, –āre, –āvī, –ātus,** love, like
**amor, –ōris,** *m.,* love
**amphitheātrum, –ī,** *n.,* amphitheater
**Anglicus, –a, –um,** English
**animus, –ī,** *m.,* mind, courage
**annus, –ī,** *m.,* year
**ante,** *adv. and prep. w. acc.,* before ( *of time or space* )
**antecēdō, –ere, –cessī, –cessūrus,** go before, take the lead
**antīquus, –a, –um,** ancient
**appellō, –āre, –āvī, –ātus,** call
**Appius, –a, –um,** *adj.,* of Appius, Appian; **Appius, –pī,** Appius
**aptus, –a, –um,** fit, suitable ( *w. dat.* )
**apud,** *prep. w. acc.,* among, with
**aqua, –ae,** *f.,* water
**aquaeductus, –ūs,** *m.,* aqueduct
**Aquītānus, –ī,** *m.,* an Aquitā'nian
**arcus, –ūs,** *m.,* arch, bow
**arēna, –ae,** *f.,* sand, arena
**argentum, –ī,** *n.,* silver
**arma, –ōrum,** *n. pl.,* arms, weapons
**ascendō, –ere, ascendī, ascēnsus,** climb (up), ascend
**atque (ac),** *conj.,* and
**ātrium, ātrī,** *n.,* atrium, hall
**attingō, –ere, attigī, attāctus,** touch, reach
**auctor, –ōris,** *m.,* maker, author
**auctōritās, –tātis,** *f.,* authority, influence
**audācia, –ae,** *f.,* boldness
**audāx,** *gen.* **audācis,** daring

**409**

audiō, –īre, –īvī, –ītus, hear
augeō, –ēre, auxī, auctus, increase
aureus, –a, –um, golden
aurīga, –ae, m., charioteer
aurum, –ī, n., gold
aut, or; aut . . . aut, either . . . or
autem, conj. (never first word), however
auxilium, –lī, n., aid; pl., reinforcements
āvertō, –ere, āvertī, āversus, turn from
avus, –ī, m., grandfather
axis, –is, m., axle

## B

barbarus, –a, –um, foreign, barbarous;
  barbarus, –ī, m., foreigner, barbarian
Belgae, –ārum, m. pl., the Belgians
bellum, –ī, n., war
bene, adv., well, well done; comp. melius,
  better; superl. optimē, best, very good
beneficium, –cī, n., kindness, benefit
benignus, –a, –um, kind
bibō, –ere, bibī, ——, drink
bonus, –a, –um, good; comp. melior,
  melius, better; superl. optimus, –a,
  –um, best
Britannia, –ae, f., Britain
Britannus, –ī, m., a Briton

## C

C., abbreviation for Gāius
cadō, –ere, cecidī, cāsūrus, fall
Caecilius, –lī, m., Caecilius (Sēsil'ius)
caelum, –ī, n., sky
Caesar, –aris, m., Caesar
canis, –is, m., dog
canō, –ere, cecinī, cantus, sing
capiō, –ere, cēpī, captus, take, seize, capture; cōnsilium capiō, adopt a plan
Capitōlium, –lī, n., the Capitol, temple of
  Jupiter at Rome; the Capitoline Hill
captīvus, –ī, m.; captīva, –ae, f., prisoner
caput, capitis, n., head
carmen, –minis, n., song
carrus, –ī, m., cart, wagon
Carthāginiēnsēs, –ium, m. pl., the Car-
  thaginians (Carthajin'ians)
Carthāgō, –ginis, f., Carthage, a city in
  Africa; Carthāgō Nova, New Carthage,
  in Spain
casa, –ae, f., house
castra, –ōrum, n. pl., camp
cāsus, –ūs, m., fall, chance, accident
Catilīna, –ae, m., Catiline
causa, –ae, f., cause, reason, case
cēdō, –ere, cessī, cessūrus, move, retreat,
  yield

celer, celeris, celere, swift
celeritās, –tātis, f., swiftness
celeriter, adv., quickly
Celtae, –ārum, m. pl., Celts, a people of
  Gaul
cēna, –ae, f., dinner
centum, hundred
cēra, –ae, f., wax
Cerēs, –eris, f., Ceres (Sē'rēs), goddess
  of agriculture
cernō, –ere, crēvī, crētus, separate, discern, see
certē, adv., certainly
certus, –a, –um, fixed, sure
cibus, –ī, m., food
Cicerō, –ōnis, m., Cicero (Sis'ero)
Circē, –ae, f., Circe (Sir'sē), a sorceress
circum, prep. w. acc., around
circus, –ī, m., circle, circus, esp. the
  Circus Maximus at Rome
cīvis, cīvis, m., citizen
cīvitās, –tātis, f., citizenship, state
clam, adv., secretly
clāmō, –āre, –āvī, –ātus, shout, cry out
clāmor, –ōris, m., shout
clārē, adv., clearly
clārus, –a, –um, clear, famous
claudō, –ere, clausī, clausus, close
cognōmen, –minis, n., cognomen, sur-
  name
cognōscō, –ere, –nōvī, –nitus, learn, recognize; perf., know, understand
cōgō, –ere, coēgī, coāctus, drive together,
  collect, compel
colō, –ere, coluī, cultus, till, inhabit, worship
colōnus, –ī, m., settler
Colossēum, –ī, n., the Colossē'um, an
  amphitheater at Rome
committō, –ere, –mīsī, –missus, join together, commit, entrust; proelium committō, begin battle
commodē, adv., suitably
commodus, –a, –um, suitable, convenient
commoveō, –ēre, –mōvī, –mōtus, disturb
commūnis, –e, common
comprehendō, –ere, –hendī, –hēnsus,
  understand
concordia, –ae, f., harmony
condiciō, –ōnis, f., condition, terms
cōnficiō, –ere, –fēcī, –fectus, do up, complete, exhaust
cōnfidō, –ere, cōnfīsus, have confidence
  (in)
cōnfirmō, –āre, –āvī, –ātus, make firm,
  encourage, establish
cōnservō, –āre, –āvī, –ātus, save, preserve
cōnsilium, –lī, n., plan, advice

cōnsistō, –ere, cōnstitī, cōnstitūrus, stand still, stop
cōnspiciō, –ere, –spexī, –spectus, catch sight of, see
cōnsul, –ulis, *m.*, consul, *the highest Roman official*
cōnsulō, –ere, –suluī, –sultus, consult
contendō, –ere, –tendī, –tentūrus, struggle, hasten
contineō, –ēre, –uī, –tentus, hold (together), contain
contrā, *prep. w. acc.*, against
conveniō, –īre, –vēnī, –ventūrus, come together
convocō, –āre, –āvī, –ātus, call together
cōpia, –ae, *f.*, supply, abundance
cor, cordis, *n.*, heart
corōna, –ae, *f.*, crown
corpus, –poris, *n.*, body
crēdō, –ere, –didī, –ditus, believe, entrust (*w. dat.*)
Crēta, –ae, *f.*, Crete
cum, *prep. w. abl.*, with
cupiditās, –tātis, *f.*, desire
cupiō, –ere, cupīvī, cupītus, desire
cūr, *adv.*, why
cūra, –ae, *f.*, care, concern; (cum) magnā cūrā, very carefully
cūrō, –āre, –āvī, –ātus, care for, cure
currō, –ere, cucurrī, cursūrus, run
currus, –ūs, *m.*, chariot

## D

dē, *prep. w. abl.*, from, down from, about
dea, –ae, *f.*, goddess
dēbeō, –ēre, dēbuī, dēbitus, owe, ought
decem, ten
December, –bris, *m.*, December
dēfendō, –ere, dēfendī, dēfēnsus, defend
dēligō, –ere, dēlēgī, dēlēctus, select
dēmōnstrō, –āre, –āvī, –ātus, show
dēpōnō, –ere, dēposuī, dēpositus, put *or* lay aside
dēscendō, –ere, dēscendī, dēscēnsus, descend
dēserō, –ere, dēseruī, dēsertus, desert
dēsiliō, –īre, dēsiluī, dēsultūrus, jump down
dēspiciō, –ere, dēspexī, dēspectus, look down on, despise
deus, –ī, *m.*, god
dēvorō, –āre, –āvī, –ātus, swallow
dīcō, –ere, dīxī, dictus, say, tell
dictātor, –ōris, *m.*, dictator
dictātūra, –ae, *f.*, dictatorship
dictum, –ī, *n.*, word
diēs, diēī, *m.*, day

difficilis, –e, difficult
digitus, –ī, *m.*, finger
dīligentia, –ae, *f.*, diligence
dīmittō, –ere, dīmīsī, dīmissus, let go, send away
discēdō, –ere, –cessī, –cessūrus, go away, depart
disciplīna, –ae, *f.*, training, instruction
discipulus, –ī, *m.*, discipula, –ae, *f.*, learner, pupil
dissimilis, –e, unlike
dīvidō, –ere, dīvīsī, dīvīsus, divide
dō, dare, dedī, datus, give, put; poenam dō, pay the penalty
doceō, –ēre, docuī, doctus, teach
dominus, –ī, *m.*, master; domina, –ae, *f.*, mistress
domus, –ūs, *f.*, house, home
dōnō, –āre, –āvī, –ātus, give, present
dormiō, –īre, –īvī, –ītus, sleep
dubitō, –āre, –āvī, –ātus, hesitate, doubt
dūcō, –ere, dūxī, ductus, lead, draw
dulcis, –e, sweet
dum, *conj.*, while
duo, –ae, –o, two
duodecim, twelve
dūrus, –a, –um, hard, harsh
dux, ducis, *m.*, leader, general

## E

ē, ex, *prep. w. abl.*, from, out from, out of
ecce, look, here!
ēdūcō, –ere, ēdūxī, ēductus, lead out
efficiō, –ere, effēcī, effectus, make (out), bring about, complete
ego, meī, I
ēgregius, –a, –um, distinguished, excellent
elephantus, –ī, *m.*, elephant
emō, –ere, ēmī, ēmptus, take, buy
Ēpīrus, –ī, *f.*, Ēpī′rus, *a province in Greece*
equus, –ī, *m.*, horse
ērumpō, –ere, ērūpī, ēruptus, burst forth
et, *conj.*, and, even; et . . . et, both . . . and
etiam, *adv.*, also, even, too
Etrūscī, –ōrum, *m. pl.*, the Etruscans
Eumaeus, –ī, m., Eumaeus (Ūmē′us)
Eurōpa, –ae, *f.*, Europe
ēvādō, –ere, ēvāsī, ēvāsūrus, go out, escape
ēvocō, –āre, –āvī, –ātus, summon
excēdō, –ere, excessī, excessūrus, depart
exemplum, –ī, *n.*, example
exerceō, –ēre, exercuī, exercitus, keep busy, train

exercitus, –ūs, m., (trained) army
exīstimō, –āre, –āvī, –ātus, think
exit, he goes out
expediō, –īre, –īvī, –ītus, set free
expellō, –ere, expulī, expulsus, drive out
explicō, –āre, –āvī, –ātus, unfold, explain
explōrō, –āre, –āvī, –ātus, investigate, explore
expugnō, –āre, –āvī, –ātus, capture by assault
exspectō, –āre, –āvī, –ātus, look out for, await, wait
exstinguō, –ere, exstīnxī, exstīnctus, extinguish
extrēmus, –a, –um, farthest, last, end of

## F

fābula, –ae, f., story
facile, adv., easily
facilis, –e, easy
faciō, –ere, fēcī, factus, do, make; verba faciō, speak, make a speech
factum, –ī, n., deed
fallō, –ere, fefellī, falsus, deceive
fāma, –ae, f., report, fame
familia, –ae, f., family
familiāris, –e, of the family, friendly; as noun, friend
fātum, –ī, n., fate; often personified, the Fates
ferrum, –ī, n., iron
fīlius, –lī, m., son; fīlia, –ae, f., daughter
fīnis, fīnis, m., end; pl., borders, territory
fīnitimus, –a, –um, neighboring, near; as noun, neighbor
firmus, –a, –um, strong, firm
flūmen, flūminis, n., river
fluō, –ere, flūxī, flūxus, flow
focus, –ī, m., hearth
fōrma, –ae, f., shape, image, form
fortasse, adv., perhaps
fortis, –e, strong, brave
fortiter, adv., bravely
fortūna, –ae, f., fortune
forum, –ī, n., market place; Forum (at Rome)
frangō, –ere, frēgī, frāctus, break
frāter, frātris, m., brother
frōns, frontis, f., forehead, front
frūmentum, –ī, n., grain
fuga, –ae, f., flight
fugiō, –ere, fūgī, fugitūrus, flee
fulmen, –minis, n., lightning
futūrus, see sum

## G

Gāius, –ī, m., Gā′ius
Gallia, –ae, f., Gaul, ancient France

Gallicus, –a, –um, Gallic
Gallus, –ī, m., a Gaul
gēns, gentis, f., people, nation
genus, generis, n., birth, kind
Germānia, –ae, f., Germany
Germānus, –ī, m., a German
gerō, –ere, gessī, gestus, carry on, wear
gladiātor, –ōris, m., gladiator
glōria, –ae, f., glory
Graecia, –ae, f., Greece
Graecus, –a, –um, Greek; Graecus, –ī, m., a Greek
grātē, adv., gratefully
grātia, –ae, f., gratitude, influence; grātiam habeō, feel grateful; grātiās agō, thank
grātus, –a, –um, pleasing, grateful
gravis, –e, heavy, severe
graviter, adv., heavily, seriously

## H

habeō, –ēre, habuī, habitus, have, hold, consider; grātiam habeō, feel grateful (w. dat.); ōrātiōnem habeō, deliver an oration
habitō, –āre, –āvī, –ātus, live
haereō, –ēre, haesī, haesus, stick
Hannibal, –alis, m., Hannibal, a Carthaginian general
herba, –ae, f., grass, plant
Hibernia, –ae, f., Ireland
hic, haec, hoc, this; as pron., he, she, it
hiems, hiemis, f., winter
Hispānia, –ae, f., Spain
Hispānus, –a, –um, Spanish
homō, hominis, m., man, human being
honestās, –tātis, f., honor
honor, –ōris, m., honor, office
hōra, –ae, f., hour
hospita, –ae, f., guest
hostis, hostis, m., enemy (usually pl.)
humilis, –e, low, humble

## I

iaciō, –ere, iēcī, iactus, throw
iam, adv., already; nōn iam, no longer
ibi, adv., there
īdem, eadem, idem, same
ignis, –is, m., fire
ille, illa, illud, that; as pron., he, she, it
impedīmentum, –ī, n., hindrance; pl., baggage
impediō, –īre, –īvī, –ītus, hinder
imperātor, –ōris, m., commander, general
imperium, –rī, n., command, power
imperō, –āre, –āvī, –ātus, command (w. dat.)
impetus, –ūs, m., attack

in, *prep. w. acc.*, into, to, against; *w. abl.*, in, on
incertus, −a, −um, uncertain
incipiō, −ere, incēpī, inceptus, take to, begin
incitō, −āre, −āvī, −ātus, urge on, arouse
incolō, −ere, incoluī, incultus, live, inhabit
īnferior, īnferius, lower
inimīcus, −a, −um, unfriendly; *as noun*, enemy
iniūria, −ae, *f.*, wrong, injustice, injury
inquit, said (he)
īnstō, −āre, īnstitī, —, threaten
īnstruō, −ere, īnstrūxī, īnstrūctus, arrange, provide, draw up
īnsula, −ae, *f.*, island
integer, −gra, −grum, untouched, fresh
intellegō, −ere, −lēxī, −lēctus, understand
inter, *prep. w. acc.*, between, among
intercipiō, −ere, −cēpī, −ceptus, intercept
interclūdō, −ere, −clūsī, −clūsus, cut off
interficiō, −ere, −fēcī, −fectus, kill
interim, *adv.*, meanwhile
intermittō, −ere, −mīsī, −missus, let go, stop, interrupt
inveniō, −īre, invēnī, inventus, come upon, find
iō, *interj.*, hurrah!
ipse, ipsa, ipsum, −self, very
īra, −ae, *f.*, anger
is, ea, id, this, that; *as pron.*, he, she, it
ita, *adv.*, so
Italia, −ae, *f.*, Italy
itaque, *adv.*, and so, therefore
iter, itineris, *n.*, journey, road, march
iterum, *adv.*, again
iubeō, −ēre, iussī, iussus, order
iūdicō, −āre, −āvī, −ātus, judge
Iūlius, −lī, *m.*, Julius; Iūlia, −ae, *f.*, Julia
iungō, −ere, iūnxī, iūnctus, join (to)
Iūnō, −ōnis, *f.*, Juno, *a goddess, wife of Jupiter*
Iuppiter, Iovis, *m.*, Jupiter, *king of the gods*
iūs, iūris, *n.*, right
iūstē, *adv.*, justly
iūstus, −a, −um, just


## L

labor, −ōris, *m.*, work, hardship
labōrō, −āre, −āvī, −ātus, work
lacrima, −ae, *f.*, tear
lacrimō, −āre, −āvī, −ātus, weep
lanterna, −ae, *f.*, lantern
Lār, Laris, *m.*, Lar, *a household god*
lassitūdō, −tūdinis, *f.*, weariness

lātē, *adv.*, widely
Latīnus, −a, −um, Latin, belonging to Latium; Latīnī, −ōrum, *m.*, the Latins
Latīnus, −ī, *m.*, Latī'nus
latrō, −ōnis, *m.*, bandit
lātus, −a, −um, wide
laudō, −āre, −āvī, −ātus, praise
lavō, −āre, lāvī, lautus, wash
lēgātus, −ī, *m.*, envoy
legō, −ere, lēgī, lēctus, gather, choose, read
levis, −e, light (*in weight*)
leviter, *adv.*, lightly
lēx, lēgis, *f.*, law
liber, librī, *m.*, book
līber, −era, −erum, free
līberē, *adv.*, freely
līberī, −ōrum, *m.*, children
līberō, −āre, −āvī, −ātus, free
lībertās, −tātis, *f.*, freedom
ligō, −āre, −āvī, −ātus, bind
lingua, −ae, *f.*, tongue, language
littera, −ae, *f.*, letter (*of the alphabet*), *pl.*, letter (*epistle*), letters (*if modified by an adjective such as* multae), literature
locus, −ī, *m.* (*pl.* loca, locōrum, *n.*), place
longus, −a, −um, long
Lūcīlius, −lī, *m.*, Lucilius (Lūsil'ius)
lūdō, −ere, lūsī, lūsus, play
lūdus, −ī, *m.*, game, school
Lūsitānia, −ae, *f.*, Portugal
lūx, lūcis, *f.*, light, daylight


## M

M., *abbreviation for* Mārcus
magister, −trī, *m.*, teacher
magnus, −a, −um, large, great; *comp.* maior, maius, greater; *superl.* maximus, −a, −um, greatest, very great
maior, *see* magnus
malus, −a, −um, bad; *comp.* peior, peius, worse; *superl.* pessimus, −a, −um, very bad, worst; malum, −ī, *n.*, trouble
mandō, −āre, −āvī, −ātus, entrust
maneō, −ēre, mānsī, mānsūrus, remain
manus, −ūs, *f.*, hand
Mārcius, −cī, *m.*, Marcius (Mar'shius)
mare, maris, *n.*, sea
marītus, −ī, *m.*, husband
Mārs, Mārtis, *m.*, Mars, *god of war*
māter, mātris, *f.*, mother
māteria, −ae, *f.*, matter, timber
mātrimōnium, −nī, *n.*, marriage
mātūrō, −āre, −āvī, −ātūrus, hasten
maximē, *adv.*, very greatly, especially

maximus, *see* magnus
medicus, –ī, *m.*, doctor
Mediterrāneum (Mare), Mediterranean
 Sea
medius, –a, –um, middle (of)
mel, mellis, *n.*, honey
melior, *see* bonus
memoria, –ae, *f.*, memory; **memoriā
 teneō**, remember
mēnsa, –ae, *f.*, table
mēnsis, –is, *m.*, month
mercātor, –ōris, *m.*, merchant
Mercurius, –rī, *m.*, Mercury
mereō, –ēre, meruī, meritus, deserve, earn
mēta, –ae, *f.*, goal, turning post, *in the
 Circus*
meus, –a, –um, my, mine
migrō, –āre, –āvī, –ātūrus, depart
mīles, mīlitis, *m.*, soldier
mīlle, *pl.* mīlia, thousand
minimē, *adv.*, not at all
minimus, minor, *see* parvus
miser, –era, –erum, unhappy, poor
mittō, –ere, mīsī, missus, let go, send
modus, –ī, *m.*, manner
moneō, –ēre, monuī, monitus, remind,
 warn
mōns, montis, *m.*, mountain
mōnstrō, –āre, –āvī, –ātus, point out,
 show
mors, mortis, *f.*, death
mōs, mōris, *m.*, custom
moveō, –ēre, mōvī, mōtus, move
mox, *adv.*, soon
mulier, mulieris, *f.*, woman
multus, –a, –um, much; *pl.*, many; *comp.*
 plūrēs, plūra, more; *superl.* plūrimus,
 –a, –um, most
mūniō, –īre, –īvī, –ītus, fortify; **viam
 mūniō**, build a road
mūnus, mūneris, *n.*, duty, service, gift
mūtō, –āre, –āvī, –ātus, change

## N

nam, *conj.*, for
nārrō, –āre, –āvī, –ātus, relate
nātūra, –ae, *f.*, nature
nauta, –ae, *m.*, sailor
nāvigō, –āre, –āvī, –ātus, sail
nāvis, nāvis, *f.*, ship
–ne, *introduces questions*
nec, *see* neque
neglegentia, –ae, *f.*, negligence
negōtium, –tī, *n.*, business
nēmō, *dat.* nēminī, *acc.* nēminem (*no
 other forms*), no one
Neptūnus, –ī, *m.*, Neptune, *god of the sea*

neque (*or* nec), and not, nor; **neque . . .
 neque**, neither . . . nor
neuter, –tra, –trum, neither (*of two*)
nihil, nothing
nōbilis, –e, noble
nōbīscum = cum nōbīs
noceō, –ēre, nocuī, nocitūrus, do harm
 to (*w. dat.*)
nōmen, nōminis, *n.*, name
nōn, *adv.*, not; **nōn iam**, no longer
nōs, we, *pl. of* ego
nōscō, –ere, nōvī, nōtus, learn; *perf.*, have
 learned, know
noster, –tra, –trum, our
nōtus, –a, –um, known, familiar
novem, nine
novus, –a, –um, new, strange
nox, noctis, *f.*, night
nūllus, –a, –um, no, none
numerus, –ī, *m.*, number
numquam, *adv.*, never
nunc, *adv.*, now
nūntiō, –āre, –āvī, –ātus, report, announce
nūntius, –tī, *m.*, messenger

## O

ob, *prep. w. acc.*, toward, on account of,
 for
obtineō, –ēre, obtinuī, obtentus, hold, obtain
occultus, –a, –um, secret
occupō, –āre, –āvī, –ātus, seize
Ōceanus, –ī, *m.*, ocean
octō, eight
oculus, –ī, *m.*, eye
officium, –cī, *n.*, duty
omnis, omne, all, every
oppidum, –ī, *n.*, town
opprimō, –ere, oppressī, oppressus, overcome, surprise
optimē, *see* bene
optimus, *see* bonus
opus, operis, *n.*, work
ōrātiō, –ōnis, *f.*, speech
ōrātor, –ōris, *m.*, orator
ōrdō, ōrdinis, *m.*, order, rank
ōrnāmentum, –ī, *n.*, jewel, costume
ostendō, –ere, ostendī, ostentus, (stretch
 out), show
ōtium, ōtī, *n.*, leisure, peace

## P

P., *abbreviation for* Pūblius
pār, *gen.* paris, equal
parātus, –a, –um, prepared, ready

parō, –āre, –āvī, –ātus, get, get ready, prepare

pars, partis, f., part, side

parvus, –a, –um, small; comp. minor, minus, less; superl. minimus, –a, –um, least

pāstor, –ōris, m., shepherd

pater, patris, m., father

patria, –ae, f., fatherland, country

paucī, –ae, –a, few

Paulus, –ī, m., Paul

paupertās, –tātis, f., poverty

pāx, pācis, f., peace

pecūnia, –ae, f., sum of money, money

peior, see malus

pellō, –ere, pepulī, pulsus, drive, defeat

Penātēs, –ium, m., the Penā'tēs, household gods

Pēnelopē, –ae, f., Penĕl'ope, wife of Ulysses

per, prep. w. acc., through, by

perficiō, –ere, –fēcī, –fectus, finish

perīculum, –ī, n., danger

permittō, –ere, –mīsī, –missus, let go through, allow, entrust (w. dat.)

permoveō, –ēre, –mōvī, –mōtus, move (deeply)

permūtātiō, –ōnis, f., exchange

perpetuus, –a, –um, constant

persōna, –ae, f., character

perveniō, –īre, –vēnī, –ventūrus, come through, arrive

pēs, pedis, m., foot; pedibus, on foot

pessimus, see malus

petō, –ere, petīvī, petītus, seek, ask (for)

Phrygia, –ae, f., Phrygia (Frij'ia), a country of Asia Minor

pictūra, –ae, f., picture

pila, –ae, f., ball

plācō, –āre, –āvī, –ātus, calm

plānus, –a, –um, level

plēbs, plēbis, f., the common people

plicō, –āre, –āvī, –ātus, fold

plūrēs, plūra, more, see multus

plūrimus, see multus

plūs, see multus

Plūtō, –ōnis, m., Plū'tō

poena, –ae, f., penalty, punishment

poēta, –ae, m., poet

Polyphēmus, –ī, m., Polyphē'mus, a man-eating giant

pompa, –ae, f., parade

pōnō, –ere, posuī, positus, put, place; castra pōnō, pitch camp

pōns, pontis, m., bridge

pontifex, –ficis, m., priest

populus, –ī, m., people; pl., peoples, nations

porta, –ae, f., gate

portō, –āre, –āvī, –ātus, carry

portus, –ūs, m., harbor

possum, posse, potuī, —, can, be able

post, adv. and prep. w. acc., behind (of place); after (of time)

posteā, adv., afterwards

postquam, conj., after

potestās, –tātis, f., power

prae, prep. w. abl., before, in front of

praeceps, gen. praecipitis, headlong, steep

praeda, –ae, f., loot

praeficiō, –ere, –fēcī, –fectus, put in charge of

praemittō, –ere, –mīsī, –missus, send ahead

praemium, –mī, n., reward

praesidium, –dī, n., guard, protection

praesum, –esse, –fuī, –futūrus, be in charge of

praetextus, –a, –um, (woven in front), bordered; toga praetexta, crimson-bordered toga

premō, –ere, pressī, pressus, press, press hard

pretium, –tī, n., price

prīmō, adv., at first

prīmum, adv., for the first time

prīmus, –a, –um, first

prīnceps, –cipis, m., leader

prō, prep. w. abl., in front of, before, for

probō, –āre, –āvī, –ātus, test, prove, approve

prōcēdō, –ere, –cessī, –cessūrus, go forward, advance

prōdūcō, –ere, –dūxī, –ductus, lead out, prolong

proelium, –lī, n., battle

prohibeō, –ēre, –hibuī, –hibitus, prevent, keep from

properō, –āre, –āvī, –ātūrus, hasten

prōpōnō, –ere, –posuī, –positus, put forward, offer

proprius, –a, –um, (one's) own

prōvideō, –ēre, –vīdī, –vīsus, foresee

prōvincia, –ae, f., province

proximus, –a, –um, nearest, very near, next

pūblicē, adv., publicly

pūblicus, –a, –um, public

Pūblius, –lī, m., Pub'lius

puella, –ae, f., girl

puer, puerī, m., boy

pugna, –ae, f., battle

pugnō, –āre, –āvī, –ātus, fight

pulcher, –chra, –chrum, beautiful

Pūnicus, –a, –um, Punic, Carthaginian

putō, –āre, –āvī, –ātus, think
Pyrrhus, –ī, m., Pỹr'rhus, *king of Epirus*

## Q

quadrīgae, –ārum, *f. pl.*, a four-horse team, a chariot
quam, *conj.*, than
quārtus, –a, –um, fourth
quattuor, four
–que (*joined to second word*), and
quī, quae, quod, *relat. pron.*, who, which, what, that; *interrog. adj.*, what
quīndecim, fifteen
quīnque, five
quīntus, –a, –um, fifth
quis, quid, *interrog. pron.*, who, what
quod, *conj.*, because
quondam, *adv.*, once (upon a time)

## R

raeda, –ae, *f.*, carriage, omnibus
rapiō, –ere, rapuī, raptus, carry off
ratiō, –ōnis, *f.*, account, reason
recipiō, –ere, recēpī, receptus, take back, recover, receive
reddō, –ere, reddidī, redditus, give back
redigō, –ere, redēgī, redāctus, drive back, reduce
redūcō, –ere, redūxī, reductus, lead back, bring back
rēgīna, –ae, *f.*, queen
regiō, –ōnis, *f.*, region
rēgnum, –ī, *n.*, royal power, kingdom
regō, –ere, rēxī, rēctus, rule, guide
relinquō, –ere, relīquī, relīctus, leave (behind), abandon
reliquus, –a, –um, remaining, rest (of)
remaneō, –ēre, remānsī, remānsūrus, remain
remedium, –dī, *n.*, remedy
remittō, –ere, remīsī, remissus, relax, send back
removeō, –ēre, remōvī, remōtus, remove
repellō, –ere, reppulī, repulsus, drive back, repulse
rēs, reī, *f.*, thing, matter, affair; rēs pūblica, public affairs, government
respondeō, –ēre, respondī, respōnsus, answer
restō, –āre, restitī, —, remain
retineō, –ēre, retinuī, retentus, hold (back), keep
revertō, –ere, revertī, reversūrus, return
rēx, rēgis, *m.*, king
Rhēnus, –ī, *m.*, the Rhine river
rīdeō, –ēre, rīsī, rīsus, laugh (at)

rogō, –āre, –āvī, –ātus, ask
Rōma, –ae, *f.*, Rome
Rōmānus, –a, –um, Roman; *as noun*, a Roman
ruīna, –ae, *f.*, ruin

## S

saccus, –ī, *m.*, sack
sacer, –cra, –crum, sacred
saepe, *adv.*, often
salūs, salūtis, *f.*, health, safety
sapientia, –ae, *f.*, wisdom
satis, *adv. and indecl. adj.*, enough
Sāturnus, –ī, *m.*, Saturn, *a god*
saxum, –ī, *n.*, rock
scēptrum, –ī, *n.*, scepter
sciō, –īre, scīvī, scītus, know
Scīpiō, –ōnis, *m.*, Scipio (Sip'io)
scrībō, –ere, scrīpsī, scrīptus, write
sēcum = cum sē
secundus, –a, –um, second
sed, *conj.*, but
sedeō, –ēre, sēdī, sessūrus, sit
semper, *adv.*, always
senātor, –ōris, *m.*, senator
senātus, –ūs, *m.*, senate
sententia, –ae, *f.*, feeling, opinion, motto
sentiō, –īre, sēnsī, sēnsus, feel, realize
sēparō, –āre, –āvī, –ātus, separate
septem, seven
sepulchrum, –ī, *n.*, tomb
sermō, –ōnis, *m.*, talk
servō, –āre, –āvī, –ātus, save, guard, preserve
servus, –ī, *m.*; serva, –ae, *f.*, slave
sex, six
sī, *conj.*, if
Sicilia, –ae, *f.*, Sicily (Sis'ily)
signum, –ī, *n.*, sign, standard, signal
silva, –ae, *f.*, forest, woods
similis, –e, like
sine, *prep. w. abl.*, without
singulī, –ae, –a, *pl. only*, one at a time
socius, –cī, *m.*, comrade, ally
sōl, sōlis, *m.*, sun
sōlus, –a, –um, alone, only
solvō, –ere, solvī, solūtus, loosen, pay
somnus, –ī, *m.*, sleep
sordidus, –a, –um, dirty
soror, –ōris, *f.*, sister
spatium, –tī, *n.*, space, time, lap (*in a race*)
speciēs, speciēī, *f.*, appearance
spectō, –āre, –āvī, –ātus, look (at)
spērō, –āre, –āvī, –ātus, hope (for)
spēs, speī, *f.*, hope
spīrō, –āre, –āvī, –ātus, breathe

spondeō, –ēre, spopondī, spōnsus, promise, engage

statua, –ae, f., statue

statuō, –ere, statuī, statūtus, establish, determine

stō, stāre, stetī, stātūrus, stand

stomachus, –ī, m., stomach

studium, –dī, n., eagerness, interest; pl., studies

sub, prep., under, close to (w. acc. after verbs of motion; w. abl. after verbs of rest or position)

subigō, –ere, –ēgī, –āctus, subdue

submittō, –ere, –mīsī, –missus, let down, furnish

suī, reflexive pron., of himself, herself, itself, themselves

sum, esse, fuī, futūrus, be

summus, –a, –um, highest, top of

sūmō, –ere, sūmpsī, sūmptus, take

super, prep. w. acc., over, above

superbia, –ae, f., pride

superbus, –a, –um, haughty

superō, –āre, –āvī, –ātus, overcome, excel

supersum, –esse, –fuī, –futūrus, be left over, survive

supplicium, –cī, n., punishment

suscipiō, –ere, –cēpī, –ceptus, undertake

sustineō, –ēre, –tinuī, –tentus, hold up, maintain, endure

suus, –a, –um, reflexive adj., his, her, its, their; his own, her own, etc.

**T**

taberna, –ae, f., shop, tavern

tamen, adv., nevertheless

tandem, adv., at last

tangō, –ere, tetigī, tāctus, touch

tardē, adv., slowly

tardus, –a, –um, slow, late

Tarentīnī, –ōrum, m. pl., the people of Tarentum

Tēlemachus, –ī, m., Telĕm'achus

tēlum, –ī, n., weapon

templum, –ī, n., temple

tempus, temporis, n., time

tendō, –ere, tetendī, tentus, stretch

teneō, –ēre, tenuī, tentus, hold, keep; memoriā teneō, remember

terminus, –ī, m., end, boundary

terra, –ae, f., land, earth

terreō, –ēre, terruī, territus, scare, frighten

tertius, –a, –um, third

texō, –ere, texuī, textus, weave

theātrum, –ī, n., theater

Ti., abbreviation for Tiberius

Tiberis, –is, m., the Tī'ber, a river in Italy

Tiberius, –rī, m., Tībē'rius

timeō, –ēre, timuī, —, fear, be afraid

timidē, adv., timidly

timidus, –a, –um, timid

Tīrō, –ōnis, m., Tī'rō

toga, –ae, f., toga (cloak)

tōtus, –a, –um, whole

trādō, –ere, –didī, –ditus, give or hand over, surrender, relate

trādūcō, –ere, –dūxī, –ductus, lead across

trahō, –ere, trāxī, trāctus, draw, drag

trānō, –āre, –āvī, –ātus, swim across

trāns, prep. w. acc., across

trānsportō, –āre, –āvī, –ātus, transport

trēs, tria, three

tribūnus, –ī, m., tribune, a Roman official

tribuō, –ere, tribuī, tribūtus, grant

trīgintā, thirty

triumphō, –āre, –āvī, –ātus, triumph

triumphus, –ī, m., triumph

Troia, –ae, f., Troy

Troiānus, –a, –um, Trojan; as noun, a Trojan

tū, tuī, you

tum, adv., then

tuus, –a, –um, your, yours (referring to one person)

**U**

ubi, adv., where; when

Ulixēs, –is, m., Ūlys'sēs

ūllus, –a, –um, any

ulterior, ulterius, farther

ultimus, –a, –um, last, farthest

unda, –ae, f., wave

ūnus, –a, –um, one

urbs, urbis, f., city

ūtilis, –e, useful

uxor, –ōris, f., wife

**V**

valeō, –ēre, valuī, valitūrus, be strong, be well; imper. valē, farewell

vāllum, –ī, n., wall

variē, adv., variously

varius, –a, –um, changing, varying, various

vāstō, –āre, –āvī, –ātus, destroy

veniō, –īre, vēnī, ventūrus, come

ventus, –ī, m., wind

Venus, –eris, f., Vēnus, goddess of love and beauty

vēr, vēris, n., spring

verberō, –āre, –āvī, –ātus, beat

verbum, –ī, n., word

vertō, −ere, vertī, versus, turn
vērus, −a, −um, true
Vestālis, −e, Vestal, of Vesta
vester, −tra, −trum, your, yours (*referring to two or more persons*)
vestis, −is, *f.*, garment, clothes
via, −ae, *f.*, way, road, street
victor, −ōris, *m.*, victor
victōria, −ae, *f.*, victory
videō, −ēre, vīdī, vīsus, see; *passive*, seem
vīgintī, twenty
vīlla, −ae, *f.*, country home
vincō, −ere, vīcī, victus, conquer
vīnum, −ī, *n.*, wine
vir, virī, *m.*, man
virgō, −ginis, *f.*, virgin, maiden
virīlis, −e, of a man
virtūs, −tūtis, *f.*, manliness, courage
vīs, —, *f.*, force, violence; *pl.*, vīrēs, −ium, strength
vīta, −ae, *f.*, life
vīvō, −ere, vīxī, vīctus, live
vīvus, −a, −um, alive
vix, *adv.*, scarcely
vocō, −āre, −āvī, −ātus, call, invite
vōs, *pl. of* tū
vōx, vōcis, *f.*, voice, remark
Vulcānus, −ī, *m.*, Vulcan, *god of fire*
vulnerō, −āre, −āvī, −ātus, wound
vulnus, vulneris, *n.*, wound

*Above, Jupiter looks down on a modern room in Roman style in the home of Walter H. Mayer (cf. p. 369). At the right, atrium of a house in ancient Herculaneum.*

# ENGLISH–LATIN

## A

able (be), possum, posse, potuī, —
about, dē, w. abl.
absent (be), absum, abesse, āfuī, āfutūrus
accuse, accūsō, –āre, –āvī, –ātus
across, trāns, w. acc.
advice, cōnsilium, –lī, n.
affair, rēs, reī, f.
affect, afflict, afficiō, –ere, affēcī, affectus
afraid (be), timeō, –ēre, timuī, —
after, use abl. abs.; post (prep. w. acc.);
   postquam (conj.)
aid, auxilium, –lī, n.
all, omnis, –e
ally, socius, –cī, m.
alone, sōlus, –a, –um
always, semper
and, et, –que
another, alius, –a, –um
appearance, speciēs, speciēī, f.
approach, accēdō, –ere, accessī, accessūrus (w. ad)
approve, probō, –āre, –āvī, –ātus
arms, arma, –ōrum, n.
arouse, incitō, –āre, –āvī, –ātus
arrive, perveniō, –īre, –vēnī, –ventūrus
as, use abl. abs.
ask, rogō, –āre, –āvī, –ātus
await, exspectō, –āre, –āvī, –ātus
away (be), absum, –esse, āfuī, āfutūrus

## B

bad, malus, –a, –um
battle, pugna, –ae, f.; proelium, –lī, n.
be, sum, esse, fuī, futūrus
beautiful, pulcher, –chra, –chrum
because, quod; use particip. or abl. abs.
begin, incipiō, –ere, –cēpī, –ceptus
between, inter, w. acc.
bind, ligō, –āre, –āvī, –ātus
blame, accūsō, –āre, –āvī, –ātus
body, corpus, corporis, n.
book, liber, librī, m.
boy, puer, puerī, m.
brave, fortis, –e; bravely, fortiter
breathe, spīrō, –āre, –āvī, –ātus
brother, frāter, frātris, m.
but, sed
by, ā, ab, w. abl.

## C

call, vocō, –āre, –āvī, –ātus; appellō, –āre,
   –āvī, –ātus; call out, ēvocō; call together, convocō

camp, castra, –ōrum, n.; pitch camp,
   castra pōnō
can, possum, posse, potuī, —
cannot, nōn possum
capture, expugnō, –āre, –āvī, –ātus
care, cūra, –ae, f.
carefully, cum cūrā
carry, portō, –āre, –āvī, –ātus; carry on,
   gerō, –ere, gessī, gestus
catch sight of, cōnspiciō, –ere, –spexī,
   –spectus
cause, causa, –ae, f.
certainly, certē
chance, cāsus, –ūs, m.
(put in) charge of, praeficiō, –ere, –fēcī,
   –fectus
children, līberī, –ōrum, m.
citizen, cīvis, cīvis, m.
citizenship, cīvitās, –tātis, f.
city, urbs, urbis, f.
clearly, clārē
climb, ascendō, –ere, ascendī, ascēnsus
close, claudō, –ere, clausī, clausus
colonist, colōnus, –ī, m.
come, veniō, –īre, vēnī, ventūrus; come
   together, conveniō, –īre, –vēnī, –ventus
complete, cōnficiō, –ere, –fēcī, –fectus
comrade, socius, –cī, m.
constant, perpetuus, –a, –um
contain, contineō, –ēre, –uī, –tentus
country, patria, –ae, f.
courage, animus, –ī, m.
cry out, clāmō, –āre, –āvī, –ātus

## D

danger, perīculum, –ī, n.
daughter, fīlia, –ae, f.
day, diēs, diēī, m.
deceive, fallō, –ere, fefellī, falsus
deep, altus, –a, –um
(deeply) move, permoveō, –ēre, –mōvī,
   –mōtus
defend, dēfendō, –ere, dēfendī, dēfēnsus
depart, excēdō, –ere, excessī, excessūrus
desert, dēserō, –ere, dēseruī, dēsertus
deserve, mereō, –ēre, meruī, meritus
desire, cupiō, –ere, cupīvī, cupītus
destroy, vāstō, –āre, –āvī, –ātus
determine, statuō, –ere, statuī, statūtus
dinner, cēna, –ae, f.
dismiss, dīmittō, –ere, dīmīsī, dīmissus
divide, dīvidō, –ere, dīvīsī, dīvīsus
do, faciō, –ere, fēcī, factus; do harm to,
   noceō, –ēre, nocuī, nocitūrus (w. dat.)
drag, draw, trahō, –ere, trāxī, trāctus

drive, agō, –ere, ēgī, āctus
duty, officium, –cī, n.

# E

eagerness, studium, –dī, n.
easy, facilis, –e; easily, facile
end, fīnis, fīnis, m.
endure, sustineō, –ēre, –tinuī, –tentus
enemy, inimīcus, –ī, m. (personal); hostis,
  –is, m. (national)
entrust, mandō, –āre, –āvī, –ātus; committō, –ere, –mīsī, –missus; crēdō, –ere,
  crēdidī, crēditus
equal, pār, gen. paris
establish, cōnfirmō, –āre, –āvī, –ātus
every, omnis, –e
example, exemplum, –ī, n.
excel, superō, –āre, –āvī, –ātus
excellent, ēgregius, –a, –um
explore, explōrō, –āre, –āvī, –ātus

# F

fall, cadō, –ere, cecidī, cāsūrus
fame, fāma, –ae, f.
familiar, nōtus, –a, –um
family, familia, –ae, f.
famous, clārus, –a, –um
farmer, agricola, –ae, m.
father, pater, patris, m.
fear, timeō, –ēre, timuī, —
feel grateful, grātiam habeō
few, paucī, –ae, –a
field, ager, agrī, m.
fifth, quīntus, –a, –um
fight, pugnō, –āre, –āvī, –ātus
find, inveniō, –īre, invēnī, inventus
firmly, firmē
first, prīmus, –a, –um
fit, aptus, –a, –um
flee, fugiō, –ere, fūgī, fugitūrus
fold, plicō, –āre, –āvī, –ātus
food, cibus, –ī, m.
foot, pēs, pedis, m.; on foot, pedibus
for (conj.), nam; (prep.), prō, w. abl.;
  ob, w. acc.
foreigner, barbarus, –ī, m.
foresee, prōvideō, –ēre, –vīdī, –vīsus
forest, silva, –ae, f.  ·
fortify, mūniō, –īre, –īvī, –ītus
four, quattuor
free (adj.), līber, –era, –erum; (v.),
  līberō, –āre, –āvī, –ātus
freedom, lībertās, lībertātis, f.
fresh, integer, –gra, –grum
friend, amīcus, –ī, m.
friendship, amīcitia, –ae, f.

from, out from, ē, ex, w. abl.; (away)
  from, ā, ab, w. abl.
furnish, submittō, –ere, –mīsī, –missus

# G

Gaul, Gallia, –ae, f.; a Gaul, Gallus, –ī, m.
general, dux, ducis, m.
get, get ready, parō, –āre, –āvī, –ātus
girl, puella, –ae, f.
give, dōnō, –āre, –āvī, –ātus; dō, dare,
  dedī, datus
go away, discēdō, –ere, –cessī, –cessūrus
god, deus, –ī, m.
good, bonus, –a, –um
grain, frūmentum, –ī, n.
(be or feel) grateful, grātiam habeō,
  –ēre, –uī, –itus
great, magnus, –a, –um
guard, praesidium, –dī, n.

# H

hand, manus, –ūs, f.
harm, do harm to, noceō, –ēre, nocuī,
  nocitūrus (w. dat.)
harmony, concordia, –ae, f.
harsh, dūrus, –a, –um; harshly, dūrē
hasten, mātūrō, –āre, –āvī, –ātūrus;
  properō, –āre, –āvī, –ātūrus
have, habeō, –ēre, –uī, –itus
he, is; hic; ille; often not expressed
head, caput, capitis, n.
health, salūs, salūtis, f.
hear, audiō, –īre, –īvī, –ītus
heavy, gravis, –e
her (poss.), eius; (reflex.), suus, –a, –um
hesitate, dubitō, –āre, –āvī, –ātus
high, altus, –a, –um
himself (intens.), ipse; (reflex.), suī
hinder, impediō, –īre, –īvī, –ītus
his (poss.), eius
hold, teneō, –ēre, tenuī, tentus
hope (v.), spērō, –āre, –āvī, –ātus;
  (noun), spēs, speī, f.
horse, equus, –ī, m.
hour, hōra, –ae, f.
house, casa, –ae, f.; domus, –ūs, f.
how (in what manner), quō modō

# I

I, ego, meī; often not expressed
if, abl. abs.
in, in, w. abl.
increase, augeō, –ēre, auxī, auctus

**influence,** addūcō, –ere, addūxī, adductus; (*noun*), grātia, –ae, *f.;* auctōritās, –tātis, *f.*
**instruction,** disciplīna, –ae, *f.*
**interest,** studium, –dī, *n.*
**into,** in, *w. acc.*
**island,** īnsula, –ae, *f.*
**it,** id; hoc; illud; *often not expressed*

## J

**journey,** iter, itineris, *n.*
**just,** aequus, –a, –um; iūstus, –a, –um

## K

**kill,** interficiō, –ere, –fēcī, –fectus
**king,** rēx, rēgis, *m.*
**kingdom,** rēgnum, –ī, *n.*
**know,** *perfect tense of* nōscō, –ere, nōvī, nōtus, *or of* cognōscō, –ere, –nōvī, –nitus; sciō, –īre, scīvī, scītus

## L

**land,** terra, –ae, *f.;* **native land,** patria, –ae, *f.*
**large,** magnus, –a, –um
**late,** tardus, –a, –um
**lead,** dūcō, –ere, dūxī, ductus; **lead across,** trādūcō; **lead back,** redūcō; **lead out,** prōdūcō
**leader,** dux, ducis, *m.;* prīnceps, prīncipis, *m.*
**learn,** nōscō, –ere, nōvī, nōtus; cognōscō, –ere, –nōvī, –nitus
**leisure,** ōtium, –ī, *n.*
**letter** (*of alphabet*), littera, –ae, *f.;* (*epistle*), litterae, –ārum, *f.*
**level,** plānus, –a, –um
**life,** vīta, –ae, *f.*
**little,** parvus, –a, –um
**live** (a life), agō, –ere, ēgī, āctus; **dwell,** habitō, –āre, –āvī, –ātus
**long,** longus, –a, –um; **no longer,** nōn iam
**look at,** spectō, –āre, –āvī, –ātus
**loot,** praeda, –ae, *f.*
**lose,** āmittō, –ere, āmīsī, āmissus
**love,** amō, –āre, –āvī, –ātus
**lower,** īnferior, īnferius

## M

**maintain,** sustineō, –ēre, –uī, –tentus
**make,** faciō, –ere, fēcī, factus
**man,** vir, virī, *m.;* homō, hominis, *m.*
**manner,** modus, –ī, *m.*

**many,** multī, –ae, –a
**messenger,** nūntius, –tī, *m.*
**middle of,** medius, –a, –um
**money,** pecūnia, –ae, *f.*
**month,** mēnsis, –is, *m.*
**most,** plūrimī, –ae, –a
**mother,** māter, mātris, *f.*
**motto,** sententia, –ae, *f.*
**mountain,** mōns, montis, *m.*
**move,** moveō, –ēre, mōvī, mōtus; migrō, –āre, –āvī, –ātus
**much,** multus, –a, –um; magnus, –a, –um
**my,** meus, –a, –um

## N

**name,** nōmen, nōminis, *n.*
**nation,** gēns, gentis, *f.*
**native land,** patria, –ae, *f.*
**nature,** nātūra, –ae, *f.*
**neighboring,** fīnitimus, –a, –um
**neither** (*adj.*), neuter, –tra, –trum
**neither . . . nor** (*conj.*), neque . . . neque
**never,** numquam
**new,** novus, –a, –um
**next,** proximus, –a, –um
**no longer** (*adv.*), nōn iam; **no one** (*noun*), nēmō, *dat.* nēminī, *m.*
**noble,** nōbilis, –e
**nor,** neque
**not,** nōn
**nothing,** nihil, *indecl. n.*
**now,** nunc
**number,** numerus, –ī, *m.*

## O

**obtain,** obtineō, –ēre, obtinuī, obtentus
**on,** in, *w. abl.;* **on account of,** ob, *w. acc.*
**one at a time,** singulī, –ae, –a; **one . . . the other,** alter . . . alter
**opinion,** sententia, –ae, *f.*
**order,** iubeō, –ēre, iussī, iussus
**other,** alius, –a, –ud; **the other** (**of two**), alter, –era, –erum
**ought,** dēbeō, –ēre, dēbuī, dēbitus
**our,** noster, –tra, –trum
**ourselves** (*intens.*), ipsī; (*reflex.*), nōs
**out of,** ē, ex, *w. abl.*
**owe,** dēbeō, –ēre, dēbuī, dēbitus

## P

**part,** pars, partis, *f.*
**peace,** pāx, pācis, *f.*
**people,** populus, –ī, *m.*

pitch camp, castra pōnō, –ere, posuī, positus

place, locus, –ī, *m.; pl.* loca, –ōrum, *n.*

plan, cōnsilium, –lī, *n.*

pleasing, grātus, –a, –um

poor, miser, –era, –erum

praise, laudō, –āre, –āvī, –ātus

prepare, parō, –āre, –āvī, –ātus

present (be), adsum, –esse, adfuī, adfutūrus

present, dōnō, –āre, –āvī, –ātus; prōpōnō, –ere, –posuī, –positus

price, pretium, –tī, *n.*

prisoner, captīvus, –ī, *m.*

prove, probō, –āre, –āvī, –ātus

province, prōvincia, –ae, *f.*

public, pūblicus, –a, –um

punishment, poena, –ae; *f.;* supplicium, –cī, *n.*

put, pōnō, –ere, posuī, positus; put in charge of, praeficiō, –ere, –fēcī, –fectus

## Q

queen, rēgīna, –ae, *f.*

quickly, celeriter

## R

rank, ōrdō, ōrdinis, *m.*

rather, *expressed by comparative*

read, legō, –ere, lēgī, lēctus

ready, parātus, –a, –um; get ready, parō, –āre, –āvī, –ātus

receive, accipiō, –ere, accēpī, acceptus

region, regiō, –ōnis, *f.*

reinforcements, auxilia, –ōrum, *n.*

remain, maneō, –ēre, mānsī, mānsūrus

remember, memoriā teneō, –ēre, tenuī, tentus

remove, removeō, –ēre, remōvī, remōtus

report, nūntiō, –āre, –āvī, –ātus

rest (of), reliquus, –a, –um

reward, praemium, –mī, *n.*

right, iūs, iūris, *n.*

river, flūmen, flūminis, *n.*

road, via, –ae, *f.;* iter, itineris, *n.*

rule, regō, –ere, rēxī, rēctus

run, currō, –ere, cucurrī, cursūrus

## S

sacred, sacer, –cra, –crum

safety, salūs, –ūtis, *f.*

sail, nāvigō, –āre, –āvī, –ātus

sailor, nauta, –ae, *m.*

same, īdem, eadem, idem

save, servō, –āre, –āvī, –ātus; cōnservō

say, dīcō, –ere, dīxī, dictus

scare, terreō, –ēre, terruī, territus

sea, mare, maris, *n.*

see, videō, –ēre, vīdī, vīsus

seek, petō, –ere, petīvī, petītus

seize, occupō, –āre, –āvī, –ātus

send, mittō, –ere, mīsī, missus; send away, dīmittō; send back, remittō

settler, colōnus, –ī, *m.*

severe, gravis, –e

shape, fōrma, –ae, *f.*

sharply, ācriter

she, ea; haec; illa; *often not expressed*

ship, nāvis, nāvis, *f.*

shout, clāmō, –āre, –āvī, –ātus

show, mōnstrō, –āre, –āvī, –ātus; dēmōnstrō

(catch) sight of, cōnspiciō, –ere, –spexī, –spectus

signal, signum, –ī, *n.*

since, *use abl. abs.;* quod (*conj.*)

sister, soror, sorōris, *f.*

sit, sedeō, –ēre, sēdī, sessūrus

slave, servus, –ī, *m.*

small, parvus, –a, –um

soldier, mīles, mīlitis, *m.*

some . . . others, aliī . . . aliī

son, fīlius, –lī, *m.*

speech, ōrātiō, –ōnis, *f.*

spend (years), agō, –ere, ēgī, āctus

stand, stō, –āre, stetī, stātūrus

standard, signum, –ī, *n.*

state, cīvitās, –tātis, *f.*

strange, novus, –a, –um

street, via, –ae, *f.*

stretch, tendō, –ere, tetendī, tentus

studies, studia, –ōrum, *n.*

suitable, commodus, –a, –um

summer, aestās, –tātis, *f.*

supply, cōpia, –ae, *f.*

swift, celer, celeris, celere

swiftly, celeriter

swiftness, celeritās, –tātis, *f.*

## T

take, capiō, –ere, cēpī, captus

teach, doceō, –ēre, docuī, doctus

teacher, magister, –trī, *m.*

terms, condiciō, –ōnis, *f.*

than, quam

thank, grātiās agō, –ere, ēgī, grātiae āctae (*w. dat.*)

that (*demonst.*), ille, illa, illud; is, ea, id; (*relat.*) quī, quae, quod

their, eōrum, eārum, eōrum

themselves (*intens.*), ipsī, –ae, –a; (*reflex.*), suī

then, tum

they, eī, eae, ea; illī, illae, illa; *often not expressed*

thing, rēs, reī, f.; often not expressed
think, putō, –āre, –āvī, –ātus
third, tertius, –a, –um
this (demonst.), hic, haec, hoc; is, ea, id
three, trēs, tria
through, per, w. acc.
till, colō, –ere, coluī, cultus
timber, māteria, –ae, f.
time, tempus, –oris, n.; one at a time,
  singulī, –ae, –a
to, ad, w. acc.; dat. of indir. obj.
too, expressed by comparative
touch, tangō, –ere, tetigī, tāctus
town, oppidum, –ī, n.
train, exerceō, –ēre, exercuī, exercitus
transport, trānsportō, –āre, –āvī, –ātus
truly, vērē
two, duo, duae, duo

## U

under, sub, w. acc. or abl.
understand, intellegō, –ere, –lēxī, –lēctus
undertake, suscipiō, –ere, –cēpī, –ceptus
unfold, explicō, –āre, –āvī, –ātus
upon, in, w. abl.
urge on, incitō, –āre, –āvī, –ātus
useful, ūtilis, –e

## V

varying, varius, –a, –um
very, expressed by superlative; very carefully, magnā cūrā
victory, victōria, –ae, f.

## W

wagon, carrus, –ī, m.
wait, exspectō, –āre, –āvī, –ātus
war, bellum, –ī, n.
warn, moneō, –ēre, –uī, –itus
water, aqua, –ae, f.
we, nōs; often not expressed
well, bene
what (pron.), quis, quid; (adj.), quī,
  quae, quod
which, quī, quae, quod
who (rel. pron.), quī, quae, quod; (interrog. pron.), quis, quid
whole, tōtus, –a, –um
why, cūr
wide, lātus, –a, –um
winter, hiems, hiemis, f.
with, cum, w. abl.; sometimes abl. alone
without, sine, w. abl.
woods, silva, –ae, f.
word, verbum, –ī, n.
work (verb), labōrō, –āre, –āvī, –ātus;
  (noun), opus, operis, n.
worse, peior, peius; worst, pessimus, –a,
  –um
wound, vulnus, vulneris, n.
write, scrībō, –ere, scrīpsī, scrīptus

## Y

year, annus, –ī, m.
you, tū (sing.); vōs (pl.); often not
  expressed
your, tuus, –a, –um; vester, –tra, –trum;
  yourselves (reflex.), vōs

The Emperor Marcus Aurelius (161–180 A.D.) erected this column in imitation of Trajan's (cf. p. vi). It is in the heart of the modern city.

The Vendôme column in Paris also imitates that of Trajan. Napoleon built it to commemorate his campaign of 1805.

424

*Tombs in a Roman cemetery near Ostia. They are tiny houses, like large doll houses. A dead town, one might say.*

*Caught by death. The ashes that covered Pompeii suffocated many people. Centuries after the ashes hardened, archeologists, finding hollowed places in them, poured in plaster, thus making casts like this.*

*Gladiators in the arena. One is heavily armed like a soldier, the other has only a trident (like a pitchfork) and a net, used like a lasso. From the motion picture "Demetrius and the Gladiators."*

*Modern painting of an ancient scene: gladiator celebrating after a victory.*

# Index

Numbers in roman type refer to the text; those in italic, to the illustrations.

ē, ex, 69, 70; as prefix, 70
economic conditions, Roman, 347
education, see schools
ego, declension of, 162, 395
egoist, *164*
Egypt, *252*
Eisenhower, *21*
eject, *305*
election posters, 110; *109*
elephants, 337; *337*
Elizabeth II, *10*
emphatic verb forms, 17, 390
endings, 29
England, *8, 10, 62, 82, 216, 252, 321*
English, see word studies
Etna, Mt., *12*
Etruscans, 4, 284, 292
extent of time or space, accusative of, 357, 402
extrēmus, use of, 338

Fabius Maximus, 165
Fabricius, 340, 375; *340*
fasces, *342*
Faustina, Temple of, *130*
Faustulus, *254*
fifth declension, 365, 392
Finland, *217*
fire protection in Rome, 146
first conjugation, 17, 177, 396
first declension, 10, 46, 392
    adjectives, 46, 72, 78, 393
floors, 262; *125, 169, 231, 264*
food and meals, 175; *176, 185, 298, 317*
Forti, E., *118, 179*
Forum, the, 130, 145, 314; *3, 5, 20, 24, 28, 55, 74, 93, 130, 151, 184, 223, 315, 368;* imperial fora, *55, 101, 102;* of Augustus, *49, 101, 102;* of Caesar, *32, 102;* of Trajan, *vi, 55, 101, 102;* of Pompeii, *87*
fountains, *8, 116, 176*
fourth conjugation, 102, 124, 399
fourth declension, 361, 392
France, *42, 44, 46, 85, 147, 158, 203, 222, 424*
Francesco di Giorgio, *139*
Frankfort, *149*
Frascati, *19*
French, Latin words in, 50, 76
furniture, Roman, etc., 261; *298, 317, 318*
future active infinitive, 307, 312
future active participle, 300
future perfect tense, 159, 390; passive, 170

future tense, 389; active, 36, 59, 118, 124; passive, 137

games, 6, 161, 196, 226, 234; *15, 22, 57, 118, 125, 161, 182, 235*
gardens, 261; *116, 298*
gates, see arches
Gaul, 42, 203, 222, 353; see **France**
gender, 20, 388
    in the first declension, 20
    in the second declension, 20, 78
    in the third declension, 214, 253
    in the fourth declension, 362
    in the fifth declension, 365
genitive case, 33, 389, 402
    of description, 369
    of nouns and adjectives in *–ius,* 67; in *–ium,* 79
    of possession, 33, 389
Genius, 291
Georgia, *331*
Germany, *71*
Giants, 271; *271*
girls, *15, 45, 125, 161, 206, 220*
gladiators, *68, 92, 109, 426;* gladiatorial shows, 110, 196, 236; *109;* see **amphitheaters**
glimpses of Roman life, see **Roman life**
gods, 269, 291
good, *50*
government, Roman, 375
Gracchi, 347, 360
grammar, basic, 385
grammar summaries, 29, 55, 85, 112, 149, 177, 238, 265, 296, 322, 378
Greece, *123, 142, 158, 287*
Gregory, Pope, 225
Gyselaer, P., *329*

hair, 52; *15, 52, 220*
Hannibal, 165, 365
hats, 52
Havana, *115*
Herculaneum, *27, 283, 290, 362, 418*
hic, declension of, 272, 395
holidays, Roman, 234, 291, 371
homo and vir, 374
hoops, *182*
Horace, 306; *306, 309, 313, 377*
Horatius, 284, 375; *284*
horses, *106, 107, 116*
hotels, Roman, 27, 110; see **inns**

tōtus and omnis distinguished, 289
towns and businesses with classical names,
see under word studies
toys, 234; *15, 118, 182, 235, 277*
trades and occupations, 317; *16, 57*; see
also shops
Trajan, Column of, *vi*
transitive verbs, 140, 387
translating, see reading
travel, 26, 372; see roads, ships, vehicles
treason, *346*
trēs, declension of, 345, 394
Treves, *71*
tribunes, 375
Trieste, *379*
Tripolitania, *158*
triumphs, Roman, 353; *352*
Trojan Horse, 77; *77, 80*
Trojans, Troy, 77, 126; *77*; see also
Aeneas
tū, declension of, 162, 395
tunic, 51; *65, 112*
Tunisia, *25, 268, 278*
Turner, J. M. W., *212*
Turnus, 168
Twelve Tables, 207, 375
Twinkle, Twinkle, 5


Ulysses, 77, 213, 229, 243, 246, 250; *212,
215, 229, 242, 250*
unit reviews, see reviews
United States, *ii, vi, 2, 7, 31, 72, 78, 85,
90, 91, 95, 96, 98, 100, 115, 124,
127, 135, 148, 149, 155, 159, 166,
171, 188, 251, 292, 294, 300, 301,
302, 303, 306, 311, 320, 321, 331,
333, 342, 359, 369, 376, 380, 423*
University of Alabama, *148*; of Virginia,
*188*
ūnus, declension of, 288, 394


Van Dyck, A., *157, 168*
Vatican, *14*
vehicles, *61, 106, 332*
Venezuela, *372*
Venus, 126, 139, 157, 269; *152, 168, 369;*
Temple of, *32, 102*; of Venus and
Rome, *60, 315*
verbal noun, 89
verbs, 15, 387, 396
    agreement of, with subject, 24, 142,
    354, 389, 402
    auxiliary, 17, 387

verbs (*continued*)
    conjugation of, see conjugations
    intransitive, 140, 387
    irregular, 401
    personal endings of, 16, 66; passive,
    137
    position of, 24
    principal parts of, 169, 177, 188, 197,
    204, 217
    progressive and emphatic forms of, 17,
    390
    stems of, 17, 66, 188
    summary of, 396
    tense of, 15, 389, 403
    transitive, 140, 387
    voice of, 390
Vesta, 269, 291, 314; Temple of, *20,
130*
Vestal Virgins, 314; *5, 151, 314, 315*
Vesuvius, 109; *87, 181*
Vettii, *16, 201*
Victoria, *198*
Victory, *271*
villas, Roman, 27, 262
Virgil, 325; *131, 154, 186, 339, 376*
Virginia, *31, 85, 188, 306, 359*
vīs, declension of. 305, 393
vocabulary reviews, see reviews
vocative case, 69, 403
voice, 136, 390
vowel changes, 103
vowels, 383; quantity of, 383; shortening
of, 17; contraction of, 67, 69, 79
Vulcan, 169, 269; *168*


wall paintings, 262; *16, 57, 77, 81, 116,
128, 141, 185, 201, 205, 208, 212,
220, 241, 288, 360, 404*
walls, 146; *163, 216*
Washington, D. C., *ii, 2, 72, 98, 100, 124,
127, 135*
Washington, State of, *166*
water supply, see aqueducts
Waterloo, *271*
wax tablets, 207; *4, 208, 220, 328*
weaving, *179, 248*
White House, 98
Wilson, Richard, *172*
window, *262*
winds, *134, 142*
wine shop, *65*
Wisconsin, *369, 418*
Wooden Horse, 77; *77, 80*
word formation, see word studies

word order, 13, 23, 24, 39, 69, 107, 113, 273
word sense, how to develop, 99, 255
word studies, English and Latin
abbreviations, 2, 34, 256, 277, 283, 367
assimilation, 73, 76, 122, 171, 190, 290
doublets, 343
French influence, 76
importance of verb, 206; of third declension, 274
intensive prefixes, 195
Latin base in English words, 97, 100, 363
Latin forms in English, see loan words
Latin forms of English names, 64; of names of states, 355
Latin influence upon English, 1, 218, 225
Latin phrases and quotations used in English, 6, 34, 44, 91, 108, 119, 143, 156, 174, 202, 215, 221, 228, 249, 256, 259, 277, 283, 301, 336, 339, 367
legal phrases in English, 336
loan words of first declension, 11, 18, 61; of second declension, 21, 73, 79, 80, 221; of third declension, 245, 249, 253; of fourth and fifth declensions, 367; of irregular comparative and superlative forms, 339; of verb forms, 61, 67, 133
months, names of, 280
names, Latin forms of English, 64; of months, 280; of states, 355
names of gods, etc., used today, see towns, etc.
Norman-French influence, 286
planets, Latin names of, 270
prefixes, intensive, 195

word studies (continued)
prefixes, Latin (and English), ab–, dē–, ex–, 70; ad–, 73; in–, 76; con– (com–), 122; re–, 125; prō–, 156; in– (neg.), dis–, 160; sub–, per–, 171; inter–, ob–, 190; ante–, trāns–, 206; ne–, circum–, contrā–, prae–, super–, 359
Renaissance, effect of, on English speech, 343
Roman numerals, 14
Romance languages, 1, 50
root words, 70, 138
spelling helps, English, 290, 309, 313, 346
suffixes, Latin (and English), –ia, 164; –tia, 167; –tās, 256; –or, 305; –ant, –ent, 309; –antia, –entia, 313; –iō, 332; –ilis, –bilis, –āris, –ārius, –ānus, –icus, –tūdō, 370
synonyms, derivatives of, 374
third declension, importance of, 274
towns and businesses with classical names, 25, 80, 91, 129, 133, 138, 143, 167, 171, 174, 199, 215, 233, 245, 249, 256, 270, 305, 316, 328, 355, 370, 374
verb, importance of, 206
vowel changes, 103
word families, 138, 233
word formation, see prefixes, root words, suffixes, vowel changes, word families
words, choice of, 99, 255
words often confused, 289, 355
Wright Brothers Memorial, 333
writing, 4, 207; writing materials, x, 4, 71, 208, 220, 323, 328

Zama, 365

# LATIN ABBREVIATIONS, WORDS, AND PHRASES
## FREQUENTLY USED IN ENGLISH

You will be reminded daily that Latin is a living language. Almost every time you open a book, a magazine, or even a newspaper you will find an abbreviation or a phrase in Latin. A knowledge of the forms on these two pages, their meanings, and how to use them correctly is one of the marks of an educated American. You will have found throughout the book many other Latin forms used in English. Below is a list of commonly used Latin abbreviations and one of words or phrases you will frequently read or hear in conversation.

## ABBREVIATIONS

**A. D.** (anno Domini), in the year of our Lord
**A. M.** (ante meridiem), before midday
**ad fin.** (ad finem), near the end [of the page]
**ad lib.** (ad libitum), at pleasure
**B. A.** (Baccalaureus Artium), Bachelor of Arts
**B. S.** (Baccalaureus Scientiae), Bachelor of Science
**cf.** (confer), compare
**d.** (denarius), penny [in Britain]
**D. V.** (Deo volente), God willing
**e. g.** (exempli gratia), for example
**et al.** (et alii), and others
**etc.** (et cetera), and so forth
**ibid.** (ibidem), in the same place
**id.** (idem), the same [as mentioned above]
**i. e.** (id est), that is
**J. C. D.** (Juris Civilis Doctor), Doctor of Civil Law
**£** (Libra), pound [British monetary unit]
**LL. B.** (Legum Baccalaureus), Bachelor of Laws
**LL. D.** (Legum Doctor), Doctor of Laws
**loc. cit.** (loco citato), in the place quoted
**M.** (meridies), midday
**M. A.** (Magister Artium), Master of Arts
**M. D.** (Medicinae Doctor), Doctor of Medicine
**N. B.** (nota bene), note well
**op. cit.** (opere citato), the work cited
**P. M.** (post meridiem), after midday
**P.S.** (post scriptum), written after [at the end of a letter]
**per cent** (per centum), by the hundred; for or in every hundred
**Ph. D.** (Philosophiae Doctor), Doctor of Philosophy
**pro tem.** (pro tempore), for the time; temporarily
**prox.** (proximo [mense]), proximo; i.e., in or of next month
**Q. E. D.** (quod erat demonstrandum), which was to be shown or proved
**℞** (*recipe*), used at the head of medical prescriptions
**ulto.** (ultimo [mense]), ultimo; i.e., in or of the month preceding

## WORDS AND PHRASES

**ad infinitum,** to infinity; i.e., without limit
**ad nauseam,** to [the point of] disgust
**alma mater,** kindly mother—applied to schools or colleges
**alter ego,** second self; close friend
**ante bellum,** before the war
**amicus curiae,** friend of the court

argumentum ad hominem, argument using one's opponent's own words or acts as
  evidence for one's views
Ars longa, vita brevis, "Art is long, time is fleeting"
bona fides, good faith
Carpe diem, Seize the day; i. e., the opportunity
Cave canem, Beware the dog!
corpus delicti, (lit., body of the transgression) the substantial facts that prove a crime
cum grano salis, with a grain of salt
cum laude, with honor
de facto, from the fact; i. e., existing with or without the right
de jure, from the right; i. e., existing by right
de novo, from a new [start]; anew
e pluribus unum, one from many
Ecce homo! Behold the man!
ex officio, out of [a result of] one's office
Errare humanum est, To err is human
ex libris, from the books [of]
ex tempore, (lit., according to the time) without preparation
Hic jacet, Here lies —
homo sapiens, man the wise; i. e., the human race
in absentia, in absence
in loco parentis, in place of a parent
in medias res, into the middle of things
in memoriam, to the memory of
in re, in the matter of
in rem, against a thing, as a legal proceeding to recover it
in toto, in all; wholly
inter alia, among other things
Ipse dixit, He [himself] has said it
ipso facto, by the fact itself; thereby
lex non scripta, the unwritten law
lex scripta, the written law
Magna Charta, the Great Paper
magnum bonum, great good
magnum opus, a great work, masterpiece; one's chief work
mirabile dictu, marvelous to say!
modus operandi, method of operating
ne plus ultra, no more beyond; the acme
Pater Noster, Our Father
Pax vobiscum, Peace be with you
per annum, by the year
per capita, by head or by individual
persona non grata, unacceptable person
post hoc, ergo propter hoc, after this, therefore because of this
pro bono publico, for the public good
pro forma, for [as a matter of] form
pro patria, for [one's] country
quid pro quo, something for something ("tit for tat")
rara avis, rare bird, a rarity
sic, so; thus; often used in parentheses or brackets to indicate that the original has been
  copied exactly
sine die, without a day; adjournment without specified date for a next meeting
sine qua non, (lit., without which [it is] not [possible]) a necessity
sub rosa, under the rose; i. e., secretly
summum bonum, the supreme good
sursum corda, [lift] up your hearts
Tempus fugit, Time flies
terra firma, dry land
ultima Thule, farthest north; the farthest limit or point possible
vice versa, conversely; in reverse